American Language Hub

STARTER
Teacher's Book

GARY PATHARE

macmillan education

Macmillan Education Limited
4 Crinan Street
London N1 9XW

Companies and representatives throughout the world

American Language Hub Starter Teacher's Book ISBN 978-0-230-49669-9
American Language Hub Starter Teacher's Book with
Teacher's App ISBN 978-0-230-49670-5

Written by Gary Pathare

The author has asserted their right to be identified as the author of this work in accordance with the Copyright, Designs and Patents Act 1988.

First published 2020

Teacher's Edition credits:
Original design by emc design ltd
Page make-up by SPi Global
Cover design by Macmillan Education, based on an original design by Restless
Cover photograph by Getty Images/valentinrussanov
Picture research by Emily Taylor

Author's acknowledgements
For Emma Pathare

The author and publishers would like to thank the following for permission to reproduce their photographs:

Alamy Stock Photo/Action Plus Sports Images W25, Alamy Stock Photo/Cultura Creative(RF) W46, Alamy Stock Photo/dpa picture alliance archive W4, Alamy Stock Photo/Fritz Liedtke W22, Alamy Stock Photo/Fco Javier Rivas Martin W23(tr5), Alamy Stock Photo/Kertu Saarits W19, Alamy Stock Photo/LightField Studios Inc. W5(cl2), Alamy Stock Photo/Magdalena Rehova W23(tr6), Alamy Stock Photo/PCN Photography W6(bl2), Alamy Stock Photo/Vadym Drobot W32; **Getty Images**/Bertlmann W14(cr1), Getty Images/BJI/Blue Jean Images W2, Getty Images/Blend Images/Kevin Dodge W12(tc), Getty Images/Blend Images/KidStock W10(cr), Getty Images/bhofack2/iStockphoto/Thinkstock Images W14(cl2), Getty Images/Brand X Pictures W7 (cl1), Getty Images/Cavan Images/Cavan W5(cl4), Getty Images/Caiaimage/Tom Merton W36, W41(tr1), Getty Images/Caiaimage/Lukas Olek W9(cl2), Getty Images/Caiaimage/Robert Daly W12(tr1), Getty Images/Cebas/Getty Images Plus/iStock Editorial W41(tr2), Getty Images/Cultura RF/Henn Photography W24, Getty Images/Cultura RF/Judith Haeusler W12(tr2), Getty Images/Compassionate Eye Foundation/Justin Pumfrey W5(tl), Getty Images/DigitalVision/Jose Luis Pelaez Inc W12(tr3), Getty Images/Dusan Ilic/E+ W45(tr2), Getty Images/DragonImages/iStockphoto W5(cl1), Getty Images/ewg3D/ iStockphoto W7(c), Getty Images/EyeEm/Laura Vernocchi W7(cr3), Getty Images/EyeEm/Paolo Gallo W6(bl1), Getty Images/EyeEm/Jaromir Chalabala W35, Getty Images/EyeEm/Reina Smyth W6(tr2), Getty Images/Frederick Breedon W6(bc), Getty Images/f9photos/ iStockphoto W1(cl2), Getty Images/GaryAlvis/E+ W7(tr2), Getty Images/GenerationClash/Getty Images Plus/iStock W6(br1), Getty Images/Getty Images Plus/Tony Anderson/The Image Bank W23(tl4), Getty Images/iStockphoto/pius99 W1(cr1), Getty Images/iStockphoto/runningguy W1(tl1), Getty Images/PhotoDisc W7(tl1), Getty Images/Ryan McVay/Thinkstock W7(tl3), Getty Images/iStockphoto/TPopova W7(tl4), Getty Images/Nomad W12(tl2), Getty Images/pagadesign W7(tr3), Getty Images/Thinkstock Images/Vacclav W7(cl2), Getty Images/gnagel/iStockphoto W7(cl3), Getty Images/iStockphoto/Nadezhda1906 W9(cr1), Getty Images/PeopleImages.com W9(br), Getty Images/Lonely Planet Images/Russell Mountford W9(tl1), Getty Images/PhotoDisc W9(tr1), Getty Images/simonkr,Tomaz Levstek W37, Getty Images/Image Source W39, Getty Images/iStockphoto/jacoblund W40(t), Getty Images/MattJeacock W40(tr), Getty Images/Peopleimages W41(tl1), Getty Images/Laurence Griffiths W41(tl2), Getty Images/martin-dm W43, Getty Images/Mint Images RF W14(cr2), Getty Images W14(cl1), Getty Images/Tetra images RF W23(tl5), Getty Images/iStockphoto/koksharov dmitry/Thinkstock W21(bl1), Getty Images/Tetra images RF/Yuri Arcurs W23(tl3), Getty Images W23(tl6), Getty Images/iStockphoto/South_agency W44, Getty Images/Victor Cardoner W1(tl3), Getty Images/iStockphoto/scanrail W7(tl2), Getty Images/Zu Sanchez Photography,ZU SANCHEZ W45(tr1), Getty Images/4FR,NILS KAHLE - 4FR PHOTOGRAPHY W45(tl1), Getty Images/Wavebreak Media/Wavebreakmedia Ltd,Wavebreak Media LTD W10(tl1), Getty Images/Westend61 W10(tl2), Getty Images/PhotoDisc W12(tl1); **Macmillan Education Limited**/Andy Keylock(Beehive Illustrations)/MACMILLAN MEXICO W26, Macmillan Education Limited/Anton Gvozdikov/iStockphoto W45(tl1), Macmillan Education Limited/Blend Images - RF/Granger Wootz W17, Macmillan Education Limited/Blend Images - KidStock/Brand X Pictures W10(tr), Macmillan Education Limited/Blend/JGI/Jamie Grill W23(tr1), Macmillan Education Limited/Bojana Dimitrovski(Advocate Art)/MACMILLAN MEXICO W28(bl, bc), Macmillan Education Limited/bokan76/iStockphoto/Milenko Bokan W23(tr4), Getty Images/Granger Wootz W34, Macmillan Education Limited/CORBIS/Royalty Free W1(cl1), Macmillan Education Limited/CORBIS W28(tc), Macmillan Education Limited/Daniel Grill/Tetra images W23(tl2), Macmillan Education Limited/Stockbyte Royalty Free Photos W9(cl1), Macmillan Education Limited/iStockphoto/LittleBee80 W10(cl), Macmillan Education Limited/iStockphoto/Lumina Stock, Lumina Images W9(tr2), Macmillan Education Limited/iStockphoto/Miles Davies W7(cr1), Macmillan Education Limited/ImageSource W9(bl), W27, W30, Macmillan Education Limited/Johner Images W23(tl1), Macmillan Education Limited/MACMILLAN/Wholly Owned W1(tl4), Macmillan Education limited/Photodisc/Getty Images W1(tr), Macmillan Education Limited/PhotoDisc W9(tl2), Macmillan Education Limited/MACMILLAN W23(tr4), Macmillan Education Limited/MACMILLAN MEXICO/Michael Crampton (Art Resource Ltd TA Meiklejohn Illustration) W29, Macmillan Education Limited/Macmillan Publishers/Peter Day W23(c), Macmillan Education Limited/PHOTODISC W7(cr2), Macmillan Education Limited/STOCKBYTE W7(tr1), Macmillan Education Limited/STOCKBYTE W7(tr4), Macmillan Education Limited/www.imagesource.com W9(cr2), Macmillan Education Limited/Westend61 W1(cr2), Macmillan Education Limited/10'000 Hours/Digital Vision W21(bl2), Macmillan Education Limited/Zero Creatives GmbH W12(tl3); **VIEW Pictures Ltd** W22(bl).

The author and publishers are grateful for permission to reprint the following copyright material:

Extracts from: '700 Classroom Activities New Edition' © David Seymour and Maria Popova 2005. Published by Macmillan Education. Used by Permission. All Rights Reserved.

Extracts from: 'Learning Teaching 3rd Edition Student's Book' © Jim Scrivener 2011. Published by Macmillan Education Limited. Used by Permission. All Rights Reserved.

Student's Book credits:
Text, design and illustration © Macmillan Education Limited 2020
Written by Ingrid Wisniewska and Ed Price

The authors have asserted their right to be identified as the authors of this work in accordance with the Copyright, Designs and Patents Act 1988.

The right of Sue Kay and Vaughan Jones to be identified as authors of the Speaking Pages in this work has been asserted by them in accordance with the Copyright, Designs and Patents Act 1988.

Designed by emc design ltd
Picture research by Emily Taylor

Full acknowledgements for illustrations and photographs in the facsimile pages can be found in the Student's Book ISBN 978-1-380-01655-3.

Printed and bound in Argentina

2021

10

Contents

Student's Book Introduction

American Language Hub is a new six-level general English course for adult learners, which takes the complexity out of teaching English. It is designed to promote effective communication and helps to build learners' confidence with regular opportunities for meaningful practice. With its firm pedagogic foundation and syllabus aligned to the revised CEFR, American Language Hub has clear learning outcomes which make it easy to use in a variety of teaching situations.

1 NICE TO MEET YOU!

The language of friendship is not words but meanings.
Henry David Thoreau

A gondolier in Venice, Italy.

OBJECTIVES
- talk about where you're from
- introduce a friend
- greet people
- fill in a form

Work with a partner. Discuss the questions.
1 Look at the picture. Which country is the man in?
2 What language(s) do you think he speaks?
3 What language(s) do you speak?

NICE TO MEET YOU! 1

The engaging photograph and famous quotation help teachers to focus students and familiarize themselves with the ideas in the unit. Teachers can also encourage students to label the picture.

Student's Book unit opener
The first page of every American Language Hub unit is the unit opener. It is an exciting visual opportunity for students to engage with the theme of the unit and see at a glance the CEFR learning objectives for each lesson.

There is a quick warm-up speaking activity. Teachers can use this time to prepare the class for their lesson and delay the main start for five minutes until all the students arrive.

Student's Book Lesson 1

Vocabulary

American Language Hub teaches vocabulary in topic-related sets to help students categorize the new words they learn. Key vocabulary sets are built on and reviewed in the back of the book.

Reading and Listening

Reading and listening sections allow students to practice their receptive skills. All sections have tasks that move from global to detailed understanding so students can achieve a good overall comprehension. The key skills focus is clearly marked in the activity titles. The texts and scripts also present target vocabulary, grammar or pronunciation.

Grammar

The American Language Hub approach to grammar is inductive. Students are exposed to new language in context. Each grammar section prompts the student to notice the feature in context and to discover its form and use. Students then have further opportunities for controlled practice before using their new language in more authentic spoken or written output.

1.1 Say hello — Talk about where you're from

V – countries P – syllables and syllable stress V – numbers 0–10 G – simple present *be: I, you*

VOCABULARY
Countries

A SPEAK Work in pairs. Say hello. Say your name.

A: Hi, I'm Victor.
B: Hello, Victor. I'm Anna. Nice to meet you.
A: Hi Anna! Nice to meet you, too!

B Complete the greetings with names of countries.

Argentina Australia Brazil Britain Canada Egypt Italy Japan Mexico Morocco Spain ~~Turkey~~

C SPEAK Work in pairs. Ask about each picture.

A: Where is it? *B: It's in Egypt.*

A pyramid in Egypt
Mount Fuji
Sydney Opera House
The leaning tower of Pisa

PRONUNCIATION
Syllables and syllable stress

In English, we stress a different part of different words. A stressed syllable is loud and strong.

Ar-gen-**ti**-na

A 1.1 Listen. Underline the stressed syllable in each word. Which word only has one syllable?

1 Argentina
2 Australia
3 Brazil
4 Canada
5 China
6 Egypt
7 Italy
8 Japan
9 Mexico
10 Morocco
11 Spain
12 Turkey

B SPEAK Work in pairs. Ask your partner about these cities. Then underline the stressed syllable.

1 Berlin, Germany
2 Budapest, Hungary
3 Bogotá, Colombia
4 Jakarta, Indonesia
5 Moscow, Russia
6 Stockholm, Sweden

A: Where's Berlin?
B: It's in Germany.

2 NICE TO MEET YOU!

1.1

LISTENING

A PREDICT Look at the photo. Read the information. Where are they?

B 1.2 **LISTEN FOR SPECIFIC INFORMATION** Listen to the conversation. Which city is the student from?

C 1.2 **LISTEN FOR DETAIL** Listen again. Find and correct three mistakes in the form.

Application for Language School

First name:	Luisa
Last name:	Fuentez
Country:	Italy
Phone number:	07647 293387

D SPEAK Work in pairs. Ask and answer.

A: Where are you from?
B: I'm from Turkey.

VOCABULARY
Numbers 0–10

A 1.3 Listen and repeat each number.

0 1 2 3 4 5
6 7 8 9 10

B 1.4 Listen to Lisa's phone number. How does she say the numbers in bold?

07647 293387

C 1.5 Listen and complete the phone numbers.

CONTACTS
1 01501 __77 2__9
2 767__ 022 14__4
3 0231 74__ 852__
4 073__ 630 433__

D SPEAK Work in a group. Ask each person for their phone number. Make a list.

A: What's your phone number?
B: It's 07790 521006.

GRAMMAR
Simple present *be: I, you*

A 1.6 Listen to the examples. Underline the verbs.

I'm from Spain.
Are you from Madrid?
No, I'm not. I'm from Bilbao.

I am = I'm

B WORK IT OUT Circle the correct verb.

am/are		
I	[1]'m / 're	from Spain.
You	[2]'m / 're	from Turkey.
I	[3]'m not / aren't	from New York.
You	[4]'m not / aren't	from Toronto.
[5]Am / Are you from Brazil?		No, I [6]'m not / aren't.

C Go to the Grammar Hub on page 98.

SPEAKING

A PREPARE Read the conversation. Practice the conversation with a partner.

A: Hi! I'm Thomas. I'm from Argentina.
B: Nice to meet you, Thomas. I'm Anna. I'm from Germany.
A: Are you from Berlin?
B: No, I'm not. I'm from Hamburg.
A: Nice to meet you, too.

B PLAN Change the underlined words so the information is about you and your partner.

C PRACTICE Work in pairs. Practice your conversation.

D REPEAT Find a new partner. Practice the conversation again.

Talk about where you're from

NICE TO MEET YOU! 3

Pronunciation

In American Language Hub, lessons focus on both word-level and sentence-level pronunciation. This not only allows students to improve their accuracy but also their fluency through sentence-level intonation, which helps students understand how to add meaning through pronunciation.

Speaking

Each lesson starts with a CEFR unit objective which the lesson is designed to address. Students will often use the grammar, vocabulary and pronunciation from the lesson to complete a speaking activity linked to the unit objective. American Language Hub allows students to safely practice speaking in pairs after most sections. This ensures that they feel confident to take an active role in the final speaking task.

Student's Book Lesson 2

Reading and Listening Skill

Every unit includes a task designed to practice a key reading or listening skill. This ensures students are given the tools they need to effectively process a wide variety of texts and scripts. By the end of each book, students will have been exposed to 12 different key skills for reading or listening.

Topics

American Language Hub topics contextualize the language input for the lesson. They have been selected to allow opportunities for personalization.

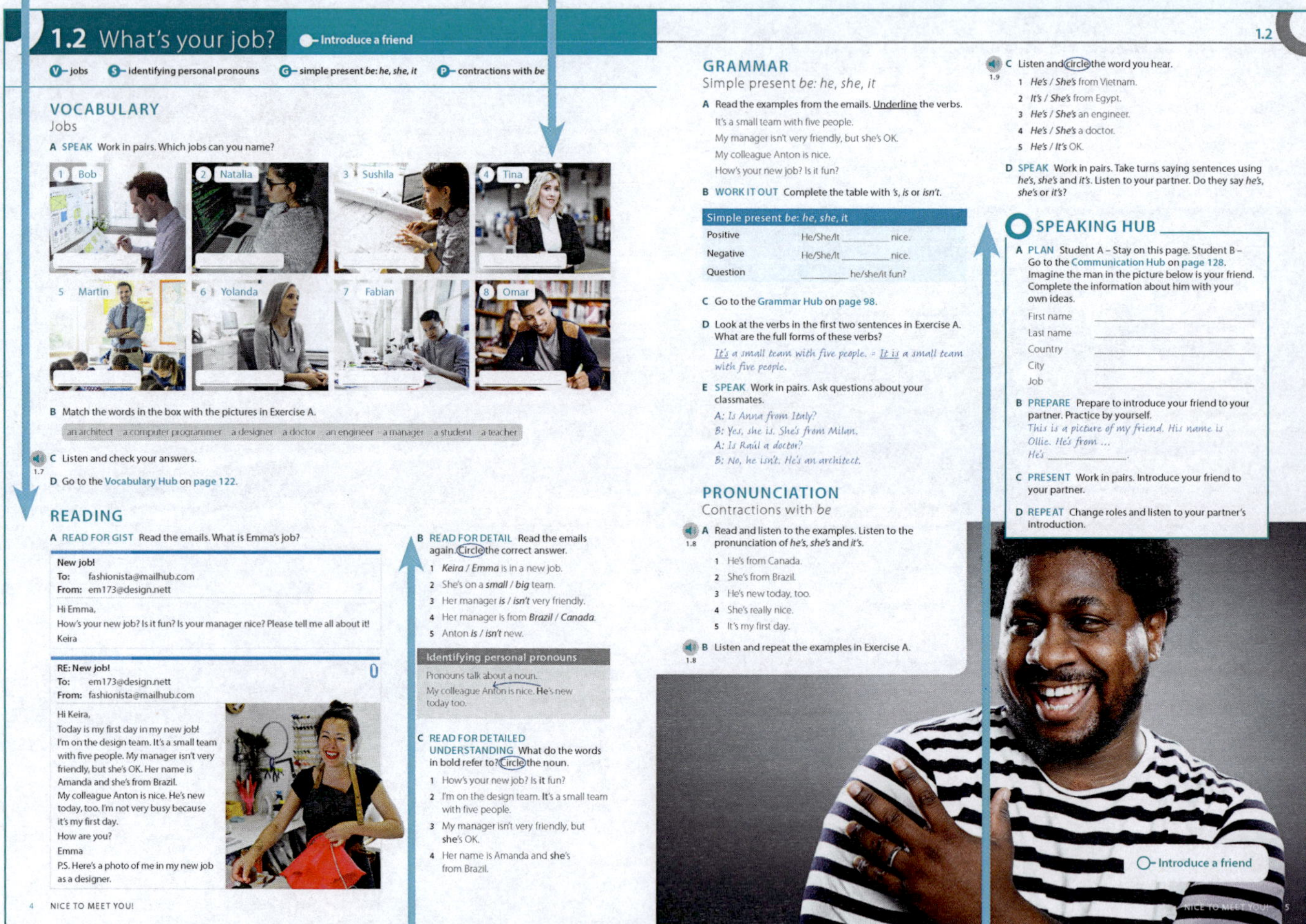

1.2 What's your job?

Introduce a friend

V – jobs S – identifying personal pronouns G – simple present *be: he, she, it* P – contractions with *be*

VOCABULARY

Jobs

A SPEAK Work in pairs. Which jobs can you name?

1 Bob 2 Natalia 3 Sushila 4 Tina 5 Martin 6 Yolanda 7 Fabian 8 Omar

B Match the words in the box with the pictures in Exercise A.

an architect a computer programmer a designer a doctor an engineer a manager a student a teacher

1.7 C Listen and check your answers.

D Go to the Vocabulary Hub on page 122.

READING

A READ FOR GIST Read the emails. What is Emma's job?

New job!
To: fashionista@mailhub.com
From: em173@design.nett

Hi Emma,
How's your new job? Is it fun? Is your manager nice? Please tell me all about it!
Keira

RE: New job!
To: em173@design.nett
From: fashionista@mailhub.com

Hi Keira,
Today is my first day in my new job!
I'm on the design team. It's a small team with five people. My manager isn't very friendly, but she's OK. Her name is Amanda and she's from Brazil.
My colleague Anton is nice. He's new today, too. I'm not very busy because it's my first day.
How are you?
Emma
P.S. Here's a photo of me in my new job as a designer.

B READ FOR DETAIL Read the emails again. Circle the correct answer.

1 *Keira / Emma* is in a new job.
2 She's on a *small / big* team.
3 Her manager *is / isn't* very friendly.
4 Her manager is from *Brazil / Canada*.
5 Anton *is / isn't* new.

Identifying personal pronouns

Pronouns talk about a noun.
My colleague Anton is nice. **He**'s new today too.

C READ FOR DETAILED UNDERSTANDING What do the words in bold refer to? Circle the noun.

1 How's your new job? Is **it** fun?
2 I'm on the design team. **It**'s a small team with five people.
3 My manager isn't very friendly, but **she**'s OK.
4 Her name is Amanda and **she**'s from Brazil.

4 NICE TO MEET YOU!

1.2

GRAMMAR

Simple present *be: he, she, it*

A Read the examples from the emails. Underline the verbs.

It's a small team with five people.
My manager isn't very friendly, but she's OK.
My colleague Anton is nice.
How's your new job? Is it fun?

B WORK IT OUT Complete the table with *'s*, *is* or *isn't*.

Simple present *be: he, she, it*	
Positive	He/She/It ________ nice.
Negative	He/She/It ________ nice.
Question	________ he/she/it fun?

C Go to the Grammar Hub on page 98.

D Look at the verbs in the first two sentences in Exercise A. What are the full forms of these verbs?

It's a small team with five people. = It is a small team with five people.

E SPEAK Work in pairs. Ask questions about your classmates.

A: Is Anna from Italy?
B: Yes, she is. She's from Milan.
A: Is Raúl a doctor?
B: No, he isn't. He's an architect.

PRONUNCIATION

Contractions with *be*

1.8 A Read and listen to the examples. Listen to the pronunciation of *he's*, *she's* and *it's*.

1 He's from Canada.
2 She's from Brazil.
3 He's new today, too.
4 She's really nice.
5 It's my first day.

1.8 B Listen and repeat the examples in Exercise A.

1.9 C Listen and circle the word you hear.

1 *He's / She's* from Vietnam.
2 *It's / She's* from Egypt.
3 *He's / She's* an engineer.
4 *He's / She's* a doctor.
5 *He's / It's* OK.

D SPEAK Work in pairs. Take turns saying sentences using *he's*, *she's* and *it's*. Listen to your partner. Do they say *he's*, *she's* or *it's*?

SPEAKING HUB

A PLAN Student A – Stay on this page. Student B – Go to the Communication Hub on page 128. Imagine the man in the picture below is your friend. Complete the information about him with your own ideas.

First name ________
Last name ________
Country ________
City ________
Job ________

B PREPARE Prepare to introduce your friend to your partner. Practice by yourself.

This is a picture of my friend. His name is Ollie. He's from ...
He's ________.

C PRESENT Work in pairs. Introduce your friend to your partner.

D REPEAT Change roles and listen to your partner's introduction.

Introduce a friend

NICE TO MEET YOU! 5

Skill labels

By focusing students' attention on the skills labels next to each exercise number, teachers can highlight which skills are being practiced and recycled.

Speaking Hub

At the end of Lesson 2, students perform a longer speaking turn which is staged to allow for planning and ideas creation. Students should apply their learning from the whole unit in the performance of their long speaking turn.

Student's Book Lesson 3

Functional Language
Each video provides a model for functional language so that students are able to access an ever-expanding bank of phrases. This language helps students to communicate effectively in a range of real-world situations.

Café Hub
The final lesson in each unit has a focus on video. Café Hub is an amusing situation comedy series. Meet Sam, Gaby and Lucy as they enjoy life in London. Find out how Gaby arrives in a new city, has interesting experiences and makes friends along the way.

Café Hub

9.3 Pizza Roma

make recommendations

COMPREHENSION

A 00.10–01:14 **Watch the first part of the video and choose the correct options to complete the sentences.**

1 Sam is ***opening / closing*** the café.
2 Sam ***knows / doesn't know*** Metal Train.
3 Gaby ***loves / hates*** pizza.
4 Pizza Roma is ***terrible / amazing***.
5 Pizza Roma has ***big / small*** pizzas.
6 The pizzas are ***expensive / cheap***.
7 Pizza Roma is ***near / far from*** Sam's Café.

B 01:15–01:34 **Watch part of the video and choose the correct set of directions from Sam's Café to Pizza Roma.**

1 ☐
2 ☐
3 ☐

C 01:35–03:00 **Watch the second part of the video. Discuss the questions.**

1 What was Gaby's pizza like?
2 Did she eat it?
3 Where did she buy it?
4 What does Gaby eat?
5 What does Lucy do?
6 Where was Lucy's pizza from?

USEFUL PHRASES

A Who says it? Gaby (G) or Sam (S)?

1 I'm afraid I'm closing now. ______
2 Hey! That's a nice cap! ______
3 Ah, I see. ______
4 It's not far. ______
5 It's next to the station. ______
6 I've got it, thanks! ______

Glossary
shop (n) (British) = store (n) (American)

B Match the useful phrases in Exercise A with the meanings.

I understand. [1]______ [2]______
I'm sorry … [3]______
It's near here. [4]______
I like your … [5]______

C Replace the underlined phrases with useful phrases from Exercise A.

Gaby: Hi, Sam. [1]I like your T-shirt.
Sam: Thanks. It's from my friend's shop.
Gaby: Where's her shop?
Sam: Oh, [2]it's near here. Just go out the café, turn left, turn left again and it's on your right.
Gaby: Left, left, right. [3]I understand, thanks!
Sam: [4]I'm sorry. I'm going to my yoga class now. It starts in five minutes.
Gaby: Ah, [5]I understand! Bye!

FUNCTIONAL LANGUAGE
Making recommendations

A Complete the phrases with the words in the box. Then watch the video again and check your answers.

Don't Do you know There's You should

Asking for a recommendation
[1]______ /**Is there** a good restaurant near here?

Giving a recommendation
[2]______ /**I know** a really good pizza restaurant. It's called Pizza Roma.
I was there last week. And the pizza was amazing. It was really big and really cheap.
[3]______ /**Why don't you** try it.
[4]______ /**I wouldn't** go to Pizza Nova! I went there last week. The pizza was bad! It was really small and really expensive.

B Circle the correct options to complete the conversation.

Liz: [1]***Do you know / There's*** a good café near here?
Mark: Do you like big breakfasts?
Liz: I love big breakfasts.
Mark: OK. [2]***why don't you / there's*** a really good café. It's called Tom's Café. I was there this morning. The breakfast is [3]***amazing / horrible***. It's really big and really cheap. [4]You ***should / shouldn't*** go there.
Liz: Thanks! Don't go to Rachel's Café. I went there yesterday. The coffee was [5]***amazing / terrible***. It was really small and really bad.
Mark: Oh, I see. Thanks.

LOOKING BACK

9.3

GABY SAM LUCY

PRONUNCIATION

9.9 **A** Listen to the conversation and notice how the underlined words are stressed.

Frank: Do you know a good restaurant near here?
Emily: Do you like sushi?
Frank: I love Japanese food.
Emily: There's a really good Japanese restaurant. It's called Sushirama.
Frank: Great.
Emily: I was there last week. And the sushi was amazing. It was really fresh. You should try it. Don't go to Suzy's Sushi! It's really bad.

9.9 **B** Listen again and repeat the conversation. Copy the stress.

SPEAKING

A PLAN Work in pairs. Read *Restaurants near you*. Discuss the questions.

1 Which restaurant(s) would you like to go to? Why?
2 Which restaurant(s) would you **not** like to go to? Why?

B PREPARE Rewrite the conversation in Pronunciation Exercise A.

- Replace the blue phrases with new ideas from the Functional language section.
- Replace the words in red using the ideas in the reviews below.
- Create some directions and include three or more useful phrases.

C PRACTICE Work in pairs. Practice and then perform your conversation in front of the class.

D REPEAT Choose different restaurants. Change roles and have a new conversation.

Restaurants near you

Moo Burger Bar ★★★★☆
Great fries!

Bob's Burgers ★☆☆☆☆
Terrible burgers, bad fries.

Puk Yuk Thai ★★★★★
Amazing! Best Thai food in town.

Bangkok House ★☆☆☆☆
Expensive Thai food.

Pierre's French cuisine ★☆☆☆☆
Bad service. Terrible food.

Paris mon amour ★★★★★
Amazing French food.

Make recommendations

LOOKING BACK

Useful Phrases
The video also provides an opportunity to learn a variety of useful phrases. Students can use these to bring authenticity to their language output.

Variety of English
The glossary boxes on these pages point out differences between American English and British English.

Pronunciation
Lesson 3 has a focus on stress and intonation. Students notice the stress and rhythm of British and American English pronunciation in the video before preparing to speak themselves.

American Language Hub for Teachers

Student's Book Writing, Review and Hubs

Writing and Review

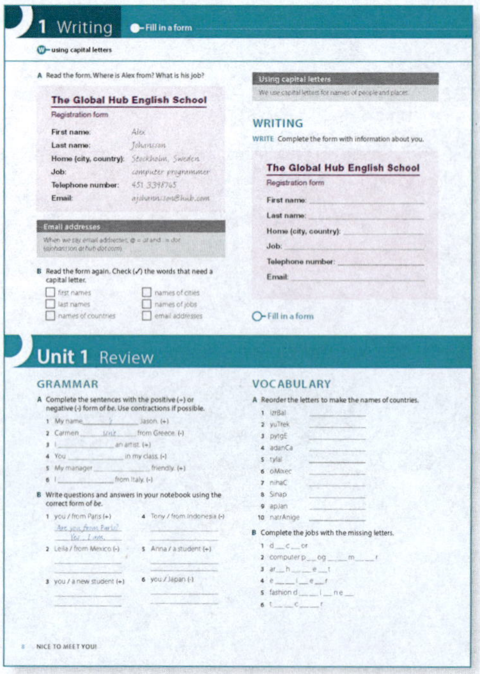
1 Writing — Fill in a form

Unit 1 Review

The Student's Book has a writing and review page at the end of each unit. Each writing lesson is aligned to the unit topic and teaches a different writing genre and skill. The review consolidates selected grammar and vocabulary from each unit.

Grammar Hub

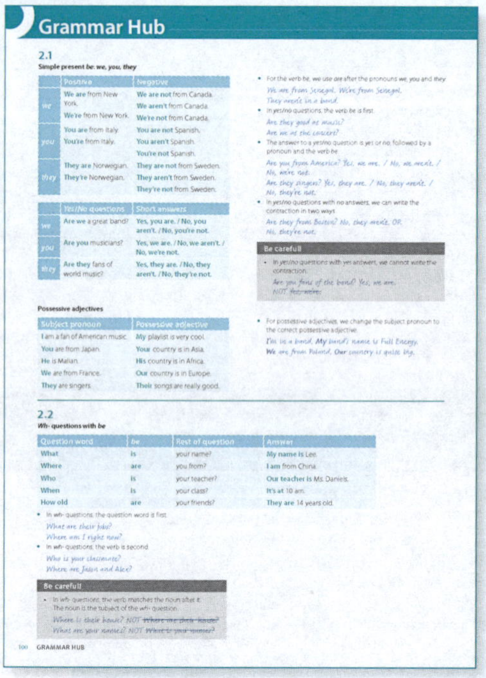
Grammar Hub

Clear explanations and further practice activities for each grammar point in the syllabus are provided at the back of the book. These can be used in class or set for homework to free up classroom time for communication.

Vocabulary Hub

Vocabulary Hub

The Vocabulary Hub provides extra practice of key vocabulary presented in each unit. As with the Grammar Hub sections, these can either consolidate work done in class or be used for further self-study.

Communication Hub

Communication Hub

The Communication Hub is used to set up longer communicative activities, such as information exchanges, quizzes and role plays.

Workbook

A Workbook is sold separately for American Language Hub. This includes 300 print activities practicing the language from the Student's Book. For each lesson, there are corresponding practice exercises of grammar, vocabulary and pronunciation. There is further practice of the reading and listening skills from Lesson 2 and extension practice of the functional language from Lesson 3. There is also a section dedicated to the unit's writing genre and skill. All of these pages develop learning from the main lessons of the Student's Book.

Vocabulary and Grammar

The Workbook practices vocabulary and grammar that students have attended to in the Student's Book. By reminding themselves of the words and skills they have recently seen, students are better able to imbed learning and have it ready for recall during speaking practice.

Listening and Reading

The Workbook provides additional listening and reading texts that explore the topics in the Student's Book. These give students the opportunity to develop the key receptive skills from the unit.

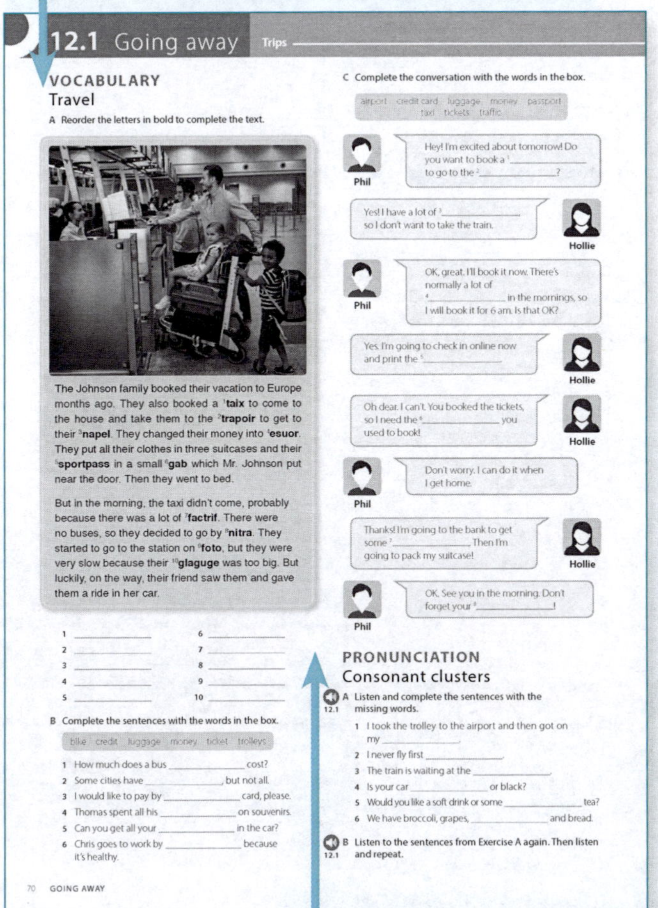
12.1 Going away — Trips

VOCABULARY
Travel

A Reorder the letters in bold to complete the text.

The Johnson family booked their vacation to Europe months ago. They also booked a [1]**taix** to come to the house and take them to the [2]**trapoir** to get to their [3]**napel**. They changed their money into [4]**esuor**. They put all their clothes in three suitcases and their [5]**sportpass** in a small [6]**gab** which Mr. Johnson put near the door. Then they went to bed.

But in the morning, the taxi didn't come, probably because there was a lot of [7]**factrif**. There were no buses, so they decided to go by [8]**nitra**. They started to go to the station on [9]**foto**, but they were very slow because their [10]**glaguge** was too big. But luckily, on the way, their friend saw them and gave them a ride in her car.

B Complete the sentences with the words in the box.

bike credit luggage money ticket trolleys

1 How much does a bus ______ cost?
2 Some cities have ______ but not all.
3 I would like to pay by ______ card, please.
4 Thomas spent all his ______ on souvenirs.
5 Can you get all your ______ in the car?
6 Chris goes to work by ______ because it's healthy.

C Complete the conversation with the words in the box.

airport credit card luggage money passport taxi tickets traffic

Phil: Hey! I'm excited about tomorrow! Do you want to book a [1]______ to go to the [2]______?
Hollie: Yes! I have a lot of [3]______ so I don't want to take the train.
Phil: OK, great. I'll book it now. There's normally a lot of [4]______ in the mornings, so I will book it for 6 am. Is that OK?
Hollie: Yes. I'm going to check in online now and print the [5]______.
Hollie: Oh dear. I can't. You booked the tickets, so I need the [6]______ you used to book!
Phil: Don't worry. I can do it when I get home.
Hollie: Thanks! I'm going to the bank to get some [7]______. Then I'm going to pack my suitcase!
Phil: OK. See you in the morning. Don't forget your [8]______!

PRONUNCIATION
Consonant clusters

12.1 A Listen and complete the sentences with the missing words.

1 I took the trolley to the airport and then got on my ______.
2 I never fly first ______.
3 The train is waiting at the ______.
4 Is your car ______ or black?
5 Would you like a soft drink or some ______ tea?
6 We have broccoli, grapes, ______ and bread.

12.1 B Listen to the sentences from Exercise A again. Then listen and repeat.

70 GOING AWAY

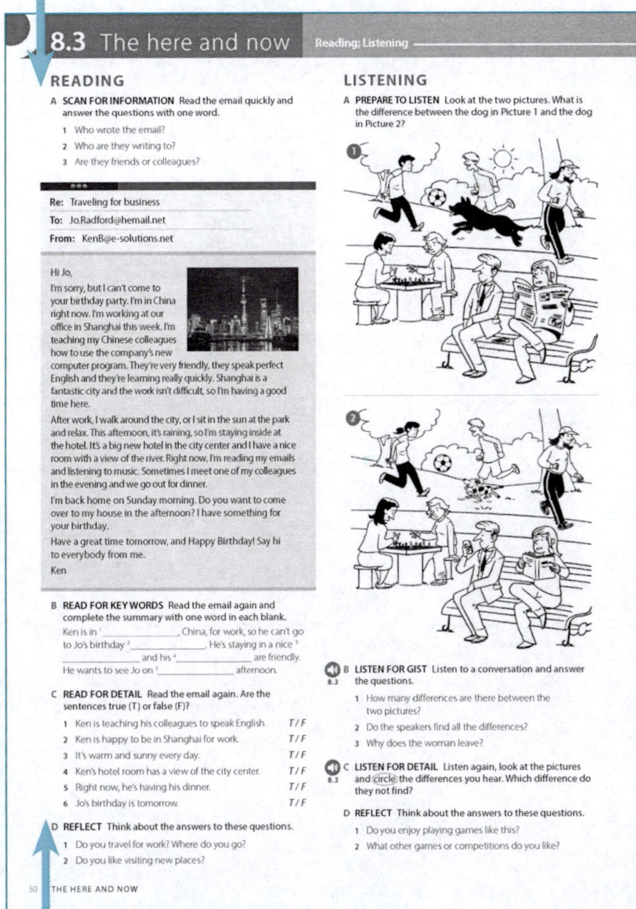
8.3 The here and now — Reading; Listening

READING

A SCAN FOR INFORMATION Read the email quickly and answer the questions with one word.

1 Who wrote the email?
2 Who are they writing to?
3 Are they friends or colleagues?

Re: Traveling for business
To: Jo.Radford@hemail.net
From: KenB@e-solutions.net

Hi Jo,

I'm sorry, but I can't come to your birthday party. I'm in China right now. I'm working at our office in Shanghai this week. I'm teaching my Chinese colleagues how to use the company's new computer program. They're very friendly, they speak perfect English and they're learning really quickly. Shanghai is a fantastic city and the work isn't difficult, so I'm having a good time here.

After work, I walk around the city, or I sit in the sun at the park and relax. This afternoon, it's raining, so I'm staying inside at the hotel. It's a big new hotel in the city center and I have a nice room with a view of the river. Right now, I'm reading my emails and listening to music. Sometimes I meet one of my colleagues in the evening and we go out for dinner.

I'm back home on Sunday morning. Do you want to come over to my house in the afternoon? I have something for your birthday.

Have a great time tomorrow, and Happy Birthday! Say hi to everybody from me.

Ken

B READ FOR KEY WORDS Read the email again and complete the summary with one word in each blank.

Ken is in [1]______ China, for work, so he can't go to Jo's birthday [2]______. He's staying in a nice [3]______ and his [4]______ are friendly. He wants to see Jo on [5]______ afternoon.

C READ FOR DETAIL Read the email again. Are the sentences true (T) or false (F)?

1 Ken is teaching his colleagues to speak English. T / F
2 Ken is happy to be in Shanghai for work. T / F
3 It's warm and sunny every day. T / F
4 Ken's hotel room has a view of the city center. T / F
5 Right now, he's having his dinner. T / F
6 Jo's birthday is tomorrow. T / F

D REFLECT Think about the answers to these questions.

1 Do you travel for work? Where do you go?
2 Do you like visiting new places?

LISTENING

A PREPARE TO LISTEN Look at the two pictures. What is the difference between the dog in Picture 1 and the dog in Picture 2?

8.3 B LISTEN FOR GIST Listen to a conversation and answer the questions.

1 How many differences are there between the two pictures?
2 Do the speakers find all the differences?
3 Why does the woman leave?

8.3 C LISTEN FOR DETAIL Listen again, look at the pictures and circle the differences you hear. Which difference do they not find?

D REFLECT Think about the answers to these questions.

1 Do you enjoy playing games like this?
2 What other games or competitions do you like?

50 THE HERE AND NOW

Pronunciation

The Workbook also consolidates the pronunciation topics from the Student's Book through further controlled practice.

Reflect

Each reading and listening page has a Reflect section so that students can use their Workbooks in class if they wish to reflect on their learning with their peers.

American Language Hub for Teachers

Teacher's Book

Worksheets
The bank of communicative worksheets at the back of the Teacher's Book provides additional controlled and freer practice of every vocabulary and grammar section.

Procedural notes
The lessons include procedural notes for teachers. These offer support to teachers on how to deliver the lesson rather than telling them how to teach. The notes are designed to be brief and easy to read.

Interleaved pages
Every level of American Language Hub has a Teacher's Book interleaved with pages of the Student's Book. The answers to all of the Student's Book activities are annotated on the page so there is no need for teachers to flip back and forth to find information.

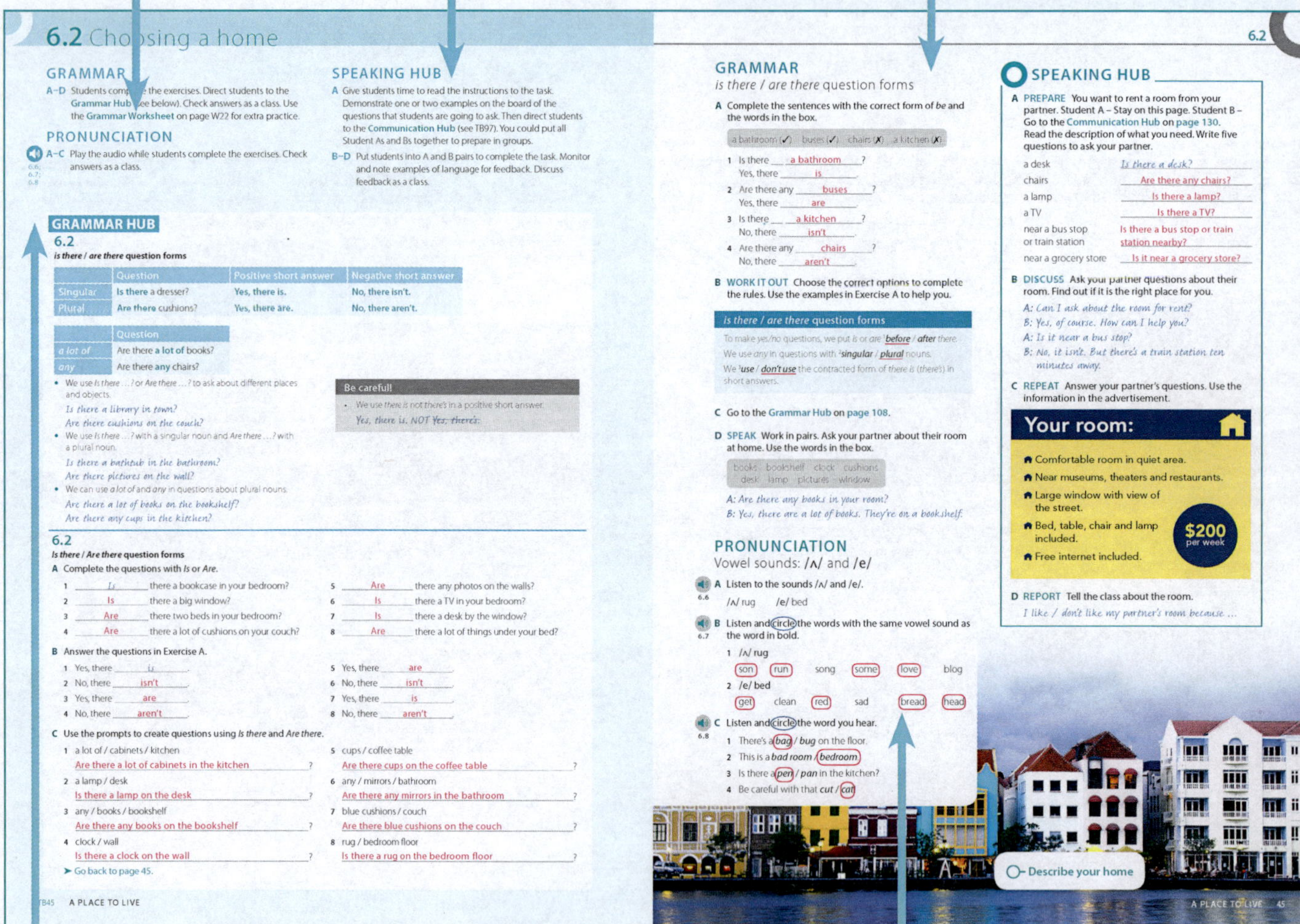
6.2 Choosing a home

GRAMMAR
A–D Students complete the exercises. Direct students to the Grammar Hub (see below). Check answers as a class. Use the Grammar Worksheet on page W22 for extra practice.

PRONUNCIATION
A–C Play the audio while students complete the exercises. Check answers as a class.

SPEAKING HUB
A Give students time to read the instructions to the task. Demonstrate one or two examples on the board of the questions that students are going to ask. Then direct students to the Communication Hub (see TB97). You could put all Student As and Bs together to prepare in groups.
B–D Put students into A and B pairs to complete the task. Monitor and note examples of language for feedback. Discuss feedback as a class.

GRAMMAR HUB
6.2
is there / are there question forms

	Question	Positive short answer	Negative short answer
Singular	Is there a dresser?	Yes, there is.	No, there isn't.
Plural	Are there cushions?	Yes, there are.	No, there aren't.

	Question
a lot of	Are there a lot of books?
any	Are there any chairs?

- We use Is there …? or Are there …? to ask about different places and objects.
  Is there a library in town?
  Are there cushions on the couch?
- We use Is there …? with a singular noun and Are there …? with a plural noun.
  Is there a bathtub in the bathroom?
  Are there pictures on the wall?
- We can use a lot of and any in questions about plural nouns.
  Are there a lot of books on the bookshelf?
  Are there any cups in the kitchen?

Be careful!
- We use there is not there's in a positive short answer.
  Yes, there is. NOT Yes, there's.

6.2
Is there / Are there question forms
A Complete the questions with Is or Are.
1 Is there a bookcase in your bedroom?
2 Is there a big window?
3 Are there two beds in your bedroom?
4 Are there a lot of cushions on your couch?
5 Are there any photos on the walls?
6 Is there a TV in your bedroom?
7 Is there a desk by the window?
8 Are there a lot of things under your bed?

B Answer the questions in Exercise A.
1 Yes, there is.
2 No, there isn't.
3 Yes, there are.
4 No, there aren't.
5 Yes, there are.
6 No, there isn't.
7 Yes, there is.
8 No, there aren't.

C Use the prompts to create questions using Is there and Are there.
1 a lot of / cabinets / kitchen — Are there a lot of cabinets in the kitchen?
2 a lamp / desk — Is there a lamp on the desk?
3 any / books / bookshelf — Are there any books on the bookshelf?
4 clock / wall — Is there a clock on the wall?
5 cups / coffee table — Are there cups on the coffee table?
6 any / mirrors / bathroom — Are there any mirrors in the bathroom?
7 blue cushions / couch — Are there blue cushions on the couch?
8 rug / bedroom floor — Is there a rug on the bedroom floor?
➤ Go back to page 45.

TB45 A PLACE TO LIVE

6.2

GRAMMAR
is there / are there question forms
A Complete the sentences with the correct form of be and the words in the box.
a bathroom (✓) buses (✓) chairs (✗) a kitchen (✗)
1 Is there a bathroom? Yes, there is.
2 Are there any buses? Yes, there are.
3 Is there a kitchen? No, there isn't.
4 Are there any chairs? No, there aren't.

B WORK IT OUT Choose the correct options to complete the rules. Use the examples in Exercise A to help you.
is there / are there question forms
To make yes/no questions, we put is or are before / after there.
We use any in questions with singular / plural nouns.
We use / don't use the contracted form of there is (there's) in short answers.

C Go to the Grammar Hub on page 108.

D SPEAK Work in pairs. Ask your partner about their room at home. Use the words in the box.
books bookshelf clock cushions desk lamp pictures window
A: Are there any books in your room?
B: Yes, there are a lot of books. They're on a bookshelf.

PRONUNCIATION
Vowel sounds: /ʌ/ and /e/
A Listen to the sounds /ʌ/ and /e/.
/ʌ/ rug /e/ bed
B Listen and circle the words with the same vowel sound as the word in bold.
1 /ʌ/ rug: son run song some love blog
2 /e/ bed: get clean red sad bread head
C Listen and circle the word you hear.
1 There's a bag / bug on the floor.
2 This is a bad room / bedroom.
3 Is there a pen / pan in the kitchen?
4 Be careful with that cut / cat.

SPEAKING HUB
A PREPARE You want to rent a room from your partner. Student A – Stay on this page. Student B – Go to the Communication Hub on page 130.
Read the description of what you need. Write five questions to ask your partner.
a desk — Is there a desk?
chairs — Are there any chairs?
a lamp — Is there a lamp?
a TV — Is there a TV?
near a bus stop or train station — Is there a bus stop or train station nearby?
near a grocery store — Is it near a grocery store?

B DISCUSS Ask your partner questions about their room. Find out if it is the right place for you.
A: Can I ask about the room for rent?
B: Yes, of course. How can I help you?
A: Is it near a bus stop?
B: No, it isn't. But there's a train station ten minutes away.

C REPEAT Answer your partner's questions. Use the information in the advertisement.

Your room:
Comfortable room in quiet area.
Near museums, theaters and restaurants.
Large window with view of the street.
Bed, table, chair and lamp included.
Free internet included.
$200 per week

D REPORT Tell the class about the room.
I like / don't like my partner's room because …

Describe your home

A PLACE TO LIVE 45

Grammar explanations
Where the Student's Book asks the students to look at the Grammar Hub, the teacher can find this already annotated on the Teacher's Book page. For ease of use, the Grammar Hub reference activities at the end of the Student's Book have been added to the Teacher's Book pages at the location they will be used in the course. This makes it easier for teachers to mark homework in class or refer to succinct grammar explanations.

Annotated answers
The answers are annotated on the interleaved pages of the Student's Book. These provide a quick reference tool for teachers.

Teacher's Book: Macmillan Books for Teachers

Lead-in

Suggested lead-ins can be used to activate prior knowledge, generate interest in the lesson topic or focus on useful lexis.

Extra activities

Extra activity boxes help teachers extend the content of the lesson, both in and out of the classroom.

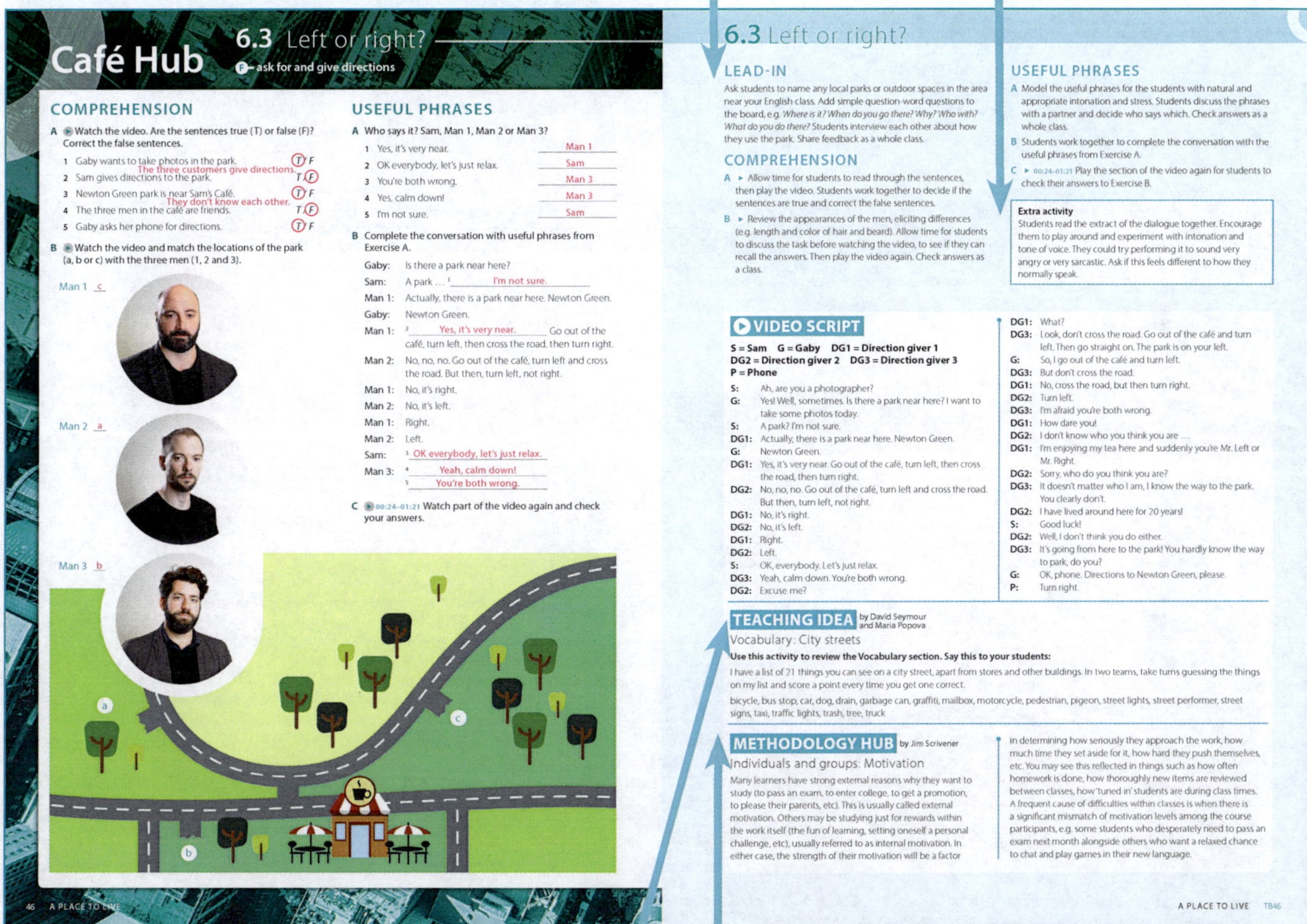

Café Hub

6.3 Left or right?

F – ask for and give directions

COMPREHENSION

A Watch the video. Are the sentences true (T) or false (F)? Correct the false sentences.

1 Gaby wants to take photos in the park. (T) F
2 Sam gives directions to the park. T (F) The three customers give directions.
3 Newton Green park is near Sam's Café. (T) F
4 The three men in the café are friends. T (F) They don't know each other.
5 Gaby asks her phone for directions. (T) F

B Watch the video and match the locations of the park (a, b or c) with the three men (1, 2 and 3).

Man 1 c
Man 2 a
Man 3 b

USEFUL PHRASES

A Who says it? Sam, Man 1, Man 2 or Man 3?

1 Yes, it's very near. Man 1
2 OK everybody, let's just relax. Sam
3 You're both wrong. Man 3
4 Yes, calm down! Man 3
5 I'm not sure. Sam

B Complete the conversation with useful phrases from Exercise A.

Gaby: Is there a park near here?
Sam: A park … 1 I'm not sure.
Man 1: Actually, there is a park near here. Newton Green.
Gaby: Newton Green.
Man 1: 2 Yes, it's very near. Go out of the café, turn left, then cross the road, then turn right.
Man 2: No, no, no. Go out of the café, turn left and cross the road. But then, turn left, not right.
Man 1: No, it's right.
Man 2: No, it's left.
Man 1: Right.
Man 2: Left.
Sam: 3 OK everybody, let's just relax.
Man 3: 4 Yeah, calm down!
5 You're both wrong.

C 00:24–01:21 Watch part of the video again and check your answers.

46 A PLACE TO LIVE

6.3 Left or right?

LEAD-IN

Ask students to name any local parks or outdoor spaces in the area near your English class. Add simple question-word questions to the board, e.g. *Where is it? When do you go there? Why? Who with? What do you do there?* Students interview each other about how they use the park. Share feedback as a whole class.

COMPREHENSION

A Allow time for students to read through the sentences, then play the video. Students work together to decide if the sentences are true and correct the false sentences.

B Review the appearances of the men, eliciting differences (e.g. length and color of hair and beard). Allow time for students to discuss the task before watching the video, to see if they can recall the answers. Then play the video again. Check answers as a class.

USEFUL PHRASES

A Model the useful phrases for the students with natural and appropriate intonation and stress. Students discuss the phrases with a partner and decide who says which. Check answers as a whole class.

B Students work together to complete the conversation with the useful phrases from Exercise A.

C 00:24–01:21 Play the section of the video again for students to check their answers to Exercise B.

Extra activity

Students read the extract of the dialogue together. Encourage them to play around and experiment with intonation and tone of voice. They could try performing it to sound very angry or very sarcastic. Ask if this feels different to how they normally speak.

VIDEO SCRIPT

S = Sam G = Gaby DG1 = Direction giver 1
DG2 = Direction giver 2 DG3 = Direction giver 3
P = Phone

S: Ah, are you a photographer?
G: Yes! Well, sometimes. Is there a park near here? I want to take some photos today.
S: A park? I'm not sure.
DG1: Actually, there is a park near here. Newton Green.
G: Newton Green.
DG1: Yes, it's very near. Go out of the café, turn left, then cross the road, then turn right.
DG2: No, no, no. Go out of the café, turn left and cross the road. But then, turn left, not right.
DG1: No, it's right.
DG2: No, it's left.
DG1: Right.
DG2: Left.
S: OK, everybody. Let's just relax.
DG3: Yeah, calm down. You're both wrong.
DG2: Excuse me?
DG1: What?
DG3: Look, don't cross the road. Go out of the café and turn left. Then go straight on. The park is on your left.
G: So, I go out of the café and turn left.
DG3: But don't cross the road.
DG1: No, cross the road, but then turn right.
DG2: Turn left.
DG3: I'm afraid you're both wrong.
DG1: How dare you!
DG2: I don't know who you think you are …
DG1: I'm enjoying my tea here and suddenly you're Mr. Left or Mr. Right.
DG2: Sorry, who do you think you are?
DG3: It doesn't matter who I am, I know the way to the park. You clearly don't.
DG2: I have lived around here for 20 years!
S: Good luck!
DG2: Well, I don't think you do either.
DG3: It's going from here to the park! You hardly know the way to park, do you?
G: OK, phone. Directions to Newton Green, please.
P: Turn right.

TEACHING IDEA by David Seymour and Maria Popova

Vocabulary: City streets

Use this activity to review the Vocabulary section. Say this to your students:

I have a list of 21 things you can see on a city street, apart from stores and other buildings. In two teams, take turns guessing the things on my list and score a point every time you get one correct.

bicycle, bus stop, car, dog, drain, garbage can, graffiti, mailbox, motorcycle, pedestrian, pigeon, street lights, street performer, street signs, taxi, traffic lights, trash, tree, truck

METHODOLOGY HUB by Jim Scrivener

Individuals and groups: Motivation

Many learners have strong external reasons why they want to study (to pass an exam, to enter college, to get a promotion, to please their parents, etc). This is usually called external motivation. Others may be studying just for rewards within the work itself (the fun of learning, setting oneself a personal challenge, etc), usually referred to as internal motivation. In either case, the strength of their motivation will be a factor in determining how seriously they approach the work, how much time they set aside for it, how hard they push themselves, etc. You may see this reflected in things such as how often homework is done, how thoroughly new items are reviewed between classes, how 'tuned in' students are during class times. A frequent cause of difficulties within classes is when there is a significant mismatch of motivation levels among the course participants, e.g. some students who desperately need to pass an exam next month alongside others who want a relaxed chance to chat and play games in their new language.

A PLACE TO LIVE TB46

Teaching Idea

Tips and ideas from the *Macmillan Books for Teachers* series are included in the teacher's notes to give some new ideas for instant communicative activities in the lesson. These can usually be used without paper preparation as warm-ups to get the class moving or as a flexible stage where there is time to fill.

Methodology Hub

Ideas for professional development from Jim Scrivener's *Learning Teaching Third Edition* are presented in every unit to help new teachers pick up helpful tips to add to their repertoire or just reflect on a new way to use American Language Hub with their class.

American Language Hub for Teachers

Teacher's App

The American Language Hub Teacher's Book comes with a Teacher's App, which gives access to the Resource Center, Test Generator and Classroom Presentation Kit.

The Classroom Presentation Kit is designed to be displayed on an interactive whiteboard (IWB) or using a projector and enables teachers to play video and audio or show interactive activities in class. It is not only user-friendly for the teacher but also for the student, with activities being clearly visible for the whole class. Answer-by-answer reveal enables teachers to elicit student responses and check answers one by one.

Tools

Embedded tools make it possible to highlight and annotate texts to prompt noticing or self-correction. Teachers have the option to turn on an audio script, which is timed to sync with the dialogue, when listening to audio.

Teachers can zoom into each activity with one click. Then they can either move smoothly through the activities or zoom out to see the whole page. They can also create a whiteboard area for additional notes.

Video

Teachers can also access the video and audio for the course, including the authentic video from *The Guardian*.

Homework

The app allows teachers to assign homework directly to their students' devices and alert them when they have activities to complete.

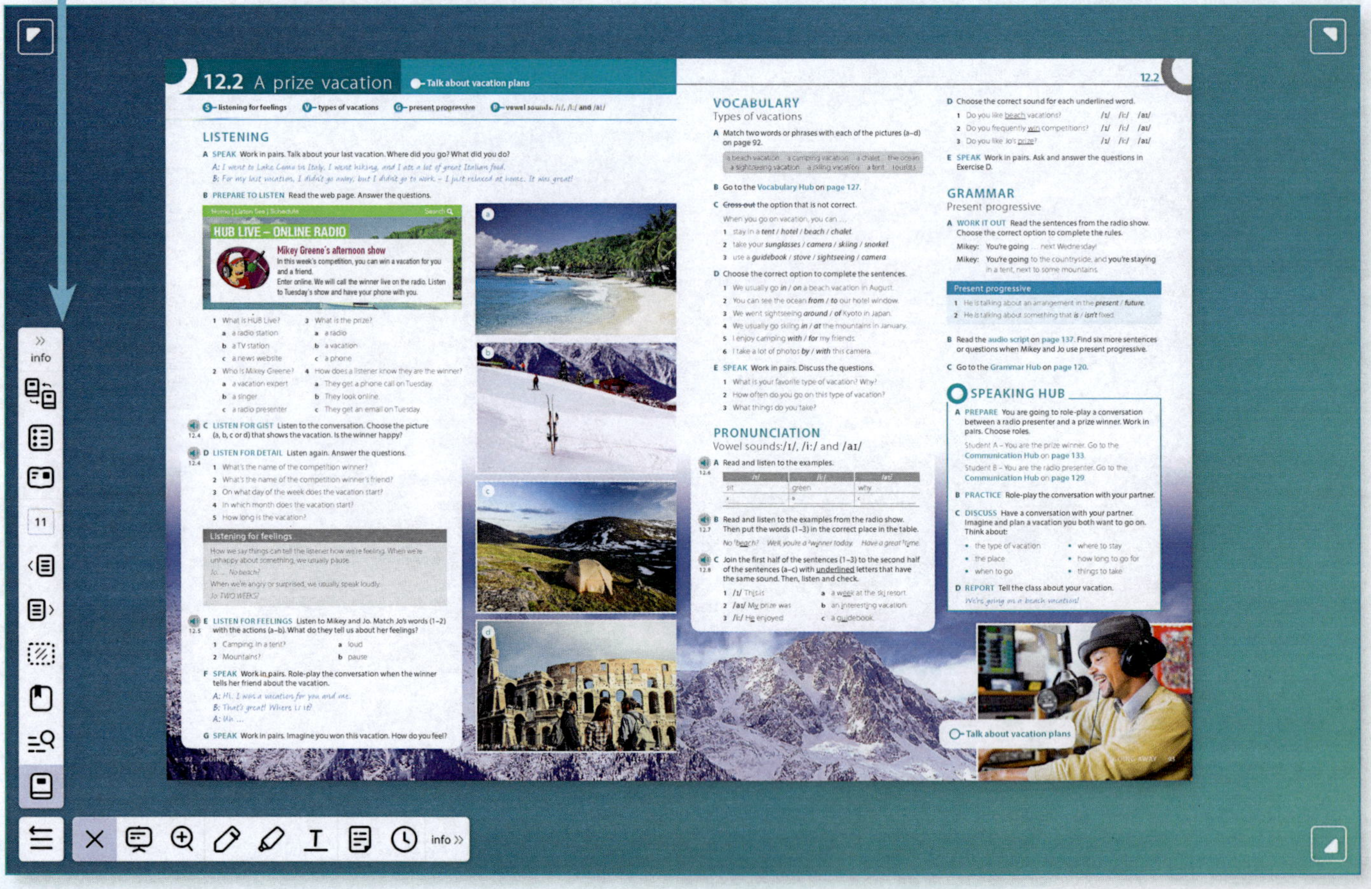

Preparation and Practice

Teachers can also configure student preparation and practice using the Teacher's App. Using the practice activities available, teachers can select and publish content to their students which they will receive through a push notification when they access their app. This enables teachers to personalize the amount and type of practice students do every week and to track their progress. Students can practice the grammar or vocabulary for the week before they go to class, allowing more time in the class for communication.

Test Generator

The Teacher's App also gives access to the Test Generator. In the Test Generator, teachers can create tests or use the pre-built tests for each level of the course and print these to assign to students. There are unit tests, mid- and end-of-course tests for each level, testing vocabulary, grammar and the four skills.

Student's App

Each Student's Book includes a code for the Student's App, to engage and encourage your students to practice their English on the move. Students can access grammar, vocabulary and pronunciation activities to prepare them for the lesson. Students are able to complete activities with varying levels of challenge and earn points.

Preparation
Allows more time for communicative activities in the class by providing pre-lesson exposure to the language covered in the Student's Book.

Practice
Provides additional practice to consolidate, review and extend areas covered in the Student's Book.

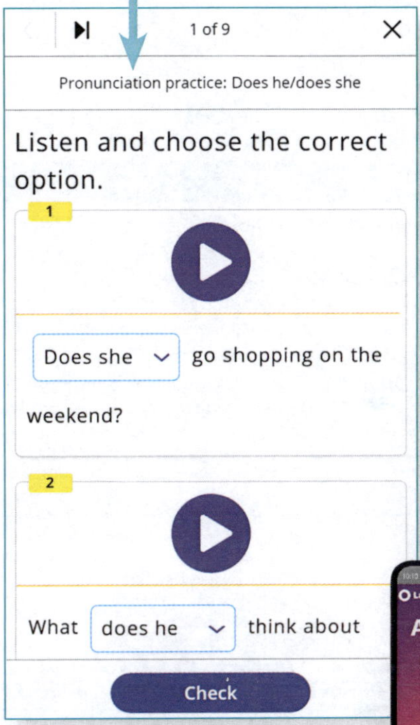

Rewards
A reward system helps to maintain student motivation.

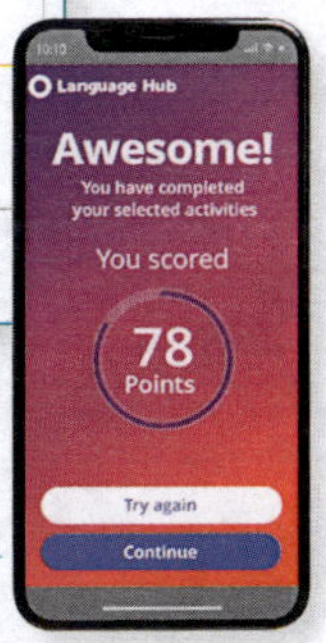

Video

Two types of video are available with the course. Café Hub is an amusing situation comedy series which models functional language. Video Hub uses content from *The Guardian* as a resource for authentic English. All the videos from the course relate to the unit topics, and offer listening practice and scaffolding for speaking output.

Video Hub

Café Hub

Student's Book Contents

Welcome

GREETINGS

A Read and listen to the conversation. 0.1

Jack: Hello! I'm Jack.
Alex: Hi. I'm Alex. Nice to meet you.
Jack: Nice to meet you, too.

B SPEAK Work in pairs. Practice the conversation. Say your name.

CLASSROOM INSTRUCTIONS

A Listen to the classroom instructions. 0.2

1

Open your book

2

Close your book

3

Read

4

Listen

5

Listen and repeat

6

Speak

7
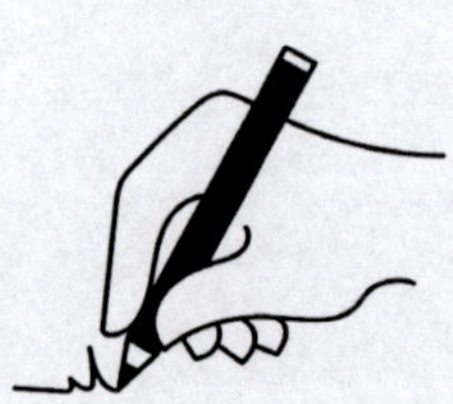
Write

8

Ask a question

B Read and listen to the conversations. 0.3

1 **Student:** What does *book* mean?
Teacher: It means *libro*.

2 **Student:** I don't understand.
Teacher: That's OK. I'll explain it again.

3 **Student:** Can you repeat that, please?
Teacher: Yes, of course.

THE ALPHABET

Aa Bb Cc Dd Ee
Ff Gg Hh Ii Jj Kk
Ll Mm Nn Oo Pp
Qq Rr Ss Tt Uu
Vv Ww Xx Yy Zz

***a*, *e*, *i*, *o*, and *u* are vowels.**
The other letters are consonants.

A Listen to the alphabet. 0.4

B Listen and repeat the alphabet. 0.4

C Listen and write the names. 0.5

1 Carlos
2 Hassan
3 Erica

D SPEAK Work in pairs. Spell your name.

A: Hello. My name's Lizzie. L – i – z – z – i – e.
B: Hi, Lizzie. My name's Florian. F – l – o – r – i – a – n.

1 Nice to meet you!

A gondolier in Venice, Italy.

The phrase is used for greeting someone when you meet them for the first time, or for saying goodbye to them on that occasion.

The quote suggests that friendship goes deeper than shared words – the words that we use to have conversations and discussions, share stories or even argue. Friendship involves knowing each other on a deeper level, at a level of emotion, feelings and understanding. This deep knowledge is sometimes difficult to describe in actual words.

Henry David Thoreau (1817–1862) was an American writer, poet and philosopher. His most famous work is *Walden*. He is widely thought of as a cultural hero and a great example of the classic American writer.

Ask students to label the photo if you need time to set up the class.

OBJECTIVES

- talk about where you're from
- introduce a friend
- greet people
- fill in a form

Work with a partner. Discuss the questions.

1 Look at the picture. Which country is the man in?
2 What language(s) do you think he speaks?
3 What language(s) do you speak?

NICE TO MEET YOU! 1

OBJECTIVES

Read the unit objectives to the class.

UNIT OPENER QUESTIONS

Focus the students on the picture of Venice and the gondolier. Encourage them to guess where the man is, using clues in the picture – the canals, the gondola, his clothes. Ask them to name all the things they can see and build up a list of vocabulary in a column at the side of the board. Leave this there for the whole lesson, referring to the words as and when they come up.

Then ask students to read Questions 2 and 3. Answer the questions as a whole class. Encourage students to answer and share their ideas. Again, add vocabulary to the board for students to use throughout the class. Add sentence stems to the board to support students, or give examples yourself. *I think he speaks Italian. Maybe he speaks English for his job. I speak English and …*

WORKSHEETS

Lesson 1.1 Say hello

Vocabulary: Countries; Numbers 0–10 (W1)

Grammar: Simple present *be*: *I*, *you* (W2)

Lesson 1.2 What's your job?

Vocabulary: Jobs (W3)

Grammar: Simple present *be*: *he*, *she*, *it* (W3)

1.1 Say hello

Talk about where you're from

V countries · P syllables and syllable stress · V numbers 0–10 · G simple present *be*: *I, you*

VOCABULARY
Countries

A SPEAK Work in pairs. Say hello. Say your name.

A: Hi, I'm Victor.
B: Hello, Victor. I'm Anna. Nice to meet you.
A: Hi Anna! Nice to meet you, too!

B Complete the greetings with names of countries.

Argentina Australia Brazil Britain Canada Egypt Italy Japan Mexico Morocco Spain ~~Turkey~~

Let's chat! It's easy! It's fun! Click and say hello!

1 Hi! I'm Emine. I'm from *Turkey*.

2 Hello, everyone! I'm Camilla. I'm from Mexico.

3 Hello! I'm Alexa. I'm from Brazil.

4 Hi, everyone! I'm Laura. I'm from Argentina.

5 Hi! I'm Yasmin. I'm from Egypt.

6 Hi, everyone! I'm David. I'm from Spain.

7 Hi! I'm Matteo. I'm from Italy.

8 Hello, I'm Emily. I'm from Britain!

9 Hello, everyone. I'm Hiro. I'm from Japan.

10 Hi! I'm Charlotte. I'm from Australia.

11 Hello! I'm Mark. I'm from Canada.

12 Hi, everyone. I'm Hamid. I'm from Morocco.

C SPEAK Work in pairs. Ask about each picture.

A: Where is it? *B: It's in Egypt.*

A pyramid in Egypt

Mount Fuji

Sydney Opera House

The leaning tower of Pisa

PRONUNCIATION
Syllables and syllable stress

In English, we stress a different part of different words. A stressed syllable is loud and strong.

Ar-gen-ti-na

1.1 **A** Listen. Underline the stressed syllable in each word. Which word only has one syllable? Spain

1 Argentina
2 Australia
3 Brazil
4 Canada
5 China
6 Egypt
7 Italy
8 Japan
9 Mexico
10 Morocco
11 Spain
12 Turkey

B SPEAK Work in pairs. Ask your partner about these cities. Then underline the stressed syllable.

1 Berlin, Germany
2 Budapest, Hungary
3 Bogotá, Colombia
4 Jakarta, Indonesia
5 Moscow, Russia
6 Stockholm, Sweden

A: Where's Berlin?
B: It's in Germany.

1.1 Say hello

LEAD-IN

As students come in, smile at individuals and say *Hi/Hello, I'm* (your name). *I'm from* (your country). *Nice to meet you!* After the first few, encourage them to reply in the same way.

VOCABULARY

Countries

A Focus students on the conversation. Read it aloud while they follow. Then read it line by line and get everyone to repeat, focusing on the contraction *I'm* with a natural tone and intonation. Then read part A and ask individual students to read part B. Put students into pairs and ask them to recall the conversation. Then ask them to stand up and mingle, having the conversation, using their own names. Join in with the students, helping and correcting as necessary.

B Read aloud the names of the countries and ask students to repeat as a class. Help with pronunciation. If you have a map in the class, get students to point out the countries. Point at yourself and say *Hi! I'm* (your name). *I'm from* (your country). Focus on the weak form of *from*, with a stress on *I* and the country name, not *from*. Ask individual students to do the same. Then students complete the exercise in pairs. Check answers as a whole class.

C Show a picture of somewhere students might know, e.g. the Eiffel Tower. Ask *Where is it?* and elicit the answer, e.g. *It's in France* (insist on the country, not Paris). Then ask students to do the exercise in pairs. Walk around helping and correcting pronunciation, especially the link between *where* and *is* /weərɪz/ and the contraction of *it is* linking to *in* creating /ˈɪtsɪn/. Use the **Vocabulary Worksheet** on page W1 for extra practice.

PRONUNCIATION

1.1

A Write *Argentina* on the board and say it, with slightly exaggerated stress on the stressed syllable. Repeat, underlining the stressed syllable. Get the class to repeat after you, then ask individual students to say the word. Play the first word on the recording to show the example, then play the audio. Write the words on the board while students do the exercise. Repeat if necessary. To give feedback, play the recording word by word and underline the stressed syllables on the board. Alternatively, students could come to the board to underline the stressed syllables.

B Put students into pairs. Demonstrate the first example and write the words on the board. Get students to ask and answer; help with the stress if necessary. Then elicit the stressed syllables and underline them on the board. Practice the pronunciation as a whole class and individually. Encourage students to exaggerate the stressed syllable; show how it is more forceful and a higher pitch and that the unstressed syllables tend to be quieter and shorter.

Extra activity

Prepare a list of capital cities for each of the countries in Pronunciation Exercise A on page 2 (e.g. Ottawa – Canada). Students work in pairs or small groups. Say the capital city and the students write the country. Conduct this as a quiz. Give one point for the country and one point for correct spelling.

GRAMMAR HUB

1.1

Simple present *be*: *I, you*

	Positive	Negative
I	**I am** from Germany. **I'm** from Germany.	**I am not** from Germany. **I'm not** from Germany.
you	**You are** from Canada. **You're** from Canada.	**You are not** from Canada. **You aren't** from Canada. **You're not** from Canada.

	Yes/No questions	Short answers
you	**Are you** from Argentina?	**Yes, I am.** **No, I'm not.**

- For the verb *be*, we use *am* with *I* and *are* with *you*.

  I am happy.
  You are happy.

- We can use the long form (*I am / You are*) or the contraction (*I'm/You're*). We typically use the contraction when we speak.

  I am from London. OR I'm from London.
  You are from France. OR You're from France.

Be careful!

- Remember: I am = I'm, You are = You're.

  I'm from Peru. NOT ~~I'm am from Peru.~~
  You're from Brazil. NOT ~~You're are from Brazil.~~

1.1 Say hello

LISTENING

1.2 **A–D** Students complete Exercises A–C, checking answers in pairs and then as a class. Then students work in pairs to ask and answer where they are from. Encourage them to use full sentences.

VOCABULARY

Numbers 0–10

1.3 **A** Write numbers 0–10 on the board. Play the audio while students listen and repeat. Then practice while pointing at the numbers on the board. Ask students to listen and complete the phone numbers. Students then work in groups to practice giving and writing down phone numbers. They can use their own numbers or false ones if they prefer. Use the **Vocabulary Worksheet** on page W1 for extra practice.

1.4 **B** Play the audio and elicit *oh*. Highlight that in American English, we pronounce the number "0" as both *oh* and *zero*.

1.5 **C–D** Play the audio while students listen and complete the numbers. Students work in groups of four or five to complete the task. Tell them they can give false numbers if they don't want to share their real one! Use the **Vocabulary Worksheet** on page W1 for extra practice.

GRAMMAR

1.6 **A–C** Play the recording while students listen and complete the task. Students complete Exercise B alone. Encourage them to check their answers in pairs and then check as a class. Direct students to the **Grammar Hub** (see below and TB2). Use the **Grammar Worksheet** on page W2 for extra practice.

SPEAKING

A–D You could ask two stronger students to demonstrate the conversation for the class. Students practice reading in pairs. For Exercise B, demonstrate with information about yourself, and then ask students to do the same for themselves. Students have the conversation and then they can repeat with new partners. Monitor and provide feedback.

AUDIO SCRIPT

1.2

Listening, Exercise B
R = Receptionist L = Lisa

R: Good morning! Can I help you?
L: Hello! Yes, I'd like some English lessons, please.
R: Of course! What's your name?
Ex C **L:** My first name is Lisa, L-i-s-a, and my last name is Fuentes, F-u-e-n-t-e-s.
R: Thank you. Where are you from?
Ex C **L:** I'm from Spain.
R: Are you from Madrid?
Ex B **L:** No, I'm not. I am from Bilbao.
R: What's your phone number?
L: 0764 729 3387.
R: OK … Now, let's find a class for you …

GRAMMAR HUB

1.1

Simple present *be*: *I, you*

A Choose the correct options.

1 I *am* / *are* from Madrid. [am circled]
2 *You're* / *You're are* from Sweden. [You're circled]
3 *I not* / *I'm not* from Berlin. [I'm not circled]
4 You *not* / *aren't* from Hungary. [aren't circled]
5 *You are* / *Are you* from New York? [Are you circled]
6 I *are* / *am* from Germany. [am circled]
7 You *are* / *am* from the UK. [are circled]
8 *Am* / *Are* you from Indonesia? [Are circled]

B Write the negatives. Use contractions.

1 I'm from Italy.
I'm not from Italy.
2 You're from Brazil.
You aren't / You're not from Brazil.
3 I'm from China.
I'm not from China.
4 You're from Egypt.
You aren't / You're not from Egypt.
5 I'm from Japan.
I'm not from Japan.
6 You're from Turkey.
You aren't / You're not from Turkey.
7 I'm from Mexico.
I'm not from Mexico.
8 You're from Australia.
You aren't / You're not from Australia.

C Complete the conversations with the words in the box.

am ~~are~~ I I'm no not yes you

1 **A:** Are you from Italy?
B: Yes, I am.
2 **A:** Hello. Are you from Brazil?
B: Yes, I am.
3 **A:** Are you from Australia?
B: Yes, I am.
4 **A:** Are you from Morocco?
B: Yes, I am.
5 **A:** Are you from Canada?
B: No, I'm not.
6 **A:** Good morning. Are you from Argentina?
B: Yes, I am.
7 **A:** Hello Lisa. Are you from China?
B: No, I'm not.
8 **A:** Are you from Mexico?
B: No, I'm not.

➤ Go back to page 3.

LISTENING

A PREDICT Look at the photo. Read the information. Where are they? They are in a language school.

1.2 **B LISTEN FOR SPECIFIC INFORMATION** Listen to the conversation. Which city is the student from? Bilbao

1.2 **C LISTEN FOR DETAIL** Listen again. Find and correct three mistakes in the form.

Application for Language School

First name:	~~Luisa~~ Lisa
Last name:	~~Fuentez~~ Fuentes
Country:	~~Italy~~ Spain
Phone number:	07647 293387

D SPEAK Work in pairs. Ask and answer.

A: Where are you from?
B: I'm from Turkey.

VOCABULARY

Numbers 0–10

1.3 **A** Listen and repeat each number.

0 1 2 3 4 5
6 7 8 9 10

1.4 **B** Listen to Lisa's phone number. How does she say the numbers in bold?

07647 293387 0 = oh
33 = double three

1.5 **C** Listen and complete the phone numbers.

CONTACTS

1 01501 _6_ 77 2 _3_ 9
2 767 _9_ 022 14 _8_ 4
3 0231 74 _4_ 852 _0_
4 073 _5_ 630 433 _7_

D SPEAK Work in a group. Ask each person for their phone number. Make a list.

A: What's your phone number?
B: It's 07790 521006.

GRAMMAR

Simple present *be: I, you*

1.6 **A** Listen to the examples. Underline the verbs.

I'm from Spain.
Are you from Madrid?
No, I'm not. I'm from Bilbao.

I am = I'm

B WORK IT OUT Circle the correct verb.

am/are		
I	[1] *'m* / *'re*	from Spain.
You	[2] *'m* / *'re*	from Turkey.
I	[3] *'m not* / *aren't*	from New York.
You	[4] *'m not* / *aren't*	from Toronto.
[5] *Am* / *Are* you from Brazil?		No, I *'m not* / *aren't*.

C Go to the **Grammar Hub** on **page 98**.

SPEAKING

A PREPARE Read the conversation. Practice the conversation with a partner.

A: Hi! I'm Thomas. I'm from Argentina.
B: Nice to meet you, Thomas. I'm Anna. I'm from Germany.
A: Are you from Berlin?
B: No, I'm not. I'm from Hamburg.
A: Nice to meet you, too.

B PLAN Change the underlined words so the information is about you and your partner.

C PRACTICE Work in pairs. Practice your conversation.

D REPEAT Find a new partner. Practice the conversation again.

Talk about where you're from

1.2 What's your job?

Introduce a friend

V jobs   S identifying personal pronouns   G simple present *be*: *he, she, it*   P contractions with *be*

VOCABULARY

Jobs

A SPEAK Work in pairs. Which jobs can you name?

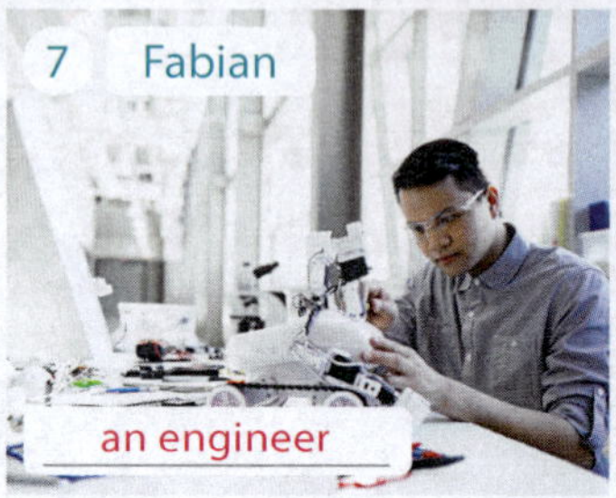

B Match the words in the box with the pictures in Exercise A.

an architect   a computer programmer   a designer   a doctor   an engineer   a manager   a student   a teacher

1.7 **C** Listen and check your answers.

D Go to the **Vocabulary Hub** on **page 122**.

READING

A READ FOR GIST Read the emails. What is Emma's job? Emma is a designer.

New job!
To: fashionista@mailhub.com
From: em173@design.nett

Hi Emma,
How's your new job? Is it fun? Is your manager nice? Please tell me all about it!
Keira

RE: New job!
To: em173@design.nett
From: fashionista@mailhub.com

Hi Keira,
Today is my first day in my new job! Ex B Q1
I'm on the design team. It's a small team Ex B Q2
with five people. My manager isn't very Ex B Q3
friendly, but she's OK. Her name is Ex B Q4
Amanda and she's from Brazil.
My colleague Anton is nice. He's new Ex B Q5
today, too. I'm not very busy because
it's my first day.
How are you?
Emma
P.S. Here's a photo of me in my new job
as a designer. Ex A

B READ FOR DETAIL Read the emails again. Circle the correct answer.

1 *Keira* / *Emma* is in a new job.
2 She's on a *small* / *big* team.
3 Her manager *is* / *isn't* very friendly.
4 Her manager is from *Brazil* / *Canada*.
5 Anton *is* / *isn't* new.

Identifying personal pronouns

Pronouns talk about a noun.
My colleague Anton is nice. **He**'s new today too.

C READ FOR DETAILED UNDERSTANDING What do the words in bold refer to? Circle the noun.

1 How's your new job? Is **it** fun?
2 I'm on the design team. **It**'s a small team with five people.
3 My manager isn't very friendly, but **she**'s OK.
4 Her name is Amanda and **she**'s from Brazil.

1.2 What's your job?

LEAD-IN

To test prior knowledge, with books closed, write some of the job titles in halves on the board:

teach *ger*

doc *er*

mana *er*

design *tor*

Invite students to come up and draw lines to match the halves. Check as a whole class. Elicit any other job titles known by students at this point and add them to a column at the side of the board. Refer to them if these words come up later in the lesson.

VOCABULARY

A–B In pairs, students look at the pictures and see if they can name the jobs. Students then match the job names to the pictures.

1.7 **C** Write the numbers 1–8 on the board. Play the audio and write the answers next to the numbers while students check their answers. Say the job titles one by one, emphasizing the stress pattern, e.g. *a designer*. Practice with students and repeat with all the jobs. Then circle the *a* in *architect* and *e* at the beginning of *engineer*, and write *an* in front. Clarify why we need *an* in front of a vowel by modeling the words with both *a* and *an* (the *n* enables us to link to the noun more easily). Write the other vowels on the board.

D Direct students to the **Vocabulary Hub** (see TB97). Students complete the exercise alone before comparing with a partner. Check the answers as a class. Teach any additional jobs that are relevant to the class. Use the **Vocabulary Worksheet** on page W3 for extra practice.

READING

A Focus students on the two emails. Ask *What is Emma's job?* Set a short time limit for students to find it.

B Students work individually to find the answers. Go through the answers together as a class, writing the correct sentences on the board. Circle *she* in sentence 2 and elicit that it refers to Emma in sentence 1 – circle *Emma* and connect the two words. Focus students on the *Identifying personal pronouns* box, and write the sentence from it on the board. Repeat the previous steps with *He/Anton*. Draw stick male and female figures and elicit which one needs *he* and which needs *she*: write the pronouns underneath. Then indicate students in the class and get the others to say *he* or *she* as appropriate.

C Students complete the exercise individually, then compare with another student before you give the answers. Add a stick picture of an animal and another of an object to your pictures on the board, e.g. a box, and write *it* next to both. Then practice the three pronouns by pointing at people and objects around the class. To extend learning for early finishers, students can create their own mini-quizzes by drawing five items (people, animals and objects). They can then test their classmates as to which is the correct pronoun.

GRAMMAR HUB

1.2

Simple present *be*: *he, she, it*

	Positive	Negative
he/she/it	**He/She is** a teacher.	**He/She is not** a teacher.
	He's/She's a teacher.	**He/She isn't** a teacher.
		He's/She's not a teacher.
	It is small.	**It is not** small.
	It's small.	**It isn't** small.
		It's not small.

	Yes/No questions	Short answers
he/she/it	**Is he** friendly?	**Yes, he is. / No, he isn't.**
	Is she the manager?	**Yes, she is. / No, she isn't.**
	Is it fun?	**Yes, it is. / No, it isn't.**

- For the verb *be*, we use *is* with *he, she* and *it*.

  He is nice.

  She is nice.

  It is nice.
- We can use the long form (*He is / She is / It is*) or the contraction (*He's / She's / It's*). We typically use the contraction when we speak.

  He is busy. OR He's busy.

  She is happy at her job. OR She's happy at her job.

  It is a big company. OR It's a big company.

Be careful!

- For negative short answers, we usually use the contraction.

  No, she isn't. NOT ~~No, she is not.~~

1.2 What's your job?

GRAMMAR

A Do the first sentence on the board as an example. Students then do the exercise in pairs while you write the other sentences on the board. Give answers and feedback on the board, and elicit what the pronouns refer to; circle and draw lines connecting the pronouns with the noun phrases, e.g. *My manager / she*.

B Students work alone to complete the table. Walk around helping as required. Give feedback by writing the full table on the board after enough time has passed. Check students understand.

C Direct students to the **Grammar Hub** (see below and TB4).

D Write *It is a small team with five people.* on the board. Say the sentence using the contraction *it's*. Erase the *i* in *is* and replace it with an apostrophe, and write it as one word. Then focus students back on Exercise A, and get them to write the verbs as full forms. Write the answers on the board.

It's a small team with five people. = It is a small team with five people.

My manager isn't very friendly, but she's OK. = My manager is not very friendly, but she is OK.

E Demonstrate the task with one or two students, then let students read the conversation. Put students into pairs and give them a few minutes to ask and answer. Help with job vocabulary if they need it. To extend the practice, students mingle, asking and answering. Use the **Grammar Worksheet** on page W3 for extra practice.

PRONUNCIATION

1.8 **A** Play the audio while students read and listen.

1.8 **B** Play the audio again sentence by sentence and get students to repeat as a whole class. Then repeat with individual students.

1.9 **C** Play the audio for students to do the task. Play it again and write the answers on the board.

D Demonstrate with the first sentence, changing the pronoun to *it*. Then put students into pairs to do the exercise.

SPEAKING HUB

A Draw a thought bubble on the board, then look at the picture and write a name, e.g. *Ollie*, in the bubble to show that it is just your imagination. Then put students into pairs A and B and direct Student B in the pair to the **Communication Hub** (see TB97) and Student A to use the current page to complete the information.

B Briefly demonstrate the activity, saying the sentences aloud. Then ask students to practice by themselves.

C Demonstrate with one student. The student introduces their 'friend' to you. Then let students work in their pairs to present their 'friends'. Make sure they use full sentences.

D Students reverse roles. Walk around listening and writing down any errors. When they finish, write any common errors on the board and get students to correct them as a whole-class activity.

Extra activity

Ask students to bring in photos of friends or to find photos of friends on their digital devices. Students write a description of their friends using the same sentence structures as in the Speaking Hub. Students then introduce their friends to their partner. You can model the activity first with a photo of one of your friends. The introduction-giving could be extended into a mingling activity.

GRAMMAR HUB

1.2

Simple present *be*: *he, she, it*

A Choose the correct options.

1 He ___ an architect.
a be (b) is

2 My friend is ___ a doctor.
(a) not b isn't

3 Maria is a manager. ___ very nice.
a It's (b) She's

4 I like my job. ___ fun.
(a) It's b She's

5 Paul isn't a teacher. ___ a student.
(a) He's b It's

6 Her name ___ Karen and she's from Canada.
(a) is b are

B Complete the email with the words in the box.

he's is (x4) ~~isn't~~ it's she's

Hi Tina!

I'm at work but I'm not very busy. My manager [1] *isn't* here today because she [2] is in New York City. Her name [3] is Sandra and [4] she's very nice. The job [5] is fun and I'm very happy here. Henri [6] is my colleague. [7] He's very friendly. We're on the design team. [8] It's a small team with four people.

See you soon!

Love,

Annette

C Write the correct short answers.

1 A: Is Marco a manager?
B: *No, he isn't.* (-)

2 A: Is your job difficult?
B: No, it isn't. (-)

3 A: Is Peter a student?
B: Yes, he is. (+)

4 A: Is Tina a teacher?
B: No, she isn't. (-)

5 A: Is your job fun?
B: Yes, it is. (+)

➤ Go back to page 5.

GRAMMAR

Simple present *be: he, she, it*

A Read the examples from the emails. Underline the verbs.

It's a small team with five people.

My manager isn't very friendly, but she's OK.

My colleague Anton is nice.

How's your new job? Is it fun?

B **WORK IT OUT** Complete the table with *'s*, *is* or *isn't*.

Simple present *be: he, she, it*		
Positive	He/She/It 's/is	nice.
Negative	He/She/It isn't	nice.
Question	Is	he/she/it fun?

C Go to the **Grammar Hub** on **page 98**.

D Look at the verbs in the first two sentences in Exercise A. What are the full forms of these verbs?

It's a small team with five people. = It is a small team with five people. isn't = is not

she's = she is

E **SPEAK** Work in pairs. Ask questions about your classmates.

A: Is Anna from Italy?
B: Yes, she is. She's from Milan.
A: Is Raúl a doctor?
B: No, he isn't. He's an architect.

PRONUNCIATION

Contractions with *be*

1.8 **A** Read and listen to the examples. Listen to the pronunciation of *he's*, *she's* and *it's*.

1. He's from Canada.
2. She's from Brazil.
3. He's new today, too.
4. She's really nice.
5. It's my first day.

1.8 **B** Listen and repeat the examples in Exercise A.

1.9 **C** Listen and circle the word you hear.

1. *He's* / *She's* from Vietnam.
2. *It's* / *She's* from Egypt.
3. *He's* / *She's* an engineer.
4. *He's* / *She's* a doctor.
5. *He's* / *It's* OK.

D **SPEAK** Work in pairs. Take turns saying sentences using *he's*, *she's* and *it's*. Listen to your partner. Do they say *he's*, *she's* or *it's*?

SPEAKING HUB

A **PLAN** Student A – Stay on this page. Student B – Go to the **Communication Hub** on **page 128**. Imagine the man in the picture below is your friend. Complete the information about him with your own ideas.

First name ______________

Last name ______________

Country ______________

City ______________

Job ______________

B **PREPARE** Prepare to introduce your friend to your partner. Practice by yourself.

This is a picture of my friend. His name is Ollie. He's from …
He's ______________.

C **PRESENT** Work in pairs. Introduce your friend to your partner.

D **REPEAT** Change roles and listen to your partner's introduction.

Introduce a friend

Café Hub

1.3 How are you?

F – greet people

COMPREHENSION

A Watch the video. Number the pictures (a–d) in the order you see them (1–4).

a 2

Sam's Café

b 4

Gaby's bedroom at night

c 3

The English School

d 1

Gaby's bedroom in the day

B Match the objects (1–8) with the places (a–d) in Exercise A. Then watch the video again and check your answers.

1 b

books

2 d

a mobile phone

3 b

an alarm clock

4 a

coffee

5 c

a computer

6 a

a credit card

7 c

a calendar

8 d

a suitcase

C Match the numbers (1–5) with the letters (a–e) to make correct sentences.

1 Gaby is in
2 The café
3 Gaby's coffee is
4 Mark is
5 Gaby's full name is

a Gabriela García Martínez.
b is Sam's Café.
c London.
d a cappuccino.
e Gaby's English teacher.

Glossary

mobile phone **(n)** **(British)** = cell phone **(n)** **(American)**

1.3 How are you?

LEAD-IN

With books closed, mime the following: ordering coffee, paying for it and then drinking the coffee. Elicit where you are and write *café* on the board. Do the same for sleeping (*bedroom*) and studying (*classroom*). To extend, students can mime other places they know the words for and have their partner or fellow students guess.

Extra activity

Ask students to look at the pictures in Exercise A and name any objects that they know. You could ask students to spell these for you, or invite them to come and write them on the board. You can then create a useful reference list on the board, adding the phonemic script and marking word stress.

COMPREHENSION

A ▸ Focus the students on the four images. Ask students to identify the places in each image. Then read through the task instructions with students. Students can predict the order of the pictures at this point. Play the video for students to watch and confirm the order. Check answers as a whole class.

B ▸ Ask students to study the images for a minute to try to memorize them and the words for them. Students then close their books as you elicit the words and spelling for each object and write these on the board. Do not correct at this point. Alternatively, students could come to the board and write their suggestions for the words and spelling. Students then open their books and check the words and the spelling. Make corrections to the words on the board. Students then work in pairs to recall which place each object was seen in the video. Play the video again for students to check.

C Read through the instructions with students and match the first parts of the sentence together. Students then work alone to complete the exercise. Allow time for students to compare in pairs before checking altogether as a group.

▶ VIDEO SCRIPT

G = Gaby S = Sam R = Receptionist M = Mark

G: Mum!
S: Good morning. Welcome to Sam's Café! Coffee?
G: Yes, a cappuccino, please.
S: Sure.
G: Ah, coffee! Thanks!
S: You're welcome.
G: Perfect! Hello!
R: Hello! Can I help you? Oh, yes. The new class starts tomorrow.
G: Great!
R: Ah! And here's your teacher.
M: Hi, I'm Mark.
G: Hi, I'm Gaby. How are you?
M: I'm fine, thanks. And you?
G: I'm fine, thanks.
M: Great. See you soon.
G: Bye!
R: OK, Gaby, what's your full name, please?
G: I'm Gabriela García Martínez.
R: Great, thank you. What's your phone number?
G: It's 07700 914865.
R: OK, thank you, Gaby. That's everything. The class starts tomorrow at nine o'clock in room seven.
G: Great, thanks. See you tomorrow at nine o'clock in room seven.
R: Yes. See you then.

METHODOLOGY HUB by Jim Scrivener

Giving instructions: Complex instructions

How can I give clearer instructions?

I propose five steps towards better instructions:

1. Become aware of your own instruction-giving (listen to yourself; record yourself; ask others to watch you and give feedback).
2. For a while, pre-plan essential instructions. Analyze the instructions beforehand so as to include only the essential information in simple, clear language, and sequence it in a sensible order. Use short sentences – one sentence for each key piece of information. Don't say things that are visible or obvious (e.g. *I'm giving you a piece of paper*). Don't give instructions that they don't need to know at this point (e.g. what they'll do after this activity is finished).
3. In class, separate instructions clearly from the other chit-chat, joking, etc that goes on. Create a silence beforehand, make eye contact with as many students as possible, find an authoritative tone, make sure they are listening before you start. Use silence and gestures to pace the instructions and clarify their meaning.
4. Demonstrate rather than explain wherever possible.
5. Check that students have understood what to do. Don't assume that everyone will automatically understand what you have said. Get concrete evidence from the students that they know what is required. Getting one or two students to tell you what they are going to do is one very simple way of achieving this.

1.3 How are you?

D ▶ 01:32–02:28 Write the form on the board without the information completed. Ask students to tell you the information by reading from the book and ask them to spell out Gabriela's name. Write the information on the form on the board. Ask students to identify any mistakes at this point if they can. Play the video for students to check the information. Check answers as a whole class.

The phone number is 07700 914865.

The classroom number is 7.

The class starts at nine o'clock.

Extra activity
For extra practice with numbers, ask students to make a grid with four squares (two rows of two squares) and to write one number from 0 to 10 in each square. Write *Bingo* on the board and your own grid to demonstrate. Say a number and write an "X" through the number if you have it on your grid. If you don't have the number, do nothing. Continue until all your numbers are crossed out and then call *Bingo!* Play the game with students as a whole class or in smaller groups.

USEFUL PHRASES

▶ 00:40–01:28 Students work in pairs to recall who says what. Play the relevant part(s) of the video again to check. Ensure all students' understanding before moving on.

FUNCTIONAL LANGUAGE

A Focus the students on the box. Highlight the three headings and mime saying hello, greeting and saying goodbye to clarify. Students complete the phrases with the words in the box.

B ▶ Play the video again for students to compare their answers. Then check answers as a whole class.

PRONUNCIATION

1.10 **A** Highlight the underlining in the conversation. Ask students to guess what this represents (*stressed syllables*). Play the conversation for students to listen and notice the stressed syllables.

1.10 **B** Play the audio again and practice with students on each line, emphasizing the stressed syllables.

Extra activity
Ask students to practice the conversation in pairs until you are confident they have memorized it word for word. Then ask students to stand up in a circle. Get the first student to say the first word of the conversation *Hello!* Then the next student says the next word, *Good*. The next student says the next word *morning*, then the next one says *How* and so on around the circle, with each student adding one word at a time. Keep going around the circle, with the students repeating the conversation one word at a time. If a student makes a mistake or hesitates, they are out of the game and have to sit down. Keep going until you have a winner. As an alternative, you could give each student three lives and the winner (or winners) is the one with the most lives left when you bring the game to an end. As the game goes on, encourage the students to get faster and faster.

SPEAKING

A Students work in pairs to practice the conversation. Monitor and remind students to stress the appropriate syllables. After one or two practices, encourage students to look up when saying their lines and highlight that they should try to speak rather than read.

B Model the activity by moving around the class and introducing yourself to individual students. Use the students' names and key phrases from the conversation in the Pronunciation section. Students then mingle, introducing themselves to their classmates.

METHODOLOGY HUB by Jim Scrivener

Use conversations

When you work with printed conversations, don't just read them silently, but get students to spend time thinking about how to say them. A useful task is to ask them to go through the text, deciding and marking which syllables are stressed. After that, students can practice them, read them out and eventually perform them without scripts. The goal is to speak naturally – which is hard to do when you are reading from text, so it's important to include some textless work. Don't worry about students learning it word-perfectly; give feedback on whether they get the feeling right or not, rather than whether they get the grammar spot-on.

METHODOLOGY HUB by Jim Scrivener

Stress and meaning

Stress typically marks out the content-carrying words in the sentence; thus it mostly affects nouns, verbs and adjectives. The content word that carries the main meaning of the sentence is usually the one you are going to stress and so the following pattern seems most likely (although others are possible):

Caroline was going to leave for Africa on Tuesday.

We can demonstrate patterns of prominence either on the board or by using Cuisenaire rods or tapping, clapping, humming the rhythm, etc. By getting the students to work out the patterns themselves, we can help to make them more aware of the importance of stress. Poetry and songs are good for focusing on stress. Shadow reading (reading simultaneously with a recording, trying to keep up with the speed and follow the rhythm) is a useful language laboratory or classroom activity.

GABY SAM LUCY

D 01:32–02:28 Watch part of the video and correct the mistakes in the numbers on the form.

ENGLISH, ENGLISH, ENGLISH, AND ENGLISH

Student Registration Form

Name:	Gabriela García Martínez
Phone number:	~~00707~~ 07700 914865
Classroom number:	~~6~~ 7
Teacher:	Mark
Time:	~~10~~ 9 am

USEFUL PHRASES

00:40–01:28 Who says it? Sam (S), Gaby (G) or the receptionist (R)? Watch part of the video and check your answers.

1 Welcome to Sam's Café! S
2 A cappuccino, please. G
3 Thanks! G
4 You're welcome! S
5 Perfect! G
6 Can I help you? R

FUNCTIONAL LANGUAGE

Greeting people

A Complete the phrases in the table with the words in the box.

fine Hello morning See soon

Saying hello	Greeting people	Saying goodbye
[1] Hello / Hi. Good [2] morning. Good afternoon. Good evening.	How are you? I'm [3] fine, thanks. And you?	Bye. See you [4] soon. [5] See you tomorrow.

B Watch the video again and check your answers to Exercise A.

PRONUNCIATION

A 1.10 Listen to the conversation. Notice how the underlined words are stressed.

Anna: Hello!
Stefani: Good morning. How are you?
Anna: Fine, thanks. And you?
Stefani: I'm fine, thanks. See you soon.
Anna: See you tomorrow.
Stefani: Bye!

B 1.10 Listen again and repeat the conversation. Copy the stress.

SPEAKING

A PREPARE Work in pairs. Practice the conversation in Pronunciation Exercise A again.

B PRACTICE Walk around the class. Greet your classmates.

A: Hi Onur. How are you?
B: I'm fine, thanks. And you?
A: I'm fine, thanks.
B: Great, see you soon.

1 Writing

Fill in a form

W – using capital letters

A Read the form. Where is Alex from? What is his job?

He is from Sweden. He is a computer programmer.

The Global Hub English School

Registration form

First name:	*Alex*
Last name:	*Johansson*
Home (city, country):	*Stockholm, Sweden*
Job:	*computer programmer*
Telephone number:	*451 3398765*
Email:	*ajohannsson@hub.com*

Email addresses

When we say email addresses, @ = *at* and . = *dot* (*ajohansson at hub dot com*).

B Read the form again. Check (✓) the words that need a capital letter.

- [x] first names
- [x] last names
- [x] names of countries
- [x] names of cities
- [ ] names of jobs
- [ ] email addresses

Using capital letters

We use capital letters for names of people and places.

WRITING

WRITE Complete the form with information about you.

The Global Hub English School

Registration form

First name: ______________________

Last name: ______________________

Home (city, country): ______________________

Job: ______________________

Telephone number: ______________________

Email: ______________________

Fill in a form

Refer students to the form as a model for the writing task.

To extend, prepare paper forms for students to complete. Then post the forms around the room for students to review. This could be further extended into a treasure hunt activity by preparing a list of questions, for example, *Find a number that ends with 8. Find a last name with 6 letters.*

Unit 1 Review

GRAMMAR

A Complete the sentences with the positive (+) or negative (-) form of *be*. Use contractions if possible.

1. My name ___'s___ Jason. (+)
2. Carmen ___isn't___ from Greece. (-)
3. I ___'m___ an artist. (+)
4. You ___aren't___ in my class. (-)
5. My manager ___is___ friendly. (+)
6. I ___'m not___ from Italy. (-)

B Write questions and answers in your notebook using the correct form of *be*.

1. you / from Paris (+)
   Are you from Paris?
   Yes, I am.
2. Leila / from Mexico (-)
   Is Leila from Mexico?
   No, she isn't.
3. you / a new student (+)
   Are you a new student?
   Yes, I am.
4. Tony / from Indonesia (-)
   Is Tony from Indonesia?
   No, he isn't.
5. Anna / a student (+)
   Is Anna a student?
   Yes, she is.
6. you / Japan (-)
   Are you from Japan?
   No, I'm not.

VOCABULARY

A Reorder the letters to make the names of countries.

1. izrBal — Brazil
2. yuTrek — Turkey
3. pytgE — Egypt
4. adanCa — Canada
5. tylaI — Italy
6. oMixec — Mexico
7. nihaC — China
8. Sinap — Spain
9. apJan — Japan
10. natrAnige — Argentina

B Complete the jobs with the missing letters.

1. d o c t or
2. computer p r og r a mm e r
3. ar c h i t e c t
4. e n g i n e e r
5. fashion d e s i g n e r
6. t e a c h e r

8 NICE TO MEET YOU!

LEAD-IN

Write your personal information in bubbles randomly on the board: your first name, last name, home city, home country, job, phone number and email address (only include the last two if appropriate or use invented ones if preferred). Get students to call out questions, e.g. *Are you a teacher?* If the question is correct, cross out the information. Continue until all the answers are crossed out.

WRITING

A Focus the students on the form. Ask *What's his name?* Show that the name includes two parts – *Alex Johansson*. Write the full name on the board. Then point at the two questions *Where is Alex from?* and *What is his job?* and get students to read and tell you the answers.

B Do the first one together, then students put a check mark in the boxes individually. Get them to compare in pairs before giving the answers. Show them the *Using capital letters* box and give some further examples to check understanding.

WRITING TASK

On the board, write *first name:* (your name) *last name:* (your name). Circle the capital letters and ask *Why?* Elicit *names*. Check that students understand they need to write about themselves. Walk around helping if necessary, making sure students use capitals correctly.

Musicians playing in a mariachi band, Guanajuato, Mexico.

Ask students to label the photo if you need time to set up the class.

The quote suggests that we do not need words to communicate. Music crosses boundaries – we do not have to speak the same language to be able to understand music and the feelings that it contains.

Henry Wadsworth Longfellow (1807–1882) was an American poet and professor. He spent time in Europe and studied French, Spanish and Italian. He translated poetry and wrote essays on French, Spanish and Italian literature. He brought European cultural traditions to American audiences.

OBJECTIVES

- talk about nationalities
- ask for and give personal information
- ask for clarification
- write an online introduction

Work with a partner. Discuss the questions.

1 Look at the picture. What type of music is it?

2 Choose two words to describe the picture.

boring happy interesting modern sad traditional

3 What do you think the quote means?

OUR MUSIC, OUR WORLD 9

OBJECTIVES

Read the unit objectives to the class.

UNIT OPENER QUESTIONS

Focus the students on the picture of the mariachi band. Ask them what kind of music it is. Elicit ideas such as *traditional* if they don't know the term *mariachi*. Explain that it is a type of music in Mexico and it is usually powerful and emotional, using many instruments and the musicians' voices. Focus students on the adjectives in the box and ask them to choose some words to describe the picture. Encourage students to use their own ideas if they want to. Discuss as a class and add any new vocabulary to the board, practicing pronunciation where appropriate.
Ask students what they think the quote means. Ask them if they agree. Ask students if they know any quotes in their own languages about music.

WORKSHEETS

Lesson 2.1 Where are they from?

Vocabulary: Languages and nationalities (W4)

Grammar: Simple present *be*: *we*, *you*, *they*; Possessive adjectives (W5)

Lesson 2.2 When are you free?

Vocabulary: Days of the week; Numbers 11–100 (W6)

Grammar: *Wh-* questions with *be* (W6)

2.1 Where are they from?

Talk about nationalities

V languages and nationalities **P** syllable stress **G** simple present *be*: *we, you, they*; possessive adjectives

READING

Esperanza Spalding – Portland, US
Fatoumata Diawara – Mali
Of Monsters and Men – Reykjavík, Iceland

A SCAN FOR INFORMATION Look at the pictures. Read the playlist. Where are the people from?

Monoswezi – Sweden, Norway, Mozambique, Zimbabwe

World Music fans!
Are you ready for some great new music?
On our playlist this week …

Esperanza Spalding is a musician from Portland in the US. She's 33 years old and she's a jazz musician. Ex B Q5
Her songs are in English, **Spanish** and **Portuguese**. We're big fans of her new album! Ex B Q2

Fatoumata Diawara is a singer and musician from **Mali**. She's 36 years old and a big star in Africa. Ex B Q6
Her album *Fatou* is one of our favorites, and our new favorite song is *Fenfo* from the new album *Fenfo (Something to Say)*!

Of Monsters and Men is a band of five people. They're from Reykjavík in Iceland. Their songs are Ex B Q1
really fun but they aren't in **Icelandic** – they're in English.

Monoswezi is an international band. Two of the band members are **Swedish**, one is **Norwegian**, one Ex B Q3
is from Mozambique and one is from Zimbabwe. Their music is a mix of African and European music. Ex B Q4
These musicians are super cool!

B READ FOR DETAIL Read the playlist and check (✓) the correct name.

	Esperanza Spalding	Fatoumata Diawara	Of Monsters and Men	Monoswezi
1 The people in this band are from one country.	☐	☐	✓	☐
2 Her songs are in three languages.	✓	☐	☐	☐
3 The people in this band are from different countries.	☐	☐	☐	✓
4 Their music is a mix of music from different countries.	☐	☐	☐	✓
5 This singer is from the US.	✓	☐	☐	☐
6 She's a big star in Africa.	☐	✓	☐	☐

C SPEAK Work in pairs. Which musicians in the playlist do you want to listen to?

VOCABULARY

Languages and nationalities

A Read the playlist again. Complete the languages and nationalities.

	Country	Language/Nationality
1	Spain	*Spanish*
2	Portugal	Portuguese
3	Iceland	Icelandic
4	Sweden	Swedish
5	Norway	Norwegian

B Work in pairs. Write the nationalities of these musicians. Choose an ending from the box.

~~-ese~~ -ian -ish

1 Midori is from Japan. She's Japan*ese*.
2 Marisa Monte is from Brazil. She's Brazilian.
3 Bono is from Ireland. He's Irish.

C Go to the **Vocabulary Hub** on **page 122**.

1

2

2.1 Where are they from?

LEAD-IN

If possible, play a short section of music from one of your favorite musicians using a digital device. Tell the class about the musician, saying their name, where they are from and the type of music they make. Invite some students to do the same.

READING

A Write the question *Where are the people from?* on the board. Elicit that they will be reading for the names of countries or cities, etc. Make sure students understand that it is important to be fast and not to read every word. Then set a time limit, e.g. one minute, to show them that scanning is a speedy activity, and show them that they should circle the place where they find the information.

B Focus the students on the table, and make sure they understand that the column headings are the names of the musicians in the text. Ask students to read sentences 1–6 and check that they understand these sentences and the task. Then show that the students need to scan first, then read carefully to answer the questions.

C Say which one of the musicians you want to listen to, using very simple language and giving simple reasons, e.g. *I want to listen to Monoswezi – they're fun and they're international. I love cool music!* Then put students into pairs to do the task. Go round encouraging them to say as much as they can, helping as required. At the end, you could decide as a class which is the most popular choice.

VOCABULARY

A Focus students on the playlist. Students complete the exercise individually, then check in pairs. Write the answers on the board and practice the pronunciation, focusing on the stressed syllables. Don't erase the board.

B Circle the last three letters of *Spanish*, *Portuguese* and *Norwegian* on the board and show that they are the same as in the box. Students complete the exercise individually. Write the new nationalities under the ones on the board, to show that these are common patterns.

C Direct students to the **Vocabulary Hub** (see TB97). Use the **Vocabulary Worksheet** on page W4 for extra practice.

GRAMMAR HUB

2.1

Simple present *be*: *we, you, they*

	Positive	Negative
we	**We are** from New York. **We're** from New York.	**We are not** from Canada. **We aren't** from Canada. **We're not** from Canada.
you	**You are** from Italy. **You're** from Italy.	**You are not** Spanish. **You aren't** Spanish. **You're not** Spanish.
they	**They are** Norwegian. **They're** Norwegian.	**They are not** from Sweden. **They aren't** from Sweden. **They're not** from Sweden.

	Yes/No questions	Short answers
we	**Are we** a great band?	**Yes, you are. / No, you aren't. / No, you're not.**
you	**Are you** musicians?	**Yes, we are. / No, we aren't. / No, we're not.**
they	**Are they** fans of world music?	**Yes, they are. / No, they aren't. / No, they're not.**

- For the verb *be*, we use *are* after the pronouns *we*, *you* and *they*.
  We are from Senegal. We're from Senegal.
  They aren't in a band.
- In *yes/no* questions, the verb *be* is first.
  Are they good at music?
  Are we at the concert?
- The answer to a *yes/no* question is *yes* or *no*, followed by a pronoun and the verb *be*.
  Are you from America? Yes, we are. / No, we aren't. / No, we're not.
  Are they singers? Yes, they are. / No, they aren't. / No, they're not.
- In *yes/no* questions with *no* answers, we can write the contraction in two ways.
  Are they from Boston? No, they aren't. OR No, they're not.

Be careful!

- In *yes/no* questions with *yes* answers, we cannot write the contraction.
  Are you fans of the band? Yes, we are.
  NOT ~~Yes, we're.~~

Possessive adjectives

Subject pronoun	Possessive adjective
I am a fan of American music.	**My** playlist is very cool.
You are from Japan.	**Your** country is in Asia.
He is Malian.	**His** country is in Africa.
We are from France.	**Our** country is in Europe.
They are singers.	**Their** songs are really good.

- For possessive adjectives, we change the subject pronoun to the correct possessive adjective.
  *I'm in a band. **My** band's name is Full Energy.*
  *We are from Poland. **Our** country is quite big.*

2.1 Where are they from?

PRONUNCIATION

2.1 **A** Write *Sweden* and *Swedish* on the board. Say the words, emphasizing the stressed first syllable. Underline the first syllable in both words, and ask *the same or different?* Write *same*. Then play the audio while students choose. To give feedback, write the words on the board and underline the stressed syllables.

2.1; 2.2 **B–D** Play the audio again and let students repeat. Make sure the students really emphasize the stressed syllables. Students then complete Exercise C, noticing any changes in syllable stress. Mark this on the board, and then ask students to listen again and repeat.

E Students complete the task in pairs. Walk around and help if needed, and check answers. Continue to group the nationalities on the board by their endings.

GRAMMAR

Simple present *be*: *we*, *you*, *they*

A Do the first sentence as an example, then students work individually to complete the exercise. Check answers as a class.

B Focus students on the table and show them that the answers are in the sentences from Exercise A. Ask students to work alone, then check answers in pairs. Elicit answers to complete the table on the board. If possible, use different colored board markers for *am*, *is* and *are*.

C Direct students to the **Grammar Hub** (see below and TB10).

D Students choose the correct part of *be*, then speak in pairs. Then get them to memorize the questions and walk around the class asking and answering the other students.

Possessive adjectives

A Say *This is our classroom* and indicate the class. Write the first sentence on the board. Demonstrate that *our* refers to you and the students. Students underline the possessive adjectives in the other two sentences while you write up the sentences. Check that they understand, pointing at students and their possessions (*their*), and a female student (if possible) and one of her possessions (*her*).

B Do the first one together, then let students work in pairs to complete the table.

C Students choose the correct answers individually, then check answers in pairs, while you monitor and help if necessary. Check answers as a whole-class activity.

D Direct students to the **Grammar Hub** (see below and TB10). Use the **Grammar Worksheet** on page W5 for extra practice.

SPEAKING

A Write the form on the board and demonstrate the activity with your own favorite musician. Ask students to work alone to complete the form.

B Demonstrate the activity, using complete sentences to describe your musician. Students work in pairs to talk about their chosen musician. Encourage them to speak in complete sentences and ask and answer follow-up questions if possible, e.g. *Is she cool?*

C Ask students to tell the class about their partners' choices. Write the names of the musicians on the board and see who is most popular.

GRAMMAR HUB

2.1

Simple present *be*: *we*, *you*, *they*; possessive adjectives

A Choose the correct options.

1 Niko and John are Greek. *They* / *We* are from Greece.
2 My best friend and I are Icelandic. *You* / *We* are from Iceland.
3 *You are* / *Are you* from Portugal?
4 Are you fans of his music? Yes, *I* / *we* are.
5 Are your friends from Chile? Yes, *we* / *they* are.
6 Are they free tonight? *No, they're not.* / *Yes, they're.*
7 I'm a fan of music. *My* / *Your* playlist is full of songs.
8 We're from Italy. *Our* / *Their* country is in southern Europe.

B Put the words in the correct order to make sentences and questions.

1 from / your friends / are / Jamaica
Are your friends from Jamaica ?
2 fans / we / of / her / music / aren't
We aren't fans of her music .
3 great / their / are / songs
Are their songs great ?
4 from / are / they / Reykjavik
Are they from Reykjavík ?
5 are / you / favorite / my / singer
You are my favorite singer !
6 big fans / new album / they're / their / of
They're big fans of their new album .
7 classmates / are / Italian / your
Are your classmates Italian ?
8 from / they're / Turkey / not
They're not from Turkey .

C Choose the correct options to complete the conversation.

Samantha:	Hi, I'm Samantha. [1] ___ in my music class?
Henry:	Hi, Samantha. I'm Henry. Yes, [2] ___ in the class together.
Samantha:	Great! [3] ___ a big fan of music like me?
Henry:	Oh, yes. [4] ___ playlist is full of great songs.
Samantha:	That's nice. [5] ___ teacher is really nice, too.
Henry:	Yes, I'm excited about [6] ___ lessons.
Samantha:	Well, see you in class!
Henry:	Bye!

1 a Are you b You are
2 a we're b are we
3 a You're b Are you
4 a Your b My
5 a Our b His
6 a your b my

➤ Go back to page 11.

PRONUNCIATION

Syllable stress

2.1 **A** Listen to the countries and nationalities. Underline the stressed syllables in the nationalities. Do the countries and nationalities have the same or different stress?

1 Sweden Swedish *same / different*
2 Egypt Egyptian *same / different*
3 Iceland Icelandic *same / different*

2.1 **B** Listen again and repeat.

2.2 **C** Listen and underline the stressed syllable in each country and nationality. Is the stress the same or different?

1 China – Chinese *same / different*
2 Turkey – Turkish *same / different*
3 Canada – Canadian *same / different*
4 Poland – Polish *same / different*
5 Italy – Italian *same / different*

2.2 **D** Listen again and repeat.

E SPEAK Work in pairs. Add another country and nationality for each ending.

Country	Nationality
1 ______	______ese
2 ______	______ish
3 ______	______(i)an

GRAMMAR

Simple present *be: we, you, they*

A Read the examples from the playlist. Underline the verbs.

Are you ready for some great new music?

They're from Reykjavík in Iceland.

... but they aren't in Icelandic – they're in English.

We're big fans of her new album.

B WORK IT OUT Complete the table with the positive and negative forms of the verb *be*.

Subject	Positive	Negative
I	'm / am	'm not
you	're / are	aren't
he/she/it	's / is	isn't
we	are / 're	aren't
you	are / 're	aren't
they	are / 're	aren't

C Go to the Grammar Hub on page 100.

D SPEAK Complete the questions. Then ask and answer them with your partner.

1 *Are / Is* you a fan of world music?
2 *Are / Is* your favorite musicians from America?

Possessive adjectives

A Read the examples. Underline the possessive adjectives.

On our playlist this week ...

Their songs are really fun.

We're big fans of her new album!

B WORK IT OUT Complete the table with possessive adjectives from the box.

Her His Its ~~My~~ Our Their Your

Subject pronoun	Possessive adjective
I am a world music fan.	1 My name is Luciana.
You are from Brazil.	2 Your songs are in Portuguese.
She is a singer from Mali.	3 Her songs are sad.
He is from Sweden.	4 His songs are in Swedish.
This is the new album.	5 Its name is *Fenfo*.
We are world music fans.	6 Our playlist is cool.
They are from Iceland.	7 Their music is full of energy.

C PRACTICE Circle the correct possessive adjective.

1 They're in a band. *Her / Their* new album is great.
2 We're fans of great music. *Our / Their* favorite music is from Brazil.
3 She's a musician. *His / Her* name is Ariane.
4 He's a singer. *Her / His* name is Michael.

D Go to the Grammar Hub on page 100.

SPEAKING

A PREPARE Write information about your favorite musician or band.

Name: ______
Country: ______
Age: ______
Name of album or song: ______

B DISCUSS Work in pairs. Tell your partner about your favorite musician or band.

C REPORT Tell the class about your partner's favorite musician or band.

Talk about nationalities

2.2 When are you free?

Ask for and give personal information

V days of the week; numbers 11–100 S identifying context G *wh-* questions with *be* P contractions in questions

VOCABULARY

Days of the week

A Read the flyer. Which class looks fun?

INTERNATIONAL CENTER

ADULT EVENING CLASSES

Learn something new!
Learn about other cultures and meet people!

All classes start at 7 pm

Ex C answers

MONDAY
Spanish guitar classes
60 mins Room 8

TUESDAY
African drums workshop
75 mins Room 24

WEDNESDAY
Arabic language class
90 mins Room 12

THURSDAY no classes

FRIDAY
Yoga for everyone
45 mins Room 18

SATURDAY AND SUNDAY no classes

2.3 **B** Listen and repeat the days of the week.

C SPEAK Work in pairs. Ask your partner questions about the classes.

A: What day is yoga?
B: Friday!

Numbers 11–100

2.4 **A** Listen and repeat the numbers. Notice the stressed syllable.

11 eleven	20 twenty
12 twelve	30 thirty
13 thirteen	40 forty
14 fourteen	50 fifty
15 fifteen	60 sixty
16 sixteen	70 seventy
17 seventeen	80 eighty
18 eighteen	90 ninety
19 nineteen	100 one hundred

B Go to the Vocabulary Hub on page 122.

2.5 **C SPEAK** Work in pairs. Circle all the numbers in the flyer and say them with your partner. Then listen and check.

LISTENING

2.6 **A LISTEN FOR GIST** Listen to three conversations. Write the number of the conversation.

Who are they?

a teachers Conversation 3
b students Conversation 2
c friends *Conversation 1*

Identifying context

Greetings such as *Good morning* or *Good afternoon* are more formal.

Hi! and *Hello!* are less formal.

2.6 **B LISTEN FOR DETAIL** Match the greetings in the box with the conversations (1–3). Conversation 1: Hi!
Conversation 2: Hi!, Hello!, Nice to meet you!

Good afternoon! Hello! Hi!
Nice to meet you! (x2)

Conversation 3: Good afternoon!, Nice to meet you!

2.6 **C LISTEN FOR DETAIL** Listen again. Choose the correct answers to complete the sentences.

1 Kara's teacher is …
a Spanish. (b) Argentinian.
2 Maria and Angelo are in classroom …
(a) 12B. b 12C.
3 Maria and Angelo are in …
a a Spanish class. (b) an Arabic class.
4 Leila is …
(a) the Arabic teacher. b the yoga teacher.

2.2 When are you free?

VOCABULARY

Days of the week

A Say *I want to learn something new*. Look at the poster. Choose one and say, e.g. *Yoga looks fun!* Then ask students to choose one of the classes. Students report their choices back and you write them on the board; let them see which is the most and least popular.

2.3 **B** Play the audio. Repeat and have students repeat after each day. Help with pronunciation; make sure they can hear that the first *d* in *Wednesday* is silent and the *o* in *Monday* sounds like a (/ʌ/) sound. Listen and repeat again.

C Demonstrate using the example. Then students work in pairs to ask and answer questions about the classes.

Numbers 11–100

2.4 **A** Write *13 thirteen* and *30 thirty* on the board. Say each one, stressing the second syllable of *thirteen* and the first syllable of *thirty*. Underline the stressed syllables. Play the audio while students listen and repeat after each number.

B Direct students to the **Vocabulary Hub** (see TB97).

2.5 **C** Students circle all the numbers individually, then complete the activity in pairs. Use the **Vocabulary Worksheet** on page W6 for extra practice.

LISTENING

2.6 **A** Give students time to read options a–c. Students listen and complete the activity. Students can check in pairs, talking about which information helped them decide. Check the answers as a class.

2.6 **B** Give students time to read the greetings in the box. Check the answers as a class and elicit ideas for why the different greetings are used (*the context – formal or informal*).

2.6 **C** Ask students to read the questions and see if they can answer any questions from memory, but don't confirm or correct them yet. Play the audio again while students listen and answer. Then play it again stopping where the answers are given. Ask students to repeat the relevant words and check answers as a class.

AUDIO SCRIPT

2.6

Listening, Exercise A
P = Pete K = Kara A = Angelo M = Maria L = Leila H = Hana

Conversation 1

Ex A Qc **P:** Hi, Kara. How are you?
Ex B **K:** Hi, Pete! Fine, thanks.
P: Are you free this evening?
K: No, I'm not. I have my Spanish guitar class this evening.
P: Oh, OK! Who's your teacher?
K: Our teacher is Ms. Sanchez.
P: Really? Where's she from?
Ex C Q1 **K:** She's from Argentina.

Conversation 2

Ex C Q2 **A:** Hi! Is this classroom 12B? Ex B
Ex C Q3 **M:** Yes, it is. Are you here for the Arabic class, too?
Ex A Qb **A:** Yes, I am. I'm a new student.
M: Great! What's your name?
A: My name's Angelo!
Ex B **M:** Hello, Angelo. I'm Maria. Nice to meet you.
A: Nice to meet you, too.

Conversation 3

Ex B **L:** Good afternoon! Are you a teacher here, too?
Ex A Qa **H:** Yes, I am! My name's Hana. I'm the yoga teacher.
Ex C Q4 **L:** Nice to meet you! My name's Leila. I'm the Arabic class teacher.
Ex B **H:** Nice to meet you! When's your class?
L: Now! Bye!
H: OK, bye!

GRAMMAR HUB

2.2

Wh-* questions with *be

Question word	*be*	Rest of question	Answer
What	**is**	your name?	**My name is** Lee.
Where	**are**	you from?	**I am** from China.
Who	**is**	your teacher?	**Our teacher is** Ms. Daniels.
When	**is**	your class?	**It's at** 10 am.
How old	**are**	your friends?	**They are** 14 years old.

- In *wh-* questions, the question word is first.
  What are their jobs?
  Where am I right now?
- In *wh-* questions, the verb is second.
  Who is your classmate?
  Where are Jason and Alex?

Be careful!

- In *wh-* questions, the verb matches the noun after it. The noun is the subject of the *wh-* question.
  Where is their house? NOT ~~*Where are their house?*~~
  What are your names? NOT ~~*What is your names?*~~

2.2 When are you free?

GRAMMAR

A Write the first question on the board and ask a few students. Underline *What* and write *question word* above it. Circle the *Wh-* and write *Wh-* in front of *question word*. Then focus students on the other questions and ask them to underline the *Wh-* question words.

B Ask students to choose words individually, then compare with a partner.

C Encourage students to use the examples in the previous exercises to help them choose the answers.

D Direct students to the **Grammar Hub** (see below and TB12).

E Read the first question with students and focus their attention on *their names*. Ask if this is singular or plural (*plural*). Then ask which form of *be* is needed for a plural (*are*). Students then complete the other questions, then match the correct answers. Check answers as a class.

F Demonstrate the first question with a student. Then students work in pairs to ask and answer the questions. Use the **Grammar Worksheet** on page W6 for extra practice.

PRONUNCIATION

2.7 **A** Write *Who is your teacher?* on the board and read it with the contraction. Erase *i* in *is* and replace it with an apostrophe; make sure students understand that the contraction is the common spoken form. Play the audio while students listen; practice the pronunciation of *who* and *how*.

B Play the audio again while students listen and repeat.

2.8 **C** Give students time to read the options. Encourage them to think what the questions would be that produce those responses. Ask them to discuss their ideas with a partner. Play the audio while students answer individually. Repeat the audio and stop after each question; give the correct answer and ask students to repeat, making sure they use the contractions.

D Write *Who's* on the board and elicit possible ways to finish the question, e.g. *your friend / your teacher*. Then put students into pairs to write the questions. Monitor and help with pronunciation. Ask them to memorize their questions and then to walk around asking other members of the class. Join in, asking the questions to students.

SPEAKING HUB

A For this information fill in the blank activity, it is vital that students don't see each other's information. Put students into pairs A and B. Direct Student Bs to the **Communication Hub** (see TB97) while Student As stay on the page. You could put all Student As and Bs together to complete the questions, or they could work alone. Students read the information cards and decide which questions they need to ask to find the missing information.

B Seat Students A and B in pairs, making sure they don't read their partner's information but speak, listen and write instead. Monitor and write a note about common mistakes and examples of good language to give feedback on when students finish.

Extra activity

Play 'Three Questions'. Tell students you are thinking of someone they know. This could be a famous person or someone you all know locally. Students can ask you three questions, e.g. *Where is the person from? How old is the person? What is his/her job?* You provide the answers. The student that guesses the name of the person then takes a turn. Students can continue to play the game in small groups.

GRAMMAR HUB

2.2

Wh-* questions with *be

A Choose the correct options.

1 What ___ your name?
(a) is b are

2 Who ___ your best friends?
a is (b) are

3 Where ___ your teacher from?
(a) is b are

4 How old ___ your parents?
a is (b) are

5 ___ your favorite artist?
a What's (b) Who's

6 ___ your favorite song?
a Where's (b) What's

B Write the correct form of the verb *be* to complete the questions.

1 Where ___are___ Tom and Joseph?
2 What ___is___ her nationality?
3 Who ___are___ your favorite musicians?
4 How old ___are___ Shannon and Michael?
5 What ___are___ his favorite apps?
6 Who ___is___ Ariana Grande?
7 How old ___is___ this movie?
8 When ___is___ your class?

C Match the questions (1–8) and the answers (a–h).

1 Where are Zara and Aliyah from? g
2 Who's your Japanese teacher? f
3 What's your favorite language? e
4 How old is your new classmate? b
5 Where's Karen from? d
6 How old are your sisters? h
7 Who are your neighbors? c
8 When's your class? a

a It's on Wednesday.
b He's 14.
c They're Mr. and Mrs. Neilson.
d She's from Sweden.
e It's Chinese.
f Mr. Watanabe.
g They're from Egypt.
h They're 24 and 28.

➤ Go back to page 13.

GRAMMAR

Wh- questions with *be*

A Read the examples. Underline the question words.

What's your name? When are you free?
Who's your teacher? How old are you?
Where's she from?

B **WORK IT OUT** Choose the correct word to complete the questions.

1 What / Who are their jobs?
2 When / How old are Kara and Pete?
3 What / Where are they from?
4 What / Who is your teacher?
5 When / What is your Spanish class?

C **WORK IT OUT** Choose the correct options to complete the rules.

wh- questions with *be*

1 In *wh-* questions, the ***verb*** / ***question word*** is first.
2 In *wh-* questions, the ***verb*** / ***question word*** is second.

D Go to the **Grammar Hub** on **page 100**.

E **PRACTICE** Complete the questions with the correct form of the verb *be*. Then match the questions (1–5) with the answers (a–e).

1 What ___are___ their names? b
2 Where ___is___ she from? e
3 When ___are___ your yoga classes? c
4 How old ___are___ your children? a
5 Who ___are___ your favorite musicians? d

a 5 and 8
b Lucia and Stefan
c On Fridays
d Of Monsters and Men and Coldplay
e Australia

F **SPEAK** Work in pairs. Use the prompts to ask and answer the questions.

1 When / your (English) classes? When are your (English) classes?
2 Who / your teacher? Who is your teacher?
3 Where / your teacher from? Where is your teacher from?

PRONUNCIATION

Contractions in questions

2.7 **A** Read and listen to these questions. Notice how *who* and *how* are pronounced.
Who is pronounced /huː/
How is pronounced /haʊ/

1 Who's your teacher? 3 Who are you?
2 How's your teacher? 4 How are you?

2.7 **B** Listen and repeat the examples in Exercise A.

2.8 **C** Listen and choose the correct answer to the questions you hear.

1 (a) He's Mr. Parker. b He's really nice.
2 a I'm a new student. (b) I'm fine, thank you.
3 (a) She's OK, thank you. b Her name's Anna.
4 (a) This is Pedro and this is Yuki. b They're great!

D **SPEAK** Work in pairs. Write four questions using *Who's*, *How's*, *Who are* and *How are*. Then ask your partner.

SPEAKING HUB

A **PREPARE** Work in pairs. Student A – Stay on this page. Student B – Go to the **Communication Hub** on **page 132**.

Read the information. What questions can you ask to find the missing information? Student A:

1 *What's his name?* 5 What's his name ?
2 How old is he ? 6 How old is he ?
3 Where is Tomoko Kogawa from ? 7 What's her name ?
4 What is Tomoko's job ? 8 What's her job ?

B **PRACTICE** Ask your partner your questions from Exercise A to complete the information about each person.

a

Name	1 Victor Moretti
Country	Argentina
Age	2 28
Job	Designer

b

Name	Tomoko Kogawa
Country	3 Japan
Age	35
Job	4 Doctor

c

Name	5 Dev Gupta
Country	India
Age	6 42
Job	Engineer

d

Name	7 Zehra Yilmaz
Country	Turkey
Age	25
Job	8 Computer programmer

Ask for and give personal information

Café Hub

2.3 I'm late

F – ask for clarification

COMPREHENSION

A Watch the video. Number the pictures (a–h) in the order you see them (1–8).

a 3

b 5

c 2

d 6

e 7

f 1

g 4

h 8

B Complete the information in the table. Watch the video again and check your answers.

Name	Gaby	3 Mark	4 Carolina	Onur	7 Marta
Nationality	1 Spanish	English	5 Brazilian	6 Turkish	Italian
Job	2 photographer	English teacher	primary school teacher	student	8 nurse

USEFUL PHRASES

A Who says it? Gaby (G), Mark (M) or Carolina (C)? Watch the video again and check your answers.

1 Please sit down. M
2 Yes, that's it. C
3 Nice to meet you. M
4 Hi, guys. G
5 Now it's your turn. M
6 I'm late! G

B Student A – Mime a phrase in Exercise A. Student B – Say the phrase. Then change roles.

2.3 I'm late

LEAD-IN

Review introductions by introducing yourself to the class. (*Hi, I'm* (name), *I'm a teacher and I'm* (nationality)). Then say to a student, recalling their information, *Hi, you're* (name), *you're a* (job/*student*) *and you're* (nationality). Students then mingle and, rather than introducing themselves first, try to recall the information about the person they are talking to.

COMPREHENSION

A ▸ Review the pictures and ask students to describe what they can see. What do they think happens in the episode? Ask students to predict the order of the scenes. Students then watch the video and number the pictures in the correct order. Allow time for students to compare answers in pairs before checking as a whole class.

B ▸ Students work in pairs to recall as many answers as possible. Then play the video for students to watch again to check answers. Complete the table on the board, asking students to come up and add answers, checking spelling for each item is correct when students add them.

USEFUL PHRASES

A ▸ Review the sentences in pairs. Students may be able to recall all of the answers at this point. Play the video again for students to check.

B Model the exercise for the students by miming one of the phrases from Exercise A. Ask students what you are doing. Students then work in pairs to mime and guess.

VIDEO SCRIPT

G = Gaby M = Mark C = Carolina O = Onur Ma = Marta

G: Oh no! I'm late for my English class!
Argh! My hair! Hello … Hi, everyone … Hi, guys … Hi, friends! They are not my friends. OK … Good morning, I'm Gabriela. No, no, no, no, no, no, no … I'm Gaby.
Hi, I'm Gaby. I'm Spanish and I'm a photographer. Perfect! I'm very, very late!

M: Good morning, everyone. My name's Mark. Nice to meet you. Please, sit down.
So, that's me. Now it's your turn. Carolina?

C: Yes. Hello, I'm Carolina. I'm Brazilian and I'm a school teacher … *primário*. How do you say *primário* in English?

M: 'Primary', I think.

C: Yes, that's it! I'm a primary school teacher.

M: Hi, Carolina.

O: Yes, OK. Hi, my name's Onur. I'm Turkish and I'm a student.

M: Hi, Onur. Nice to meet you.

Ma: Hi, I'm Marta. I'm from Italy and I'm a nurse.

G: No taxis!

C: I'm sorry, I don't understand.

O: Yes. What does 'nurse' mean?

G: Hi! Hi, I'm Gaby. I'm Spanish and I'm a photographer. Perfect.

TEACHING IDEA by David Seymour and Maria Popova

Vocabulary: Languages

Use this activity to review countries, nationalities and languages. Say this to your students:

Listen to the countries and write the nationality and the language of each one.

In small groups, compare your lists and write down any words that are new to you.

Germany (German – German)
Peru (Peruvian – Spanish, Quechua)
France (French – French)
Iran (Iranian – Farsi, Azerbaijani)
Holland (Dutch – Dutch)
Japan (Japanese – Japanese)
Brazil (Brazilian – Portuguese)
Turkey (Turkish – Turkish, Kurdish)
Switzerland (Swiss – German, French, Italian, Romance)
Senegal (Senegalese – French, Pulaar, Wolof)
Wales (Welsh – English, Welsh)
Canada (Canadian – English, French, Indian)
Kenya (Kenyan – English, Gikuyu, Swahili, etc)
Israel (Israeli – Hebrew, Arabic)
Sweden (Swedish – Swedish)
Ethiopia (Ethiopian – Amharic, Tigrigna)
Ireland (Irish – English, Gaelic)

TEACHING IDEA by David Seymour and Maria Popova

Vocabulary: Job clap

Use this activity to review the Vocabulary section. Say this to your students:

Stand in a circle. Take turns naming a job, then the workplace for that job, and then another job, and so on, e.g. *A – pilot. B – plane. C – baker.* Clap your hands to this rhythm (demonstrate) and give your answer on every fourth beat. If you miss the beat, you are out.

TEACHING IDEA by David Seymour and Maria Popova

Vocabulary: Picture board

Use this activity to review the Vocabulary section. Say this to your students:

Work in two teams. Take turns coming up to the board. I'm going to give you a job. (Write it on a piece of paper or whisper it.) You have 60 seconds to draw pictures to help your team guess the job. You must not write any letters, or speak.

waiter, doctor, gardener, bricklayer, policeman, carpenter, soldier, artist, receptionist, chef, surgeon, farmer, vet, miner, nurse, secretary

2.3 I'm late

FUNCTIONAL LANGUAGE

A Students work alone to complete the phrases with the verbs in the box.

B ▶ 02:01–02:50 Once answers are checked by watching sections of the video again, focus the students on the title of the section (*Asking for clarification*) and elicit explanations of what this means (*what we do when we don't understand completely and need more information*).

C Students reorder the words to make phrases. Build up the correct phrases on the board for students to check.

PRONUNCIATION

2.9 **A** Focus the students on the conversation. Elicit what the underline means (*stressed syllables*). Play the audio for the students to listen to and notice the stress.

2.9 **B** Model the conversation with a confident student. Then model each line one by one, practicing with the whole class. Finally, play the audio and have students listen and repeat.

Extra activity

Write the conversation on the board. Divide the class into three, and have each group be one of the three people in the conversation. Have the class say the conversation, each student in their role. Then erase a word from each line. Students say the conversation together again, recalling the missing word. Keep erasing words from the lines and having the students repeat the conversation until all or nearly all of the conversation is erased and students can remember their lines.

SPEAKING

A Students work alone to write notes about what they will say in their conversation. Monitor and help students with pronunciation, particularly word stress, for the job and nationality. Encourage students to practice the full phrases in which they will include this information. They could record themselves on their digital devices.

B Students practice their conversations in their groups. Again monitor and assist with pronunciation as required, and encourage students to record themselves on their digital devices.

C Groups present their conversations to the rest of the class. Praise and encourage, highlighting examples of effective pronunciation.

Extra activity

Write the following words on the board: *happy*, *sad*, *tired*, *scared* and *bored*. Use mime and pictures to explain what these words mean. Demonstrate the task by pointing to the word *sad* on the board and pointing to yourself while doing an exaggerated sad face. Point to the word *happy* and point to one of the stronger students. Point to yourself again and say *Angela* and point to the student again and say *Roberto*. Read Angela's first line of the conversation in a sad voice and encourage the student to read Roberto's line in a happy voice. Continue performing the conversation with you doing a sad voice for Angela's lines and the student doing a happy voice for Roberto's lines. Then put the students into pairs to do the same. You can allocate an adjective to each student or let them choose. As an extension, some of the students could perform their conversation in front of the class and the others have to guess which emotion each of them is demonstrating.

METHODOLOGY HUB by Jim Scrivener

Word stress

Stress and its opposite – unstress – are very important aspects of English pronunciation. Getting the stress wrong can seriously damage your chances of being understood.

Words have their own stress pattern; for example, water, cricket and justice are stressed on the first syllable, whereas abroad, enough and today are stressed on the second. A stressed syllable in a word is usually noticeable by being slightly louder, longer and higher in pitch than the syllables next to it.

Stress and unstress

Unstressed syllables tend to be pronounced less loudly and with a more 'relaxed' manner; vowel sounds are typically 'weak'. Check this out: try saying the words *water* and *justice* with the stress on the wrong syllable. What happens to the previously stressed syllables?

The unstressed syllables become weaker, i.e. shorter, spoken more quickly and with less well-defined (or even altered) sounds, e.g. /wɑ'tɜːr/, /dʒəs'tiːs/.

Word stress is important because when it is wrong, words sound very strange or even incomprehensible. Would anyone understand you saying *secretary*? Sometimes wrong stress changes one word into another: *desert* – *dessert*. Or it can change the class of a word: *import* (v) – *import* (n).

Marking stress

There are a variety of ways of marking stress in a written text and it's important to do this for students. Which of the following do you personally find clearest?

formation	'window	□ unhappy	□□□ impostor
magaZINE	cassette	**wat**erfall	de^light^ful

GABY

SAM

LUCY

FUNCTIONAL LANGUAGE

Asking for clarification

A Complete the phrases with the verbs in the box.

mean say understand

1 Carolina: How do you [1] ___say___ *primário* in English?
Mark: 'Primary', I think.

2 Marta: I'm a nurse.
Carolina: I'm sorry, I don't [2] ___understand___.

3 Onur: What does 'nurse' [3] ___mean___?
Mark: *Enfermeira*

B ▶ 02:01–02:50 Watch part of the video and check your answers to Exercise A.

C Reorder the words to make the phrases.

1 mean? / What / 'student' / does
What does 'student' mean?

2 you / say / in English? / How / do / *obrigado*
How do you say *obrigado* in English?

3 understand. / I'm sorry, / I / don't
I'm sorry, I don't understand.

PRONUNCIATION

A (2.9) Listen to the conversation. Notice how the underlined words are stressed.

Angela: Good morning, everyone. My name's Angela. I'm your English teacher.
Roberto: I'm Roberto. I'm from Italy. How do you say *medico* in English?
Angela: 'Doctor'.
Roberto: Oh yes, that's it. I'm a doctor.
Monika: Hi. My name's Monika. I'm Polish and I'm an architect.
Roberto: I'm sorry, I don't understand. What does 'architect' mean?

B (2.9) Listen again and repeat the conversation. Copy the stress.

SPEAKING

A PREPARE You are going to introduce yourself to a group. Think about what you want to say.

- name
- nationality
- job

B PRACTICE Work in groups. Imagine you are in a new class. Practice your conversation.

C PRESENT Perform your conversation for the rest of the class.

Glossary

primary school teacher (n) (British) = elementary school teacher (n) (American)

Ask for clarification

Unit 2 Writing

2 Writing — Write an online introduction

W — using *and* to join sentences

A Read the title and introduction of the blog post. What do you think Tina writes about?

address age birthday country job name nationality phone number teacher's name

GLOBAL HUB LANGUAGE SCHOOL

Home Forum About Login Sign up

Say hello to your classmates. Post your introductions on this page.

Posted by: Tina Gonzalez

Hi, everyone! My name's Tina and I'm from Mexico. I'm 28 years old and I'm a photographer. My English classes are on Tuesdays and Thursdays. My teacher is Mr. Sampson. He's from Ottawa in Canada. I'm a big fan of British music. My favorite bands are Coldplay and Arctic Monkeys. Their music is really cool!

Using *and* to join sentences

We use *and* to link ideas. *And* gives extra information.
I'm 28 years old *and* I'm a new student.

B Read Tina's self-introduction again. Answer the questions.

1. Where's Tina from? Mexico
2. How old is she? 28 years old
3. What's her job? She's a photographer.
4. Who's Mr. Sampson? Her teacher
5. Who are her favorite bands? Coldplay and Arctic Monkeys

WRITING

A PLAN Imagine you are at a new school. Complete the information.

What's your name?	
Where are you from?	
What's your job?	
When are your English classes?	
Who's your teacher?	
Who are your favorite musicians?	

B WRITE Write an introduction for your school web forum. Use Tina's introduction to help you. Use *and* to join sentences.

O — Write an online introduction

Refer students to the post as a model for the writing task.

Encourage students to take time to plan their writing.

Remind students to use *and* in their writing.

Unit 2 Review

GRAMMAR

A Choose the correct verb to complete the sentences.

1. We *am* / *is* / *are* from Morocco.
2. My friend *am* / *is* / *are* Portuguese.
3. *Am* / *Is* / *Are* you a fan of world music?
4. Their names *am* / *is* / *are* Paolo and Pawel.

B Write the questions for these answers.

1. He's a teacher. *What's his job?*
2. They're from Brazil. Where are they from?
3. Her name is Elise. What is her name?
4. My class is on Thursday. When is your class?
5. I'm 34 years old. How old are you?
6. My teacher is Mr. Stevens. Who is your teacher?

C Circle the correct possessive adjectives.

1. She's from Brazil and *his* / *her* songs are in Portuguese.
2. We're from Iceland, but *our* / *their* songs are in English.
3. They're from Senegal and *our* / *their* music is traditional.
4. You're from Mexico, but *my* / *your* name is German.

VOCABULARY

A Write the nationalities for these countries.

1. Brazil *Brazilian*
2. Canada Canadian
3. Iceland Icelandic
4. Turkey Turkish
5. Egypt Egyptian
6. Poland Polish
7. Japan Japanese
8. Argentina Argentinian

B Complete the days of the week.

1. M o n day
2. T u e sday
3. W e d n e s day
4. T h u r s day
5. F r i day
6. S a t u r day
7. S u n day

16 OUR MUSIC, OUR WORLD

LEAD-IN

Write the names of some famous people that the class is likely to know on pieces of paper. Give them out randomly. Students stand up and walk around introducing themselves to each other. At the end, ask students who is in the room.

WRITING

A Books closed, write the words in the box on the board, checking understanding by asking students questions as you do so, e.g. *What's your teacher's name?* Books open, focus students on the title (make sure they don't start reading the text) and ask which words on the board they think it will be about. Then set a time limit, e.g. two minutes, for students to read the text to see if they were right.

B Write *My name's* (your name). and *I'm from* (your country). on the board. Focus students on the sentence *My name's Tina and I'm from Mexico*. Elicit the fact that you can join your two sentences by erasing the period and writing *and*. Ask students to find the other example (*I'm 28 years old and I'm a photographer*). Write it on the board, erase *and* and put a period. Focus students on the rule box and the function of *and* in the sentence. Students answer individually, then check answers in pairs. Write the answers on the board and focus students on the words which gave the answers.

WRITING TASK

A Students complete the table with their information individually. Walk around helping as necessary.

B Focus students on Tina's blog post again, and ask them to write a similar blog post using their information. Tell them to connect some sentences using *and*. Walk around helping while they complete the task individually, then ask them to share their posts with other students; you could pin these on the board or share them on a social media platform if appropriate.

A collection of rubber boots.

Ask students to label the photo if you need time to set up the class.

This echoes the modern approach of cognitive psychology that what we are is a result of what we think. Our experiences and feelings – our life – are shaped by our thoughts. Avoiding negative thoughts will help us to avoid experiencing life negatively.

Marcus Aurelius (121–180) was Emperor of Rome from 161 to 180 and called the *Philosopher*, by many. His main writing, *Meditations*, is considered by some as the greatest in the history of philosophy.

OBJECTIVES

- describe everyday objects
- talk about your family
- describe people
- write a social media post

Work with a partner. Discuss the questions.

1 Choose words that match the picture.

family home job nationality school

2 Who do you think lives in the house?

3 Who is important in your life?

Suggested answers: child, children, adults, man, woman, family, mother, father

MY LIFE 17

OBJECTIVES

Read the unit objectives to the class.

UNIT OPENER QUESTIONS

Write the words from Question 1 on the board and ask students to identify the ones they think match the picture. Erase any word not mentioned. Then ask for suggestions for other connected words and add them to the board. Students copy these words and keep the list as support for the work in the unit, adding to it throughout the lessons. The lists can be used as content for 'pop-up' quizzes during and at the end of the unit.

Then ask students to read Questions 2 and 3. Answer the questions as a whole class. Encourage a lot of students to answer and share their ideas. Again, add vocabulary to the board for students to use throughout the class. Add sentence stems to the board to support students, or give examples yourself. *I think two children live here …*

WORKSHEETS

Lesson 3.1 That's my coat

Vocabulary: Objects and colors (W7)

Grammar: *a/an* and plural nouns (W8); *this*, *that*, *these*, *those* (W9)

Lesson 3.2 I have two sisters

Vocabulary: Family (W10)

Grammar: *have/has* (W11)

3.1 That's my coat

Describe everyday objects

V objects and colors G *a*/*an* and plural nouns; *this, that, these, those* P /s/, /z/ and /ɪz/

VOCABULARY
Objects and colors

A Look at the picture. Write the letter (or letters) for these words.

a hat e
a phone d
a sweatshirt j
an umbrella i
a bag a, c, f, h
a coat k, l, m, n
glasses b
headphones g

B Look at the picture again. Write the correct letter.

Which coat is …

1 blue? k
2 red? l
3 green? n
4 black? m

C Go to the Vocabulary Hub on page 123.

GRAMMAR
a/*an* and plural nouns

A WORK IT OUT Read the examples. Choose the correct options for the sentences in the box.

In the picture, …

letter j is a sweatshirt.
letter i is an umbrella.
letters k, l, m, and n are coats.

_a_/_an_ and plural nouns

1 We use *a*/*an* when there is one / more than one object.
2 We add *s* when there is *one* / *more than one* object.

B Go to the Grammar Hub on page 102.

C SPEAK Work in pairs. Say the color and name of an object in the picture. Your partner says the correct letter.

A: A blue bag
B: Letter c!
A: Correct. White glasses …

a: a red bag
b: white glasses
c: a blue bag
d: a black phone
e: a gray hat
f: a green bag
g: gray headphones
h: a white bag
i: a yellow umbrella
j: a brown sweatshirt
k: a blue coat
l: a red coat
m: a black coat
n: a green coat

PRONUNCIATION
/s/, /z/ and /ɪz/

3.1 **A** Listen and repeat the sounds and the words.

/s/ coats /z/ headphones /ɪz/ glasses

3.2 **B** Listen to the words. Choose the correct sound for the underlined letters.

1 umbrellas /s/ /z/ /ɪz/
2 hats /s/ /z/ /ɪz/
3 bags /s/ /z/ /ɪz/
4 classes /s/ /z/ /ɪz/

C SPEAK Work in pairs. Make a list of the objects from Vocabulary Exercise A that are in your classroom. Say how many.

A: an umbrella
B: sixteen black bags

LISTENING

3.3 **A** LISTEN FOR GIST Listen to the conversation. What is the problem? At first, the man gives her the wrong items.

3.3 **B** LISTEN FOR KEY WORDS Listen again. Look at the picture above and circle all the objects that you hear.

3.3 **C** LISTEN FOR DETAIL Listen again and answer the questions.

1 What's the woman's ticket number? 42
2 What color is the woman's coat? blue
3 What color are the woman's bags? green / white

3.1 That's my coat

LEAD-IN

Get a set of sticky notes and ask students to label all the objects they know in the classroom. When they're finished, check ideas and practice any pronunciation as required.

VOCABULARY

A–C Students complete the activities individually and then check their ideas in pairs. Then direct students to the **Vocabulary Hub** (see TB97). Use the **Vocabulary Worksheet** on page W7 for extra practice.

GRAMMAR

a/an and plural nouns

A–C Students complete the activities. Direct students to the **Grammar Hub** (see below and TB19). Demonstrate Exercise C with one of the objects in the picture, then put students into pairs to do the task. Use the **Grammar Worksheet** on W8 for extra practice.

PRONUNCIATION

3.1 **A** Play the audio while students listen and repeat. Focus students on the endings and demonstrate the three sounds /s/, /z/ and /ɪz/.

3.2 **B–C** Play the audio while students work individually. Students can work in pairs or groups in Exercise C. Elicit answers and check as a class.

LISTENING

3.3 **A–C** Play the audio while students listen. Elicit what the problem is. Play the audio again and students complete Exercises B and C. Check answers as a class.

AUDIO SCRIPT

3.3

Listening, Exercise A
C = Customer CA = Coatroom attendant

	C:	Hello. Can I have my coat, please?
	CA:	Yes. What's your ticket number?
Ex C Q1	**C:**	It's 42.
	CA:	42, OK … here you are.
Ex B	**C:**	Sorry, that isn't my coat. That's a red coat. My coat's blue.
	CA:	Oh, sorry. Uh … Is this your coat?
Ex C Q2	**C:**	No! My coat is blue. That coat is green. Ex B
	CA:	Oh, yes … Is this your coat?
Ex B	**C:**	No. My coat is blue! That coat is black.
	CA:	This one?
	C:	Yes, that's it.
	CA:	Here you go.
	C:	Thank you. And can I have my bags, please?
	CA:	Bags?
	C:	Yes, there are two bags. One is green and the other one is white.
	CA:	Are these your bags?
Ex B / Ex C Q3	**C:**	No! Those bags are red and blue. My bags are green and white!
	CA:	Sorry! Sorry! Are these your bags?
	C:	Yes!
	CA:	Here you go.
	C:	Thank you.

GRAMMAR HUB

3.1

a/an* and plural nouns; *this, that, these, those

a/an	Plural nouns
a hat	three hat**s**
a phone	phone**s**
a box	two box**es**
a baby	three bab**ies**
an umbrella	two umbrella**s**

- We use *a* or *an* to talk about one object.
- We use *an* when the noun starts with a vowel sound (*a, e, i, o, u*). We use *a* when the noun doesn't start with a vowel sound.
- We don't use *a* or *an* with plural nouns (= more than one object).
- We add *-s* to the end of most nouns to make them plural.
- We add *-es* to the end of nouns ending in *-ch* (e.g. *watch – watches*), *-s* or *-ss* (e.g. *class – classes*), *-sh* (e.g. *brush – brushes*), *-x* (e.g. *box – boxes*), and *-o* (e.g. *potato – potatoes*) to make them plural.
- For nouns ending in *-y*, we change the *-y* to *-i-* and add *-es* (e.g. *baby* – babies).

this, that, these, those

- We use *this* and *that* to talk about one object.
  Is this your bag?
- We use *these* and *those* to talk about more than one object.
  Those actors are Italian.
- We use *this* and *these* to talk about things that are near.
  These are my shoes.
- We use *that* and *those* to talk about things that are not near.
  That's Khaled's house over there.

3.1 That's my coat

GRAMMAR

this, that, these, those

3.4 **A** Focus students on the pictures. Ask them to name the objects in the pictures. Then play the audio while they complete the task individually. Check the answers, playing the audio again if necessary.

B Students match the rules individually, then check in pairs. Give the answers, then draw simple pictures with arrows on the board to show the meanings next to the word. Check understanding by pointing at individual and plural objects near you and far from you (make sure they understand it is from your perspective) or ask students to do this.

C Direct students to the **Grammar Hub** (see below and TB18).

D Elicit the answer to the first picture as a whole class as an example, then let students answer the rest individually before checking in pairs. Write the answers on the board. Use the **Grammar Worksheet** on page W9 for extra practice.

SPEAKING

A With a student as the customer, role-play the conversation as customer and coatroom attendant. Check that students understand the situation, then get them to practice the conversation in pairs. When they have done it once or twice, ask them to do it again by reading each line, then looking up and speaking. Then, see if they can remember the whole conversation with books closed.

B This is a simple role play. The more authentic you can make it, the more useful and fun it will be, so, if possible, bring in some simple realia and move the classroom furniture appropriately. Divide the class into small groups and choose (or ask students to choose) one member from each group to be the coatroom attendant. Direct coatroom attendants to the **Communication Hub** (see TB97). Select one stronger student to demonstrate being the coatroom attendant; if possible, ask the student to wait outside the classroom or away from the main group. Let the students prepare, then set up the objects and bring the attendant in.

C Let them do the role play without your intervention; do not correct at this point, but write notes to give feedback on language and other issues (e.g. body language, tone, etc) later.

D Give any feedback that you think would be useful, then repeat, changing the attendants and owners of the objects. Encourage students to act in their roles if they want to. Doing this in another language can be fun and different for many students.

Extra activity
Students identify which aspect of the role play in the Speaking section they would like feedback on. First, in small groups, students brainstorm a list of areas of language and communication (e.g. grammar, pronunciation, volume, body language, etc). Students then select two key areas they would individually like feedback on. Students can then perform the role play again to the class and receive the feedback from you and the other students in the group.

GRAMMAR HUB

3.1

***a/an* and plural nouns**

A Choose *a* or *an* or no article (–) to complete the sentences and questions.

1. My grandmother has *a* / *an* / – glasses.
2. *A* / *An* / – headphones are useful.
3. Aisha doesn't have *a* / *an* / – coat.
4. Is there *a* / *an* / – address on the letter?
5. This is *a* / *an* / – map of Turkey.
6. Take *a* / *an* / – umbrella with you!

B Complete the sentences and questions with the plural form of the words in parentheses.

1. Put three ___tomatoes___ (*tomato*) in the salad.
2. Our ___families___ (*family*) live on the same street.
3. When are your piano ___lessons___ (*lesson*)?
4. Which ___countries___ (*country*) are on the map?
5. My team isn't playing well – we have five ___losses___ (*loss*)!

this, that, these, those

C Complete the sentences and questions with *is* or *are*.

1. This phone ___is___ great!
2. ___Is___ that a map of Greece?
3. These ___are___ my new shoes.
4. These exercises ___are___ easy!
5. What ___is___ that thing over there?
6. ___Are___ these Olivia's headphones?

D Read the sentences and check (✓) the correct pictures.

1 This is my new hat.

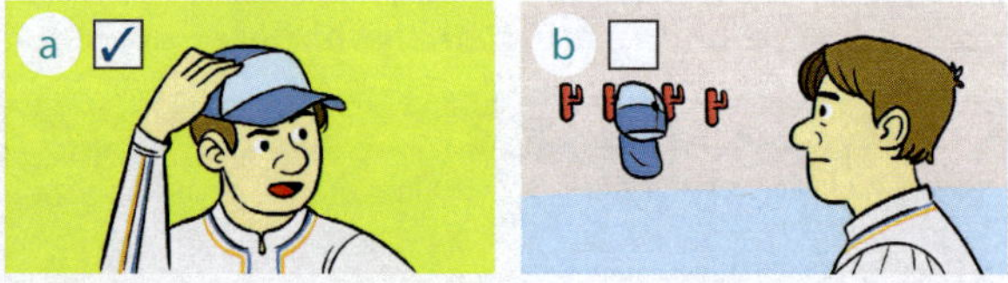

2 That is my book.

3 Those headphones are cool!

4 Are these your keys?

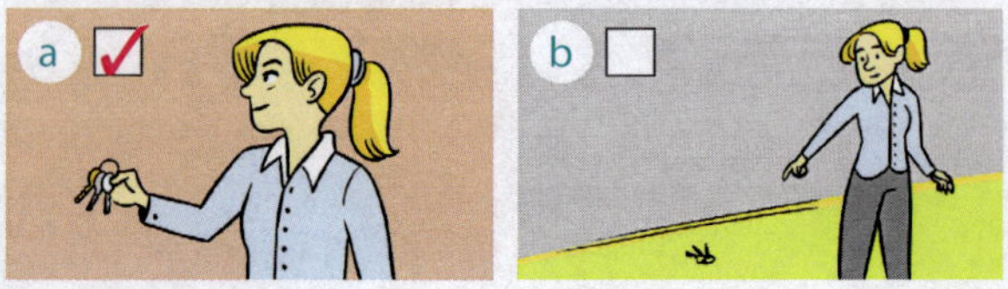

➤ Go back to page 19.

GRAMMAR

this, that, these, those

A Look at the pictures. Listen and complete the sentences from the conversation with *this, that, these* or *those*.

3.4

a

Coatroom attendant:	Is [1] ____this____ your coat?
Customer:	No! My coat is blue. [2] ____That____ coat is green.

b

Coatroom attendant:	Are [3] ____these____ your bags?
Customer:	No! [4] ____Those____ bags are red and blue.

B WORK IT OUT Look at the pictures and sentences in Exercise A again. Match the numbers (1–4) with the letters (a–d) to complete the rules.

this, that, these, those

1 We use *this* and *that* to talk about … c
2 We use *these* and *those* to talk about … a
3 We use *this* and *these* to talk about … d
4 We use *that* and *those* to talk about … b

a more than one object.
b things that are not near.
c one object.
d things that are near.

C Go the **Grammar Hub** on **page 102**.

D PRACTICE Write *this, that, these* or *those* and the name of the object for each picture.

1 ____these coats____

2 ____that hat____

3 ____those bags____

4 ____this phone____

SPEAKING

A PRACTICE Work in pairs. Practice the conversation.

Customer:	Can I have my hat, please?
Coatroom attendant:	Is this your hat?
Customer:	No. That hat is blue. My hat is green.
Coatroom attendant:	Is this your hat?
Customer:	Yes, that's my hat.

B PREPARE Work in groups. You are going to ask for your own objects at a coatroom.

One person is the coatroom attendant. Go to the **Communication Hub** on **page 129**.

The rest of the group are customers.

- Put some objects on the table. Try and put out more than one of the same type of object.
- Think about the names of the objects (hat, bag, headphones, etc).
- Think about the colors (red, blue, black, white, gray, brown, etc).
- Don't tell the attendant which object is yours.

Remember: *that/those.*

C DISCUSS Ask for your things at the coatroom. Use the conversation in Exercise A to help you.

D REPEAT Change roles and repeat.

A: Can I have my glasses, please?
B: Are these your glasses?
A: No, they aren't. Those glasses are brown. My glasses are black.

Describe everyday objects

3.2 I have two sisters

Talk about your family

S finding key information | V family | P schwa /ə/ | G *have/has*

READING

A PREPARE TO READ Look at the picture. Choose three words from the box to describe it.

cake family job party restaurant

100 YEARS YOUNG!

Local woman celebrates her 100th birthday with her family. Ex C Q1

Lilly Wenders is 100 years old this week, Ex B Q1 and there's a family party to celebrate. Ex C Q1 'A lot of my family lives in the same town as me,' Ex C Q2 says Lilly. 'I'm very lucky.'

Lilly is not the oldest person in her family. She has two **sisters**. Agatha is 103 Ex B Q2 and Hattie is 106. Ex B Q3

Lilly has two **children**, Sally and Emily, and three **grandchildren**: Katrina, Olivia and Clara. 'I don't have a **son** or a **grandson**,' says Lilly. 'My children and my grandchildren are all women.' Ex C Q3

'Do you have any men in your family?' I ask Lilly.

'Yes, I do,' says Lilly. 'I have a **husband**, Arthur. It's his birthday this week, too, but he's only 84!' Ex B Q4

Finding key information

Finding the important information first can help you to understand a text.

Examples of important information are:

- names (people, places)
- numbers (age, time, date)

B SCAN FOR INFORMATION Read the article quickly. Match the people (1–4) with their ages (a–d).

1 Lilly — b
2 Agatha — c
3 Hattie — d
4 Arthur — a

a 84
b 100
c 103
d 106

C READ FOR DETAIL Read the article again. Complete the statements with the underlined words in the article.

1 The party is for Lilly's ___birthday___.
2 Lilly lives in the same ___town___ as a lot of people in her family.
3 Lilly has a lot of ___women___ in her family.

D SPEAK Work in pairs. Answer the questions.

1 Do you know anyone who is 100 years old?
2 Do you live in the same town/city as your family?

VOCABULARY

Family

A Find the words in bold in the article. Put them in the correct place in the table.

Female	Male
mother	father
1 sister	brother
daughter	2 son
grandmother	grandfather
granddaughter	3 grandson
wife	4 husband
Female and/or male	
parents	
5 children/ grandchildren	6 grandchildren/ children

B Complete the family tree with names from the article.

C Complete the sentences with words from Exercise A.

1 Arthur: 'Lilly is my ___wife___.'

2 Hattie: 'Lilly is my ___sister___.'

3 Emily: 'Lilly is my ___mother___.'

4 Clara: 'Lilly is my ___grandmother___.'

3.2 I have two sisters

LEAD-IN

Play a quick review game: get students to choose two words each from the previous unit or lesson (any words, e.g. numbers, colors, objects, etc) and write them on a piece of paper. Don't tell students why. You choose and write a word, too. Demonstrate the activity: mime your word for students to guess. Students take turns miming one of their words to the class. Give them one point if someone guesses in less than ten seconds and give the correct guesser a point. Then ask another student, changing the timing to under five seconds and two points for a correct guess. You could bring in a small prize (e.g. a chocolate bar) for the winner, as appropriate.

READING

A Write the words in the box on the board and elicit their meaning and pronunciation. Then focus students on the picture. In pairs, students choose three words that best describe the picture. Place a check mark next to the words on the board with students' answers to see what the most popular choices were. Focus students on the *Finding key information* box and read through it with them. Write a sentence with names starting with capital letters, e.g. *Jane Howell is a doctor and she works in City Hospital.* Circle the capital letters and show that these help you find names quickly.

B Explain the task, then set a time limit, e.g. two minutes. Students do the task individually, then compare in pairs.

C Ask students to cover the Reading text. Focus students on the sentences and see if they can remember or guess any answers before they uncover the text. Then ask them to complete the task individually before checking with a partner. Check answers as a class.

D Read aloud the first question, and answer it yourself with some detail, e.g. *Yes … my grandmother's friend Angela is a hundred … she lives in New York … / No, but my grandfather is 90 …* Do the same for the second question, then put students into pairs to answer the questions. Get feedback on the information from the whole class – you could write all the ages up and compare.

VOCABULARY

A Students do the task individually, then check in pairs. Encourage them to guess if they are not sure – if they write in pencil, they can erase wrong answers later. If you help, focus students on the parts of the words, e.g. *grand*, *son*, to help them decide. Go through the answers. As an extension, you could identify what you are, e.g. *I am a daughter, a wife and a mother*, and then get students either in pairs or as a whole class to say what they are (this will be more productive with older students).

B Students use the information from the article to complete the family tree individually. Check answers.

C Do the first sentence as an example. To make sure students understand that they are looking from the perspective of the first name, point to it on the family tree and trace your finger to the relevant relationship. Use the **Vocabulary Worksheet** on page W10 for extra practice.

GRAMMAR HUB

3.2

have/has

	Positive	Negative
I/you/we/they	**I have** a phone. **You have** a phone. **We have** a phone. **They have** a phone.	**I don't have** a son. **You don't have** a son. **We don't have** a son. **They don't have** a son.
he/she	**He has** a phone. **She has** a phone.	**He doesn't have** an umbrella.

	Question	Short answers
I/you/we/they	**Do I/you/we/they have** children?	**Yes, I/you/we/they do.** **No, I/you/we/they don't.**
he/she	**Does he/she have** a red bag?	**Yes, he/she does.** **No, he/she doesn't.**

- We use *have/has* to talk about family members and things that we own.

PRONUNCIATION

3.5 **A** Play the audio while students listen. They may find the schwa sound strange and/or funny! Make the sound yourself, exaggerating the 'flatness', and get them to repeat it. Tell students that it is a very important sound in English.

3.5 **B** Students listen again and repeat the sentences.

3.6 **C** Students do the task while you write the words on the board. Play the audio to check and give feedback by underlining the schwa sounds. Repeat the audio and ask students to repeat.

D Check that students understand how the maze works and that they are looking for words with a schwa sound. Do the first word together, then put them into pairs to complete the task. Encourage students to say the words aloud to each other to help. Write the correct line of words on the board and underline the schwa in each, or ask students to come to the board and underline the schwa sounds.

GRAMMAR

A Focus students on the exercise and ask them to identify and underline examples of both. Encourage students to think about the contracted forms. Then ask them to look at the box and decide on the rule.

B Write the sentences *I have a brother. She doesn't have a sister. Do you have a son? Yes, I do.* on the board. Write *positive*, *negative*, *question* and *answer* in a column on the board and ask students to match. Use underlining and questions to help students understand the concepts. Students then work in pairs to complete the table. Write the answers on the board.

C Direct students to the **Grammar Hub** (see below and TB20). Use the **Grammar Worksheet** on page W11 for extra practice.

SPEAKING HUB

A Demonstrate by writing on the board the beginning of your family tree. Talk through it as you do it, e.g. *this is me!*, *this is my mother*, *I have three brothers …* Then students work individually to complete their own family trees.

B When students finish, divide them into groups if the class is big, and read and demonstrate the instructions. Students do the exercise. Monitor and try not to intervene unless they ask for help, but write a note about anything you want to correct at the end.

C Students take their own family trees and walk around the class talking to other students, asking and answering more questions. If they have pictures of their family members on their phones, encourage them to show them to the other students when they talk about them.

Extra activity

Students work in pairs to create their partner's family tree. Students ask their partner about family members, e.g. *Do you have a brother? How old is he?*, etc, and write a note about the answers in a list form. When both students have finished asking questions, they should have a list of people in their partner's family. They then work alone to draw the family tree of their partner, before showing to check if they are correct.

GRAMMAR HUB

3.2

have/has

A Complete the sentences with the correct form of *have*.

1 Afua *doesn't have* a coat and she's cold! (-)
2 My friends and I don't have English classes on Sundays. (-)
3 My mother has a new phone. (+)
4 I have a brother. (+)
5 Akim has a blue school bag. (+)
6 My dad doesn't have glasses. (-)
7 She has a brother and a sister. (+)
8 We have a new car. (+)
9 They don't have grandchildren. (-)
10 Sarah doesn't have a coat. (-)

B Put the words in order to make questions. Then write short answers.

1 my phone / have / Do / you
A: *Do you have my phone*?
B: No, *I don't*.

2 have / Carlo / a brother / Does
A: Does Carlo have a brother?
B: No, he doesn't.

3 have / they / a red car / Do
A: Do they have a red car?
B: Yes, they do.

4 two grandchildren / Mary and John / have / Do
A: Do Mary and John have two grandchildren?
B: Yes, they do.

5 the waiter / have / our food / Does
A: Does the waiter have our food?
B: Yes, he does.

➤ Go back to page 21.

PRONUNCIATION
schwa /ə/

3.5 **A** Listen to the sentences. Notice how the underlined letters sound.

1 Lilly is my moth<u>er</u>.
2 Arthur is my fath<u>er</u>.
3 Paul is my husb<u>a</u>nd.
4 I have three childr<u>e</u>n.

3.5 **B** Listen again and repeat.

3.6 **C** Underline the letters with the schwa sound. Listen and check.

1 daught<u>er</u> 2 par<u>e</u>nts 3 grandfath<u>er</u> 4 broth<u>er</u>

D Connect the words with the schwa sound to get out of the maze.

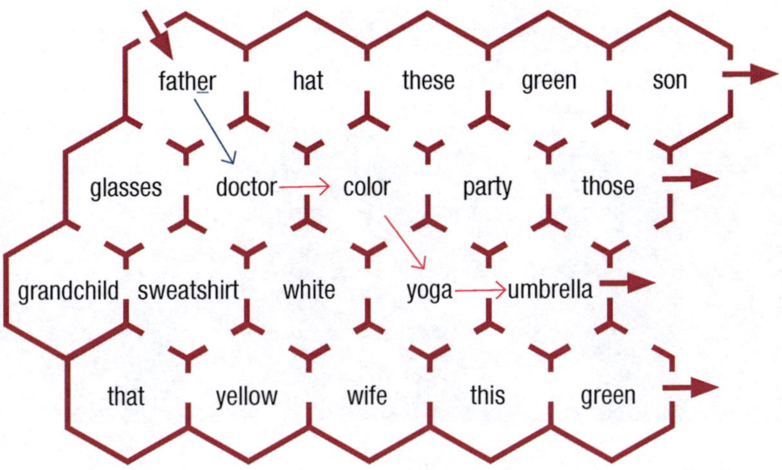

GRAMMAR
have/has

A **WORK IT OUT** Read the phrases from *100 years young!* Underline examples of *have/has*. Then choose the correct option to complete the rule.

Lilly <u>has</u> two children, …
'I <u>don't have</u> a son or a grandson, …'
'<u>Do you have</u> any men in your family?'
'Yes, I do, …' <u>I have</u> a husband, …'

have/has

We use *have/has* to talk about *somebody's age* / <u>*family members and things that we own*</u>.

B **WORK IT OUT** Complete the table with the words in the box.

do doesn't doesn't have don't have has ~~have (x3)~~

have/has	
positive (+)	I [1] ___have___ a sister She [2] ___has___ a brother.
negative (–)	I [3] ___don't have___ a brother. He [4] ___doesn't have___ a granddaughter.
question	Do you [5] ___have___ a daughter? Does she [6] ___have___ a daughter?
answer	Yes, I [7] ___do___. / No, I don't. Yes, she does / No, he [8] ___doesn't___.

C Go to the Grammar Hub on page 102.

SPEAKING HUB

A **PREPARE** Draw your family tree on a piece of paper and write the family members. Don't write their names and don't write your name.

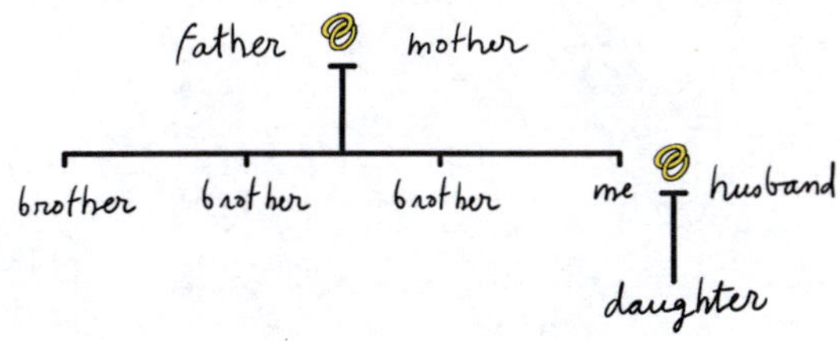

B **DISCUSS** Work in groups. Follow the instructions:

- Fold your family trees and put them in a box.
- Take out another person's family tree.
- Ask and answer questions. Find out who each family tree belongs to.

A: Do you have a sister, Nita?
B: No, I don't.
A: Do you have three brothers?
B: Yes, I do.
A: Is this your family tree?
B: Yes, it is!

C **PRACTICE** Ask each other more questions about the people in your families.

A: What's your brother's name?
B: His name's Hector.
A: How old is he?
B: He's 34.
A: What does he do?
B: He's a builder.

Talk about your family

Café Hub

3.3 Guess who

F – describe people

COMPREHENSION

A Watch the video. Number the events (a–d) in the order you see them (1–4). Is it easy for Gaby to meet Lucy? No, it isn't easy for Gaby to meet Lucy.

a 2

b 3

c 1

d 4

B Are the sentences true (T) or false (F)? Watch the video again and check your answers.

1 Gaby sees Lucy's poster in Sam's Café. (in the language school) T / (F)
2 Gaby texts Lucy first. (T) / F
3 Lucy has a yellow jacket. a green jacket T / (F)
4 Lucy is English. American T / (F)
5 Lucy has a green scarf. gray scarf T / (F)
6 At Sam's Café, all the women have green jackets. (T) / F
7 Gaby says she's not OK. she's OK T / (F)
8 Gaby is Lucy's new Spanish teacher. (T) / F

C Correct the false sentences in Exercise B.

D How many bags, chairs, etc can you see in the picture?

bags	3	laptops	1	men	2	tables	3
chairs	5	plants	4	people	7	women	5

3.3 Guess who

LEAD-IN

Ask students to look at the images and predict the storyline. Listen to all ideas and ask questions to explore the students' ideas.

COMPREHENSION

A ▸ Read through the task with students. Then play the video. Allow time for students to compare answers in pairs before checking as a whole class.

B ▸ Students work in pairs to recall as many answers as possible. Then play the video for students to watch again and check answers.

C After the second viewing, students work in pairs to correct the false sentences in Exercise B.

D With books closed, write the words from the exercise on the board (*bags, computers, men, tables, chairs, plants, people, women*). Then ask students questions, e.g. *How many bags are in the classroom?* This could be run as a treasure hunt, with a time limit and students working in small groups to check around the room. To check answers, ask individual students questions: *How many computers are in the classroom?* Then tell students they will do the same thing with the photo in the book. Set a time limit and run the exercise as a race. Check answers as a whole class.

▶ VIDEO SCRIPT

G = Gaby Ma = Marta C = Carolina L = Lucy

G: Bye!
C, Ma: Bye!
G: Lucy. Hello Lucy, my name's Gaby. I'm from Spain. I can help with your Spanish.
L: Hi Gaby, that's great! Are you free today at four o'clock?
G: Sure!
L: Do you know Sam's Café?
G: Yes! Perfect. See you then. I've got long brown hair and a yellow jacket.
L: Great! I'm American. I have light brown hair, a black bag, a green jacket and a gray scarf.
G: OK. She's got a green jacket. They've all got green jackets! Lucy's got light brown hair. Lucy's got a black bag. Lucy's got a gray scarf. What? Lucy?
L: Gaby?
G: Green jacket. Light brown hair. Black bag. Gray scarf. Lucy?
L: Gaby?
G: Yes, it's Gaby. I'm Gaby.
L: Are you OK now?
G: Yes. I'm fine, thanks.
L: So, Spanish conversation?
G: Let's do it!

METHODOLOGY HUB by Jim Scrivener

Weak forms

One important effect of prominence is to mark out a rhythm. There is also a dramatic effect on unstressed words in a sentence.

Unstressed words tend to be pronounced fairly fast, almost as if trying to cram themselves into the spaces between the beats of the rhythm (a common feature of student English is a failure to do this – giving each word in the sentence equal time in the rhythm). They also tend to be pronounced in a 'weak' manner; they typically have shorter vowel sounds: /ʊ/ rather than /uː/ and /ɪ/ rather than /iː/, etc. This use of weak forms is one of the features of connected speech that makes listening comprehension more difficult for students. If you are expecting to hear *to* pronounced as /tuː/ or *was* pronounced as /wɑz/, then you are less likely to recognize the words when you hear /tə/ or /wəz/.

The schwa

The most common weak form vowel sound (and thus the most common sound in the English language) is /ə/. It is also the only sound to be given its own name – the schwa. If your learners are anything like mine, they will take a lot of convincing that words are really pronounced with schwa weak forms in natural English; they may feel that using 'full' vowel sounds must be 'correct' English.

Because the schwa is a short and unassertive sound, there is a danger that in focusing on it in classroom sentences, it might lose its naturally weak character. Here are some awareness-raising and practice ideas.

De-schwaed texts

Prepare a short text (three or four lines long). Wherever a schwa would be said in a word, insert a blank line instead of the vowel(s). Leave all other vowels as they are. In class, give out the text and explain what you have done. Learners must now go through the text and work out the missing written vowels. This will raise awareness about the many ways that the schwa sound can be spelled in English.

3.3 Guess who

FUNCTIONAL LANGUAGE

A Students work alone to review the examples in the box. Then make a sentence about yourself (if possible) from the box and, as a whole class, ask students to make sentences. Students then work alone to complete the exercise.

B ▶ 01:39–02:20 Students watch part of the video again to check their answers to Exercise A in context. Check answers as a class.

C Students complete the descriptions of the images with the words in the box.

D Ask a strong student to help you model the example conversation. Then, if appropriate, ask students to describe the hair of other people in the class using the words from the box in Exercise C and the example conversation. Students can introduce other words (e.g. *brown*) if known and also the words for clothes they have learned.

PRONUNCIATION

3.7 **A** Focus the students on the conversation. Elicit what the underline means (*stressed syllables*). Play the audio for the students to listen to and notice the stress.

3.7 **B** Play the audio again and have students practice line by line, as a single group and individually.

C Model the conversation with a confident student. Students then work in pairs to practice the conversation. Monitor and encourage appropriate stressing.

SPEAKING

A Students work in pairs to decide the time and place they want to meet their partner. Students write notes about their hair and clothes so they can describe what they look like. Encourage students to work with notes rather than full sentences if they can.

B Students take turns 'calling' the people they want to speak to about the language classes and describe themselves in order to meet.

C Students change roles and find a new time and place to meet. If they are feeling imaginative, they could also imagine a new appearance for themselves.

Extra activity

Find a photo with a lot of people pictured. Number the people in the image, adding these numbers to the image. Then assign students (either in the whole class or large groups) a number each (students should keep this number secret) that corresponds to the numbered people in the image. Students describe the numbered person they have been assigned to the other members of the group. The students listening decide who the student is in the photo and write a note (e.g. 3 = *Monica*). After all the students have spoken, the group compares their notes to find out who got the most answers correct.

METHODOLOGY HUB by Jim Scrivener

Role play

In role play, learners are usually given some information about a 'role' (e.g. a person or a job title). These are usually printed on 'role cards'. Learners take a little preparation time and then meet up with other students to act out small scenes using their own ideas, as well as any ideas and information from the role cards.

Running a role play: some guidelines

- Make sure the students understand the idea of role play. Do they know what's going to happen? Do they know what is required of them? Are they comfortable doing that or not?
- Make sure the context or situation is clear.
- Do they understand the information on their own card? Allow reading / dictionary / thinking time (during which you go around and help if necessary).
- Give them time to prepare their ideas before they start – maybe encourage note-writing – but when the activity starts, encourage them to improvise rather than rely on prepared speeches and notes. The preparation work they have done will inform their role play but could simply get in the way if they over-rely on it. It may help to take away the cards when the role play starts.
- At the end of the role play, make sure that you give some feedback on how well (or not) the students completed the activity. Remember to comment on the language used as well as the appropriateness of what was said. Students will need to feel that they have achieved something.

GABY

SAM

LUCY

FUNCTIONAL LANGUAGE
Describing people

Subject + verb	Type	Color	Noun
I've got	long	brown	hair.
I have	light	brown	hair.
Gaby's got a		yellow	jacket.

A Put the words in 1–5 in the correct order. Use the box to help you.

1 got / a / jacket. / green / She's
She's got a green jacket.

2 got / They've all / jackets. / green
They've all got green jackets.

3 Lucy's / hair. / brown / light / got
Lucy's got light brown hair.

4 got / Lucy's / bag. / black / a
Lucy's got a black bag.

5 gray / got / Lucy's / a / scarf.
Lucy's got a gray scarf.

B 01:39–02:20 Watch part of the video and check your answers to Exercise A.

C Complete the descriptions with the words in the box.

blond curly long straight

1 short blond hair

2 long red hair

3 straight gray hair

4 curly black hair

D **SPEAK** Work in pairs. Play a game of *Guess who* in the class.

A: She has long brown hair.
B: Is it Sandra?
A: Yes it is.

PRONUNCIATION

3.7 **A** Listen to the conversation. Notice how the underlined words are stressed.

Jessica: Hi, Mark. Are you free at two o'clock?
Mark: Yes!
Jessica: Do you know Sam's Café?
Mark: Yes. See you there at two o'clock. I have light brown hair and a black coat.
Jessica: OK. I have long black hair, a green coat and a yellow scarf.

3.7 **B** Listen again and repeat the conversation. Copy the stress.

C **SPEAK** Work in pairs. Practice the conversation.

SPEAKING

A **PLAN** Work in pairs. You want to do a language exchange. Arrange to meet your partner – you don't know each other.

- Choose a time and a place to meet.
- Write notes about your appearance.

B **PRACTICE** Work in pairs. Write and practice a similar conversation to the one in Pronunciation Exercise A.

C **REPEAT** Swap roles. Choose a new time and place to meet.

Note

I've got (British) = I have (American)
She's got (British) = She has (American)

The word *got* is typically not used with *has* and *have* in standard American English.

Describe people

Unit 3 Writing

3 Writing

Write a social media post

W – using *but*

A Read the social media post. Whose birthday is it today? Match the picture with the event. It's Martina's 30th birthday.

Florence Duprey
January 24, 9:21 am

Happy birthday to my sister Martina! Here we are at home. She's wearing the yellow sweater and has a big smile – she's one in this picture! Our mom took this photo. Today it's Martina's 30th birthday party! We have the cake, but Mom is late 😊! Our little sister Talia is here, too – she's in the yellow top next to her husband Larry. Martina has a husband, too. His name is Paulo – he's the one in the white sweater. Ex B Q1 Ex B Q2 Ex B Q3 Ex B Q4

5 20 9

Using *but*

We use *but* to join ideas that are different.
*We have the cake, **but** mom is late!*

B Read the post again. These sentences are all false. Correct the sentences.

1. Martina is two years old in the first picture.
Martina is one year old in the first picture
2. Martina's mom is at Martina's 30th birthday party.
Martina's mom is late
3. Martina has one sister.
Martina has two sisters
4. Larry is wearing a white sweater.
Paulo is wearing a white sweater

WRITING

A PLAN You are going to write a social media post. Find a picture of people in your family on a special day. Plan what you want to say.

B WRITE Write a social media post for the picture.

Write a social media post

Refer students to the social media post as a model for the writing task.

Remind students to take time to plan their writing.

Encourage students to edit their own work. They can check for spelling and grammar errors.

Unit 3 Review

GRAMMAR

A Complete the sentences with *this, that, these* or *those*.

1 That bag is red.
2 This bag is blue.

3 Those bags are red.
4 These bags are blue.

B Complete the sentences with *is* or *are*.

1. This bag is green.
2. Those hats are yellow.
3. Those headphones are black.
4. These glasses are white.
5. This phone is gray.
6. Those bags are brown.

C Choose the correct option to complete the sentences.

1. I *have* / *has* a son.
2. *Do you has* / *Do you have* a brown coat? Yes, I *do*/*does*.
3. I *don't have* / *doesn't have* a brother.
4. She *don't have* / *doesn't have* a granddaughter.
5. *Does* / *Do* he have a brother? No, he *don't* / *doesn't*.

VOCABULARY

A Complete the words for objects and colors.

1. My headphones are green.
2. This umbrella is white.
3. I have a brown sweatshirt.
4. My glasses are gray.
5. That is a blue coat.
6. These are my black bags.

B Use the information. Write the names of the people.

Angela is 6. Mary is 35. Cara is 70.

1. Cara: 'Mary is my daughter.'
2. Angela: 'Cara is my grandmother.'
3. Mary: 'Angela is my daughter.'

Pietro is 10. Guillermo is 50. Giancarlo is 80.

4. Giancarlo: 'Pietro is my grandson.'
5. Guillermo: 'Giancarlo is my father.'
6. Pietro: 'Guillermo is my father.'

24 MY LIFE

LEAD-IN

Ask students to bring in photos of their families on a happy or special day, either printed images or ones on their digital devices. Demonstrate describing your own photos. Students then mix and mingle, finding out about each other's friends and family.

WRITING

A Focus students on the picture and ask them what they can see. Ask whose birthday it is today and ask students to read the post quickly to find out and match the picture. Write *It's my birthday* ________ *I am happy.* on the board. Draw a smiley face above each part. Elicit and write *and* in the blank. Change the second smiley face to a sad face. Erase *happy* and *and*, and write *sad* followed by a comma and *but* in their place. Check that students understand that the two ideas are different. Instruct students to find *We have the cake, but mom is late.* in the text, then refer them to the *Using but* box and check students understand. Focus them on the use of the comma before *but*.

B Do the first question together, then let them work individually and check in pairs. Write the correct sentences on the board.

WRITING TASK

A Make sure students know that they need a photo of a special day before the class. Refer students back to the social media post and ask them to identify the kinds of information it has in it. Write their ideas on the board. Ask if there are other things they could include and add them. Then tell them to look at their photo of a special day and decide what they will write about and in what order. Ask students to include at least one sentence with *but*.

B Students write their post. Walk around helping while they complete the task individually. Then ask them to share their posts with other students; you could pin these on the board or share them on a social media platform if appropriate.

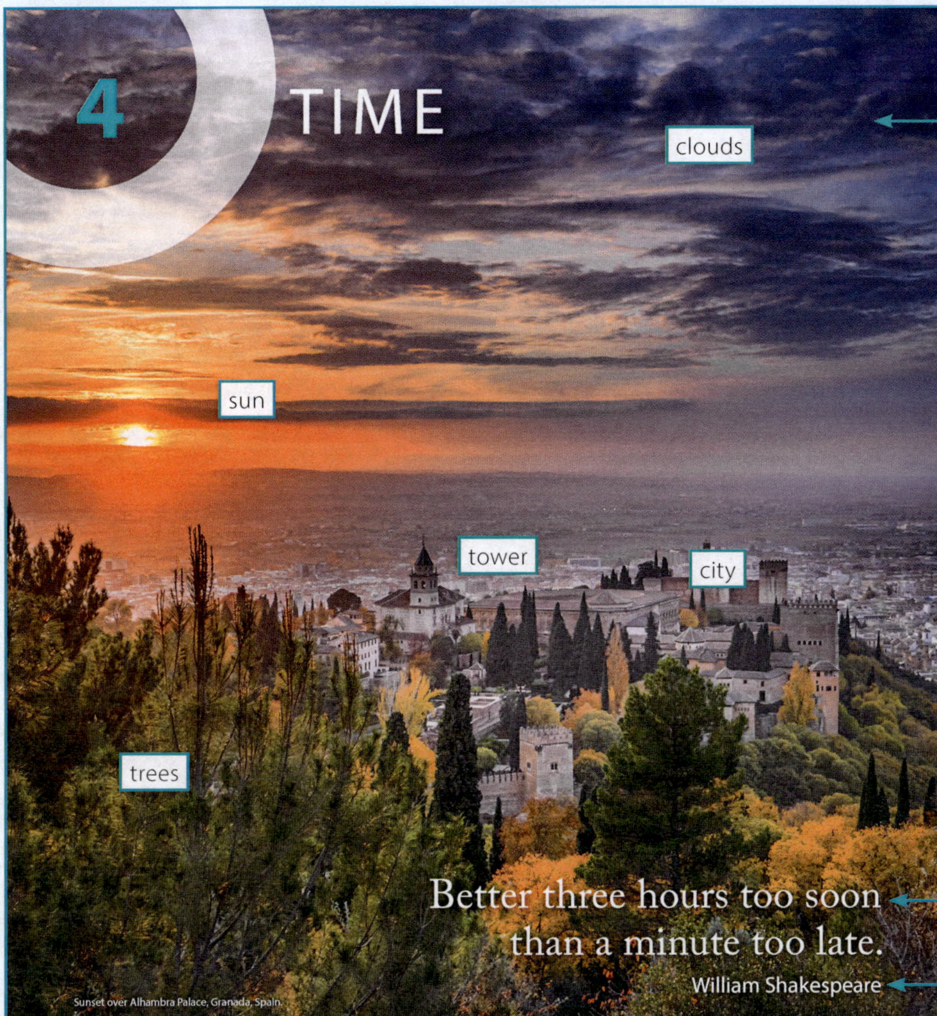

Sunset over Alhambra Palace, Granada, Spain.

Ask students to label the photo if you need time to set up the class.

From Shakespeare's *The Merry Wives of Windsor*, the quote refers to being prepared for action, rather than responding when it is too late, even if we are only a few moments too late. The amount of time doesn't alter the fact that we have missed the opportunity forever.

William Shakespeare (1564–1616) is one of the most famous English-language writers in history. He wrote many plays, at least 37, and over a hundred sonnets (a form of poetry). Many of his works are still performed today around the world, both in theaters and on screen.

OBJECTIVES

- talk about daily routines
- talk about annual routines
- order in a café
- write an email about your routine

Work with a partner. Discuss the questions.

1 Look at the picture. Which words match the picture?

city countryside moon morning night ocean sky sun

2 What's your favorite time of day?

3 Read the quote. Are you usually early or late for things?

TIME 25

OBJECTIVES

Read the unit objectives to the class.

UNIT OPENER QUESTIONS

Write the words from Question 1 on the board and ask students to identify the ones they think match the picture. Erase any word not mentioned. Then ask for suggestions for other connected words and add them to the board. Students copy these words and keep the list as support for the work in the unit, adding to it throughout the lessons. The lists can be used as content for 'pop-up' quizzes during and at the end of the unit.

Then ask students to read Questions 2 and 3. Answer the questions as a whole class. Encourage students to answer and share their ideas. Again, add vocabulary to the board for students to use throughout the class.

WORKSHEETS

Lesson 4.1 Every day

Vocabulary: Daily activities; Time (W12)

Grammar: Simple present: *I, you, we, they* (W13)

Lesson 4.2 Every year

Vocabulary: Months and seasons (W14)

Grammar: Simple present questions: *I, you, we, they* (W15)

4.1 Every day

Talk about daily routines

V daily activities; time G simple present: *I, you, we, they* P sentence stress

VOCABULARY

Daily activities

A Match the sentences (1–4) with the pictures (a–d).

1 I finish work at six ten in the evening.
2 I get up at seven o'clock in the morning.
3 I go to work at eight thirty in the morning.
4 I get home at five o'clock in the afternoon.

a 2

b 4

c 3

d 1

B Go to the **Vocabulary Hub** on **page 123**.

Time

4.1 Complete the times with the numbers in the box. Then listen and check.

eight eleven fifty forty-five nine twelve

1
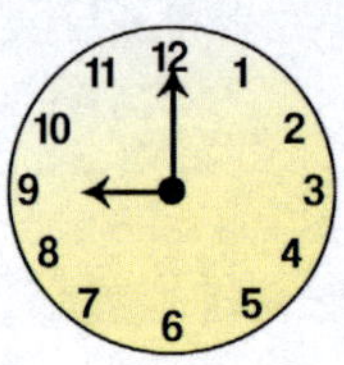

nine o'clock

2

twelve ten

3

twelve fifty

4

eleven thirty

5

eight fifteen

6

one forty-five

LISTENING

A **PREPARE TO LISTEN** Read the information about the podcast. Then choose the correct options to complete the summary.

The title of this podcast series is *My life*. In this episode, [1]*three* / *two* people talk about [2]*the people they know* / *the things they do*. The people in this episode have the same [3]*hobby* / *job*.

4.2 **B** **LISTEN FOR MAIN IDEA** Listen to the podcast and choose the correct options to complete the sentences.

1 Magne is Astrid's ...
 a brother. (b) husband.
2 Astrid and Magne live and work ...
 (a) in the same place. b in different places.
3 Astrid and Magne work ...
 a at the same time. (b) at different times.

4.2 **C** **LISTEN FOR DETAIL** Listen again. Circle the correct person: Astrid (A) or Magne (M).

1 1 am go to bed A / (M)
2 5 am get up (A) / M
3 5:15 am start work (A) / M
4 11 am get up A / (M)
5 1:30 pm start work A / (M)
6 1:30 pm finish work (A) / M
7 8 pm go to bed (A) / M
8 9:45 pm finish work A / (M)

D **DISCUSS** Work in pairs. Which person's day do you prefer? Why?

4.1 Every day

LEAD-IN

Review students' knowledge of numbers up to 100. You could prepare some bingo cards and play as a class. Or ask students to count around the class. Students can change the direction of who speaks next by saying two numbers. To make it more challenging, ask learners to count in fives.

VOCABULARY

Daily activities

A–B Students do the activity individually, then check in pairs before checking answers as a whole class. Direct students to the **Vocabulary Hub** (see TB97).

Time

4.1 Students may not be familiar with the *quarter till or half past/ thirty* way of telling the time. In that case, teach them the system using a circle on the board to represent the clock face, with a line down the middle and *half past/thirty* on the right and *quarter till* on the left. Go around eliciting examples, e.g. *quarter till five, three thirty/half past three*, etc, and show how the hour changes. (Note that in Am English, *thirty* is used over *half past* but students may have heard both terms.) Use the **Vocabulary Worksheet** on page W12 for extra practice.

LISTENING

A Focus students on the podcast information. Students complete the summary. Give the answers, checking understanding.

4.2 **B** Go through the questions with the students and ask what they think the answers will be. Then play the audio while they listen and complete the exercise. Check the answers as a group.

4.2 **C** Ask students if they can remember any answers. Play the audio again as many times as they need to complete the task to their satisfaction.

D Put students into pairs to discuss the questions. Get feedback from the whole class.

GRAMMAR HUB

4.1

Simple present: *I, you, we, they*

	Positive	Negative
I	**I work** in an office.	**I do not work** in an office. **I don't work** in an office.
you	**You start** work at eight o'clock.	**You do not start** work at eight o'clock. **You don't start** work at eight o'clock.
we	**We watch** TV in the evening.	**We do not watch** TV in the evening. **We don't watch** TV in the evening.
they	**They play** soccer.	**They do not play** soccer. **They don't play** soccer.

- We use the simple present for things that are always true or actions that always happen.
  They live in a lighthouse.
  We play soccer on Saturdays.
- For *I/you/we/they*, the verb form is the same.
  I play.
  We play.
- We form the negative with the long form (*do not*) or the contraction (*don't*) before the verb. We usually use the contraction when we speak.
  I do not start work at nine o'clock. OR I don't start work at nine o'clock.

Be careful!

- Remember that *don't* is the negative of *do not*.
  I don't work here. NOT ~~I don't not work here.~~

AUDIO SCRIPT

4.2

Listening, Exercise B
P = Presenter A = Astrid M = Magne

P: My life … the lighthouse keepers.
A: Hello. My name's Astrid. I'm a lighthouse keeper. I live and work in a lighthouse.
Ex B Q1 **M:** Hi. I'm Magne. I'm Astrid's husband. I also live and
Ex B Q2 work in the lighthouse. We work in the same place.
Ex B Q3 **A:** But we don't work at the same time. I get up very
Ex C Q2, Q3, Q6 early – at five o'clock in the morning! I start work at five fifteen, and I finish at one thirty in the afternoon.
Ex C Q5 & Q8 **M:** I don't work in the morning. I start work at one thirty in the afternoon, and I finish work late – at nine forty-five in the evening.
A: I relax and watch TV in the afternoon but I don't watch TV in the evening. I make something to eat
Ex C Q7 and then I go to bed at eight o'clock.
Ex C Q1 & Q4 **M:** I watch TV or read a book in the evening. I go to bed at one o'clock in the morning and I get up late at 11 o'clock in the morning.

4.1 Every day

GRAMMAR

A–C Ask students to complete these activities alone and then to check ideas in pairs. Ask them to discuss why they chose those answers. Then elicit ideas from students and check answers as a class.

D Direct students to the **Grammar Hub** (see below and TB26).

E Ask students what time of day doctors work. Elicit the idea of working in a hospital and the meaning of *night shift*. Then let them work in pairs to complete the text while you walk around, guiding if necessary. Check answers as a whole class.

F Say *I'm* (your age). *I get up at …* Elicit the times students think you get up. Tell them who is correct and write the answer, e.g. *I get up at eight o'clock in the morning*, on the board. Ask *what about five-year-old children?* Elicit a few suggestions, then refer students to the example. Put them into pairs to discuss their ideas. Make sure they use full sentences and correct times. Write the ages on the board, and get the class feedback. Did they agree? Encourage them to continue the discussion as a whole class if they can. Don't erase your sentence. Use the **Grammar Worksheet** on page W13 for extra practice.

PRONUNCIATION

4.3 **A** Go back to your sentence on the board and read it aloud. Ask students if they can hear which words are stressed. Focus students on the example sentences and the different color words. Play the audio while students read the sentences and decide which color represents the stressed words. Check answers as a class.

4.4 **B** Ask students to read the sentences and predict the stresses. Go through the example sentence together. Don't confirm any answers at this stage: play the audio while they listen and underline, and then give feedback.

4.5 **C** Play the audio while students listen and write individually. Repeat until they are able to complete the task. Check answers as a class.

SPEAKING

A Focus students on the activities in the list and check that they understand them by miming the actions and asking students to say which action you are miming. Alternatively, ask volunteers to mime one of the actions, and the rest of the class can guess. Then demonstrate by doing the first two (*get up* (✓) / *have breakfast* (✗)) on the board about yourself. Students complete the task individually, adding a check mark next to the activities they do every day.

B Students identify and add the times where appropriate. Say *I get up at eight o'clock, but I don't have breakfast at home*. Ask students to plan what to say in the same way – can they join some sentences or add any information?

C Put students into pairs and ask them to discuss their daily routines. Encourage them to work through two or three items at a time and compare as they go, which is more natural than 'giving a speech' by going through them all one by one. At the end, ask students to report back to another pair how they are the same and different. Ask one or two pairs to report back to the class. Are there any things that everyone in the class/ nobody does?

GRAMMAR HUB

4.1

Simple present: *I, you, we, they*

A Choose the correct options.

1 I (don't) / *not* watch TV in the mornings.
2 They *do go* / (*go*) to bed at 11 pm.
3 After work, we go home and *to relax* / (*relax*).
4 I (don't) / *not* get up early on Sundays.
5 I *am live* / (*live*) with two friends.
6 We (*start*) / *do start* work at seven in the morning.
7 You (*go*) / *to go* out on Saturdays.
8 They *play don't* / (*don't play*) games on their computers at work.

B Complete the text with the verbs in the box.

don't talk | finish | get up | go | live | relax | start | ~~work~~

I [1] *work* in an office. My friends Anna and Frieda work there too. They're very nice. We [2] start work at 8 am, so I [3] get up at 7 am. When we [4] finish work – at about five o'clock, we [5] go out. Our other friends [6] live in the town, so we meet them after work. We [7] relax and we [8] don't talk about work!

C Reorder the words to make sentences.

1 don't / at six o'clock / I / get up — *I don't get up at six o'clock*.
2 TV / in the evenings / watch / I — I watch TV in the evenings.
3 at seven o'clock / work / don't / you / start — You don't start work at seven o'clock.
4 live / we / in the same house — We live in the same house.
5 games / on my computer / play / I — I play games on my computer.
6 on Monday evenings / don't / we / go out — We don't go out on Monday evenings.
7 they / here / don't / live — They don't live here.
8 I / at home / relax — I relax at home.

➤ Go back to page 27.

GRAMMAR

Simple present: *I, you, we, they*

A Read the sentences from the podcast. Are they positive (+) or negative (–)?

a I get up at five o'clock in the morning. (+) / –

b I don't work in the morning. + / (–)

B WORK IT OUT Complete the table with the words in the box.

don't go go

Simple present: *I, you, we, they*			
subject pronoun	positive	subject pronoun	negative
I you we they	[1] go to work at eight o'clock in the morning.	I you we they	[2] don't go to work at six o'clock in the morning.

C WORK IT OUT Read the sentences again. Choose the correct option to complete the rules.

1 In positive sentences with *I*, *you*, *we*, and *they* we use <u>*verb*</u> / *do* + *verb*.

2 In negative sentences with *I*, *you*, *we*, and *they* we use *verb* / <u>*don't* + *verb*</u>.

D Go to the **Grammar Hub** on **page 104**.

E PRACTICE Complete the description with the correct positive or negative form of the verbs in the box.

finish get up (x2) go start ~~work~~

The night shift

I'm a doctor. For one week in each month, I [1] *don't work* during the day. I [2] start my job at ten o'clock in the evening and I [3] finish at eight o'clock in the morning. I [4] don't get up in the morning, like most people. I [5] get up in the evening, and I [6] go to bed in the morning.

F SPEAK Work in pairs. What times do you think these people get up and go to bed?

5-year-old children
80-year-old people
20-year-old people
People your age

PRONUNCIATION

Sentence stress

4.3 **A** Listen and repeat the sentences. Which words are stressed – the red or the blue? The red words are stressed.

1 I go to bed at ten o'clock.

2 I don't go to bed at ten o'clock.

4.4 **B** <u>Underline</u> the stressed words in the sentences. Then listen and check.

1 I <u>read</u> a <u>book</u> in the <u>evening</u>.

2 We <u>don't</u> watch <u>TV</u> in the <u>morning</u>.

3 They <u>start</u> <u>work</u> at <u>eight</u> o'<u>clock</u> in the <u>morning</u>.

4 They <u>don't</u> start at <u>eight</u> <u>thirty</u>.

5 I <u>relax</u> in the <u>evening</u>.

4.5 **C** Listen and complete the sentences.

1 I go to work at eight o'clock.

2 I watch movies in the evening.

3 They don't go to bed at ten thirty.

4 We don't relax in the afternoon.

SPEAKING

A PREPARE Think about these daily activities. Check (✓) the ones that you do every day.

- [ ] get up
- [ ] have breakfast
- [ ] go to work/school
- [ ] start work/classes
- [ ] have lunch
- [ ] finish work/classes
- [ ] go home
- [ ] have dinner
- [ ] watch TV/a movie
- [ ] read a book
- [ ] talk to friends/family
- [ ] go to bed

B PLAN Write the times you do the things in Exercise A. Prepare how to say it.

C DISCUSS Work in pairs. Compare your daily routines. What's different? What's the same?

A: I get up at seven o'clock in the morning.
B: I get up at eight o'clock in the morning.

Talk about daily routines

4.2 Every year

Talk about annual routines

V months and seasons
G simple present questions: *I, you, we, they*
S using pictures before you read
P *do you* /dʒʊ/

VOCABULARY
Months and seasons

A Match the pictures with the seasons.

fall spring summer winter

B Listen and complete the calendar.

4.6

April August December July June March May November October September

January	February	March
April	May	June
July	August	September
October	November	December

C SPEAK Work in pairs. Answer the questions.

- Which season is it now?
- Which month is it now?
- Which season is your favorite?
- Which month is your birthday in?

READING

A PREDICT Work in pairs. Look at the pictures in the article *Nomads in Mongolia* but don't read the text. What do you know about these people's lives?

Using pictures before you read

Articles on websites and in magazines and newspapers usually have pictures. Look at the pictures before you read to get an idea of what the text is about.

B PREPARE TO READ Match the words in the box with the pictures (a–d) in *Nomads in Mongolia* opposite.

hills horse river tents

C READ FOR GIST Read the article. Match the correct question (a–d) with each paragraph (1–4).

a How often do they go to a different place?
b What are nomads?
c Where do they go in different seasons?
d Do they live in houses?

D READ FOR DETAIL Read the article again. Are the statements true (T) or false (F)?

1 Mongolia is in Europe. Mongolia is in Asia. T / (F)
2 Nomads live in cities. Nomads live in the countryside. T / (F)
3 Nomads live in a type of tent. (T) / F
4 Nomads have animals. (T) / F
5 In Mongolia, September is in the spring. September is in the fall. T / (F)
6 Many nomads go to a river in the spring. (T) / F

E SPEAK Work in pairs. Answer the questions.

- Are there nomads in your country?
- Would you like to live in different places in your country at different times of the year?

NOMADS
in Mongolia

Ex D Q1 **Mongolia is a large country in Asia, north of China and south of Russia. There's a lot of space, about 1.56 million km², but there aren't a lot of people. There are about 3,000,000 (three million) people in Mongolia and many of these people are nomads.**

1 b — Nomads are people who go to different places in different months or seasons. They don't live in cities, they live in the countryside. (Ex D Q2)

2 d — No, they don't. They don't have houses, but they have tents, called *gers*, and they have horses and other animals. (Ex D Q3, Ex D Q4)

3 a — Some nomads move thirty times a year, some move four times a year. Many nomads go to a different place in the spring and in the fall. In Mongolia, spring is March, April and May, and fall is September and October. (Ex D Q5)

4 c — In the spring, they go close to a river for water. In the fall, they go to the hills. (Ex D Q6)

4.2 Every year

LEAD-IN

Put the students in a line. Ask the first student to say a word they remember from the course. If they say, e.g. *seven*, the next student has to think of a word beginning with the last letter, *n*, e.g. *not*. Continue until they can't think of the next word. Then start again asking the student who couldn't continue to start with a new word.

VOCABULARY

A Students match pictures with seasons, either individually or in pairs. Check answers, write *seasons* on the board and practice pronunciation.

4.6 **B** Students listen and write the months in the correct order. Check and practice pronunciation, and syllable stress. Highlight that in *February*, in some regions, the first *r* is silent when spoken.

Extra activity

Ask students to close their books. Write numbers 1–12 on the board. Elicit the months from the students. Write them by the numbers starting with *1* and *January*. Then tap on each month one by one and get the class to say them, starting in order, then randomizing. Then start to erase months quickly after every two or three that they say, leaving just the first letter; continue to choose these ones so students have to recall them. Eventually, you should have just the first letters. Then you can erase these one by one until you are just tapping the numbers while students say the words.

C Put students into pairs to answer the questions. Walk around and encourage them to add more information and ask more questions if possible. Get feedback from the whole class; which is the most popular season and which month has the most birthdays? Use the **Vocabulary Worksheet** on page W14 for extra practice.

READING

A Ask students about what they know about nomads and Mongolia. Don't confirm or deny their comments yet, but be positive about them all. Write notes on the board as they speak.

B Students work in pairs to match the words to the four photos (a–d). Check as a whole class.

C Ask students to quickly skim the text to see if any of their ideas from Exercise A (on the board) were correct and match the four questions (a–d) to the paragraphs. Check answers as a class.

D Students answer questions individually. Walk around and help if necessary. Help students identify the part of the text where the answer will be, then 'zoom in' and read that part in detail. Ask them to highlight the places where they found the answers; this is a good reading strategy and also helps you to give feedback.

E Put students into pairs to discuss the questions. The first is a response to the text – encourage them to talk about any traveling people (e.g. people in sales!) even if they don't have nomads. For the second question, make sure they give as much detail as they can. The focus is on fluency, so don't interrupt them; show that we value content and the ability to continue speaking for extended turns.

GRAMMAR HUB

4.2

Simple present questions: *I, you, we, they*

	Yes/No question	Positive short answer	Negative short answer
I	**Do I** live in a house?	**Yes, you do.**	**No, you don't.**
you	**Do you go** to the river?	**Yes, I/we do.**	**No, I/we don't.**
we	**Do we live** in houses?	**Yes, you do.**	**No, you don't.**
they	**Do they go** to the countryside?	**Yes, they do.**	**No, they don't.**

	Wh- questions
I/you/we/they	**What time do I start** work? **How do you relax**? **Where do we live**? **When do they go** to work?

- For *yes/no* questions, we put *do* at the beginning. We don't change the verb.

  Do you work here?

- For other questions we can use question words, e.g. *where, when, what time, who, how*, etc. We put *do* after the question word.

  Where do you live?
  When do we start work?

Be careful!

- For negative answers to *yes/no* questions, we normally use the contraction.

  No, I don't. NOT ~~*No, I do not.*~~

4.2 Every year

GRAMMAR

A Ask the students a *yes/no* question and a *Wh-* question, e.g. *Do you have breakfast at home? What time do you get up?* Refer students to the questions in the book. Students do the task, then check in pairs. Check answers as a class.

B Students work individually to complete the rules, then check in pairs. Go through the *Simple present questions: I, you, we, they* box, eliciting examples of the types of questions.

C Direct students to the **Grammar Hub** (see below and TB28).

D Do the first example on the board as a whole class, to show students the process (find the question word if there is one, then the verb form for a question). Students work individually to complete the exercise. Ask students to write the full questions out and not just number the words. Elicit answers on the board. Ask students to highlight the different parts: the question words, *do* and the verb form and the subject in between. Use different colors to highlight the patterns.

E Demonstrate the activity by asking students to choose a question to ask you and modeling an answer for them. Then put them into pairs to speak. Monitor, encouraging students to give full answers and helping them when necessary. Use the **Grammar Worksheet** on page W15 for extra practice.

PRONUNCIATION

4.7 **A** Play the audio while students read and listen to the questions in the book. Ask them to say the underlined words separately and then in sentences. Explain/Show how the phonemic script (/ʤʊ/) represents the connected sound.

4.8 **B** Students say the questions, taking turns. Play the audio and let them repeat. Encourage students to use the connected speech version.

C Demonstrate the first question, then ask students to work in pairs asking and answering each question. Monitor and encourage the use of (/ʤʊ/) for *do you*. Ask students to expand on answers to make sure that the exercise is not seen just as pronunciation practice but as having a communicative purpose. Monitor and find out if reading is popular, what time students get home, etc and discuss as a class.

SPEAKING HUB

A Demonstrate the task on the board with the first question *what/called?* Then put students into pairs and direct Student Bs to the **Communication Hub** (see TB97). You could put all Student As and Bs together, or they could work individually.

B As this exercise works as an information fill in the blank activity, make sure they cannot see their partner's information.

C Students ask and answer questions using the information they can see. Monitor, encouraging them to use clarification questions when necessary.

> **Extra activity**
> Students prepare an information fill in the blank activity about an animal they know about or choose to research. They can work together in small groups to prepare a 'key facts' list, similar to the list in Exercise C. They then prepare question prompts related to their information. Students work in pairs with partners from other groups, asking and answering the questions.

GRAMMAR HUB

4.2

Simple present questions: *I, you, we, they*

A Match the questions (1–6) and the answers (a–f).

1 Do you live in Texas? c
2 When do we start work? f
3 Where do they live? a
4 Do they work in August? d
5 How do you relax? b
6 Who do you work with? e

a In Madrid.
b I watch TV.
c Yes, I do.
d No, they don't.
e Erica.
f At six o'clock.

B Complete the sentences with the words in the box.

do (x2) don't how when where

1 **A:** Do you both live in Warsaw?
B: Yes, we do.

2 **A:** Where do you live?
B: In Switzerland.

3 **A:** Do those people work with you?
B: No, they don't.

4 **A:** How do you get to work?
B: By car.

5 **A:** When do you watch TV?
B: In the evening.

6 **A:** Do you go to bed late?
B: Yes, I do. I go to bed at about one o'clock in the morning.

C Use the prompts to write questions.

1 you / live / in a tent — Do you live in a tent?
2 where / you / work — Where do you work?
3 you / play / games — Do you play games?
4 when / you / talk / to your family — When do you talk to your family?
5 what time / you / start work — What time do you start work?
6 your friends / live here — Do your friends live here?
7 how / we / play this game — How do we play this game?
8 you / go / to the countryside — Do you go to the countryside?

➤ Go back to page 29.

GRAMMAR

Simple present questions: *I, you, we, they*

A Read two of the questions from *Nomads in Mongolia*. Match the questions (a and b) with the correct question type (1 and 2).

a Where do they go? b Do they live in houses?

1 Question b is a *yes/no* question. The answer can be *yes* or *no*.

2 Question a is a *wh-* question. The answer depends on the question word.

B WORK IT OUT Read the questions again and find their answers in the text. Complete the rules.

Simple present questions: *I, you, we, they*

1 In *yes/no* questions we use *do* before / *after I, you, we,* and *they*.

2 In *wh-* questions we use a question word (for example *what, where, when …*) before / *after do*.

3 To give short answers to *yes/no* questions we use do or don't / *repeat the main verb*.

C Go to the **Grammar Hub** on **page 104**.

D PRACTICE Reorder the words to make questions. Choose the correct question type.

1 go to work / you / when / in the morning / do

When do you go to work in the morning?

a *yes/no* b *wh-* (circled)

2 you / go / to another country / in the summer / do

Do you go to another country in the summer?

a *yes/no* (circled) b *wh-*

3 talk to / in the evening / you / do / who

Who do you talk to in the evening?

a *yes/no* b *wh-* (circled)

4 in the same place / live / you / do / all year

Do you live in the same place all year?

a *yes/no* (circled) b *wh-*

E SPEAK Work in pairs. Ask and answer the questions in Exercise D.

PRONUNCIATION

Do you /dʒʊ/

A 4.7 Read and listen to the questions. How does the speaker say the underlined words?

1 Do you live in the countryside?

2 When do you go to work?

The speaker runs these two words together, so we hear /dʒʊ/ instead of *do* and *you* separately.

B 4.8 Work in pairs. Say these questions. Then listen and repeat.

1 Do you get home at seven thirty?

2 Where do you live?

3 Do you read a book in the evening?

4 What do you do in the summer?

C SPEAK Work in pairs. Ask and answer the questions in Exercises A and B.

A: Do you live in the countryside?

B: No, I don't. I live in the city.

SPEAKING HUB

A PREPARE Work in pairs. Student A – Use the information below. Student B – Go to the **Communication Hub** on **page 131**.

Student A – Write questions to find out information about the birds in the picture above.

1 what / called What are they called?

2 where / live Where do they live?

3 where / go / August or September Where do they go in August or September?

4 where / go / May or June Where do they go in May or June?

5 how far / go How far do they go every year?

B DISCUSS Ask your partner the questions in Exercise A. Complete the missing information.

C DISCUSS Read the information about gray whales. Answer your partner's questions.

Name: Gray whales

Where: Near Alaska and near Mexico.

When: In the fall (October, November, December) they go to Alaska. In the spring (February, March, April) they go to Mexico.

How far: About 10,000–12,000 miles per year (16,000–20,000 kilometers)

Talk about annual routines

Café Hub

4.3 Coffee chaos

F– order in a café

COMPREHENSION

A Watch the video without sound. Underline the correct word or phrase.

1. The first customer *is* / ***isn't*** sure what she wants.
2. Sam *is* / ***isn't*** sure what the customer wants.
3. The line ***is*** / *isn't* long behind her.
4. The other customers are ***fast*** / *slow*.
5. Sam *is* / ***isn't*** happy to see the customer again.

B Read the list of things you can buy in Sam's Café. Watch the video again. Check (✓) the things you hear.

coffee	✓	water	☐
latte	✓	soya milk	✓
cappuccino	✓	bread	✓
mocha	☐	croissants	✓
hot chocolate	✓	snacks	☐
tea	✓	soft drinks	☐

C Use a word from each column to describe the coffee the woman buys.

a small			
a medium	**soya**	**cappuccino**	to drink in
a large		latte	**to take away**

D Who says it? Sam, the woman or the man in the line? Watch the video again and check your answers.

1. What type of coffee would you like? Sam
2. That's a great question! woman
3. Come on! man
4. What kind of bread do you have? woman
5. Medium! I mean medium. woman
6. So, let me check. Sam
7. No problem. woman
8. How big is a medium? woman

E **SPEAK** Work in pairs. What do you think the phrase 'Come on!' means in this context?

Suggested answer: Hurry up

Glossary

soya milk **(n) (British)** = soy milk **(n) (American)**

take away **(phrsal v) (British)** = take out or to go **(phrsal v) (American)**

4.3 Coffee chaos

LEAD-IN

Write the name of a café that your students will know on the board. Then write up the name of the drink you would buy there. Elicit answers from around the class, helping with vocabulary and spelling as required, building up a menu on the board. Take a class vote to see which is the most popular drink.

COMPREHENSION

A ▶ Play the video without sound. Students then work in pairs to underline the correct word or phrase. Check answers as a whole class.

B ▶ Review the list as a class, concept checking with images and actions as necessary. Students then watch the video with sound and add a check mark next to the things they hear. Allow time for students to compare in pairs before checking as a whole class.

C Ask students to use the parts of the table to say which coffee the woman finally orders in the café.

D ▶ Ask students to read the sentences from the video and see if they can remember who says each one. Students compare their answers in pairs. Then watch the video again, telling students to listen carefully for each sentence. Check answers as a class.

E Students work in pairs and discuss their ideas. Elicit ideas from different pairs and discuss as a class. Ask students if it is formal or informal (*informal*) and if it is polite or impolite (*a little impolite – the man and the woman don't know each other*). Extend the discussion to ask students how they would react: *Would they wait? Would they say something? Would they just leave and go somewhere else?*

METHODOLOGY HUB by Jim Scrivener

Video in class

In order to exploit video recordings, we need to consider what there is to exploit. What does a video recording have that my classroom / textbook / CD player doesn't have?

A video has:

- sound
- moving pictures: the pictures give context to the sounds we hear. We can see facial expressions, eye contact, physical relationships, background, etc
- a 'rewind' button: we can replay these images again and again
- a 'pause' button: we can freeze-frame images, stopping the action at any point
- a volume control: we can turn the sound off or make it quiet or very loud.

In addition, you can usually:

- accurately jump to a specific moment
- replay small sections with precision
- show subtitles in English – or any included language – on screen.

If you have a web cam or video camera, there are even more possibilities (for making programs, recording students speaking in activities, etc).

Using video recordings in class, we can divide video playback activities into three general categories:

1 Preview: what you do before you watch a section of recording
2 Viewing: what you do while you watch
3 Follow-up: what you do after watching

Any one lesson might include a number of these as different sections of the recording are used, e.g. preview first section, view first section, preview second section, view second section, follow-up first and second sections, preview third section, etc – each section might be minutes long or could be only a few seconds.

VIDEO SCRIPT

S = Sam C1 = Customer 1 C2 = Customer 2
C3 = Customer 3 C4 = Customer 4 C5 = Customer 5

S: Good morning. What can I get you?
C1: What do you have?
S: Er, bread, croissants, coffee …
C1: Coffee! Good, good. A coffee, please.
S: Sure. What type of coffee would you like?
C1: Oh. Cappuccino or latte? Latte or cappuccino? Can I have a latte, please? Do you have soya milk?
S: Yes, we do.
C1: A soya latte, please.
S: Sure. Small, medium or large?
C1: Oh. Small, medium or large. That's a great question. How big is a medium? Good, good.
C2: Come on!
C1: OK. OK. Can I have a small, please?
S: Sure!
C1: Medium! I mean medium.
S: Medium.
C1: To take away.
S: So, let me check. You want a medium, soya latte to take away?
C1: Cappuccino.
S: You said latte.
C1: Yes, sorry. I want a cappuccino.
S: So, you want a medium, takeaway soya cappuccino?
C1: Yes.
C3: Tea, please.
C4: Two cappuccinos, please.
C5: Hi, one hot chocolate, please.
S: Sorry, we're closing now.
C1: No problem. Good, good. What kind of bread do you have?

4.3 Coffee chaos

FUNCTIONAL LANGUAGE

A Students work alone to complete the phrases with the words in the box. Students then compare answers with a partner.

B ▶ Play the video again for students to check their answers.

PRONUNCIATION

4.9 **A** Focus the students on the conversation. Elicit what the underline means (*stressed syllables*). Play the audio for the students to listen and notice the stress.

4.9 **B** Model the conversation with a confident student. Then model each line one by one, practicing with the whole class. Finally, play the audio again and have students listen and repeat.

C Students work in pairs to practice the conversation. Monitor and encourage appropriate natural stressing, with students working toward looking up as they say each line, rather than reading off the page.

SPEAKING

A Display the menu to the whole class if possible. Model the activity with a student by taking the role of Student B. Replace *cappuccino* with another item from the menu. Students then work in pairs to practice.

B Again model the activity with a student. Take the role of the difficult customer and model a similar conversation to the one on the video. Students then work in pairs to practice. Monitor and help as required.

C Pairs perform their conversations for the rest of the class. Praise and encourage, highlighting examples of effective sentence stress. Take a whole-class vote on who the most difficult customer is.

Extra activity

Ask students to work in pairs or groups. Ask them to create a café. They should choose a name, create a menu and decide on prices. Students from different groups can go and order from their classmates' cafés, creating conversations similar to those in the Speaking section.

METHODOLOGY HUB by Jim Scrivener

Prominence

Stress typically marks out the content-carrying words in the sentence; thus it mostly affects nouns, verbs and adjectives. The content word that carries the main meaning of the sentence is usually the one you are going to stress and so the following pattern seems most likely (although others are possible):

<u>Car</u>oline was <u>go</u>ing to leave for <u>Af</u>rica on <u>Tues</u>day.

Effects of changing stress

Consider the effect that changing stress has on the meaning of a single sentence. Finish the explanatory notes in the same way as the first example.

1 Michael wanted to buy the red shirt. (not the red sweater)
2 Michael wanted to buy the red shirt. (not …)
3 Michael wanted to buy the red shirt. (not …)
4 Michael wanted to buy the red shirt. (not …)
5 Michael wanted to buy the red shirt. (but …)

We can demonstrate patterns of prominence either on the board or by using Cuisenaire rods or tapping, clapping, humming the rhythm, etc. By getting the students to work out the patterns themselves, we can help to make them more aware of the importance of stress. Poetry and songs are good for focusing on stress. Shadow reading (reading simultaneously with a recording, trying to keep up with the speed and follow the rhythm) is a useful language laboratory or classroom activity.

Answers

2 not steal it / borrow it, etc.
3 not Jun / Maria / Li, etc.
4 not the green one / blue one, etc.
5 but he didn't.

METHODOLOGY HUB by Jim Scrivener

Seating

However your classroom is laid out, and whatever kind of fixed or movable seating you have, it is worth taking time to consider the best ways to make use of it.

- What different seating positions are possible without moving anything?
- Are any rearrangements of seats possible?
- Which areas of the room are suitable for learners to stand and interact in?
- Is there any possibility that the room could be completely rearranged on a semi-permanent basis to make a better language classroom space?

Important considerations are:

- Can learners comfortably work in pairs with a range of different partners?
- Can learners comfortably work in small groups with a range of other learners?

For each activity you do in class, consider what grouping, seating, standing arrangements are most appropriate. Changing seating arrangements can help students interact with different people, change the focus from you when appropriate and allow a range of different situations to be recreated within the classroom, as well as simply adding variety to the predictability of sitting in the same place every time. It's difficult to sit still for a long time; it's worth including activities that involve some movement, even if only to give people the chance to stretch their legs. Students might not like it if there is a constant movement every five minutes, but some variety of working arrangements is usually helpful.

GABY

SAM

LUCY

FUNCTIONAL LANGUAGE

Ordering in a café

A Complete the phrases with the words in the box. Then complete the headings with *Customer* or *Sam*.

Can check get have kind large One please Sorry want What you

A __Sam__	B __Customer__
What can I [1] __get__ you?	[7] __Can__ I have a latte / a soya latte / a tea / a hot chocolate, please?
[2] __What__ type of coffee would you like?	Do [8] __you__ have soya milk?
Sure. Small, medium or [3] __large__?	Can I [9] __have__ a small, please?
So, let me [4] __check__: you [5] __want__ a medium soya latte to take away?	A soya latte, please.
[6] __Sorry__, we're closing now.	[10] __One__ tea / hot chocolate, please.
	Two cappuccinos, [11] __please__.
	What [12] __kind__ of bread do you have?

B Watch the video again and check your answers to Exercise A.

PRONUNCIATION

4.9 **A** Listen to the conversation. Notice how the underlined words are stressed.

Coffee seller: Good morning! What can I get you?
Customer: Can I have a coffee, please?
Coffee seller: What type of coffee would you like?
Customer: A cappuccino, please. Do you have soy milk?
Coffee seller: Sure. One soy cappuccino. Small, medium or large?
Customer: Can I have a medium, please? To go.
Coffee seller: So, you want a medium, soy cappuccino to go?
Customer: Yes, please.

4.9 **B** Listen again and repeat the conversation. Copy the stress.

C SPEAK Work in pairs. Practice the conversation.

SPEAKING

Coffee	small	medium	large
Latte	$2.00	$2.50	$3.00
Cappuccino	$2.00	$2.50	$3.00
Americano	$1.70	$2.20	$2.70
Mocha	$2.00	$2.50	$3.00
Hot chocolate	$2.00	$2.50	$3.00
Tea	$1.00	$1.50	$2.00

Croissant $2.00 Bread and jam $2.50

A PREPARE Work in pairs. Take turns being Student A and B. Replace the underlined words. Use the menu to help you.

Student A: What can I get you?
Student B: Can I have a cappuccino, please?
Student A: Small, medium or large?
Student B: Can I have a small, please?
Student A: Sure. One small cappuccino.
Student B: Thanks.

B PRACTICE Have a new conversation. Student A works in a café. Student B is a difficult customer. Practice your conversation.

C PRESENT Show your conversation to the class. Who is the best difficult customer?

Order in a café

4 Writing

Write an email about your routine

W – using contractions

A Read the email from Hadid to his friend Javier.
Where does Hadid work? Hadid works on an oil rig.

To: Javier
From: Hadid
How are you?

Hi Javier,

How are you? I don't work in Madrid anymore. I work on an oil rig. It's in the middle of the ocean. I work here every spring.
Ex B Q1 I get to the oil rig in March, and I go home in April. Ex B Q2
Ex B Q3 We get up at six o'clock in the morning, and we start work at
Ex B Q4 seven. We finish work at seven o'clock in the evening – it's a Ex B Q5
long day! I don't have time to read a book or watch TV in the evening. I eat, talk to my family on the phone and go to bed
Ex B Q6 at nine o'clock.

What about you? Where are you now? What's your job?

See you,

Hadid

Using contractions

When we write to friends or family, we can use contractions:
I'm for *I am*
it's for *it is*.

B Read the email again. Match the activities (1–6) with the months and times (a–f).

1 get to the oil rig – c March
2 go home – d April
3 get up – f 6 am
4 start work – a 7 am
5 finish work – b 7 pm
6 go to bed – e 9 pm

1	get to the oil rig	a	7 am
2	go home	b	7 pm
3	get up	c	March
4	start work	d	April
5	finish work	e	9 pm
6	go to bed	f	6 am

C SPEAK Work in pairs. Answer the question.
Do you think Hadid's routine is good? Why/Why not?

WRITING

A PLAN You are going to write an email to an old friend. Write notes about your daily routine.

B WRITE Write your email. Tell them about your daily routine. Use contractions.

Write an email about your routine

Refer students to the email as a model for the writing task.

Encourage students to only write notes, not full sentences, at this stage.

Remind students they can use contractions when writing an informal email.

Unit 4 Review

GRAMMAR

Put the words in the correct order to make sentences.

1 do / get up / you / what time
What time do you get up?
2 live / in Spain / they
They live in Spain.
3 watch / TV in the evening / you / don't
You don't watch TV in the evening.
4 like / soccer / don't / we
We don't like soccer.
5 you / start work / when / do
When do you start work?
6 they / do / why / at five o'clock / get up
Why do they get up at five o'clock?

VOCABULARY

A Complete the sentences with the words in the box.

get get up go (x2) finish watch

1 I get up at six o'clock in the morning.
2 I go to work at eight thirty in the morning.
3 I finish work at five thirty in the afternoon.
4 I get home at six ten.
5 I relax and watch TV at seven thirty in the evening.
6 I go to bed at ten forty-five at night.

B Match the sentences in Exercise A with these times.

a 5:30 pm 3
b 6 am 1
c 6:10 pm 4
d 10:45 pm 6
e 8:30 am 2
f 7:30 pm 5

C Complete the words in these sentences.

1 My birthday is in February.
2 My favorite season is winter.
3 May is the month after April.
4 In my country, the summer is June, July and August.

32 TIME

LEAD-IN

Tell the students to write three things that they do or don't do every day, but make one not true. Then ask them to walk around saying their sentences, e.g. *I get up at nine o'clock, I have breakfast and I don't go to work*. The other students have to guess which one isn't true, but tell them not to say. You can join in. At the end, share the 'untruths'! Who was the best at concealing?

WRITING

A Set a short time limit, e.g. 30 seconds, to encourage students to scan the email for the answer rather than reading every word. Check answer as a whole class.

B See if students can remember any answers with the email covered, then get them to work individually to match the activities. Check in pairs and then as a whole class.

C In pairs, students discuss each part of the routine. Monitor, making sure they give reasons for their preferences.

WRITING TASK

A Write a brief plan for your daily routine on the board, e.g. *get up/8:30, no breakfast/coffee!* … so students can see that they only need notes. Ask students to do the same for their days, individually. Help with vocabulary if necessary.

B Students write, expanding their notes into sentences. Go around helping, referring them to the model email wherever possible, to help them become more autonomous.

Two men sitting on metal drums, Perth, Australia.

OBJECTIVES

- talk about free time
- talk about food and meals
- ask for information
- write a blog about food

Work with a partner. Discuss the questions.

1 Look at the picture. Why are these people happy?
2 What's your favorite food?
3 What makes you feel happy?

TIME FOR A BREAK 33

Ask students to label the photo if you need time to set up the class.

The quote advises us to take care of our free time. It is too easy to forget that we need time off. We must remind ourselves how important free time is and make sure we keep some time set aside for ourselves.

Ralph Waldo Emerson (1803–1882) was an American writer, philosopher and poet. He was interested in the idea of individuality and personal freedom. He gave many public lectures around the US and his voice represented an alternative view to conventional society at that time. He was also a strong supporter of the anti-slavery movement later in life.

OBJECTIVES

Read the unit objectives to the class.

UNIT OPENER QUESTIONS

Ask students to describe what they can see in the picture, and add useful words to the board. Students then work in pairs to list three ideas for why the men might be happy. They then compare their ideas with another pair. Working alone, students then list three things that make them happy. This can be run as a mingling *Find someone who* activity. Once students have their list of three things, they mingle with other students asking *What makes you feel happy?* They should write a note about students who give the same answer as they have on their list. Students report back to the class at the end, saying how many people they shared answers with. Finally, write up a list of favorite foods on the board and find out which is the most popular with the class.

WORKSHEETS

Lesson 5.1 Relax and be happy

Vocabulary: Free-time activities (W16)

Grammar: Simple present: *he*, *she*, *it* (W17)

Lesson 5.2 When's your lunch break?

Vocabulary: Food and meals (W17)

Grammar: Adverbs of frequency (W18)

5.1 Relax and be happy

Talk about free time

V free-time activities **G** simple present: *he, she, it* **P** *does he / does she*

VOCABULARY

Free-time activities

A Look at the pictures. What is the same about all these activities? They all show people taking a break, relaxing, having a good time, not working.

1

___go___ for a walk

2

___sit___ in the backyard

3

___cook___ a meal

4

___take___ a bath

5

___go___ shopping

6

___play___ chess

7

___go___ to the gym

8

___go___ running

B Match the verbs with the pictures. Listen and check. 5.1

cook go (x4) take play sit

C SPEAK Work in pairs. What do you do to relax?

LISTENING

A LISTEN FOR GIST Listen to an interview. Which of the free-time activities from Vocabulary Exercise A do the people talk about? 5.2 cook a meal; take a bath; go to the gym; go running

B LISTEN FOR DETAIL Listen again. Are these sentences true (T) or false (F)? 5.2

1 The man eats lunch in his office. (T) / F
2 The woman goes to the gym on her lunch break. T / (F) Her friend goes to the gym.
3 The woman goes for a walk after work. T / (F) The woman goes home and cooks a meal and watches TV.
4 The woman watches TV in the evening. (T) / F
5 The man goes running after work. (T) / F
6 The woman goes running on the weekend. (T) / F

5.1 Relax and be happy

LEAD-IN

Ask students to create a short survey to find out how much free time their classmates have. Students can ask questions, e.g. *What time do you start/finish work?* Report back as a class.

VOCABULARY

5.1 **A–B** Students work individually, then check in pairs. See if students can see any patterns, e.g. *play games*, but *go running/shopping*. There is no need to give the word *collocation* but try to show that some words go with each other.

C As an example, tell students what you do to relax, giving a few details such as the time, the days you do it, where you do it and how you feel. Then put students into pairs to talk about their activities. Use the **Vocabulary Worksheet** on page W16 for extra practice.

LISTENING

5.2 **A** Students listen and identify which activities they hear from Vocabulary Exercise A. Check answer as a class.

5.2 **B** Give students time to read the sentences and predict/remember any answers. Then play the audio as many times as they need to answer all the questions.

AUDIO SCRIPT

5.2

Listening, Exercise A
I = Interviewer W = Woman M = Man

I: Hi! Do you have a minute? I'd like to ask you some questions.
W: OK. What's it about?
I: It's about how you relax in your free time.
W: OK!
M: Sure!
I: Thanks! Do you work near here?
W: Yes, we both work in the offices over there.
I: Great! Question 1: What do you do in your lunch break?
Ex B Q1 **M:** Um … I have lunch at my desk; I don't have time to take a break.
W: Yes, he works all the time! He doesn't even take coffee breaks!
Ex A **I:** Do you go to the gym on your lunch break?
Ex B Q2 **W:** No, I don't. My friend has a gym at her office and she goes there on her lunch break.
I: That sounds good. Does she go to the gym every day?
W: No, she doesn't. She goes about twice a week.
I: OK. The next question is: What do you do to relax after work?
Ex B Q3 & Q4 **W:** I usually go home and cook a meal and watch TV. Ex A
Ex B Q5 **M:** Yeah, I go running after work. After that, I go home and take a bath!
I: OK. Question 3: What do you do to relax on the weekend?
Ex B Q6 **W:** Umm … well … I go running … Ex A
M: Yeah, she goes running and I go food shopping. She doesn't like food shopping!
W: Then I relax in the evening. I cook a nice meal and watch a movie on TV.
I: That's great. Thanks for your time today. Please take a free one-day pass to our new gym!
W: Ooh! Thanks …!
M: Thank you …!

GRAMMAR HUB

5.1

Simple present: *he, she, it*

	Positive	Negative
he/she/it	**He cooks** dinner every day. **She washes** the dishes after dinner.	**He doesn't go running** in the morning. **She doesn't do** the laundry every day.

	Yes/No question	Short answer
he/she/it	**Does Henry take** a bath in the evening? **Does it clean** the floor?	**Yes, he does. / No, he doesn't.** **Yes, it does. / No, it doesn't.**

- In positive sentences with *he, she* or *it*, we use the main verb plus *-s* or *-es*.
  He cooks dinner for his family.
  She does housework in the afternoon.
- In negative sentences with *he, she* or *it*, we use *doesn't* plus the main verb without *-s*.
  Brad doesn't clean the bathroom.
  She doesn't watch TV all the time.
- In *yes/no* questions with *he, she* or *it*, we use *does* followed by the subject and the main verb without *-s*.
  Does your mom do your laundry for you?
- In *wh-* questions with *he, she* or *it*, we use a subject and *does* plus the main verb without *-s*.
  When does Martin make his bed?
- We use *does* in short answers to *yes/no* questions. We do not repeat the main verb.
  Does Tom clean the kitchen? Yes, he does. NOT ~~*Yes, he does clean.*~~

Be careful!

- Some verbs take *-es* for the ending in *he/she/it* simple present. Some examples are *do* and *go* and verbs that end in *-sh* or *-ch*.
  He does the laundry at night. NOT ~~*He dos the laundry at night.*~~
  She washes dishes with her sister. NOT ~~*She washs dishes with her sister.*~~

5.1 Relax and be happy

GRAMMAR

A Write the first sentence on the board and do it together as a class. Then write the other sentences up while the students complete the exercise. Give feedback by underlining on the board or asking a volunteer to do it. Discuss any problems and check students understand.

B Students work individually, then check in pairs. Go around helping, but don't give answers; direct students back to the examples so they can work it out for themselves. Give answers as a whole class and deal with any problems.

C Do the first sentence together, referring to the *Simple present: he, she, it* rule box. Get students to write the number of the rule from the box after each question when they complete the exercise. Check answers and reasons as a class.

D Direct students to the **Grammar Hub** (see below and TB34).

E Students complete the conversation in pairs. Check answers. You can ask the pairs to read/act out the conversation, to get further speaking practice and confidence with the grammar. Use the **Grammar Worksheet** on page W17 for extra practice.

PRONUNCIATION

5.3 **A** Play the audio while students read and listen. Ask them to repeat the sounds of the underlined words. Practice the sounds.

5.4 **B** Play audio while students listen and circle the words. Check answers as a class.

5.4 **C** Repeat the audio while students listen and repeat.

SPEAKING

A Demonstrate using your own free-time activities, then students work individually to complete the table. Help with vocabulary where needed.

B Make sure students are seated so they cannot see each other's notes, e.g. face to face but not side by side. Demonstrate the activity with a strong student, then let them discuss and fill in the information. Monitor, encouraging full sentences and follow-up questions.

C Students report on their partner's activities. They could come to the front of the class to do this if they feel confident doing so.

GRAMMAR HUB

5.1

Simple present: *he, she, it*

A Choose the correct options.

1 He ___ for a walk every weekend.
a go (b) goes

2 She ___ meals for her children.
a cook (b) cooks

3 George doesn't ___ in the backyard at night.
(a) sit b sits

4 What gym does Monica ___ to?
a goes (b) go

5 Does Taylor ___ chess every day?
a plays (b) play

6 Does he go running late at night? Yes, he ___.
(a) does b runs

7 Kelly ___ TV on Saturday mornings.
a watchs (b) watches

8 What time does Jenny ___ a bath?
(a) take b takes

B Check (✓) the correct sentences and put an (✗) for the incorrect sentences.

1 David sits in the backyard in the evening. ✓
2 Mike go running every Sunday. ✗
3 Jill cooks meals for her family. ✓
4 Paula doesn't plays chess every day. ✗
5 Does Josh goes to the gym? ✗
6 **A:** Does Henry go shopping?
B: Yes, he does. ✓
7 **A:** Does Amy take a bath every day?
B: No, she doesn't do! ✗
8 Where Erika goes for a walk? ✗

C Complete the sentences with the correct form of the words in parentheses.

1 Michelle ___*sits*___ (*sit*) in the backyard in the summer.
2 My dad ___takes___ (*take*) a bath every night.
3 She ___goes___ (*go*) for a walk every weekend.
4 When ___does he do___ (*he / do*) the laundry?
5 **A:** Does your grandmother go running?
B: No, she ___doesn't___ (*do not*).
6 Lily ___doesn't go___ (*not go*) to the gym.
7 **A:** Does your brother play chess?
B: Yes, he ___does___ (*do*).

➤ Go back to page 35.

GRAMMAR

Simple present: *he, she, it*

A Read the examples. Underline the verbs.

He <u>works</u> all the time! He <u>doesn't</u> even <u>take</u> coffee breaks.

<u>Does</u> she <u>go</u> to the gym every day?

No, she <u>doesn't</u>. She <u>goes</u> about twice a week.

She <u>doesn't have</u> time to relax!

B **WORK IT OUT** Complete the rules with words in the box.

does doesn't main verb question word without

Simple present: *he, she, it*

1 In positive sentences, we use the ___main verb___ plus *-s* or *-es*.

2 In negative sentences, we use ___*doesn't*___ plus the main verb without *-s*.

3 In *yes/no* questions, we use *Does* followed by the subject and the main verb ___without___ *-s*.

4 In short answers, we use ___*does*___ or *doesn't*.

5 In *wh-* questions, we use a ___question word___ and *does* plus the main verb without *-s*.

C **PRACTICE** Choose the correct option to complete the sentences.

1 Martin *cook* / *<u>cooks</u>* dinner in the evening.

2 Anna *don't* / *<u>doesn't</u>* go shopping after work.

3 Does Paolo *<u>play</u>* / *plays* chess?

4 What does Shyama *<u>do</u>* / *does* on the weekend?

5 **A:** Does Akira *takes* / *<u>take</u>* a bath after work?

B: Yes, he *takes* / *<u>does</u>*.

D Go to the **Grammar Hub** on **page 106**.

E **PRACTICE** Complete the conversation.

Anna: What do you [1] ___do___ to relax on the weekend? Do you go shopping?

Bea: No, I don't. My husband [2] ___goes___ shopping, and I [3] ___go___ running. What about you?

Anna: I [4] ___go___ to the gym and my husband [5] ___watches___ TV and [6] ___plays___ computer games.

Bea: That sounds good. What kind of games [7] ___does___ he play?

Anna: He [8] ___plays___ action games.

PRONUNCIATION

does he / does she

A 5.3 Read and listen to the questions. Notice how the speaker links the underlined words together. We hear /dʌziː/ and /dʌʃiː/.

1 <u>Does he</u> go the gym?

2 <u>Does she</u> go running?

B 5.4 Listen to each question and circle the words you hear.

1 *(Does he)* / *Does she* cook dinner every night?

2 *Does he* / *(Does she)* go shopping on the weekend?

3 What *does he* / *(does she)* do at lunchtime?

4 What kind of food *(does he)* / *does she* cook?

C 5.4 Listen and repeat the questions in Exercise B.

SPEAKING

A **PREPARE** Complete the table with your free-time activities. Write three activities in each box.

	Me	My partner
On your lunch break		
In the evening		
On the weekend		

B **DISCUSS** Work in pairs. Ask your partner questions to complete the table. How many things are the same for both of you?

What do you do on your lunch break? Do you go for a walk?

C **REPORT** Tell the class about your partner.

Anton goes shopping on the weekend. He doesn't cook meals at home.

5.2 When's your lunch break?

Talk about food and meals

V food and meals **S** skimming **G** adverbs of frequency **P** linking with /j/

VOCABULARY
Food and meals

A Look at the pictures. Which food do you eat for breakfast, lunch or dinner?

a  apples

b  bread

c  cheese

d  eggs

e  potatoes

f  noodles

g  beans

h  cereal

i  chicken

j  fish

k  rice

l  pasta

B Match the words in the box to the pictures.

apples beans bread cereal cheese chicken eggs fish noodles pasta potatoes rice

C Go to the **Vocabulary Hub** on **page 124**.

D **SPEAK** Make a list of food you eat every day. Tell your partner. What's the same? What's different?

READING

A **PREPARE** Work in pairs. Look at the pictures. Which foods can you name? Where do you think they come from?

READING Ex B answers

Sara

bento lunch box from Japan

Natalia

tortillas with beans, chicken and rice from Central America / Mexico

Davide

pasta with tomato sauce from Italy

Skimming

When you skim a text, you read it quickly to get the general idea.

B **SKIM** Read *Lunch breaks around the world* and match the correct people with the pictures in Exercise A.

C **READ FOR GIST** Read the article. Which questions do all three people answer? Check (✓) the questions.

- **a** What do you eat for lunch? ✓
- **b** Is your lunch expensive? ☐
- **c** What time is your lunch break? ✓
- **d** Who do you eat lunch with? ✓
- **e** Where do you eat lunch? ✓
- **f** Do you eat a big lunch? ☐

D **READ FOR DETAIL** Read the article again. Write the correct names.

1. Natalia eats soup for lunch.
2. Davide doesn't eat rice for lunch.
3. Sara eats lunch at work.
4. Natalia doesn't talk about a drink.
5. Davide has lunch with family.
6. Natalia has more than an hour for lunch.

LUNCH BREAKS AROUND THE WORLD

More and more people in the US don't take a lunch break. They eat lunch at their desk instead. Here we take a look at countries around the world and what workers do on their lunch breaks.

Sara, Japan

We always take our lunch break at the same time every day, from 12 to 1. Some people bring a lunchbox from home, but I always go to the office cafeteria to eat with my colleagues. Ex D Q3 The food is usually really good. I usually have rice with fish or chicken and some vegetables. After lunch, I have a cup of green tea. I drink a lot of green tea every Ex B Q4 day because it's good for my health.

Davide, Italy

Our lunch break is from 1:30 to 2:30. Sometimes we go to a local restaurant for lunch, but I usually go home. Ex D Q5 My wife always comes home for lunch, and we eat together. Ex D Q2 We usually have a small dish of pasta. After that we have some freshly cooked meat or fish. My favorite is chicken in tomato sauce. For dessert, we always have some fruit and finally a cup of coffee. Ex B Q4

5.2 When's your lunch break?

LEAD-IN

Ask learners to name any food or drink items that they know in English. Write the items down on strips of paper, or keep a list. When you have a complete list, ask learners to come to the front, then show them an item on the list and ask them to either draw or describe the item for the rest of the class. The first person to guess correctly gets a point. You could offer a bonus point if they can spell the item correctly for you. Continue until there are no more items on the list.

VOCABULARY

A Write *breakfast/lunch/dinner* on the board. Ask *What time?* Write times above, e.g. *8:00 breakfast*. Then show students the pictures and get them to say what they eat – if they know the words, write them under the three meals on the board.

B Students work in pairs to label the pictures. Encourage students to work it out by elimination if necessary. If students need further support, write the words from the box on the board in three groups matching the pictures. Go through the answers, practicing pronunciation, e.g. the schwa sound (/ə/) in the first syllable of *potatoes*, the different sound for *ea* in *bread* (/e/) and *beans* (/iː/) and the final syllable (/z/) in *apples/noodles*.

C Direct students to the **Vocabulary Hub** (see TB97).

D Walk around helping while students make their lists. Help with vocabulary if necessary. Then demonstrate the activity, e.g. Say *I have juice every day, but I don't have apples*. Then ask students to speak. Go around encouraging them to produce complete sentences and to ask and answer questions. Get feedback from the whole class; write the names of the foods on the board and add a check mark next to them whenever they are mentioned again. Which foods are the most popular? Use the **Vocabulary Worksheet** on page W17 for extra practice.

READING

A Students work in pairs to name the foods and identify their origin. Write their ideas on the board.

B Focus students on the *Skimming* box. Elicit times that they might skim read, e.g. when they first look at a text, when they are looking at a newspaper or magazine for something interesting to read, etc. Give students a short time limit, e.g. two minutes, to complete the task. Check answers, asking students to identify the words that helped them decide.

C Go through the questions with the students, checking they understand them and the task. Then give them a time limit, e.g. five minutes, to do the task individually, highlighting the relevant sections of the text if possible. Ask students to check with a partner before you give feedback.

D Students work individually, then check with a partner. Go through the answers. If possible, get responses to the content of the texts, asking questions if necessary, e.g. *Who has the best lunch?*

GRAMMAR HUB

5.2

Adverbs of frequency

100% ↑ … ↓ 0%

Adverb	Examples with *be*	Examples with other verbs
always	I'm **always** hungry!	I **always** drink coffee with breakfast.
usually	He's **usually** thirsty after running.	He **usually** eats dinner at 7 pm.
frequently	They're **frequently** late for dinner.	They **frequently** eat lunch in their office.
sometimes	You're **sometimes** tired and hungry.	You **sometimes** have coffee after lunch.
seldom	We are **seldom** free for coffee.	You **seldom** have dessert.
never	I'm **never** late for dinner.	I **never** drink orange juice.

- We put adverbs of frequency after the verb *be*.
  He's usually very hungry before lunch.
  They're sometimes busy on weekends.
- We put adverbs of frequency before other verbs.
  I usually have a large salad for supper.
  She frequently drinks water at lunchtime.
- We can also put the adverbs *usually* and *sometimes* at the beginning of the sentence.
  Usually, I have fruit for my breakfast.
  Sometimes, I have coffee.

Be careful!

- We don't put the adverbs *always*, *seldom* or *never* at the beginning of a sentence.
  She always has rice. NOT ~~Always, she has rice.~~

Be careful!

- We do not use *never* with *don't* or *doesn't*.
  I never eat late at night. NOT ~~I don't never eat late at night.~~

5.2 When's your lunch break?

GRAMMAR

A Do the first sentence together. Students continue individually and check in pairs. Go through the answers together and write the adverbs on the board.

B Students complete the chart. Draw a line with 0% at one end and 100% at the other, and place the adverbs along the line. Leave the chart up on the board.

C Students work in pairs. Give them time to think about the questions before giving feedback. Ask them to give examples from Exercise A to support their answers.

D Direct students to the **Grammar Hub** (see below and TB36).

E Demonstrate the conversation with a student and draw everyone's attention to the verbs and adverbs. Students complete the activity in pairs while you monitor. Try not to interrupt, but correct subtly if necessary, and encourage them to use the adverbs of frequency from the board. Use the **Grammar Worksheet** on page W18 for extra practice.

PRONUNCIATION

5.5 **A** Explain that the symbol (/j/) represents a sound. Play the recording and ask students to repeat the sentence, drawing their attention to how the words link together with the (/j/) sound.

5.6 **B** Play the first sentence and ask students to identify the sound and the words linked by it. Repeat until they hear it. Write the sentence on the board and circle the linked words. Then play the rest of the sentences. Write them all up and elicit answers from the class.

5.6 **C** Highlight that we link words with /j/ when one word ends with the /aɪ/, /iː/, /eɪ/ or /ɔɪ/ sound and the next word starts with a vowel sound. Play the audio again while students listen and repeat. Show how the linking 'smooths out' connection between the words, making them easier to say.

SPEAKING HUB

A Focus students on the survey. Check that they remember what a survey is. Do the first question together, then let students finish it individually. Walk around monitoring and helping.

B Go through the example conversation, then ask students to ask you some of the questions as a demonstration; answer in full sentences and get them to ask a follow-up question for each one. Then get students to walk around asking and answering the questions.

C Ask some of the students to report back their findings to the class.

Extra activity
Students prepare a presentation to report the findings of their surveys to the class. The presentation could include visuals, e.g. hand-drawn charts or presentation slides including images and charts which can be projected. Students can share their skills and teach each other how to create the charts, presentation slides, etc.

GRAMMAR HUB

5.2

Adverbs of frequency

A Choose the correct adverbs of frequency.

1 I ___ have coffee in the morning, but not every day.
a always (b) frequently

2 She ___ has salad for lunch. She has it three or four times a week.
a never (b) frequently

3 He ___ eats eggs for breakfast. He doesn't like them!
a sometimes (b) never

4 They ___ have dinner at home, five or six days a week.
a never (b) usually

5 She's ___ early for class, two or three times a month.
(a) sometimes b always

6 We ___ cook chicken and rice. My wife and I don't like it.
(a) never b usually

7 John is ___ busy on Fridays. He has a lot of work on that day.
(a) always b never

8 You ___ eat snacks, almost every day of the week!
a sometimes (b) frequently

B Choose the correct options to complete the sentences.

1 Mike (*usually has*) / *has usually* juice with his cereal.
2 She *cooks frequently* / (*frequently cooks*) dinner for the family.
3 They *frequently are* / (*are frequently*) late for class.
4 We *drink never* / (*never drink*) milk at breakfast.
5 I (*am sometimes*) / *sometimes am* hungry for breakfast.
6 He (*seldom eats*) / *eats seldom* vegetables.
7 You *always aren't* / (*aren't always*) busy for lunch.
8 Helena doesn't *never* / (*usually*) eat bananas.

C Put the words in the correct order to make sentences.

1 drink / usually / for / I / breakfast / tea
I usually drink tea for breakfast.
2 home / cooks / she / dinner / at / frequently
She frequently cooks dinner at home.
3 in / hungry / morning / the / he / is / always
He is always hungry in the morning.
4 breakfast / eat / we / never
We never eat breakfast.
5 don't / pizza / usually / they / have
They don't usually have pizza.
6 for / are / never / we / work / late
We are never late for work.

➤ Go back to page 37.

GRAMMAR
Adverbs of frequency

A Find and complete the sentences with adverbs from *Lunch breaks around the world*.

1 The food is ___usually___ really good.
2 I ___usually___ have rice with fish or chicken and some vegetables.
3 ___Sometimes___ we go to a local restaurant for lunch.
4 My wife ___always___ comes home for lunch.
5 I ___never___ have dessert.
6 I ___frequently___ have some fruit or something sweet as a special treat.

B Complete the chart with *sometimes*, *usually* and *never*.

seldom ↓ — frequently ↓ — always ↓

0% ——————————— 100%

↑ [1] ___never___ ↑ [2] ___sometimes___ ↑ [3] ___usually___

C **WORK IT OUT** Read the sentences in Exercise A and choose the correct option to complete the rules.

Adverbs of frequency

We use adverbs of frequency to say how often we do things. We put them …

1 *before* / *after* the verb *be* (in positive and negative sentences).
2 *before* / *after* other verbs (in positive sentences).

D Go to the **Grammar Hub** on **page 106**.

E **SPEAK** Work in pairs. How often do you eat these kinds of food? When do you eat them? Tell your partner.

bread cheese chocolate coffee fish fruit ice cream milk rice tea

A: I usually have coffee for breakfast.
B: I frequently have coffee, but I sometimes have tea.

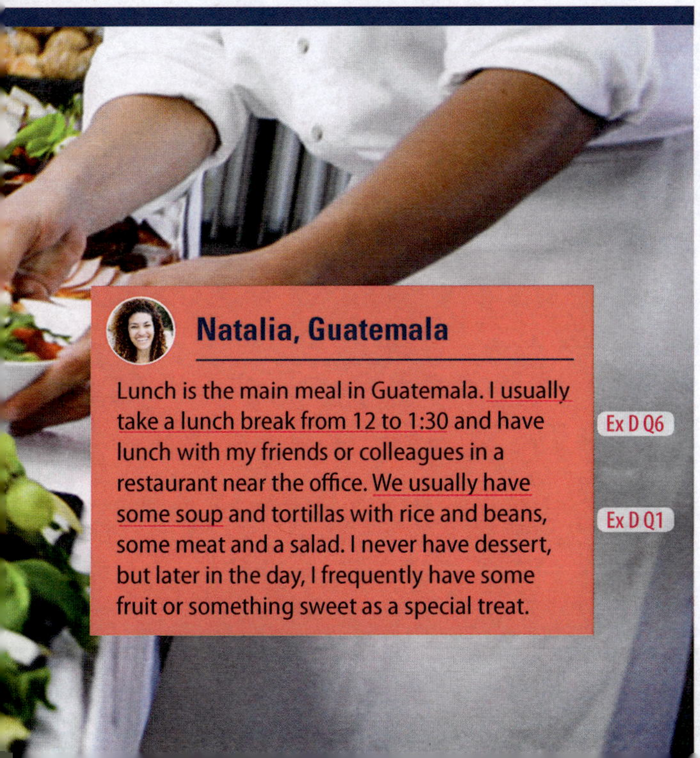

Natalia, Guatemala

Lunch is the main meal in Guatemala. I usually take a lunch break from 12 to 1:30 and have lunch with my friends or colleagues in a restaurant near the office. We usually have some soup and tortillas with rice and beans, some meat and a salad. I never have dessert, but later in the day, I frequently have some fruit or something sweet as a special treat.

Ex D Q6

Ex D Q1

PRONUNCIATION
Linking with /j/

5.5 **A** Listen to the sentence. Notice how the /j/ sound links the words joined with a ‿.

She‿always eats lunch at work.

5.6 **B** Read and listen. Draw a ‿ to show the words linked with a /j/ sound.

1 He‿always drinks coffee.
2 I‿usually have a salad.
3 She‿eats pasta for lunch.
4 We‿all eat fish and rice.

5.6 **C** Listen again and repeat the examples.

SPEAKING HUB

A **PREPARE** You are going to take a survey of eating habits in your class. Complete the questions (1–6).

EATING HABITS SURVEY

1 Do you ___usually drink coffee for breakfast___?
a ______ usually drinks coffee for breakfast.
2 Do you ___always cook dinner at home___?
b ______ always cooks dinner at home.
3 Do you ___frequently eat lunch at work___?
c ______ frequently eats lunch at work.
4 Do you ___sometimes eat pizza for lunch___?
d ______ sometimes eats pizza for lunch.
5 Do you ___(ever) eat chocolate___?
e ______ never eats chocolate.
6 Do you ___regularly eat meat___?
f ______ seldom eats meat.

B **PRACTICE** Ask your classmates the survey questions. Write names in sentences a–f. Ask each person another question to get more information.

A: Do you usually drink coffee for breakfast?
B: No, I don't.
A: What do you usually drink for breakfast?
B: I usually drink tea or hot chocolate.

C **REPORT** Tell the class about your answers.

Jerome doesn't drink coffee for breakfast. He usually drinks tea or hot chocolate.

Talk about food and meals

Café Hub

5.3 No battery

F– ask for information

COMPREHENSION

A ▶ Watch the video. Complete the information about the train ticket.

2 3 85 afternoon return

1 Gaby wants a ticket to Manchester on Saturday afternoon.
2 It leaves at 3 pm.
3 It takes about 2 hours.
4 She wants a return ticket.
5 It costs £ 85.

B ▶ Watch the video again and put the events (a–f) in the correct order (1–6).

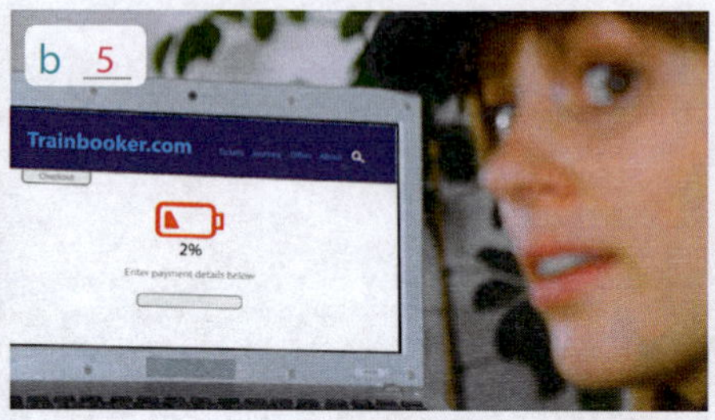

C ▶ Match the phrases (1–6) with the pictures (a–f) in Exercise B. Then watch the video again and check your answers.

1 It worked! e
2 Gaby hates computers. d
3 Lucy needs Gaby's credit card. c
4 There's no battery. b
5 Lucy has an idea. f
6 The wi-fi stops working. a

USEFUL PHRASES

A Complete the useful phrases with the words in the box.

expensive idea matter news see worked

1 I have an idea!
2 Let me see.
3 Good news!
4 What's the matter?
5 Wow, that's expensive!
6 It worked!

B ▶ Watch the video again and check your answers to Exercise A.

C SPEAK Work in pairs. Complete the conversations with useful phrases from Exercise A. Practice the conversations.

1 A: I don't have a ticket.
B: Good news – I have a ticket for you!

2 A: It's $150.
B: Wow, that's expensive!

3 A: What time does it leave?
B: Let me see.

4 A: Oh no!
B: What's the matter?

5 A: I don't know what to do!
B: I have an idea!

6 A The code doesn't work.
B: Here – try this number.
A: It worked!

5.3 No battery

LEAD-IN

Write the names of some famous online shopping platforms on the board. Add two columns, one with a smiley face at the top and one with a sad face at the top. Elicit good things and bad things about buying online, e.g. good – quick, easy; bad – technology problems, battery problems. Use pictures and mime to help to clarify for students and build up lists of words and pictures in the columns, as appropriate.

Then, ask students to open books and identify the two problems Gaby and Lucy have with online purchasing (*wi-fi and battery*).

COMPREHENSION

A ▸ Review the pictures and ask students to describe what they can see. Ask students to predict how to complete the sentences with the words and numbers in the box. Students then watch the video and check and complete the sentences. Allow time for students to compare answers in pairs before checking as a whole class.

B ▸ Students work together to discuss and order the events. Elicit answers from the class.

C ▸ Do the first one as a whole class to make sure students understand the task. Students then work alone to complete the task. Play the video again for everyone to check.

USEFUL PHRASES

A Students review the useful phrases in pairs. Ask them to complete the phrases with the words in the box.

B ▸ Play the video again for students to check their answers to Exercise A.

C Students work alone to complete the conversations with the useful phrases. After comparing answers in pairs, check as a whole class. Then model some of the conversations with individual students. Highlight how to say the price in conversation 2 (*one hundred and fifty dollars*). Pairs then work together to practice all the conversations.

▶ VIDEO SCRIPT

G = Gaby L = Lucy

G: I need to buy a train ticket. But I hate computers! I like people.
L: I have an idea! Hello, ma'am. Can I help you?
G: Yes, please. I'd like a ticket to Manchester on Saturday afternoon.
L: Saturday afternoon. Let me see. Good news! There is a train.
G: Amazing! What time does it leave?
L: What time does it leave? Let me see. It leaves at 3 pm.
G: How long does it take?
L: How long does it take? Hold on. It takes about two hours.
G: Perfect. Can I book a ticket, please?
L: Of course, ma'am. Single or return?
G: A return, please.
L: Oh.
G: What's the matter?
L: The wi-fi's not working.
G: I've got an idea!
L: No, no, no, yes! That's it. OK, let's book a return. Wow. That's expensive!
G: Really? How much is it?
L: £85.
G: £85!
L: I know! OK, I need your credit card details.
G: Hold this.
L: Oh no! There's no battery!
G: Got it! Here.
L: No!
G: It worked!
L: Yes!
G: Not today!

METHODOLOGY HUB by Jim Scrivener

What is lexis?

When teaching, should we consider every set of letters that is bordered by spaces as a separate entity? Or does it make more sense to take some combinations of words as a single grouping, a single meaning, a single **lexical item**?

Computer and *water* are familiar one-word vocabulary items, but what about *stock market*? These two words are regularly found together with a fixed meaning; this surely counts as a single item of vocabulary (it has its own entry in the dictionary). How useful would it be to only teach *stock* and *market* separately and hope that the learners will somehow find a way of combining them to make a new meaning? *Stock market* is an example of a single lexical item, in this case with two words rather than one.

A more difficult problem is provided by expressions such as *It's up to you*. Is this a single lexical item, or is it a sentence that a speaker (knowing the rules of grammar) constructs afresh every time he needs it? Consider some other examples: *it's all the same to me, what on earth …, minding my own business, funny you should say that, sorry I'm late, wouldn't you rather …, it'll do*, etc. These items would probably not be found in most dictionaries, but, all the same, they do seem to have an element of being fixed items, in the same way that individual words do. It is now generally believed that native speakers do not construct expressions of this type word by word but rather extract ready-made **chunks** of language from an internal store and then put them together with other language items in order to express complete meanings.

5.3 No battery

FUNCTIONAL LANGUAGE

A As a whole class, elicit which phrases are said by the customer and which by the ticket seller.

B Students match the phrases with the responses.

PRONUNCIATION

5.7 **A** Highlight that some parts of words are underlined. Play the audio and confirm that the underlining shows the stressed syllables.

5.7 **B** Play the audio again line by line for students to listen and repeat. Encourage the students to use stress naturally, focusing on producing the stressed syllable but also on reducing volume, length and pitch of unstressed syllables.

SPEAKING

A Focus the students on the timetable and ask questions to check understanding, e.g. *What time does the train arrive in New York City? How much is a round-trip ticket to Boston?* Students then work in pairs to complete the conversation with information from the timetable.

B As a class, elicit how a useful phrase can be added to the conversation (e.g. *Let me see* before *It leaves at* ...). Students then work with their partners to add useful phrases to their conversations from Exercise A. Monitor and assist as required.

C Students practice their conversations. Monitor and encourage students to look up and say their parts, focusing on appropriate stress. Students can record themselves on their digital devices and watch their performances to improve for next time.

D Model parts of the conversation with different students around the class, choosing different information each time. Students then change roles in their pairs and improvise using different information from the timetable.

Extra activity

To extend the Speaking section and allow students further practice of the language, set a new context for practice. Students could choose new destinations and prices for train tickets (or bus tickets). Alternatively, students could find current timetables and prices for local or foreign destinations and use that information to build new conversations.

METHODOLOGY HUB by Jim Scrivener

The communicative purpose of language learning

It is important to remember that no one area of skills or language systems exists in isolation: there can be no speaking if you don't have the vocabulary to speak with; there's no point learning words unless you can do something useful with them.

The purpose of learning a language is usually to enable you to take part in exchanges of information: talking with friends, reading instructions on a package of food, understanding directions, writing a note to a colleague, etc.

METHODOLOGY HUB by Jim Scrivener

Speaking: Fluency, accuracy and communication

Imagine a switch inside your head – it swings between two settings: 'working mainly on accuracy' and 'working mainly on fluency' (see Figure 5.1).

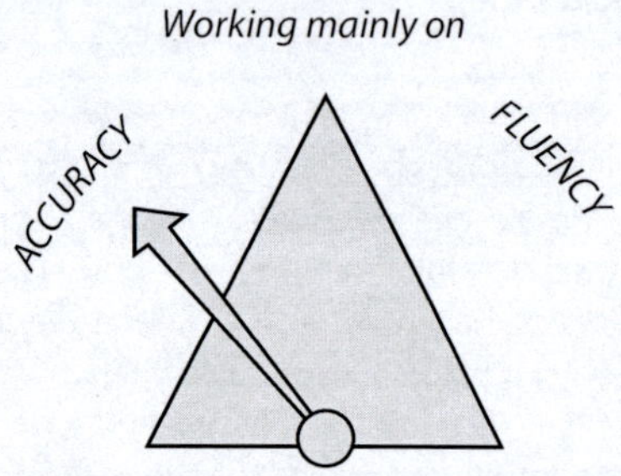

FIGURE 5.1 Accuracy/fluency switch

It's probably a huge simplification, but I suspect that something like this is at work in my head through most of my language teaching, changing its setting from activity to activity, stage to stage – and, in some teaching, changing moment by moment in response to things happening in class. And I think that initially getting that switch installed and working may be a key skill for anyone learning to be a language teacher.

Certainly there are activities in which you are arguably working on both accuracy and fluency in relatively equal measure, but many everyday language-teaching lesson stages are focused on one more than the other, and at any one moment, in any one activity, it is likely that you will be trying to focus on accuracy rather than fluency, or fluency rather than accuracy. The danger of correcting students in the middle of a mainly fluency task is that you interrupt their flow and take the focus off their message. Students frequently find it hard to continue after a correction, while others in class may become more reluctant to speak for fear of similar interruptions.

It is therefore important for you to be clear about what is involved in accuracy-focused work as compared with fluency-focused work. And it's especially important to be clear about the differing goals – and consequently different classroom procedures – of the two.

GABY

SAM

LUCY

FUNCTIONAL LANGUAGE

Asking for information

A Write *Customer* or *Ticket seller* in the correct column, A or B.

A ___Customer___	B ___Ticket seller___
1 I'd like a ticket to New York on Saturday afternoon.	**a** That's $85, please.
2 What time does it leave?	**b** It takes about two hours.
3 How long does it take?	**c** Saturday afternoon. Yes, there is a train.
4 Can I book a ticket, please?	**d** One-way or round-trip?
5 Round-trip, please.	**e** It leaves at 3 pm.

B Match the phrases (1–5) with the responses (a–e).

Glossary

pounds (n) (British) = dollars (n) (American)
return ticket (n) (British) = round-trip ticket (n) (American)
single ticket (n) (British) = one-way ticket (n) (American)

PRONUNCIATION

5.7 **A** Listen to the conversation and notice how the underlined words are stressed.

Ticket seller: Can I help you?
Customer: Yes, I'd like a ticket to Boston on Friday morning, please.
Ticket seller: Friday morning. Let me see. Yes, there is a train.
Customer: What time does it leave?
Ticket seller: It leaves at 10:30.
Customer: How long does it take?
Ticket seller: It takes about three hours.
Customer: How much is it?
Ticket seller: Thirty-five dollars.
Customer: Can I book a ticket, please?
Ticket seller: One-way or round-trip?

SPEAKING

DESTINATION	DEPARTURE	ARRIVAL	PRICE one-way	PRICE round-trip
Washington, D.C.	10:30	12:30	$30	$55
Baltimore	10:45	11:45	$20	$30
New York City	11:00	1:30	$45	$60
Boston	11:15	3:00	$55	$80

A PREPARE Work in pairs. Complete the conversation using information in the timetable.

I'd like a ticket to ____________, please.
There is a train to ____________ this morning.
What time ____________?
It leaves at ____________.
How long ____________?
It takes ____________.
How much ____________?
One-way or ____________?
____________, please.
That's $____________, please.

B PLAN Work in pairs. Add three or more useful phrases to the conversation.

C PRACTICE Work in pairs. Practice the conversation.

D REPEAT Change roles. Choose a new destination.

Ask for information

Unit 5 Writing

5 Writing

Write a blog about food

W– using object pronouns

A Read Bob's blog. What is the blog post about?

a an everyday lunch
(b) a special lunch
c how to cook lunch
d Bob's favorite lunch

BOB'S DAILY BLOG

A pot-luck lunch at work

Ex B Q1 Once a month at work, we have a pot-luck lunch. Everyone cooks some food at home and we bring it
Ex B Q2 to the large meeting room. Some of my colleagues are really good cooks! They bring all kinds of food from their home countries. One of my colleagues is from Mexico and she makes a great chicken dish with
Ex B Q3 chocolate. It's amazing!
Ex B Q4 I'm not a good cook and I usually just bring a
Ex B Q5 salad. We eat and share all the food together – it's a great way to make friends at work!

B Read Bob's blog again. Are these statements true (T) or false (F)?

1 They have a pot-luck lunch every week. T (F) Once a month.
2 They eat the pot-luck lunch in a restaurant. T (F) They eat in a meeting room.
3 A colleague makes delicious Mexican food. (T) F
4 Bob is very good at cooking. T (F) He's not a good cook.
5 Bob always brings cupcakes or cookies. T (F) He usually brings a salad.

Using object pronouns

We use pronouns so we don't need to repeat the noun.

*Everyone cooks some **food** at home and we bring **it** to the large meeting room.*

C Complete the sentences with the correct pronoun.

1 **My brother** works near my office. I meet ___him___ for lunch every week.
2 We bring different **dishes** to work and share ___them___ with each other.
3 **My sister** works in Mexico. I visit ___her___ there every year.
4 I don't go out for **lunch**. I eat ___it___ at my desk.

WRITING

A PREPARE You are going to write a blog about a special meal tradition in your life. Think about the following points.

- What's special about the meal?
- How often do you have it?
- Where is it?
- What kind of food do you have?
- What's good about this meal?

B WRITE Write your blog.

C REVIEW Read another person's blog. Ask questions to get more information.

Write a blog about food

Refer students to the blog as a model for the writing task.

You could do an example about yourself. Describe a special meal tradition in your life, making sure you cover all the points. When you finish, elicit what you said for each point and write notes about the students' answers on the board. Then number the notes in the order you would write about them, telling students what you are doing. As you do this, group and number the notes on the board, draw arrows, erase, etc so that students can see that planning your writing is a fluid, flexible process.

Unit 5 Review

GRAMMAR

A Choose the correct words to complete the sentences.

1 Sasha *sit* / *sits* in the backyard after work.
2 Eric *doesn't cook* / *cook* dinner during the week.
3 Where does Maria *eat* / *eats* lunch?
4 Does Maha *have* / *has* lunch at school?
5 A: *Do* / *Does* Antonio and Sofia eat at home on Friday?
B: No, they *doesn't* / *don't*.
6 A: Does Jana *drink* / *drinks* tea every day?
B: Yes, she *do* / *does*.

B Add the adverb to each sentence.

1 I am ^never late for work. (never)
2 We ^sometimes eat breakfast in a café. (sometimes)
3 I ^frequently cook dinner at home. (frequently)
4 Vicky and Sue ^usually have pizza on Friday. (usually)
5 Carey is ^always very busy on the weekend. (always)

VOCABULARY

A Complete the phrases to describe recreational activities.

1 go for a w a l k
2 take a b a t h
3 cook a m e a l
4 go r u n n i n g
5 go to the g y m
6 play c h e s s

B Label the pictures with the correct words.

a pasta

b eggs

c noodles

d grapes

e bread

f fish

40 TIME FOR A BREAK

LEAD-IN

Tell the class that they are going to prepare a meal together. Ask everyone to think of a dish. Compile a menu on the board. Write *Pot Luck* at the top and explain that it is something people frequently do in America. Ask if students have this kind of communal meal in their culture.

WRITING

A Give students a time limit, e.g. 30 seconds, to encourage them to scan the blog rather than read in detail. Check the answer and ask students to identify which words helped them decide.

B Students work individually to answer the questions, then check in pairs. Go through the answers as a whole class.

C Write *him/her/it* on the board. Ask which is for a man, a woman and an object. Students complete the exercise. Write the answers on the board.

WRITING TASK

A Ask students to read through the five points. Students work individually to write notes and put them in order.

B Give students time to write. Monitor as they write, helping but avoiding giving too much input yourself; refer students back to the model wherever possible.

C Ask students to swap blogs with another student. Ask them to think about something positive they can say about their partner's blog and any places where they would like more information.

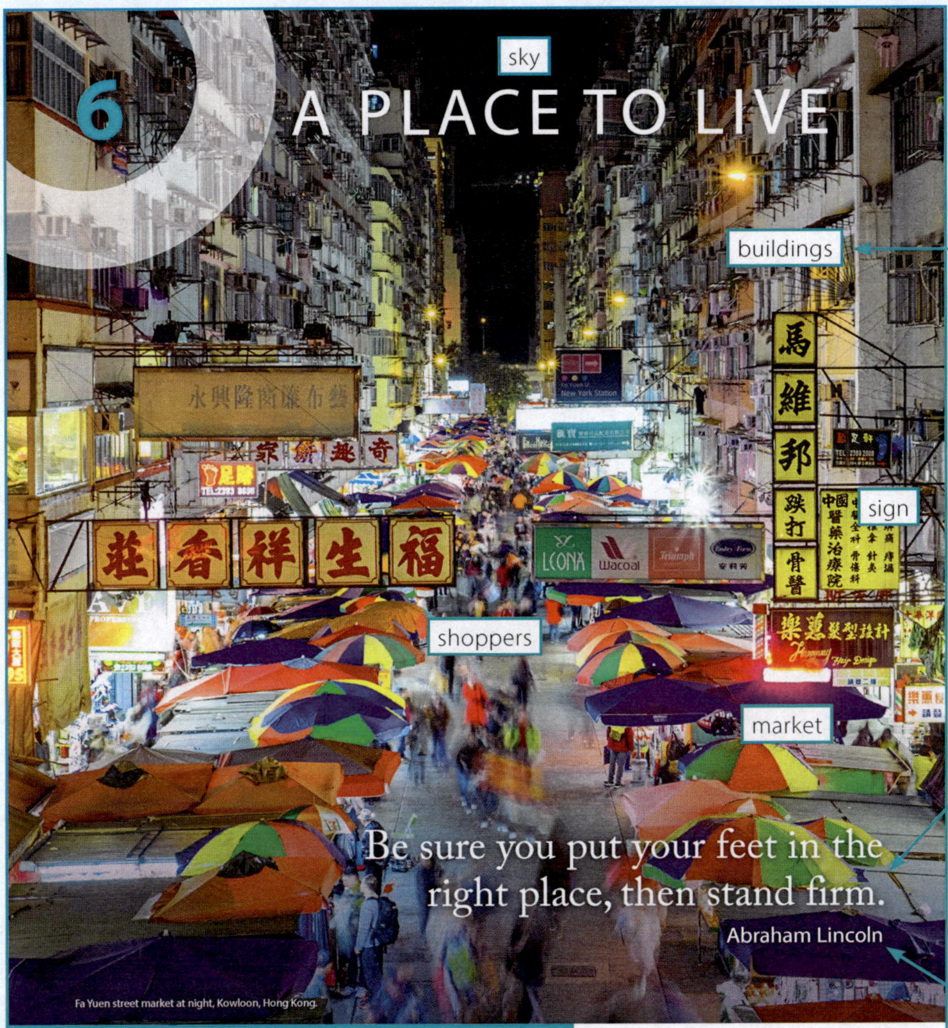

Fa Yuen street market at night, Kowloon, Hong Kong.

Ask students to label the photo if you need time to set up the class.

A two-step approach is advisable, when standing up for beliefs, rights and ideas. First, be sure and think the situation through: put our 'feet in the right place'. Be convinced and convincing; we need to 'stand firm', confident in our position when talking with others who may not share our views.

Abraham Lincoln (1809–1865) was the 16th president of the US. He was born into a hard-working family, fighting to get himself an education, and it was this drive and ambition which drove him to reach the highest office in the US.

- describe your town or city
- describe your home
- ask for and give directions
- write a review of a café

Work with a partner. Discuss the questions.

1 Where do you live?
2 Look at the picture. Is this a good place to live? Why/Why not?
3 Complete the sentence in your own words: *Life in a big city is … because …*

cheap dangerous difficult easy expensive horrible nice safe

A PLACE TO LIVE 41

OBJECTIVES

Read the unit objectives to the class.

UNIT OPENER QUESTIONS

Write *I live in* (your town/city). on the board. Write *Where do you live?* on the board and ask students to come up and write the answer as it applies to them. If you have a multinational class, you could display a map and mark the students' countries. Then draw students' attention to the picture and write on the board *Is this a good place to live?* Ask them to describe their thoughts on the picture and then to say whether they think it would be a good place to live or not. Ask them to share their ideas about the picture, making observations about specifics in the picture that would make it a good place to live or not. Ask several members of the class to get a broad range of views. Then ask them to think about where they live and if it is a good place to live or not. Share ideas as a whole class. Add ideas to the board so students can use these for support and inspiration when discussing and answering the question *Life in a big city is … because …* Add all new ideas to the board.

WORKSHEETS

Lesson 6.1 Around town

Vocabulary: Places in a town (W19)

Grammar: *there is / there are*; *some* and *any* (W20)

Lesson 6.2 Choosing a home

Vocabulary: Furniture and rooms; Prepositions of place (W21)

Grammar: *is there / are there* question forms (W22)

6.1 Around town

Describe your town or city

V places in a town G *there is / there are*; *some* and *any* P *there is / there are*

VOCABULARY
Places in a town

6.1 **A** Match the places (1–10) with the words in the box. Then listen and check your answers.

art gallery café hotel market museum park restaurant store station theater

1 station

6 café

2 hotel

7 market

3 theater

8 museum

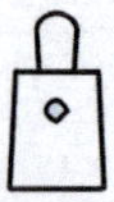
4 store

9 park

5 restaurant

10 art gallery

6.1 **B** Listen and repeat.

C Complete the sentences with the names of places in a town.

1 I sometimes go to the __theater__ on the weekend to see a play.
2 We usually buy fresh fruits and vegetables at the __market__.
3 Let's visit the __art gallery__ to see the paintings.
4 We frequently visit the __museum__ to learn about history.
5 Let's go out to a __restaurant__ for dinner tonight!
6 We frequently stay in a __hotel__ on vacation.
7 I usually take my children to the __park__ to play soccer.
8 Let's go to a __café__ for some coffee and ice cream!
9 Suzanna frequently goes to the __store__ to buy clothes or shoes.
10 How far is it to the __station__? My train is at 3 pm.

D SPEAK Work in pairs. Which of these places do you go to in your town?

READING

A PREPARE TO READ Look at the pictures in *What's special about your home town?* Find these things in the pictures.

boat bridge building canal market

B READ FOR GIST Read *What's special about your home town* Choose the best summary of the main idea.

a Only tourists enjoy Venice.
b Venice is a very difficult place to live.
(c) Life in Venice is interesting and fun.

C READ FOR GIST Which topics are in the forum post? Check (✓) the answers.

- [x] art
- [x] food
- [ ] hotels
- [ ] jobs
- [ ] music
- [ ] schools
- [x] transportation

D READ FOR DETAIL Are the sentences true (T) or false (F)?

1 Venice is a modern city. T / (F) — Some buildings are over 500 years old.
2 Venice is a good city to see art. (T) / F
3 There are hundreds of bridges in Venice. (T) / F
4 There are a lot of cars and buses in the city center. T / (F) — There aren't any.
5 The writer takes a water taxi to work. T / (F) — He/she walks to work every morning.

E SPEAK Work in groups. Answer the questions.

1 Is Venice a good place to live, in your opinion? Why/Why not?
2 Is Venice similar to or different from your home town or city

What's special about
YOUR HOME TOWN?

March 17, 6:57 Reply | Like

Highlighting = GRAMMAR Ex A answers

I live in Venice, in Italy. It's famous all over the world and there are a lot of tourists. But it's an exciting place to live and work, too. Ex B

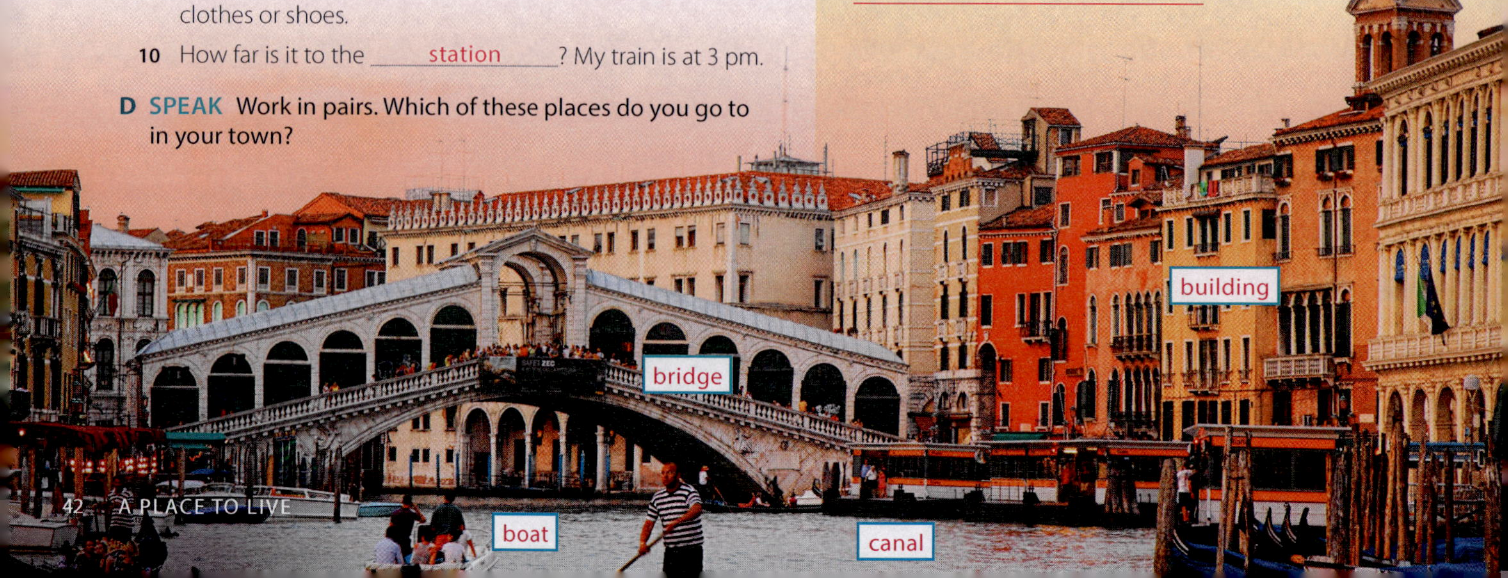

6.1 Around town

LEAD-IN

Ask students to write down the name of their favorite place in town. Students then walk around, saying, e.g. *My favorite place is the Italian restaurant.* When they finish, write the places on the board. Which was the most popular?

VOCABULARY

6.1 **A** Focus students on the images and the words in the box, and elicit one answer as an example. Students match words and places individually, then check in pairs. Play the audio for them to check. Write the words up on the board and practice pronunciation; focus on the /aːr/ sound in *market*, *park* and *art*, the shortened sound of *restaurant*, the stress on the second syllable of *hotel* and the diphthong in *station* (/eɪ/) and *café* (/eɪ/).

6.1 **B** Play the audio again while students listen and repeat.

C Read the first sentence and complete it for yourself, as an example. Then let students work in pairs to complete the exercise. Monitor and help as necessary. Go through the answers with the whole class. For the appropriate sentences (e.g. 1, 2, 4, etc), encourage students to make sentences with the same or a different adverb of frequency to describe how often they do each of these things.

D Tell the class your answer to the question, extending your answers by explaining why and when you go to the places (or why not). Students then discuss the question in pairs before reporting back to the whole class. Use the **Vocabulary Worksheet** on page W19 for extra practice.

READING

A Focus students on the photos of Venice and the words in the box. Give them time to match the words, then go through the answers, practicing pronunciation, especially the silent *u* in *building* (/bɪldɪŋ/).

B Check that students understand the three options, and then remind students that reading for gist means not reading in detail; give them a time limit for the task (e.g. one minute) to reinforce this. Ask them to justify their choices before giving the answer.

C See if students can remember the topics from the first reading, then ask them to read the text again quickly. Check answers, asking students to identify the words that gave them the answers.

D Students work individually to answer the questions. Ask them to circle, underline or highlight the parts of the text that give the answers. Go through the answers with the whole class.

E Check that students understand the questions, then ask them to work in small groups of three or four to discuss them. Monitor, but try not to correct; encourage fluency rather than accuracy at this point. Note any common issues and deal with them after the speaking activity.

GRAMMAR HUB

6.1

there is / there are

	Singular	Plural
Positive	**There is** a bus stop. **There's** a bus stop.	**There are** a lot of boats.
Negative	**There isn't** an airport.	**There aren't** any buses.

- We use *there is/isn't* or *there are/aren't* to say that something exists (or doesn't exist). We can use *there is / there are* to describe different places or things in a house, town, etc.

  There are a lot of flowers in the yard.

  There's a bookstore in the center of town.
- We use *there is* with a singular noun and *there are* with a plural noun.

  There's a bank in the city center.

  There are bus stops on this street.
- We use *some* and *a lot of* with plural nouns in positive sentences.

  There are some nice cafés in my neighborhood.

  There are a lot of hotels in this city.
- We use *any* and *a lot of* with plural nouns in negative sentences.

  There aren't any museums in my town.

  There aren't a lot of tourists here.

	some / a lot of / any
Positive	There are **some** big buildings. There are **a lot of** museums.
Negative	There aren't **any** islands. There aren't **a lot of** stores.

Be careful!

- In sentences with more than one noun, the verb agrees with the first noun.

  There's a hotel and a grocery store.

  There are ten stores and a large hotel.

  There's a park and two swimming pools.

6.1 Around town

GRAMMAR

A Students work individually to find and underline examples. Do the first one together as a class to support students.

B In pairs, students work out the rules. Monitor, referring students to examples rather than giving the answers. When everyone has finished, go through the answers, writing examples from the text on the board to illustrate the points. Check that everyone understands; practice some examples of positive and negative singular and plural nouns.

C Direct students to the **Grammar Hub** (see below and TB42).

D Ask students to read the example conversation; encourage them to notice the use of short forms. Then put them into pairs to talk. Monitor and note mistakes, and give feedback at the end; ask one or two students to say what there is/isn't/are/aren't to the class, and check if they all agree. Use the **Grammar Worksheet** on page W20 for extra practice.

PRONUNCIATION

6.2 **A** Write the first sentence on the board and read it out in two ways – first carefully, then more naturally. Elicit the differences in the way the words are connected, and draw a symbol to show the elisions and connected speech. Then play the audio while students listen and read.

6.2 **B** Replay the audio and ask students to repeat. Make sure they use the elisions and that they understand that this is a natural way to speak – it is not wrong or lazy!

SPEAKING

A Check that students understand the headings in the table, then ask them to work individually to fill it in before checking answers with a partner.

B With the same partner, students discuss the three questions and decide if they are true or false. Get feedback from the whole class.

C In small groups of three or four, students discuss their town or city. Encourage fluent discussion including their opinions about the places and when and why they go or don't go there.

Extra activity

Tell the class that the area where the English class is located is going to be the site for a new building. Elicit the names of different places from the lesson (e.g. *grocery store*, *café*, *hotel*, *market*, etc) and write them on the board. Ask students to work individually in choosing three of these places they think should be built. Students then work in small groups, sharing their top three. Together the group should decide on their top three overall. Then regroup the students. Students work together in their new groups discussing and choosing their number one choice. Share the number one choice from each group and add them to the board. Take a whole-class vote for which place should be built in the area. Throughout, encourage the students to explain and justify their choices.

GRAMMAR HUB

6.1

There is / There are

A Choose the correct options to complete the sentences.

1 There aren't ***some*** / ***any*** cars in Venice. [any]
2 There are ***a lot of*** / ***any*** water taxis. [a lot of]
3 There ***'s*** / ***are*** 350 boats (called 'gondolas') in Venice. [are]
4 There are about 400 boatmen but there***'s*** / ***are*** only one woman! ['s]
5 There are ***a*** / ***some*** narrow streets in Venice. One street is only 53 centimeters wide! [some]
6 There are ***some*** / ***any*** very old buildings in Venice – the Palazzo Grimani Museum is more than 500 years old! [some]

B Complete the description with *there is/there isn't* or *there are/aren't*.

I live in a small town and [1] ___there aren't___ a lot of restaurants. [2] ___There's / There is___ one small café where you can get tea and coffee or juice. [3] ___There aren't___ a lot of things to do in my town – it's very boring really – but [4] ___there's / there is___ a nice park. I usually play soccer there with my friends on Saturdays. It's a very small place, so [5] ___there aren't___ any art galleries and [6] ___there isn't___ a museum. You have to go to the city to find those, but [7] ___there are___ two small stores. [8] ___There's / There is___ a train station and that's very important for me and my friends because we get the train into the city. In the city, [9] ___there's / there is___ a big shopping mall and we go there to buy clothes.

C Complete the sentences with the correct form of the noun in parentheses. Add *a* or *an* if necessary.

1 There are a lot of ___flowers___ (*flower*) in our yard.
2 There's a TV and ___a computer___ (*computer*).
3 There aren't any ___books___ (*book*) on the bookshelf.
4 There are ten ___chairs___ (*chair*) and a big table.
5 There's ___a fridge___ (*fridge*) in the kitchen.
6 There isn't ___an apple tree___ (*apple tree*) in the backyard.
7 There aren't a lot of ___plants___ (*plant*) on the balcony.
8 There are some ___cushions___ (*cushion*) on the floor.

➤ Go back to page 43.

GRAMMAR

there is / there are; some and *any*

A Read the post again. Underline examples of *there is, there are, some* and *any*.

B **WORK IT OUT** Complete the table using the examples in Exercise A to help you.

there is / there are; some and *any*		
	Singular	Plural
Positive +	There [1] is a really good café.	There [2] are over 400 bridges.
Negative -	There [3] isn't a really large grocery store..	There [4] aren't any cars.
Some and *a lot of*	We use *some* and *a lot of* with [5] *singular* / *plural* nouns. *Some* means a [6] *small* / *big* number. *A lot of* means a [7] *small* / *big* number. We usually use them in [8] *positive* / *negative* sentences.	
Any	We use *any* in [9] *negative* / *positive* sentences and in questions.	

C Go to the **Grammar Hub** on **page 108**.

D **SPEAK** Work in pairs. Talk about places near where you are. Use *there is* or *there are* and the words in the box.

art gallery cafés hotel museum restaurants stores

A: There's an art gallery near the school, but there isn't a museum.

B: There are cafés near the school, but there aren't any restaurants.

Venice is a city with a lot of history – I love it! Ex D Q1
There are some buildings that are over 500 years old! Venice is great for art. There are museums and art galleries everywhere. Ex D Q2 There are over 400 bridges in Venice. Ex D Q3 Why? Because there are a lot of canals! There aren't any cars in this area, but there's a train station outside the city center. There aren't any buses in the center either – people go to work by water taxi! Ex D Q4 There isn't a really large grocery store, but there's a great market with a lot of fresh fruits and vegetables.

I walk to work every morning and look at the buildings and the canals and the bridges. They're amazing! There's a really good café near my home. They make great coffee and fresh sandwiches and I eat breakfast there every morning when I go to work. I think Venice is a great place to live! Ex D Q5

PRONUNCIATION

there is / there are

A Read and listen to the examples. 6.2

1 There's a restaurant.
2 There's a grocery store.
3 There are some stores.
4 There are some hotels.

B Listen and repeat the sentences in Exercise A. 6.2

SPEAKING

A **PLAN** Write the names of places in the chart. Use the words from the Vocabulary section on page 42.

Everyday life	Weekend fun	Food and drink
market	art gallery	café
park	hotel	restaurant
station	museum	
store	theater	

B **PREPARE** Work in pairs. Are these sentences true or false about your town?

1 There are a lot of parks in my town and there's a museum.
2 There aren't any theaters, but there's an art gallery.
3 There's a large grocery store and there are also a lot of small stores.

C **DISCUSS** Work in groups. Talk about places in your town.

There are a lot of parks in my city. There's a big park near the river and I usually go there with my friends on the weekend.

Describe your town or city

6.2 Choosing a home

Describe your home

V – furniture and rooms; prepositions of place
G – *is there / are there* question forms
S – predicting
P – vowel sounds: /ʌ/ and /e/

VOCABULARY

Furniture and rooms

A Look at the picture. What kind of person do you think lives here? The person who lives here is probably a musician or music student because of the guitar and the poster of a guitarist.

B Complete the description with the words in the box.

bed bookshelf chair clock closet cushion desk lamp wall window

The [1] ___chair___ and the [2] ___desk___ are blue. The [3] ___lamp___ is green. The [4] ___clock___ is yellow. The [5] ___bookshelf___ is red. The [6] ___window___ is big. The [7] ___closet___ is brown. The [8] ___bed___ is gray. The [9] ___cushion___ is orange. The [10] ___wall___ is light yellow.

6.3 **C** Listen and check your answers to Exercise B .

D Go to the **Vocabulary Hub** on **page 124**.

E **SPEAK** Work in pairs. What furniture do you have in your room at home or your classroom?

Prepositions of place

A Look at the picture in Vocabulary Exercise A again. Complete the description below using *in*, *on* or *under*.

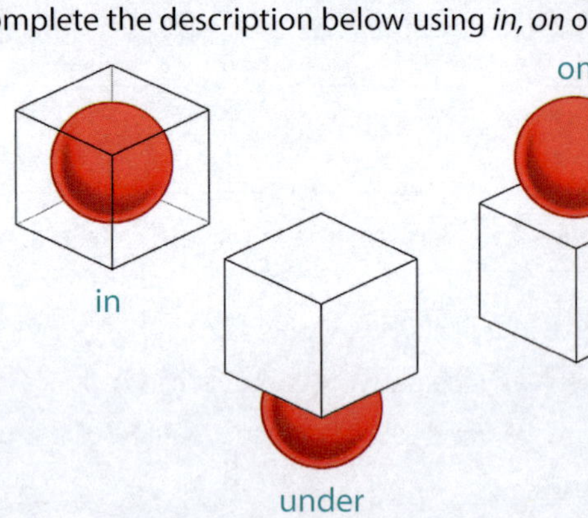

There's a desk and a chair [1] ___in___ the room. There's a lamp [2] ___on___ the desk. There are clothes [3] ___in___ the closet. There are books [4] ___on___ the bookshelf. There's a small table next to the bed. There's a clock [5] ___on___ the table. There's a cushion [6] ___on___ the chair. There's a bag [7] ___under___ the desk. There's a picture [8] ___on___ the wall.

6.4 **B** Listen to a description of the room. Find four differences between the picture opposite and the description you hear.

C **SPEAK** Work in pairs. Look at the picture again. Describe the location of one thing. Say the object your partner is describing.

A: It's on the desk.
B: Is it the lamp?

D Student A – Go to the **Communication Hub** on **page 128**. Student B – Go to the **Communication Hub** on **page 132**.

LISTENING

A **PREPARE TO LISTEN** Read the information about a studio apartment and answer the questions.

1 Where is the studio? central Manhattan
2 What is near the studio? bus stop, grocery store
3 How can you get more information? call the agency

> **NYC RENTALS**
> **Studio** for rent in central Manhattan.
> Close to a bus stop and a grocery store.
> Must see! Call for an appointment.
> **646-755-8318**

> **Predicting**
> Before you listen, try to think about which topics will be in the conversation. Predicting helps to make the information easier to understand.

B **PREDICT** Look at the form in Exercise D. Check (✓) the topics that you think you will hear in the conversation.

- [x] location
- [ ] neighbors
- [x] number of rooms
- [ ] pets
- [x] money
- [x] stores
- [x] size

6.5 **C** **LISTEN FOR GIST** Listen to the conversation and check your answers to Exercise B. Does the man decide to rent the apartment? No, he doesn't.

6.5 **D** **LISTEN FOR DETAIL** Listen to the conversation again. Complete the form with the correct information.

> **STUDIO FOR RENT**
> Address: ___25B___ East 23rd Street
> Time to bus stop: ___10___ minutes
> Furniture:
> - [ ] desk
> - [ ] chair
> - [x] bookshelf
> - [x] lamp
> - [ ] closet
> - [ ] couch
> - [ ] armchair
> - [x] bed
>
> Window with view of ___park___
> Bathroom: **yes**/**no** (yes underlined) Kitchen: **yes**/**no** (no underlined)
> Price per month: ___$2,000___

6.5 **E** **LISTEN FOR DETAIL** Listen again. Why doesn't the man like the room? There's no kitchen or bathtub and it's too expensive.

6.2 Choosing a home

LEAD-IN

Bring some magazine pictures of stylish homes in. Put them around the class. Get students to walk around and say which ones they like and don't like. Then take a whole-class vote on the favorite home/room.

VOCABULARY

Furniture and rooms

A Focus students on the picture. Get their ideas of who lives there and write them on the board. Ask if they like the room and why/why not.

B Students work individually to complete the exercise, then check in pairs. Don't help until students have completed the exercise – it is important that they try to find the answers by eliminating the ones they know in order to develop autonomy and linguistic awareness.

6.3 **C** Play the audio while students listen and repeat. Focus them on the difficult pronunciations, e.g. the *z* sound and the following schwa in *closet* /ˈklɑzət/, the schwa in *cushion* /ˈkʊʃ(ə)n/ and the final sound in *window* /ˈwɪndoʊ/.

D Direct students to the **Vocabulary Hub** (see TB97).

E Talk briefly about your room at home as an example, then students work in pairs to discuss their own rooms. Monitor but don't overcorrect – encourage fluency and extended speaking turns. At the end, ask one or two students to describe their partner's room.

Prepositions of place

A Pre-teach the three prepositions using an object and placing it in various places in relation to a table, for example. Then students work individually to complete the exercise before checking in pairs. Go through the answers with the whole class.

6.4 **B** Play the audio while students listen and look at the picture. Ask if they noticed any differences but don't confirm them yet. Tell the students there are four differences, then play the audio again. Check answers.

In the picture, there's only one chair; the lamp is on the desk (not on the table next to the bed); the clock is next to the bed (not under it); there's only one picture on the wall.

C Demonstrate with one or two examples from the picture, then put students into pairs to take turns describing and guessing. Monitor without interrupting too much.

D Students go to the **Communication Hub** (see TB97). Use the **Vocabulary Worksheet** on page W21 for extra practice.

LISTENING

A Give students time to read the questions, then focus the students on the advertisement to answer them. Check answers.

B Students predict the topics they will hear – help with vocabulary if necessary. Ask for ideas but do not confirm them at this point.

6.5 **C** Play the audio while students listen and check. Ask if the man decides to rent the apartment, and ask how they know. Play the audio again stopping at the relevant places to check the answers.

6.5 **D** See if students can remember any information while they go through the form, then play the audio again while they complete the information.

6.5 **E** Play the audio again while students listen for the answer to the question. Check the answer, repeating the audio if necessary.

AUDIO SCRIPT

6.4

Vocabulary, Exercise B
M = Martin

M: Hi everyone, my name's Martin and I'm looking for someone to rent my room. As you can see, there's a desk and two chairs. There's a big closet. You can put your clothes in there. There's a bookshelf. All my books are on it right now. There's a small table with a lamp on it next to the bed. Oops, my clock is under the bed. Sorry about that! Those are a couple of my pictures on the wall. And there's a window with a nice view of the yard. All this for 200 dollars a month!

6.5

Listening, Exercise C
R = Realtor M = Man

R: Hi! This is New York City Rentals. How can I help you?
M: Hello. I'd like some information about the studio for rent on East 23rd Street.
Ex D **R:** Sure! No problem. Let's see. That's number 25B, the studio? What would you like to know?
M: Are there any buses on that street?
Ex D **R:** Yes, there are. It's about a 10-minute walk to the bus stop.
M: OK. Are there any stores nearby?
R: Yes, there are. There's a grocery store on the corner and there are a lot of restaurants nearby.
M: Is there a living room and a bedroom?
R: No, it's a studio. There's only one room.
M: Oh, I see. What about the furniture? What's in the room? Are there any chairs?
Ex D **R:** No, there aren't. There are some bookshelves, a lamp and a bed. That's all. It's a small studio …
M: There's no desk and no chair. Hmm. Is there a large window?
Ex D **R:** Yes, there's a large window with a view of the park.
M: Is there a bathroom?
Ex D **R:** Yes, there is. There's a small bathroom with a shower, but no bathtub.
M: Is there a kitchen?
R: No, there isn't. It's just one room!
Ex C Ex D **M:** No kitchen and no bathtub, and you want $2,000 a month! You must be joking!

6.2 Choosing a home

GRAMMAR

A–D Students complete the exercises. Direct students to the **Grammar Hub** (see below). Check answers as a class. Use the **Grammar Worksheet** on page W22 for extra practice.

PRONUNCIATION

6.6; 6.7; 6.8

A–C Play the audio while students complete the exercises. Check answers as a class.

SPEAKING HUB

A Give students time to read the instructions to the task. Demonstrate one or two examples on the board of the questions that students are going to ask. Then direct students to the **Communication Hub** (see TB97). You could put all Student As and Bs together to prepare in groups.

B–D Put students into A and B pairs to complete the task. Monitor and note examples of language for feedback. Discuss feedback as a class.

GRAMMAR HUB

6.2

is there / are there **question forms**

	Question	Positive short answer	Negative short answer
Singular	**Is there** a dresser?	**Yes, there is.**	**No, there isn't.**
Plural	**Are there** cushions?	**Yes, there are.**	**No, there aren't.**

	Question
a lot of	Are there **a lot of** books?
any	Are there **any** chairs?

- We use *Is there …?* or *Are there …?* to ask about different places and objects.

  Is there a library in town?

  Are there cushions on the couch?
- We use *Is there …?* with a singular noun and *Are there …?* with a plural noun.

  Is there a bathtub in the bathroom?

  Are there pictures on the wall?
- We can use *a lot of* and *any* in questions about plural nouns.

  Are there a lot of books on the bookshelf?

  Are there any cups in the kitchen?

Be careful!

- We use *there is* not *there's* in a positive short answer.

  Yes, there is. NOT ~~*Yes, there's.*~~

6.2

Is there / Are there **question forms**

A Complete the questions with *Is* or *Are*.

1 *Is* there a bookcase in your bedroom?
2 Is there a big window?
3 Are there two beds in your bedroom?
4 Are there a lot of cushions on your couch?
5 Are there any photos on the walls?
6 Is there a TV in your bedroom?
7 Is there a desk by the window?
8 Are there a lot of things under your bed?

B Answer the questions in Exercise A.

1 Yes, there *is*.
2 No, there isn't.
3 Yes, there are.
4 No, there aren't.
5 Yes, there are.
6 No, there isn't.
7 Yes, there is.
8 No, there aren't.

C Use the prompts to create questions using *Is there* and *Are there*.

1 a lot of / cabinets / kitchen
Are there a lot of cabinets in the kitchen?
2 a lamp / desk
Is there a lamp on the desk?
3 any / books / bookshelf
Are there any books on the bookshelf?
4 clock / wall
Is there a clock on the wall?
5 cups / coffee table
Are there cups on the coffee table?
6 any / mirrors / bathroom
Are there any mirrors in the bathroom?
7 blue cushions / couch
Are there blue cushions on the couch?
8 rug / bedroom floor
Is there a rug on the bedroom floor?

➤ Go back to page 45.

GRAMMAR

is there / are there question forms

A Complete the sentences with the correct form of *be* and the words in the box.

a bathroom (✓) buses (✓) chairs (✗) a kitchen (✗)

1 Is there ___ a bathroom ___?
Yes, there ___ is ___.

2 Are there any ___ buses ___?
Yes, there ___ are ___.

3 Is there ___ a kitchen ___?
No, there ___ isn't ___.

4 Are there any ___ chairs ___?
No, there ___ aren't ___.

B WORK IT OUT Choose the correct options to complete the rules. Use the examples in Exercise A to help you.

is there / are there question forms

To make *yes/no* questions, we put *is* or *are* [1]*before* / *after there*.

We use *any* in questions with [2]*singular* / *plural* nouns.

We [3]*use* / *don't use* the contracted form of *there is* (*there's*) in short answers.

C Go to the **Grammar Hub** on **page 108**.

D SPEAK Work in pairs. Ask your partner about their room at home. Use the words in the box.

books bookshelf clock cushions desk lamp pictures window

A: Are there any books in your room?
B: Yes, there are a lot of books. They're on a bookshelf.

PRONUNCIATION

Vowel sounds: /ʌ/ and /e/

6.6 **A** Listen to the sounds /ʌ/ and /e/.

/ʌ/ rug /e/ bed

6.7 **B** Listen and circle the words with the same vowel sound as the word in bold.

1 /ʌ/ rug
son **run** song **some** **love** blog

2 /e/ bed
get clean **red** sad **bread** **head**

6.8 **C** Listen and circle the word you hear.

1 There's a **bag** / *bug* on the floor.
2 This is a *bad room* / **bedroom**.
3 Is there a **pen** / *pan* in the kitchen?
4 Be careful with that *cut* / **cat**.

SPEAKING HUB

A PREPARE You want to rent a room from your partner. Student A – Stay on this page. Student B – Go to the **Communication Hub** on **page 130**. Read the description of what you need. Write five questions to ask your partner.

a desk	*Is there a desk?*
chairs	Are there any chairs?
a lamp	Is there a lamp?
a TV	Is there a TV?
near a bus stop or train station	Is there a bus stop or train station nearby?
near a grocery store	Is it near a grocery store?

B DISCUSS Ask your partner questions about their room. Find out if it is the right place for you.

A: Can I ask about the room for rent?
B: Yes, of course. How can I help you?
A: Is it near a bus stop?
B: No, it isn't. But there's a train station ten minutes away.

C REPEAT Answer your partner's questions. Use the information in the advertisement.

Your room:

- Comfortable room in quiet area.
- Near museums, theaters and restaurants.
- Large window with view of the street.
- Bed, table, chair and lamp included.
- Free internet included.

$200 per week

D REPORT Tell the class about the room.

I like / don't like my partner's room because …

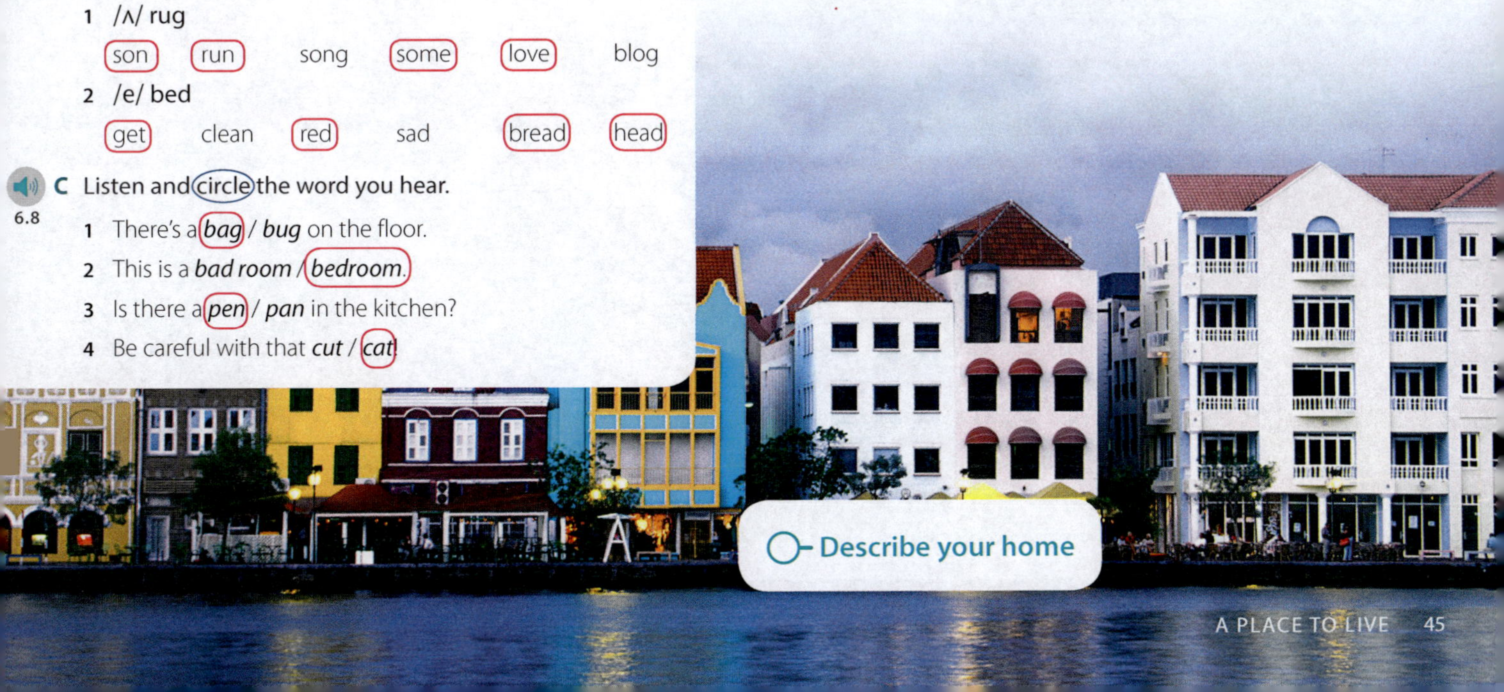

Describe your home

Café Hub

6.3 Left or right?

F– ask for and give directions

COMPREHENSION

A ▶ Watch the video. Are the sentences true (T) or false (F)? Correct the false sentences.

1 Gaby wants to take photos in the park. (T) / F
2 Sam gives directions to the park. T / (F) — The three customers give directions.
3 Newton Green park is near Sam's Café. (T) / F
4 The three men in the café are friends. T / (F) — They don't know each other.
5 Gaby asks her phone for directions. (T) / F

B ▶ Watch the video and match the locations of the park (a, b or c) with the three men (1, 2 and 3).

Man 1 c

Man 2 a

Man 3 b

USEFUL PHRASES

A Who says it? Sam, Man 1, Man 2 or Man 3?

1 Yes, it's very near. Man 1
2 OK everybody, let's just relax. Sam
3 You're both wrong. Man 3
4 Yes, calm down! Man 3
5 I'm not sure. Sam

B Complete the conversation with useful phrases from Exercise A.

Gaby: Is there a park near here?
Sam: A park ... [1] I'm not sure.
Man 1: Actually, there is a park near here. Newton Green.
Gaby: Newton Green.
Man 1: [2] Yes, it's very near. Go out of the café, turn left, then cross the road, then turn right.
Man 2: No, no, no. Go out of the café, turn left and cross the road. But then, turn left, not right.
Man 1: No, it's right.
Man 2: No, it's left.
Man 1: Right.
Man 2: Left.
Sam: [3] OK everybody, let's just relax.
Man 3: [4] Yeah, calm down!
[5] You're both wrong.

C ▶ 00:24–01:21 Watch part of the video again and check your answers.

6.3 Left or right?

LEAD-IN

Ask students to name any local parks or outdoor spaces in the area near your English class. Add simple question-word questions to the board, e.g. *Where is it? When do you go there? Why? Who with? What do you do there?* Students interview each other about how they use the park. Share feedback as a whole class.

COMPREHENSION

A ▶ Allow time for students to read through the sentences, then play the video. Students work together to decide if the sentences are true and correct the false sentences.

B ▶ Review the appearances of the men, eliciting differences (e.g. length and color of hair and beard). Allow time for students to discuss the task before watching the video, to see if they can recall the answers. Then play the video again. Check answers as a class.

USEFUL PHRASES

A Model the useful phrases for the students with natural and appropriate intonation and stress. Students discuss the phrases with a partner and decide who says which. Check answers as a whole class.

B Students work together to complete the conversation with the useful phrases from Exercise A.

C ▶ 00:24–01:21 Play the section of the video again for students to check their answers to Exercise B.

Extra activity

Students read the extract of the dialogue together. Encourage them to play around and experiment with intonation and tone of voice. They could try performing it to sound very angry or very sarcastic. Ask if this feels different to how they normally speak.

▶ VIDEO SCRIPT

S = Sam G = Gaby DG1 = Direction giver 1
DG2 = Direction giver 2 DG3 = Direction giver 3
P = Phone

S: Ah, are you a photographer?
G: Yes! Well, sometimes. Is there a park near here? I want to take some photos today.
S: A park? I'm not sure.
DG1: Actually, there is a park near here. Newton Green.
G: Newton Green.
DG1: Yes, it's very near. Go out of the café, turn left, then cross the road, then turn right.
DG2: No, no, no. Go out of the café, turn left and cross the road. But then, turn left, not right.
DG1: No, it's right.
DG2: No, it's left.
DG1: Right.
DG2: Left.
S: OK, everybody. Let's just relax.
DG3: Yeah, calm down. You're both wrong.
DG2: Excuse me?
DG1: What?
DG3: Look, don't cross the road. Go out of the café and turn left. Then go straight on. The park is on your left.
G: So, I go out of the café and turn left.
DG3: But don't cross the road.
DG1: No, cross the road, but then turn right.
DG2: Turn left.
DG3: I'm afraid you're both wrong.
DG1: How dare you!
DG2: I don't know who you think you are ...
DG1: I'm enjoying my tea here and suddenly you're Mr. Left or Mr. Right.
DG2: Sorry, who do you think you are?
DG3: It doesn't matter who I am, I know the way to the park. You clearly don't.
DG2: I have lived around here for 20 years!
S: Good luck!
DG2: Well, I don't think you do either.
DG3: It's going from here to the park! You hardly know the way to park, do you?
G: OK, phone. Directions to Newton Green, please.
P: Turn right.

TEACHING IDEA by David Seymour and Maria Popova

Vocabulary: City streets

Use this activity to review the Vocabulary section. Say this to your students:

I have a list of 21 things you can see on a city street, apart from stores and other buildings. In two teams, take turns guessing the things on my list and score a point every time you get one correct.

bicycle, bus stop, car, dog, drain, garbage can, graffiti, mailbox, motorcycle, pedestrian, pigeon, street lights, street performer, street signs, taxi, traffic lights, trash, tree, truck

METHODOLOGY HUB by Jim Scrivener

Individuals and groups: Motivation

Many learners have strong external reasons why they want to study (to pass an exam, to enter college, to get a promotion, to please their parents, etc). This is usually called external motivation. Others may be studying just for rewards within the work itself (the fun of learning, setting oneself a personal challenge, etc), usually referred to as internal motivation. In either case, the strength of their motivation will be a factor in determining how seriously they approach the work, how much time they set aside for it, how hard they push themselves, etc. You may see this reflected in things such as how often homework is done, how thoroughly new items are reviewed between classes, how 'tuned in' students are during class times. A frequent cause of difficulties within classes is when there is a significant mismatch of motivation levels among the course participants, e.g. some students who desperately need to pass an exam next month alongside others who want a relaxed chance to chat and play games in their new language.

6.3 Left or right?

FUNCTIONAL LANGUAGE

A Look through the symbols with students, concept checking the meaning of each one with gesture and questions. Students then complete the phrases with the words in the box. Elicit answers from the class. Clarify and practice the pronunciation of *straight* (/streɪt/) and the linking heard in *straight ahead* (i.e. *straight‿ahead* /streɪ təhɛd/).

B Students work alone at first to use the map to complete the directions. Allow time for students to compare their answers with a partner, adjusting as necessary. Then check answers as a whole class.

PRONUNCIATION

6.9 **A** Review the conversation and elicit the meaning of the underline (*stressed syllables*). Students listen to the conversation and follow along in their books.

6.9 **B** Model the conversation with a student for the rest of the class. Highlight the stressed syllables and show how the other syllables are reduced in volume, length and vowel clarity. Students then work in pairs to repeat the conversation. Monitor and encourage natural, appropriate stress.

C Ask students to change pairs and practice the conversation again with new partners.

SPEAKING

A Read through the task with students, and go through the example. Students then work in pairs to take turns asking for and giving directions from Sam's Café. Monitor and write a note about language use for feedback afterward. Help students problem-solve any issues with language at the end of this stage to prepare them for the next exercise.

B Students work in threes to write a conversation. Read through the instructions for each student to ensure each is clear about his or her role. Students then practice their conversations. Monitor and encourage appropriate stress on key information words. Also encourage students to work toward saying their part of the conversation rather than reading it from the page.

C Students then perform their conversations for the whole class. Students decide which conversation was the best.

Extra activity
Students work in pairs to prepare directions to a place near the location of your English class. Students then give the directions to the class without saying what the destination is. The rest of the class must guess.

METHODOLOGY HUB by Jim Scrivener

Classroom activities: Planning an activity

The basic building block of a lesson is the activity or task. We'll define this fairly broadly as 'something that learners do that involves them using or working with language to achieve some specific outcome'. The outcome may reflect a 'real-world' outcome (e.g. learners role-play buying train tickets at the station) or it may be a purely 'for-the-purposes-of-learning' outcome (e.g. learners fill in the blanks in 12 sentences with present perfect verbs). By this definition, all of the following are activities or tasks:

- Learners do a grammar exercise individually then compare answers with each other in order to better understand how a particular item of language is formed.
- Learners listen to a recorded conversation in order to answer some questions (in order to become better listeners).
- Learners write a formal letter requesting information about a product.
- Learners discuss and write some questions in order to make a questionnaire about people's eating habits.
- Learners read a newspaper article to prepare for a discussion.
- Learners play a vocabulary game in order to help learn words connected with cars and transportation.
- Learners repeat a number of sentences you say in order to improve their pronunciation of them.
- Learners role-play a store scene where a customer has a complaint.

Some things that happen in the classroom are not tasks. For example, picture a room where the teacher has started spontaneously discussing in a lengthy or convoluted manner the formation of passive voice sentences. What are students doing that has an outcome? Arguably, there is an implied task, namely, that students should 'listen and understand', but by not being explicit, there is a real danger that learners are not genuinely engaged in anything much at all.

This is a basic, important and frequently overlooked consideration when planning a lesson. As far as possible, make sure that your learners have some specific thing to do, whatever the stage of the lesson. Traditional lesson planning has tended to see the lesson as a series of things that the teacher does. By turning it around and focusing much more on what the students do, we are likely to think more about the actual learning that might arise and create a lesson that is more genuinely useful. (And if you plan everything in terms of what the students will do, you might find you worry less about what the teacher has to do!) Even for stages when you are 'presenting' language, be clear to yourself what it is that students are supposed to be doing and what outcome it is leading to. Think of a complete lesson as being a coherent sequence of such learner-targeted tasks.

GABY

SAM

LUCY

FUNCTIONAL LANGUAGE

Asking for and giving directions

A Complete the phrases with the words in the box.

Cross Go left near on out there Turn

Asking for directions

Is [1] there a park [2] near here?

Giving directions

Go [3] out of the café. 

Turn [4] left. 

[5] Turn right. 

[6] Cross the street. 

[7] Go straight ahead. 

The park is [8] on your left. 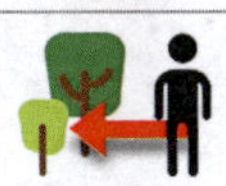

B Look at the map of the town in the Speaking section. Complete the correct directions to go from Sam's Café to Newton Green.

Go [1] out of the café and turn [2] right. Then turn [3] right and go [4] straight ahead. Then turn [5] left and then turn [6] right. The park is on your [7] left.

PRONUNCIATION

6.9 **A** Listen to the conversation and notice how the underlined words are stressed.

James: Is there a restaurant near here?

Sarah: Yes. Go out of the café and turn right. Then turn right and go straight ahead. Then turn right again and then turn left. The restaurant is on your left.

James: So, I go out of the café and turn right.

Sarah: Yes. Then turn right and go straight ahead.

James: Then turn right again and then left and the restaurant is on my left. Perfect.

6.9 **B** Work in pairs. Listen again and repeat the conversation. Copy the stress.

C SPEAK Work in pairs. Practice the conversation in Exercise A.

SPEAKING

A PREPARE Work in pairs. Take turns asking for and giving directions from Sam's Café. Use the map below.

A: Is there a movie theater near here?

B: Yes. Go out of Sam's Café and turn left. Then turn left and then left again. The movie theater is on your left.

B PRACTICE Work in groups of three. Write and practice a conversation. Use the map above or use a local map. Include three or more useful phrases.

Student A

- Ask for directions to a place on the map.

Student B

- Give wrong directions.

Student C

- Disagree and give the correct directions.

C PRESENT Perform your conversation for the class. Which conversation is the best?

Ask for and give directions

Unit 6 Writing

6 Writing — Write a review of a café

W — using *because*

A Work in pairs. Describe the picture. Use the words in the box to help you.

chair floor lamp table wall window

B Read the text. Why did the writer write it?

a to ask people to visit the café
(b) to say what he thinks about the café
c to tell the story of his visit to the café

Amazing hot chocolate! ★★★★☆

I love this café because it's modern and clean. There are really cool chairs and tables. The hot chocolate is excellent, but it's a little expensive! It's usually very busy and I sometimes wait 20 minutes or more for my hot chocolate. There's free internet so it's the perfect place to read your emails and text messages.

♡ 7 ⟲ 2

C Read the text again. What are the positive and negative things about the café?

Positive	Negative

Using *because*

We use *because* to give reasons and answer the question *why?*
I love this café *because* it's modern and clean.

D SPEAK Work in pairs. What is your opinion of this café?

WRITING

A PREPARE Think of a café that you like or don't like. Complete the table with your reasons.

Like	Dislike

B WRITE Write a short review of your café. Use the review in Exercise B as a model.

C PRESENT Read your review to your partner. Listen to your partner. When they finish ask questions for more information.

○— Write a review of a café

Answers

Positive
It's modern and clean.
There are really cool chairs and tables.
The hot chocolate is excellent.
There's free internet.
Negative
The hot chocolate is expensive.
It's usually busy.

Refer students to the review as a model for the writing task.

Students can swap reviews and edit their partner's writing.

Unit 6 Review

GRAMMAR

A Choose the correct options to complete the sentences.

1 *There's* / *There are* three theaters in my town.
2 *Are there* / *There are* any art galleries?
3 There aren't any *stores* / *park*.
4 *There's* / *Is there* a new café near my home.
5 A: Is there a market?
B: Yes, *there is* / *there's*.

B Complete the conversation with the correct form of *there is* or *there are*.

Aya: Please tell me about your new apartment. [1] Is there a living room?
Kay: Yes, [2] there is a living room. [3] There are also two bedrooms.
Aya: [4] Are there any stores nearby?
Kay: No, [5] there aren't. But [6] there's a large grocery store near the station.

VOCABULARY

A Complete the words to describe places in a town.

1 I always buy fresh food at the m a r k e t.
2 My friends sometimes play soccer in the p a r k.
3 They usually stay in a h o t e l when they go on vacation.
4 I go to the s t a t i o n every morning at 8 am to get the train.
5 We sometimes eat dinner at a r e s t a u r a n t near our house.

B Complete the sentences with prepositions of place and words for furniture.

There are two chairs and a desk in this room. There's a cushion [1] on one chair. There's a bag [2] under the other chair. There's a [3] lamp/clock and a [4] clock/lamp on the desk. There are books on the [5] bookshelf. There's a mirror [6] on the wall. There are some clothes in the [7] closet. There's a small [8] rug on the floor.

48 A PLACE TO LIVE

LEAD-IN

Write the names of local cafés on pieces of paper. Give one to each student. They each say three facts about their café, and the others guess. This can be a competition; the person who guesses first 'gets' the café, and the person with the most cafés wins.

WRITING

A Students take turns describing the picture; they could use three words each from the box, or they could both describe it.

B Students read the options first, then the text. Check the answer, making sure students identify the reasons for their choice in the text.

C Do one example first, e.g. *clean – positive*. Then students work individually to complete the task before checking in pairs and then with the whole class. Focus students on the *Using because* box, then check understanding and use by asking questions about the text, e.g. *Why is it a good place to read emails? Because there's free internet.*

D Students work in pairs. Encourage them to use *because* when giving reasons; you could demonstrate briefly first, if necessary.

WRITING TASK

A Students prepare individually. Encourage them to choose different cafés.

B While students write, monitor and help if necessary; refer them to the model answer rather than giving help directly.

C Students read their reviews to a partner, then answer questions about it. When students finish, you could ask them to walk around and do the same with other partners, and/or display their work on a board and read each other's. As an extra authentic activity, they could choose a café to meet in, if appropriate.

Performer with the Chinese State Circus, London, England.

A skill is a particular ability that involves special training and experience.

Ask students to label the photo if you need time to set up the class.

The quote urges us to be confident in our skills and abilities. As the ultimate decision-maker, if we decide something is possible for us, then we will be able to achieve this. It makes reference to the power of positive thinking.

John Burroughs (1837–1921) was an American writer and naturalist who was deeply interested in the natural world. He was a teacher and farmer but then began writing full time when he moved to the Hudson River Valley. His writing on nature was more literary than scientific and included poems as well as essays.

OBJECTIVES

- talk about your abilities
- talk about people's talents
- make polite requests
- write a competition entry

Work with a partner. Discuss the questions.

1 Look at the picture. What can you see?

2 Look at the picture again. Choose the correct options to complete the description.

There is a [1]*man / woman*. He has a lot of things on his [2]*head / hand*. He has [3]*black / gray* hair. There's a [4]*bag / bird* at the top.

3 Read the quote. Do you agree?

SKILLS 49

OBJECTIVES

Read the unit objectives to the class.

UNIT OPENER QUESTIONS

Focus the students on the picture of the circus performer and the act he is performing. Encourage them to guess things about the performer – his abilities, his training, how long it might have taken him to learn the balancing act. Ask them to name all the things they can see and build up a list of vocabulary in a column on the side of the board. Leave this there for the whole lesson referring to the words as and when they come up.

Then ask students to look at the description in Question 2. Go through the answers as a class. Next, ask students to read the quote again and ask if they agree or disagree. Encourage students to tell their partner and discuss their answers. Elicit views from several students and add vocabulary to the board for support for expressing their opinions.

WORKSHEETS

Lesson 7.1 What can you do?

Vocabulary: Abilities (W23)

Grammar: *can/can't* (W24)

Lesson 7.2 He's amazing!

Vocabulary: Adjectives (W25)

Grammar: Possessive *'s* (W26)

7.1 What can you do?

Talk about your abilities

G – *can/can't* P – *can/can't*: /æ/ and /ə/ V – abilities

READING

A PREPARE TO READ Work in pairs. Look at the pictures (a–c) in the article and discuss the questions.

Suggested answers

1 What can you see in the pictures? sports; people; mountains; rock; sea/ocean
2 What sport do you think each picture shows? climbing; flying; diving; swimming

B READ FOR MAIN IDEA Read the article quickly. Choose the correct options.

1 This article is about what some …
a animals can't do. (b) people can do.
2 This writer talks to three people about …
(a) their abilities. b their pets.
3 The people can do …
(a) amazing things. b useful things.

C READ FOR KEY INFORMATION Read the article again. Choose the correct numbers to complete the sentences.

2 4 (x2) 6 80 500

1 Luis can climb ___500___ meters up a mountain in ___4___ hours.
2 Seon-Yeong can fly for ___4___ kilometers. She can be in the air for ___2___ minutes.
3 Ireen can swim down ___80___ meters. She can be underwater for ___6___ minutes.

ANIMALS VS HUMANS

As we all know, animals can do many things that humans can't do. Birds can fly, fish can swim and breathe underwater, and monkeys can climb. Humans can't. Or can we? This week we talk to three amazing humans about their abilities. Ex D Q1 Ex B

Interviewer: Luis, what exactly is a free climber?

A free climber doesn't use ropes to help them climb, only to stop them from falling. Sometimes it's a little bit dangerous. I can't climb for very long because it's difficult and I get tired. I can climb about 500 meters in four hours. Ex D Q2

Interviewer: Seon-Yeong, can you really fly?

Yes, I can! I'm a wingsuit flyer in my free time. Birds take off from the ground, but I can't. I jump from somewhere really high, like the top of a mountain or from a plane. I can fly for about four kilometers, and I'm usually in the air for two minutes. Ex D Q3

Interviewer: Ireen, you're a free diver – how long can you stay underwater?

I can hold my breath for about six minutes. I don't have an air tank, so I am very careful when I dive. I can dive about 80 meters down and then I need to come up again. I love it, it's so quiet underwater! Ex D Q4

a

b

c

D READ FOR DETAIL Read the article again. Are the statements true (T) or false (F)?

1 Animals and humans have some of the same skills. (T) / F
2 Free climbing is very dangerous. T / (F) Sometimes it's a little bit dangerous.
3 Wingsuit flyers need to take off from a high place. (T) / F
4 Free divers don't take any extra air when they go underwater. (T) / F

E SPEAK Work in groups. Answer the questions

1 Which sport in the text do you want to try?
2 Are there other sports you want to try?

I want to try wingsuit flying – it looks really fun!

GRAMMAR

can/can't

A WORK IT OUT Read the examples from the article. Choose the correct option to complete the rule.

Animals can do many things that humans can't do.

A: Can you really fly?

B: Yes, I can!

can/can't

We use *can/can't* to talk about abilities / *routines*.

B WORK IT OUT Read the examples again. Choose the correct options to complete the rules.

can/can't

1 After *can* and *can't* we use a **verb with *to*** / **verb without *to***. We always use the same form of the verb with all subjects.
2 We **use** / **don't use** *do* and *don't* in questions and negative sentences with *can/can't*.

C Go to the Grammar Hub on page 110.

7.1 What can you do?

LEAD-IN

On the board, write some activities the students might know, e.g. *swim*, *speak English*, *cook*, *drive a car*. Then draw a scale numbered 1 to 5, with *very easy* at one end and *very difficult* at the other. Write the activities above the numbers to show how easy/difficult you find each activity. Explain to the students. Students then create a similar scale for themselves and compare their scales in small groups to find who they are most similar to.

READING

A Students work in pairs to discuss the questions. Encourage them to give as many ideas as they can about the pictures.

B Check that students understand the options, then they read individually to answer them. Set a short time limit to encourage gist reading rather than close reading – demonstrate first how they could do this, e.g. by drawing a finger down the page and looking for key words. Check answers with the whole class.

C Students read individually, then check in pairs. Go through the answers as a whole class.

D Students read the questions first, and see if they can remember any answers. Then they read the article carefully – encourage close reading. Monitor, directing them back to the text if they have any difficulties, rather than giving answers. Check answers with the whole class, asking students to justify their choices by reading out the parts of the text that give the information.

E Direct students to read the questions and check that they understand the task. Then ask a strong student to read the example aloud. Students work in small groups of three or four to discuss their answers. Elicit some feedback and write some preferences on the board; use it to show/discuss the most popular choices.

GRAMMAR

A Put students into pairs to read the examples, discuss and choose the correct rule. Give the answer and check understanding.

B Students work in pairs to complete the rule box. Write the answers on the board and check understanding; give some examples, then check by asking, e.g. *can – to drive – he?* Elicit *He can drive*.

C Direct students to the **Grammar Hub** (see below and TB51).

D Write the first question and answer on the board, and ask students to call out the correct order for each. Write them up. Then ask students to continue the exercise. Elicit and write the questions and answers on the board. Use the **Grammar Worksheet** on page W24 for extra practice.

GRAMMAR HUB

7.1

can / can't

	Positive	Negative
I/you/he/she/it/we/they	**I can** swim. **They can** fly.	**I can't** swim. **They can't** fly.

- We use *can/can't* when we want to talk about someone's ability or skills.

  I can run.

  I can't drive a car.
- The form of *can/can't* never changes.

  He can swim. NOT ~~*He cans swim.*~~

  She can't climb. NOT ~~*She cans not climb.*~~

	Question	Positive short answer	Negative short answer
I/you/he/she/it/we/they	**Can you** climb? **Can they** live underwater?	**Yes, I/we can.** **Yes, they can.**	**No, I/we can't.** **No, they can't.**

- We also ask *wh-* questions with *can*.

  What can you do?

  Which animals can fly?

Be careful!

- *Can* is followed by a verb without *to*.

  I can swim. NOT ~~*I can to swim.*~~

7.1 What can you do?

PRONUNCIATION

7.1

A Play the audio while students listen. Play it again while students listen and repeat. Play the audio as many times as necessary if students have difficulty hearing the difference between the sounds. Write the phonemes on the board and practice the pronunciation of them in isolation.

B Demonstrate one or two examples with you and a student, then put students into pairs to ask and answer the questions. Monitor, encouraging students to use correct pronunciation of the three sounds in *can/can't* (**/kæn/**, **/kən/**, **/kænt/**).

VOCABULARY

A Students complete the sentences individually, then check in pairs. Practice pronunciation of the vocabulary items.

B Do the first question with students as an example, then ask them to work individually or in pairs. Monitor and help as necessary, then check answers with the class.

C Students write the phrases under the pictures individually. Give the answers to the whole class.

D Direct students to the **Vocabulary Hub** (see TB97). Use the **Vocabulary Worksheet** on page W23 for extra practice.

SPEAKING

A Go through the list, demonstrating the actions and saying, e.g. *I can't ride a motorcycle – I can draw!* Add another to show that they can go beyond the list, e.g. *I can speak German*. Then put students into pairs and tell them to choose five abilities.

B Students work in pairs to write five questions using their ideas in a list (1–5) on a piece of paper or their notebook; both students need to write them. Then tell them to draw two columns, one with a check mark (✓) and one with an (✗), after the questions.

C Tell the pairs of students to stand up and walk around, asking their questions to other pairs. Tell them to add a check mark or an (✗) next to the answers, so they are doing a survey to find people who can do the activities on the list.

D Put one student from each pair into groups. Ask them to report their survey findings, as in the examples. Monitor, but try not to correct at this stage – write a note about any feedback you want to give after the activity. When they have finished, ask students what surprising results came out of the activity, e.g. three students can ski but no students can cook! As a follow-up, they could write up the results in a paragraph and display it on the wall or share it on a group site.

GRAMMAR HUB

7.1

can / can't

A Choose the correct options.

1. I can (*walk*) / *to walk* all day.
2. He (*can't*) / *not* speak English.
3. (*Can you*) / *You can* play chess?
4. I can swim but my brother *isn't* / (*can't*).
5. *They can* / (*Can they*) climb with a rope?
6. **A:** Can you swim?
   B: Yes I (*can*) / *swim*.
7. What things (*can you*) / *you can* do?
8. Dogs can swim but they *not* / (*can't*) fly.

B Write *can* or *can't* to complete the sentences.

1. We ___can___ climb this mountain – it's not that big!
2. Fish ___can't___ fly.
3. My brother ___can't___ speak French – he's terrible at languages.
4. Sam's manager ___can___ play the guitar. She's very talented.
5. She can drive a car but she ___can't___ ride a motorcycle.

C Complete the short answers.

1. Can you swim? Yes, ___I can___.
2. Can you play guitar? No, ___I can't___.
3. Can they swim? Yes, ___they can___.
4. Can John speak French? Yes, ___he can___.
5. Can she speak Spanish? No, ___she can't___.
6. Can fish fly? No, ___they can't___.

D **PRACTICE** There is one mistake in each sentence. Correct the sentences.

1. I can to climb without ropes.
   ___I can climb without ropes.___
2. We not can jump very high.
   ___We can't jump very high.___
3. It can flies for hundreds of kilometers.
   ___It can fly for hundreds of kilometers.___
4. He cans swim underwater for a long time.
   ___He can swim underwater for a long time.___
5. Do you can dive ten meters down?
   ___Can you dive ten meters down?___
6. No, I don't can!
   ___No, I can't!___
7. They can do play musical instruments.
   ___They can play musical instruments.___
8. We can to run very far.
   ___We can run very far.___
9. She can speaks English.
   ___She can speak English.___
10. Yes, I do can.
    ___Yes, I can!___

➤ Go back to page 50.

D PRACTICE Order the words to make questions and answers.

1 A: you / swim / can

Can you swim ?

B: can / yes, / I

Yes, I can .

2 A: a monkey / fly / can

Can a monkey fly ?

B: no, / can't / it

No, it can't .

3 A: you / can / what / do

What can you do ?

B: can / a mountain / I / climb

I can climb a mountain .

4 A: which / can / live / animal / underwater

Which animal can live underwater ?

B: live / can / underwater / a fish

A fish can live underwater .

PRONUNCIATION

can/can't: /æ/ and /ə/

7.1 **A** Listen and repeat the sounds, words and examples.

/æ/ can — **A:** Can you climb?
B: Yes, I can.

/ə/ can — **A:** What can you do?
B: I can swim.

/æ/ can't — I can't fly.

B SPEAK Work in pairs. Ask questions like the ones in Exercise A. Give answers that are true for you.

A: Can you climb?

B: Yes, I can. I can't climb a mountain. I can climb a tree! What can you do?

VOCABULARY

Abilities

A Complete the sentences with the verbs in the box.

cook dance draw juggle sing ski

1 Helia can draw .

2 Gus can ski .

3 Gina can cook .

4 Pablo can dance .

5 Mira can sing .

6 Alex can juggle .

B Match the verbs (1–6) to the nouns (a–f) to make phrases.

1 drive e — 3 do b — 5 ride f

2 play c — 4 paint d — 6 speak a

a French — c the guitar — e a car

b yoga — d a picture — f a motorcycle

C Write the correct phrases from Exercise B under each picture.

a ride a motorcycle

b speak French

c do yoga

d drive a car

e play the guitar

f paint a picture

D Go to the **Vocabulary Hub** on **page 125**.

SPEAKING

A PREPARE You are going to interview your classmates. Work in pairs. Choose five abilities from the ideas below or use your own ideas.

ride a motorcycle draw
swim climb a mountain
juggle ski play the piano
speak Spanish dance
cook drive a car

B PLAN Write one question about each ability you chose.

Can you ride a motorcycle?

C PRACTICE Go around the class. Find people who can do each activity on your list.

A: Can you ride a motorcycle?

B: Yes, I can.

D REPORT Work in groups. Tell the group the results of your survey.

A: Three people can ride a motorcycle.

B: Six people can draw.

Talk about your abilities

7.2 He's amazing!

Talk about people's talents

S listening for pronoun reference V adjectives G possessive 's P possessive 's

LISTENING

A PREPARE TO LISTEN Look at the picture. Choose the correct words to complete the sentences. There are three words you don't need.

cellos dancers guitars musicians pianos violins

1 These people are ___musicians___.
2 Two people have ___cellos___.
3 Three people have ___violins___.

B LISTEN FOR GIST (7.2) Listen to a radio show. Find and correct three mistakes in the summary.

Sheku Kanneh-Mason is a musician. He has ~~eight~~ six brothers and sisters. ~~They all~~ Braimah, Isata and Sheku study at the Royal Academy of Music. Their parents ~~play~~ don't play musical instruments.

Listening for pronoun reference

We use pronouns (*I*, *you*, *we*, *they*, *he*, *she*, *it*, *this*, *that*) and adverbs (*there*, *here*) so we don't need to repeat names of people and places. Listen for a name or a place and think about the pronoun or adverb the speaker will use in their next sentence.

*Sheku Kanneh-Mason's an amazing musician. **He**'s the winner of the 2016 BBC Young Musician of the Year Award.*

*Oliver: Are they students at the **Royal Academy of Music**, as well?*

*Carrie: No, they don't go **there** – not yet anyway.*

C LISTEN FOR DETAIL (7.2) Listen again. Match the names of people and places (1–6) with their connection to Sheku (a–f).

1 Braimah — c
2 Isata — b
3 Kadiatu and Stuart — a
4 Nottingham — d
5 Royal Academy of Music — e

a his parents
b his sister
c his brother
d where he lives
e where he studies

D SPEAK Work in pairs. Answer the questions.

1 Can you play a musical instrument? Which one(s)?
2 Who is talented in your family? What can they do?

VOCABULARY
Adjectives

A Read the sentences from the radio show. The underlined word in sentence 1 is an adjective. Underline the adjectives in sentences 2 and 3.

1 *Every day we talk about an interesting person.*
2 *Today's person is a young musician.*
3 *It's difficult to find the time to play an instrument ...*

B Match the adjectives in Exercise A with their definitions.

1 Someone who is ___young___ has lived for only a short time.
2 Something that is ___difficult___ is not easy to do or understand.
3 Something, or someone, that is ___interesting___ is exciting and unusual.

C Read the sentences in Exercise A again. Choose the correct option to complete the rules.

1 We use adjectives ***before*** / ***after*** a noun.
2 We use adjectives on their own ***before*** / ***after*** the verb *be*.

D Underline the adjectives in these sentences.

1 He's an amazing musician.
2 My sisters are all great swimmers.
3 Fionn and Carla are both bad dancers.
4 Lois's singing is terrible.
5 Oliver's a talented artist.
6 Juan's dad is awful at cooking.
7 This is a boring book.
8 I eat a lot of healthy food.

E Work in pairs. Complete the table with the adjectives in Exercise D. Are they positive (+) or negative (–)?

Positive	Negative
amazing	bad
great	terrible
talented	awful
healthy	boring

F SPEAK Use the adjectives in the box to complete the sentences so they are true for you. Tell your partner.

amazing bad boring difficult easy good OK talented terrible

1 I'm a(n) ________ musician.
2 I think it's ________ to play the cello.
3 I think it's ________ to have a big family.
4 I think music with violins and cellos is ________.

7.2 He's amazing!

LEAD-IN

Write a list of five activities on the board such as *sing*, *play the piano*, *dance*, etc and clarify meaning by miming as required. Then make a sentence about each using *I can* or *I can't*. Students have to guess which are true and which are false. Students then do the same in small groups.

LISTENING

7.2 **A–D** Focus students on the picture. Ask if they know anything about these people or this type of music. Students listen and complete the exercises. They can check in pairs, then check as a class.

VOCABULARY

A Focus students' attention on the example and draw a line from the adjective to show that it describes the person. Then ask students to underline the adjectives in 2 and 3. Elicit the answers and start to create a list of adjectives on the board.

B–F Students do the exercises individually, then check in pairs. Check answers as a class. Use the **Vocabulary Worksheet** on page W25 for extra practice.

AUDIO SCRIPT

7.2

Listening, Exercise B
O = Oliver C = Carrie

O: Welcome to *The People Show*. Today's special person is a very interesting young musician.
Ex C Q4 His name's Sheku Kanneh-Mason and he's from Nottingham in the UK. Tell us more, Carrie.

C: Hi, Oliver. Sheku Kanneh-Mason's an amazing musician. He's the winner of the 2016 BBC Young Musician of the Year Award, and he was a musician at Prince Harry and Meghan Markle's wedding in May 2018.

O: What instrument does he play?

Ex B **C:** He plays the cello. But Sheku isn't the only musician in his family. He has six brothers and sisters, and they're all wonderful musicians.

O: Six? Wow! So, there are seven children in the Kanneh-Mason family?

Ex C Q1 & Q2 Ex C Q5 **C:** That's right. Braimah is Sheku's brother. He plays the violin. Isata is Sheku's sister, and she plays the piano. They are all students at London's Royal Academy of Music. Sheku also has four younger sisters.

O: What instruments do they play?

C: Konya and Aminata play the violin, and Jeneba and Mariatu play the cello. These four can all also play the piano.

Ex B **O:** Are they students at the Royal Academy of Music, as well?

C: No, they don't go there – not yet anyway. They're too young right now.

O: So, is everyone in the Kanneh-Mason family a musician?

Ex C Q3 Ex B **C:** No, they aren't. Sheku's parents' names are Kadiatu and Stuart. They don't play any musical instruments.

O: I'm not surprised. It's difficult to find the time to play an instrument when you have seven children!

GRAMMAR HUB

7.2

Possessive 's

Singular noun	This is **John's** sister.
Singular noun ending with -s	Is that **Chris's** brother? Is that **Chris'** brother?
Plural noun	These are the **girls'** friends.

- We use a possessive 's to show that something belongs to someone.
  This is Mark's bag. = This bag belongs to Mark.
- With a singular noun, we add 's to show something belongs to that person.
  This is the boy's dad.
- With a singular noun that ends in -s, we can add 's or ' after the -s.
  This is James's sister.
  This is James' sister.
- For plural nouns that end in -s, we add the ' after the -s.
  My cousins' house. (= I have more than one cousin and they share the same house.)
  What are your parents' names? (= You have more than one parent.)

Be careful!

- We also use 's as a contraction of *is* or *has*.
  His name's Bill. (= his name is)
  He's been out with his brother. (= he has)

7.2 He's amazing!

GRAMMAR

A Do an example on the board, using people in the class, e.g. *Jan is Eric's friend*. Then ask students to underline the words with the possessive *'s* in their books before checking answers in pairs.

B–F Students work individually to complete the activities before discussing their ideas with a partner. Then check answers as a class.

G Direct students to the **Grammar Hub** (see below and TB52).

H Tell the students about your family (or friends), using the model as an example. Then put students into pairs to talk about the topics. Monitor and help if necessary.

I Put one of each pair of students into groups to talk about their partner. Monitor, encouraging fluency, making sure students use the possessive *'s* where necessary. Ask them to share any interesting information with the whole class, and encourage students to ask follow-up questions if possible. Use the **Grammar Worksheet** on page W26 for extra practice.

PRONUNCIATION

7.3 **A** Read aloud the names in the table and focus on the final *s* sounds. Play the audio while students listen. Play it again while students repeat.

7.4; 7.5 **B–C** Students listen and identify the different sounds. Check answers as a class.

SPEAKING HUB

A Put students into pairs of A and B, and direct Student Bs to the **Communication Hub** (see TB97).

B You could group all Student As together and all Student Bs together to help each other write the questions.

C Pair As and Bs together to ask and answer questions. Since this is an information fill in the blank exercise, it is important to seat them so that they cannot see the information but have to speak and listen to complete the exercise, e.g. face to face or back to back.

D Students repeat the exercise with the new information and a different partner.

E Give students a few minutes to think about someone they find amazing. Demonstrate with someone you find amazing first, then put students into pairs to talk about their choices. Try to encourage fluency rather than accuracy at this stage, but write down any relevant mistakes and effective examples of language use and give feedback on them to the whole class at the end.

Extra activity

In a whole-class circle, start the chain by saying, e.g. *My favorite day is Wednesday*. The student next to you repeats your sentence using the possessive *s* and then adds another sentence, e.g. *X's favorite day is Wednesday. My favorite color is blue*. The next student continues the chain by repeating the two sentences using possessive *s* and adding their own sentence, choosing the topic of the sentence. Continue until the chain breaks. Then start again from that point. See how long the chain can get.

GRAMMAR HUB

7.2

Possessive *'s*

A There is one mistake in each sentence. Find and correct the mistakes.

1. This is my ~~friend~~ *friend's* sister, Mary.
2. Sebastian is ~~Fiona~~ Fiona's brother.
3. John's ~~brothers~~ brothers' names are Philip and Frederick.
4. My ~~sisters'~~ sister's name is Sandra.
5. I like ~~Davids'~~ David's house.
6. Do you know ~~Angus~~ Angus's/Angus' manager?
7. These are my ~~parent's~~ parents, Jill and Greg.
8. Where is Harry's ~~parents~~ parents' house?

B Rewrite the phrases using *'s* or *'*.

1. the uncle of my friend = *my friend's uncle*
2. the office of Costas = Costas's/Costas' office
3. the names of my parents = my parents' names
4. the favorite restaurant of Keith = Keith's favorite restaurant
5. the daughter of my manager = my manager's daughter
6. the company of his cousins = his cousins' company
7. the school of their sons = their sons' school
8. the desk of Peter = Peter's desk

C Read the text and write *'s* or *'* in the correct places. There are six changes, including the example.

I have a busy week this week. On Monday, there's an all-day meeting in my manager*'s* office, starting at 9 am. Then, I have to go to my son's school (I have a son and a daughter) to talk to his teachers. On Tuesday, I go to Tampa for three days. We usually go in my colleague's car. I always stay at a friend's house in Tampa. My parents live near there, so I usually see them. My parents' house is very small, so I can't stay there. Then, on Friday, we have a meeting at our company's Orlando office. Finally, my vacation starts on Saturday!

➤ Go back to page 53.

GRAMMAR
Possessive 's

A Read the sentences from the radio show. Underline the words with the possessive 's.

1 Braimah is Sheku's brother.
2 Sheku's parents' names are Kadiatu and Stuart.

B **WORK IT OUT** Choose the correct option to complete the rule.

We use 's and ' to say that someone or something *belongs to* / *happens to* someone or something.

C **WORK IT OUT** Read the sentences again. Add 's or ' to complete the rules and examples.

Possessive 's

We use [1] 's after singular nouns: *Sheku is Braimah* [2] 's *brother.*
We use [3] ' after plural nouns ending in -s: *His sisters* [4] ' *names are Isata, Konya, Jeneba, Aminatu and Mariatu.*

D **PRACTICE** Add 's or ' in the correct place to complete the sentences.

1 My mother name is Kali. *My mother's name is Kali.*
2 Luke's favorite instrument is the violin.
3 My two cousins' house is in the city.
4 Alice's parents' names are Olive and Oscar.
5 All of the musicians' instruments are in the next room.
6 Alberto is Carlos's brother.

E **WORK IT OUT** Read the information and choose the correct options.

Possessive 's, *is* and *has*

We also use 's as a short form of *is* or *has*.
His name's Sheku Kanneh-Mason. (= his name [1] *is* / *has*)
He's done his homework. (= he [2] *is* / *has*)

F **PRACTICE** Choose the correct meaning of 's in these sentences.

1 Mark's my father. *is* / *has* / *possessive 's*
2 My father's name is Mark. *is* / *has* / *possessive 's*
3 Mark's gone to the store. *is* / *has* / *possessive 's*

G Go to the **Grammar Hub** on **page 110**.

H **SPEAK** Work in pairs. Tell your partner about the following things …

- your family
- your home
- your hobby

My sister is a musician. My home is in Costa Rica. My hobby is swimming.

I **SPEAK** Work in groups. Tell them about your partner. Use possessive 's.

Erica's sister is a musician. Erica's home is in Costa Rica. Erica's hobby is swimming.

PRONUNCIATION
Possessive 's

A 7.3 Listen to how we say the *s* at the end of each of the names in the table.

/z/	/s/	/ɪz/
Aminata's	Albert's	Angus's
Anna's	Juliet's	Alex's

B 7.4 Listen to three more names. Write them in the table.

Alex's Anna's Juliet's

C 7.5 Choose the correct pronunciation for the possessive 's at the end of the names. Listen, check and repeat.

1 Marcus's /z/ /s/ /ɪz/
2 Tom's /z/ /s/ /ɪz/
3 Junko's /z/ /s/ /ɪz/
4 Carlos's /z/ /s/ /ɪz/
5 Bec's /z/ /s/ /ɪz/
6 Max's /z/ /s/ /ɪz/

SPEAKING HUB

A Work in pairs. Student A – Stay on this page. Student B – Go to the **Communication Hub** on **page 133**.

B **PREPARE** Read the information about this person. Write questions to find the missing information.

Student A answers:
HIFUMI ABE is from [1] Japan. He is good at judo. He is a world champion. His sister's name is [2] Uta. She is good at judo, too. [3] Uta is the 2017 Junior World Champion. They are the winners of the 2017 Tokyo Grand Slam.

1 Where is Hifumi from? 2 What …? 3 Who …?

C **DISCUSS** Work in pairs. Ask your partner questions to complete the missing information. Answer your partner's questions.

D **REPEAT** Repeat with the information below.

Student A answers:
JONATHAN BROWNLEE is from England. He is good at [1] triathlons – three events in one race. He can swim, ride a bicycle and run – and he's fast! His brother is good at [2] triathlons, too. His brother's name is Alistair. They both have [3] Olympic medals.

E **REFLECT** Think of another amazing person. Tell your partner about them.

Talk about people's talents

Café Hub

7.3 New hair

F– make polite requests

COMPREHENSION

A ▶ 00.54–02:41 Watch the first part of the video and answer the questions.

1 Who is Lisa? the hairdresser

2 What sort of hairstyle does Gaby want? something different

3 What do you think Gaby's new hairstyle is like? Students' own answers

B ▶ 02:42–02:57 Watch the end of the video. What is Gaby's new hairstyle? Do you like it?
Gaby has purple hair / the same hair as Lisa.

C When Gaby says *Wow!* what does she mean?

1 I love it.

(2) I hate it.

3 It's OK.

D Complete the sentences with the words in the box.

concert	hairstyle	Lisa's Hair	magazine	Spain	three o'clock

a Gaby arrives at the hairdresser's at three o'clock. 5

b Lucy invites Gaby to a friend's concert. 1

c Gaby calls Lisa's Hair. 3

d The hairdresser loves Spain. 4

e Gaby wants to change her hairstyle. 2

f Gaby reads a magazine. 6

E ▶ Put the events (a–f) in Exercise D in the correct order (1–6). Then watch the video again and check your answers.

FUNCTIONAL LANGUAGE

Making polite requests

A Underline the polite phrases. Who said it?

1 So, Gaby what ***do you want*** / ***would you like***?
a Gaby (b) Lisa

2 ***I'd like*** / ***I want*** something different, please.
(a) Gaby b Lisa

B Complete the phrases by putting the word in parentheses in the correct place.

1 Three o'clock is fine. Can I *have* your phone number, please? (have)

2 I'd like to book an appointment, please. (to)

3 Is that Lisa's Hair? (that)

4 Do you have time today? (Do)

5 Yes, it is. (it)

6 Yes, today's good. What time would you like to come? (like)

7 Yeah sure! When would you like to come? (would)

7.3 New hair

LEAD-IN

Ask students to describe what they can see in the picture and to guess where the place is, giving reasons for their answer. When they guess *hairdresser's* (you can ask students to search the text on the page for clues to help them to guess), share some information about your hairdresser, if appropriate. For example, *I go to Lulu's every two months. I pay $12. It takes 20 minutes.* Students can share similar details.

COMPREHENSION

A ▸ 00:54–02:41 Read through the questions with students and then play the video. Students compare their answers with a partner before checking as a whole class.

B ▸ 02:42–02:57 Encourage a personal response to the final question (there is obviously no correct answer) and ask students to explain their views.

C Say *Wow* with appropriate intonation and then elicit what Gaby means when she says it. (You could show how important intonation is at this point by saying *Wow* with different intonation and, therefore, different meaning, asking the students to decipher the meaning.)

D Students work in pairs to complete the sentences with the words in the box. Check answers as a whole class.

E ▸ Students number the events in Exercise D in order. Play the video again for students to check.

FUNCTIONAL LANGUAGE

A Work together as a class to identify the correct words to complete the polite phrases and to decide who says them.

B Students look at the example phrases and then work alone to add the word in parentheses to the correct place in the sentences. Students then compare with a partner. (They will use the video in Exercise D to give their answers a final check.)

VIDEO SCRIPT

L = Lucy G = Gaby Li = Lisa

L: Hi Gaby, would you like to come to my friend's concert tonight?
G: Yes! What time?
L: Eight o'clock. It's at the Hackney Club.
Li: Hiya!
G: Hola! Sorry, hi! Is that Lisa's Hair?
Li: Yeah.
G: Great! I'd like to …
Li: Are you Spanish?
G: Yes, I'm Spanish. I'd like to …
Li: Oh, really? I love Spain! Sunshine, tapas. Oh, I need a holiday.
G: Yes, holidays are great. Anyway, I'd like to book an appointment, please.
Li: Yeah, sure! When would you like to come?
G: Do you have time today?
Li: Yes. Today is good. What time would you like to come?
G: Er, three o'clock?
Li: Three o'clock is fine. Can I have your phone number, please?
G: Sure.
Li: So, Gaby. What would you like?
G: I'd like something new and different, please.
Li: Different. I know exactly what to do. Just relax. OK, Gaby. Are you ready to see the new you?
G: Yes.
Li: So? What do you think?
G: Wow.

METHODOLOGY HUB by Jim Scrivener

Working on appropriacy

A lot of work in the area of function is to do with common sense and common politeness – and most of all to do with an awareness of audience. This, of course, is partly cultural. We can help students become more aware of appropriacy by getting them to consider:

- Who are you talking/writing to? How well do you know them?
- How formal/informal is the relationship?
- Where are you? What unwritten rules or codes of conduct apply?

Some ideas for integrating functional work into a course:

- focusing on a functional area and studying a number of exponents;
- role plays: considering what to say in particular relationships;
- listening: working out relationships between speakers;
- deciding how different situations make one sentence mean different things;
- building dialogues and picture-story conversations;
- acting out play scripts;
- writing letters to different people;
- altering written conversations to change the relationship.

C Concept check the diagram with students so they understand it represents a conversation with two people speaking. Students then work in pairs to complete the conversation with phrases from Exercise B.

D ▶ 01:01–02:05 Play the section of the video for students to check their answers.

> **Extra activity**
> Build up the conversation from Exercise C on the board, and run a disappearing dialogue activity.
> Write the full conversation on the board and ask learners to practice it in pairs. Once students are comfortable with the exchanges, remove a couple of words from each of the turns. Students continue to practice the conversation, recalling the words to fill in the blanks you have created. Continue in the same way until the dialogue has completely disappeared from the board. Students continue to practice the conversation until eventually they can recall everything.

PRONUNCIATION

7.6 **A** Clarify the meaning of intonation through modeling *Wow* again, writing it on the board and adding arrows to show your intonation. Highlight that intonation provides meaning and also organization to what we say.

7.6 **B** Students listen and repeat the conversation as a whole class. Use gestures to help the students to fully engage with intonation and the direction it is moving at the end of the questions (*up for* yes/no *questions and down for* Wh- *questions*).

> **Extra activity**
> Ask students to make the dialogue impolite. Elicit what they would have to change, e.g. language, intonation, tone or gestures if face to face. Students could write a new dialogue where either the customer or the person they are booking the appointment with is rude. They can practice and perform the conversation for the class. Discuss what aspects make the person impolite and whether this is the same in different languages and cultures.

SPEAKING

A Read through the task with students, adding one line of the conversation to the board and demonstrating which information to change. Students then create a new conversation in pairs, using information from the table to help.

B Demonstrate completing the diary with check marks to show when you are free. Ask students to add six check marks to the diary, covering *today* and *tomorrow* (they should obviously include times for *today* which are later than the time doing the activity).

C Read through the conversation in the book with a strong student. Clarify how the people in the conversation manage to find a time which suits both and that this appointment can be written in the student's diary. Then model an improvised conversation with a student, showing that information has been changed. Students mingle and complete their diaries with appointments.

METHODOLOGY HUB by Jim Scrivener

Intonation

Intonation is sometimes referred to as the 'music' of the language, and we use it as a kind of oral equivalent of written punctuation. It is closely connected to prominence, for the main movement of intonation begins at the tonic syllable. This movement can be upwards (a rise), downwards (a fall), a rise with a fall (a rise–fall), a fall with a rise (a fall–rise) or flat. Intonation has a definite effect on meaning and also gives us information about the speaker's attitude.

It is hard to teach intonation systematically because, although there are some common patterns, there are few clear rules, and many people with an 'unmusical' ear find it hard to recognize or categorize intonation patterns. It is, however, so important that it is essential to include work on intonation in most courses. Many learners speak English with a flat intonation, which can sound boring or uninteresting. Using wrong intonation can also give offense.

Some ideas for working on intonation:

- Get students to mark intonation patterns on conversations. (How can you mark them? Arrows? Lines? Music? Write the words in a wiggly way to reflect the movement.)
- Get students to say the same single word (e.g. *hello*) with different intonation to convey completely different meanings.
- Use these differences to prepare and practice some one-word conversations, e.g.:

  A: Lunch?

  B: No.

  A: Tomorrow?

  B: Maybe.
- Hum/whistle/sing the sentence without words before you say it.
- Indicate intonation with hand gestures, waves, etc.
- Exaggerate intonation (this can be very funny).
- Exaggerate lack of intonation.
- Encourage students to 'feel' the emotion as they speak. Emotions of anger, interest, surprise, boredom, etc can naturally power the intonation.

GABY

SAM

LUCY

C Complete the conversation with the phrases from Exercise B.

1 *Is that Lisa's Hair?*

Yes, 2 it is.

3 I'd like to book an appointment, please.

4 Yeah sure! When would you like to come?

5 Do you have time today?

6 Yes, today's good. What time would you like to come?

7 *Three o'clock?*

8 Three o'clock is fine. Can I have your phone number, please?

Sure.

D 01:01–02:05 Watch part of the video again and check your answers to Exercises B and C.

PRONUNCIATION

7.6 **A** Listen to the conversation and notice how the intonation goes up (↗) or goes down (↘) in questions.

Ben: Is this Dr. Jones? (↗)
Dr. Jones: Yes, it is.
Ben: Can I book an appointment, please? (↗)
Dr. Jones: Sure. When would you like to come? (↘)
Ben: Do you have time today? (↗)
Dr. Jones: Yes, today's good. What time? (↘)
Ben: Is two o'clock OK? (↗)
Dr. Jones: Two o'clock's fine. Can I have your phone number, please? (↗)

7.6 **B** Listen again and repeat the conversation. Copy the intonation.

SPEAKING

A PREPARE Work in pairs. Replace the red words in Pronunciation Exercise A with different people, times and places. Use the ideas below or your own ideas. Practice the dialogue.

Person	Day	Time
Dr. Smith	tomorrow	noon
Johanna Mendelsohn, mechanic	Monday	two thirty
Mr. Roberts, bank manager	next Tuesday	four o'clock

B PLAN Make appointments with other students in the class. Put a check mark (✓) next to the six times when you are free today and tomorrow.

	TODAY	TOMORROW
09:00		
10:00		
11:00		
12:00		
1:00		
2:00		
3:00		
4:00		
5:00		
6:00		
7:00		
8:00		

C PRACTICE Go around the class and make appointments with other students. Then change roles and do the activity again.

A: Is this (name of person)?
B: Yes, it is.
A: Can I book an appointment, please?
B: Yes. When would you like to come?
A: Is today at 11 o'clock OK?
B: Sorry, I'm not free. Is 12 o'clock OK?
A: 12 o'clock's fine.

Make polite requests

7 Writing

Write a competition entry

W – using commas in lists

A Read the two texts. Then choose the correct option to complete the sentence.

The texts are applications for a *talent competition* / *sports competition*.

B Work in pairs. Complete the applications with the words in the box.

artist cello dance person picture Spanish

Anyone Can Do It!

Name: Imelda Suarez **Age:** 29
About you: I'm Imelda and I'm from Spain. I love music and I can play the guitar, the piano and the [1] ___cello___. I can also sing and [2] ___dance___. I also love languages and I can speak [3] ___Spanish___, Italian and English.

Anyone Can Do It!

Name: Lucas Johnson **Age:** 32
About you: I'm Canadian, but I live in Mexico. I really love art. I'm a(n) [4] ___artist___, and I'm really fast! I can draw, and I can paint a(n) [5] ___picture___ of any animal, [6] ___person___ or thing, and I can do it in one or two minutes!

Using commas in lists

We use a comma (,) when we write more than two words in a list. We don't usually use a comma before *and*.

I can play the guitar, the piano and the cello.

C Add the missing commas to these sentences.

1 My brother can speak English, Turkish and Arabic.
2 Kyle swims, runs and rides his bike every week.
3 I go to Spanish classes on Mondays, Wednesdays and Fridays.

WRITING

WRITE Imagine that this is your application for the talent show. Complete the missing information. Write a short paragraph. Use commas.

Anyone Can Do It!

Name: ____________
Age: ____________
What can you do?
I can … ____________

Write a competition entry

Refer students to the applications as models for the writing task.

Remind students they can write notes and plan what they want to say before they start writing.

Unit 7 Review

GRAMMAR

A Choose the correct options to complete the sentences.

1 My brother *can* / *can to* swim underwater for three minutes.
2 Lyra can *jump* / *jumps* six meters.
3 A: *Do you can* / *Can you* draw?
B: Yes, I *can* / *draw*.
4 What *do you can* / *can you do*?
5 I *can't drive* / *drive can't* a car, but I *do* / *can* ride a motorcycle.

B Find and correct the mistake in each sentence.

1 ~~Johns~~ John's brother can play the piano.
2 My ~~sisters~~ sisters' names are Jo and Leah.
3 ~~Alexs~~ Alex's hobby is wingsuit flying.
4 What are your ~~parents~~ parents' names?
5 My ~~friends~~ friend's/friend is an amazing dancer.
6 Paulo's ~~friends~~ friend's/friend has played the cello.

VOCABULARY

A Complete the phrases with the correct letters.

1 paint a picture
2 play the guitar
3 drive a car
4 speak Turkish
5 ride a bicycle
6 play soccer

B Complete the sentences with the adjectives in the box.

boring difficult good long old terrible

1 Niall's a ___good___ musician. He can play a lot of instruments.
2 Yoga is ___difficult___. I can't do it.
3 My grandmother is ___old___. She's 97.
4 My Spanish is ___terrible___. I can't say anything.
5 I do yoga for a ___long___ time every day. I sometimes do it for four hours.
6 I don't like shopping at the grocery store. I think it's ___boring___.

56 SKILLS

LEAD-IN

Ask students to think of three things they can do. Then ask them to add one that is not true. Have them take turns saying the four things; the other students have to guess the one that isn't true. Demonstrate it yourself first.

WRITING

A Check that students understand the two choices, then ask them to quickly look at the texts and decide what they are about. Give the correct answer, and ask what words tell them that.

B Check that students understand *application* and the words in the box, then put them into pairs to complete the applications. Don't help too much; let them make mistakes and correct them. When they have finished, go through the answers.

C Students work individually to complete the exercise, then check in pairs. Write the full sentences on the board and tell students to give you the answers.

WRITING TASK

Start completing the missing information in the form yourself as an example, showing that you are giving true information. Then students work individually to complete the forms. Go around helping with vocabulary. Get students to check each other's work in pairs, then post the applications on the wall and get all the students to see who they think has the most talent.

A man in front of the Northern Lights, Alaska.

The phrase is used to describe the present moment.

Ask students to label the photo if you need time to set up the class.

The quote mirrors the popular modern idea of mindfulness. It places importance on the moment we are in now, and the need to find happiness now, rather than in the future, or regretting the past. We are only ever in the present moment; accept this and be content in the here and now.

Omar Khayyam (1048–1131) was a Persian poet, mathematician and astronomer from the north of Iran. He created the Jalali solar calendar and did important work on cubic equations. Several works of poetry are attributed to him, and many became popular in English in the 19th century and were translated by Edward FitzGerald in 1859.

OBJECTIVES

- describe what people are doing
- talk about clothes
- shop for clothes
- write a short message

Work with a partner. Discuss the questions.

1 Look at the picture. Which words from the box describe it? Suggested answers: amazing, beautiful, cold, green, night

amazing boring beautiful blue cold day green warm night ugly

2 Would you like to visit this place? Why/Why not?

3 Read the quote. Tell your partner three good things about today.

THE HERE AND NOW 57

OBJECTIVES

Read the unit objectives to the class.

UNIT OPENER QUESTIONS

Students work in pairs. Ask students to look at the picture of the man in front of the Northern Lights and then to use the words in the box to describe what they can see, highlighting the words in the box to help them to do this. Add any other useful words from the students' ideas to the board to help students during the remainder of the lesson. Elicit how the image makes students feel. Ask students what other words they might know to describe the picture. Add any other ideas to the board to add to the helpful vocabulary. Students can then discuss if they would like to visit this place. Encourage them to give reasons for their answers. Elicit if anybody has experience of the Northern Lights. Where and when did they see them?

Discuss the meaning of the quote as a class and ask students to share their good things with the class if they wish and build a list on the board. Students could write their ideas on large pieces of paper and post these around the room to lend an air of positivity to the lesson.

WORKSHEETS

Lesson 8.1 What's he doing?

Vocabulary: Verb phrases (W27)

Grammar: Present progressive (W28)

Lesson 8.2 The gray coat

Vocabulary: Clothes (W29)

Grammar: Adjective order (W30)

8.1 What's he doing?

Describe what people are doing

G present progressive **V** verb phrases **P** different ways to pronounce *a*

LISTENING

A PREPARE TO LISTEN Look at the pictures. Match the things (1–6) with the correct picture (a–d).

1 a bench	b	4 a phone	d
2 a book	a	5 a sandwich	b
3 coffee	b	6 trees	c

B PREPARE TO LISTEN Look at the comic strip again. Choose the correct options.

1 Picture a: The man is talking to a *woman* / *police officer*.
2 Picture b: The man is having lunch *with friends* / *alone*.
3 Picture c: The man is lying *under a tree* / *on a bench*.
4 Picture d: The man is looking at his *watch* / *phone*.

8.1 **C LISTEN FOR THE MAIN IDEA** Listen to a conversation. Put the pictures (a–d) in the correct order.

D SPEAK Work in pairs. Discuss the questions.

1 Do the police have the right man? No
2 What item of clothing is the right man wearing?
The 'right man' is wearing a gray coat, not a green coat.

GRAMMAR

Present progressive

8.2 **A** Listen to a part of the conversation again. Complete the missing words.

Officer A: Can you see the [1] ___man___?
Officer B: Yes. I'm watching him [2] ___now___.
Officer A: What's he doing?
Officer B: He's having [3] ___lunch___.
Officer A: Is he talking to [4] ___anyone___?
Officer B: No, he isn't. He's by himself.
Officer A: Is he in a [5] ___café___?
Officer B: No, he's sitting on a [6] ___bench___. He's eating a [7] ___sandwich___ and drinking [8] ___coffee___.

B WORK IT OUT Read the conversation in Exercise A. Underline the verbs that end with *-ing*. Choose the correct option to complete the rule.

We use present progressive (verb + *-ing*) to talk about *right now* / *every day*.

C WORK IT OUT Read the examples of the present progressive in the conversation again. Choose the correct options.

Present progressive

1 We make present progressive with *subject* + *be* + *to* + *verb* / *subject* + *be* + *verb* + *-ing*.
2 In questions, the subject (*I, you, he, she, it* ...) goes *before* / *after be*.
3 In short answers, we use *subject* + *be* / *subject* + *be* + *verb* + *-ing*.

D WORK IT OUT Complete the table with the correct form of the verbs in the box. Use Exercise A to help you.

eat have sit

Verb (base form)	Spelling rule	Verb + *-ing*
do watch [1] eat	Verb + *-ing*	doing watching [4] eating
live [2] have	Verb (without *-e*), + *-ing*	living [5] having
get [3] sit	Verb (add extra last consonant) + *-ing*	getting [6] sitting

E Go to the Grammar Hub on page 112.

F SPEAK Work in pairs. Choose a picture from the comic strip but don't tell your partner which one. Describe it to your partner. Which picture is it?

A: I can see a man.
B: What's he doing?
A: He's sitting on a bench. He's ...
B: Is it picture ...?

8.1 What's he doing?

LEAD-IN

Focus learners on the images at the top of the page. Elicit what kind of images they are, e.g. are they decorative or do they tell a story?

LISTENING

8.1 **A–D** Students work in pairs to match the words and pictures. Students then choose the correct options in Exercise B. Play the audio while students complete the activity. Students discuss the answers. Ask them to find the 'right man' in the pictures.

GRAMMAR

8.2 **A–F** Ask students if they can recall any of the words in the blanks before you play the audio. Students complete the exercises individually and then check in pairs. Direct students to the **Grammar Hub** (see below and TB59). Use the **Grammar Worksheet** on page W28 for extra practice.

AUDIO SCRIPT

8.1

Listening, Exercise C
A = Officer A B = Officer B

A: Can you see the man?
B: Yes. I'm watching him now.
A: What's he doing?
B: He's having lunch.
A: Is he talking to anyone?
B: No, he isn't. He's by himself.
A: Is he in a café?
Ex C 1b **B:** No, he's sitting on a bench. He's eating a sandwich and drinking coffee.
B: OK … he's finishing his lunch.
A: Where's he going now?
B: He's stopping at the bank.
A: The bank! OK. This is it.
Ex C 2d **B:** Wait. He isn't going to the bank. He's looking at his phone. I think he's reading a message. OK. He's walking. He's going to … the library.
A: The library? OK. Stay with him.
B: He's in the library.
A: Right. What's he doing there?
Ex C 3a **B:** He's talking to someone. She's showing him something.
A: What is it?
B: It's …
A: Yes?
B: It's a book!
A: A book. What's happening now?
B: He's leaving.
A: Stay with him.
B: I can see him.
A: What's he doing?
B: He's going to the bank.
A: The bank! OK. This time … This is it.
B: Wait. He's not going to the bank. He's going to the park.
A: The park? Is he meeting anyone?
B: No, he isn't.
A: Argh. What's he doing?
Ex C 4c **B:** He's lying down. He's taking a nap. I think he's sleeping.
A: What? Are you watching the right man?
B: Yes, I am! He's tall, he has gray hair and he's wearing a green coat.
Ex D **A:** No, that's not him. Our man has a gray coat, not a green coat. You're watching the wrong man. What's that noise?
B: Um … It's coming from the bank.

GRAMMAR HUB

8.1

Present progressive

A Choose the correct options.

1 I'm *walking* / *walk* down the street. (walking)
2 You *are* / *is* sitting on my coat. (are)
3 We're not *watch* / *watching* the movie now. (watching)
4 *Is she* / *She is* meeting her friend now? (Is she)
5 He's *stand* / *standing* up right now. (standing)
6 They're *not looking* / *looking not* at clothes. (not looking)
7 Are you *have* / *having* lunch now? (having)
8 We're *going* / *go* to the park. (going)

B Choose the correct answers to the questions.

1 Are you texting Darren?
a No, you're not. **(b)** No, I'm not.
2 Is your sister having lunch?
(a) Yes, she is. b Yes, she has.
3 Are they going to the bank?
a No, they're not going. **(b)** No, they're not.
4 Am I wearing your T-shirt?
a Yes, it is. **(b)** Yes, you are.
5 Is he lying down right now?
a Yes, he's lying. **(b)** Yes, he is.
6 Is Harry sleeping?
(a) No, he's not. b No, he not sleeping.
7 Are they talking to someone?
a No, they're not talking. **(b)** No, they aren't.
8 Are you watching the soccer game?
(a) Yes, I am. b Yes, I'm.

C Complete the sentences with the present progressive form of the verbs in parentheses.

1 He ___is walking___ (*walk*) to the park.
2 She ___'s/is eating___ (*eat*) dinner now.
3 They ___'re/are sitting___ (*sit*) on a bench.
4 I ___'m/am having___ (*have*) a salad.
5 ___Are you wearing___ (*you / wear*) your new coat?
6 Look! The car ___isn't / is not stopping___. (*not stop*)
7 ___Is she making___ (*she / make*) dinner?
8 I ___'m/am putting___ (*put*) money in the bank.

➤ Go back to page 58.

8.1 What's he doing?

VOCABULARY

A–B Students work individually to complete the exercises, then check in pairs. Go through the answers, showing how these words go together in English. Check the collocations against the students' L1; where there is a difference, they need to be careful not to simply translate. Practice the pronunciation of the whole phrases, emphasizing that they are said quickly, as a language 'chunk'. Use the **Vocabulary Worksheet** on page W27 for extra practice.

PRONUNCIATION

A (8.3) Elicit the different sounds from students to see if they are already familiar with the phonemes. Isolate and practice each one, then listen and repeat the examples.

B (8.4) You could ask learners to say the words aloud and predict where they will go in the table. Play the audio to complete the activity. Check answers as a class.

C (8.5) Play the audio while students listen and complete the questions. Repeat if necessary, then check answers.

D Model the first question with a strong student as an example, then put them into pairs to ask and answer the questions.

SPEAKING

Put students into pairs and ask Student A to stay on the page and direct Student B to the **Communication Hub** (see TB97). Remind students to use language for clarification if they are having difficulty with the task, asking their partner to repeat information or say it in a different way. Let them do the exercise while you walk around; monitor, but try not to intervene. Write a note about any feedback to give when they finish.

Extra activity

Students work in pairs. One of each pair sits with their back to the board, faced by their partner. On the board, write verb phrases, e.g. *read a newspaper*, *take a selfie*. The students facing the board have to mime the activities (in any order) while their partner guesses, using the present progressive, e.g. *You're taking a selfie*. You can run this as a competition with the winning pair guessing/miming finishing first and then able to give all the sentences correctly, e.g. *She is reading a newspaper*.

GRAMMAR HUB

8.1

Present progressive

	Positive	Negative
I	**I am talking** to my neighbor. **I'm talking** to my neighbor.	**I am not wearing** a green coat. **I'm not wearing** a green coat.
you/we/they	**We are sitting** in a café. **We're sitting** in a café.	**They are not leaving** the park. **They aren't leaving** the park. **They're not leaving** the park.
he/she/it	**It is raining** right now. **It's raining** right now.	**She is not working** at her desk. **She isn't working** at her desk. **She's not working** at her desk.

	Question	Positive short answer	Negative short answer
I	**Am I sitting** in your chair?	**Yes, you are.**	**No, you aren't. / No, you're not.**
you/we/they	**Are you drinking** coffee?	**Yes, I am.** **Yes, we are.**	**No, I'm not.** **No, we aren't. / No, we're not.**
he/she/it	**Is he taking** a selfie?	**Yes, he is.**	**No, he isn't. / No, he's not.**

- We use the present progressive to talk about things that happen now.
  I'm going to the library right now.
- We make the present progressive with the subject + *am/is/are* + verb + *-ing*.
  We're walking down the street.
  She's standing up now.
- In questions, the subject goes after *am/is/are*.
  Are you meeting your friends?
- In positive short answers, we use the subject + *am/is/are*.
  Is Malcolm watching TV right now? Yes, he is.
- In negative short answers with *you/he/she/it/we/they*, there's a choice of negative.
  Is Greg watching TV right now? No, he isn't. OR No, he's not.

Be careful!

- We cannot use the present progressive to talk about things we do every day, only for things we're doing right now.
  I'm drinking tea with my breakfast today. NOT ~~I'm drinking tea with my breakfast every day.~~
- We add *-ing* to the verb to make the present progressive. Some verbs have special spelling rules. For verbs that end in a consonant + *-e*, such as *have*, *come* and *make*, we cut the *-e* and add *-ing*.
  He's coming from the library. NOT ~~He's comeing from the library.~~
- For most verbs that end in consonant + vowel + consonant, such as *sit*, *stop* and *put*, we double the consonant and add *-ing*.
  They're stopping at the bank. NOT ~~They're stoping at the bank.~~

VOCABULARY

Verb phrases

A Choose the correct verbs to complete the phrases. Use each verb only once.

go have look meet read take talk watch

1 meet
a friend

2 look
at your phone

3 take
a selfie

4 have
a good time

5 read
the newspaper

6 watch
a movie

7 go
to the bank

8 talk
to a friend

B Match the verbs from Exercise A with the words and phrases.

1 *have* lunch / a meeting / coffee
2 watch TV / a soccer game / someone do something
3 read a book / a message / a magazine
4 go out / to the library / shopping
5 talk to a teacher / on the phone / about something
6 take a photo / a break / a taxi
7 look at a picture / in the mirror / at someone
8 meet someone at a party / at nine o'clock / at the station

PRONUNCIATION

Different ways to pronounce *a*

8.3 **A** Listen and repeat the words in the table.

/æ/	/eɪ/	/ɔː/	/ɑ /
have	take	walk	watch
catch	play	call	want
match	stay	fall	wash

8.4 **B** Listen to the words in the box and put them in the correct place in the table.

call catch fall match play stay want wash

8.5 **C** Listen and complete the questions.

1 What do you play: ball games or board games?
2 Who do you talk to every day?
3 What do you usually have for lunch?
4 What do you want to watch: a soccer game or a movie?

D **SPEAK** Work with a partner. Ask the questions in Exercise C. Give full answers.

SPEAKING

Work in pairs. Student A – Look at the instructions below. Student B – Go to the Communication Hub on page 131.

Student A

- Look at the picture.
- Describe the people and what they are doing to your partner.
- Listen to your partner's description of their picture.
- Find six differences.

1 In Student A's picture, the woman sitting on the bench is eating an apple. In Student B's picture, she's eating a banana.
2 In Student A's picture, the woman sitting on the bench is drinking tea. In Student B's picture, she's drinking juice.
3 In Student A's picture, the man reading a newspaper is sitting down. In Student B's picture, he's standing up.
4 In Student A's picture, the girl under the tree is lying down. In Student B's picture, she's sitting down.
5 In Student A's picture, the boy is looking at his phone. In Student B's picture, he isn't looking at his phone.
6 In Student A's picture, the man walking in the background is not on the phone. In Student B's picture, he's on the phone.

Describe what people are doing

8.2 The gray coat

Talk about clothes

V – clothes P – vowel sounds: /iː/, /ɜː/, /uː/ and /ɔː/ S – identifying key words G – adjective order

VOCABULARY

Clothes

A Look at Person 1 in the picture. What clothes is he wearing? Choose words from the box to complete the description.

shorts sneakers socks T-shirt

He's wearing a white [1] T-shirt and blue [2] shorts. He's wearing red [3] sneakers and white [4] socks. He also has a green backpack.

B Go to the **Vocabulary Hub** on **page 125**.

C SPEAK Work in pairs. Choose someone in the picture. Ask and answer questions. Who is your partner describing?

A: She's wearing a dress.
B: Is she wearing a hat?
A: Yes, she is.

PRONUNCIATION

Vowel sounds: /iː/, /ɜː/, /uː/ and /ɔː/

8.6 **A** Complete the sentences with a word in the box that has the same sound as the <u>underlined</u> letters. Listen and check.

a coat ~~a hat~~ jeans a shirt shorts a suit

1 Hannah's wearing a c<u>a</u>p. Izzie's wearing *a hat*.
2 Ally's wearing a sk<u>ir</u>t and a shirt.
3 Paulo's wearing a suit and sh<u>oe</u>s.

8.7 **B** Listen to the words for clothes. Then listen and repeat.

jeans shirt shoes shorts

8.8 **C** Match the words in the box with the correct vowel sound in questions 1–4. Then listen and check.

bird clean do door green sports who word

1 /iː/ jeans clean, green
2 /ɜː/ shirt bird, word
3 /uː/shoes do, who
4 /ɔː/ shorts door, sport

D SPEAK Work in pairs. Look around you. Describe different people.

A: Eva's wearing jeans. *B: Elliot's wearing a shirt.*

READING

Suggested answers: The people are at the station. Some of them are standing, and some of them are sitting. Some people are looking at their phones.

A PREPARE TO READ Look at the picture at the top of the page again. What are the people doing?

B READ FOR KEY WORDS Read the messages and look at the picture. Which person (1–11) is Claus? Which person is Imogen?

Claus 3 Imogen 9

Identifying key words

Looking for key words can help you understand the topic of a text or sentence quickly.

I'm wearing a gray ***sweatshirt****. [Topic = clothes]*

Claus

Hi Claus, I'm at the station. <u>Where are you?</u> Ex C Q1

Ex C Q2 I'm here, too. <u>I have the bag, but I can't see you</u>. What are you wearing?

An <u>old</u> blue sweatshirt and a yellow cap.

Sorry, I can't see you. Where are you?

<u>I'm standing near the store.</u> Ex C Q3
What are you wearing?

A <u>long</u> gray coat.

I think I can see you. Are you wearing a red cap?

Yes, I am.

I can see you! I think the police are watching.

The police? Why are the police watching?

Something's happening at the bank. It's on the radio. <u>The police are looking for a man with a gray coat and a bag with a lot of money.</u> Ex C Q4

Ex C Q5 <u>I have a bag, but it doesn't have any money in</u>
Ex C Q6 <u>it! It's your bag ... from the restaurant last night.</u>

I know, thank you! I'm coming over to you now.

8.2 The gray coat

LEAD-IN

Make strips of paper with activities on it, e.g. *I'm swimming*, and put them in a bag. Ask a student to come and take one, then mime it. The other students must say what the activity is, e.g. *You're swimming*. The person who guesses correctly goes next; continue until all students have had a chance and all the strips are used.

VOCABULARY

A Students complete the exercise individually. Encourage students to use the language they already know (colors) and to think about sentence structure (singular or plural) to help them. Check answers as a class.

B Direct students to the **Vocabulary Hub** (see TB97).

C Students read the conversation, then you can demonstrate the activity by describing a (unnamed) student using the same format. Put students into pairs to complete the activity. If there is time, put them into different pairs and practice again. Use the **Vocabulary Worksheet** on page W29 for extra practice.

PRONUNCIATION

8.6 **A** Write the first example on the board and read it aloud, focusing on the vowel sound /æ/ in *cap* and *hat*. Check that students understand that they need to find sounds that sound the same by contrasting the sound with *jeans* /dʒiːnz/ and asking if that word has the same or a different sound (*different*). They can work in pairs; encourage them to try saying the words. Then play the audio to check answers.

8.7 **B** Play the audio while students read and listen, then play it again and ask them to repeat.

8.8 **C** Write the symbols for the four sounds across the top of the board and say them; ask students to repeat. Then write the example word under each sound, and say it while students listen and repeat. Check that they can hear the different sounds. Point out that when the vowel sound pronounced "aw" as in law (/ɔː/) is followed by the *R* consonant (as in shorts), the sound changes slightly due to the mouth's position to blend the *AW* and *R* sounds; however, this is still represented by the same phonetic symbol. Have students work in pairs to match the words, saying them aloud if possible. Play the audio while they check, then play it again and write the words in the columns on the board. Practice the pronunciation of the words in each list.

D Put students into pairs to do the exercise; monitor and help with the sounds if necessary.

READING

A Focus students on the pictures again. Ask: *What are the people doing?* Go through the pictures with the whole class, making sure they use the present progressive accurately.

B Go through the *Identifying key words* box with the students. Give one or two more examples, e.g. *he's making lunch* (*topic = food*). Then set the task by doing the first one with the class; ask students to identify the key words. Let students work on it individually before checking in pairs. Go through the answers with the whole class and write them on the board.

METHODOLOGY HUB by Jim Scrivener

Sounds: Vowels

Vowels

A vowel is a voiced sound made without any closure or friction so that there is no restriction to the flow of air from the lungs. You may find a mnemonic of some kind helpful while you are learning the phonemes. Your students might also like this idea: you could write a simple story for them (e.g. 'Eat this good food', said the bird …) or, better still, get them to devise their own sentences. You could also attempt more 'poetic' versions, as with the diphthongs.

Students of most other foreign languages will find that, while a number of English phonemes are familiar, some will be distinctly different from the ones they use. Particular problems arise when:

- English has two phonemes for a sound that seems, to an untrained ear, to be a single sound. A common example of this is the distinction between /ɪ/ and /iː/ (as in hip vs heap), which sound the same to some students.
- English has a phoneme that does not exist in the students' own language.

In both cases, getting students to produce the sounds themselves can be difficult; it is necessary to raise their awareness of the fact that there is something to work on, and the first step is to get them to hear the difference. Receptive awareness comes before productive competence.

GRAMMAR HUB

8.2

Adjective order

	Size	Age	Color
Adjectives	big short long	new old	red yellow green blue gray white
Example sentences	It's a **big red** coat. He's wearing **old green** shorts. We're wearing our **new blue** shoes.		

- We can put more than one adjective before a noun.
  I'm wearing a new red shirt.
  He has a big gray hat.
- The color adjective usually goes after the adjective for size or age.
  It's an old yellow dress. NOT ~~*It's a yellow old dress.*~~

Be careful!

- Remember to use the right article before the adjective. We use *an* in front of adjectives that start with a vowel.
  She's wearing an old blue dress. NOT ~~*She's wearing a old blue dress.*~~

8.2 The gray coat

C Students read the text again and answer the questions, then check with a partner. Go through the answers with the whole class, asking them to justify their answers by identifying the words that give them. Elicit the idea that Claus is also wearing a gray coat, like the man the police are looking for, and he has a bag.

D Ask students to read the summary. Ask if it is good or bad. Tell them it is bad – there are five mistakes! Ask them to read the original text again and identify the five mistakes. When they have finished, go through the answers, eliciting the corrections.

GRAMMAR

A Using an item in the class, write, e.g. *a small new red bag*, on the board. Ask students to identify the adjectives. Underline them. Ask *size, color or age?* and write the words above each one. Then ask students to find examples of adjectives for size, color and age in the text. Add them to the columns on the board. Practice pronunciation, and ask students to point out examples of them in the class.

B Students work in pairs to work out the rules. Give answers and do some more examples on the board using items in the classroom, writing them on the board in the columns.

C Direct students to the **Grammar Hub** (see below and TB60).

D Do the first example on the board, then let students work individually and check in pairs. Add the answers to the lists on the board.

E Demonstrate with a few examples of people in the class, then put students into pairs to describe the people in the pictures. Monitor, but do not overcorrect; note any general problems and give feedback when students have finished. Use the **Grammar Worksheet** on page W30 for extra practice.

SPEAKING HUB

A Elicit some ideas for the first picture, writing brief notes on the board, including what you are wearing, then let students work individually to write notes for all three pictures for themselves.

B Students work in pairs to do the exercise. Let them use their phones for this if appropriate; they could be out of sight of each other to make it feel more authentic.

C Students work with a different partner. Encourage them to make different choices of clothes and activities.

Extra activity

Run the Speaking Hub activity in reverse. Elicit a list of situations, e.g. *at the gym*, *camping*, *in the mountains*. Then ask students to write a note about what they are wearing in each situation (you can include what they are doing, too, to make the next stage easier if you wish). Students then work in small groups. One student says what he or she is wearing (and doing), while the others guess the situation from the list.

GRAMMAR HUB

8.2

Adjective order

A Choose the correct options.

1 It's a ___ coat.
  (a) new red b red new
2 She has ___ shoes.
  a green old (b) old green
3 He's wearing a ___ hat.
  (a) big blue b blue big
4 Do you have a ___ dress?
  (a) new green b green new
5 I like your ___ skirt.
  a yellow long (b) long yellow
6 They don't have ___ sneakers.
  a white new (b) new white
7 It's a(n) ___ sweatshirt.
  a gray old (b) old gray
8 Michelle is wearing a ___ coat.
  (a) short white b white short

B Check (✓) the correct sentences and put an (✗) for the incorrect sentences.

1 She's wearing red long socks. ✗
2 He likes old yellow hats. ✓
3 It's a gray big dress. ✗
4 Those aren't new brown shoes. ✓
5 They're not wearing long green skirts. ✓
6 We have blue old T-shirts. ✗
7 I want a big white sweatshirt. ✓
8 Do you have green new shoes? ✗

C Put the words in the correct order to make sentences and questions.

1 socks / brown / they're / old
  They're old brown socks.
2 has / red / coat / she / a / big
  She has a big red coat.
3 wearing / green / they're / old / T-shirts
  They're wearing old green T-shirts.
4 you / hat / new / a / have / brown / do
  Do you have a new brown hat?
5 coat / like / I / blue / your / long
  I like your long blue coat.
6 a / sweatshirt / yellow / that's / big
  That's a big yellow sweatshirt.

➤ Go back to page 61.

C READ FOR SPECIFIC INFORMATION Read the messages again. Answer the questions.

1 Can Imogen see Claus when she arrives at the station? No. She writes 'Where are you?'.
2 Can Claus see Imogen? No. He writes 'What are you wearing?'.
3 Where is Imogen? Near the store.
4 Why are the police watching Claus? Gray coat and a bag; wearing same clothes as man police are looking for.
5 Is Claus the man the police are looking for? No. He has a bag, but it doesn't have any money.
6 Is the bag Claus's bag or Imogen's bag? Imogen's

D READ FOR DETAIL Read the messages again. Find and correct the five mistakes in the summary.

Claus is at the ~~park~~ station. He's meeting Imogen. Claus has a ~~blue~~ gray coat and a bag. The police are looking for a man with a gray ~~sweatshirt~~ coat and a bag. Claus has Imogen's ~~coat~~ bag. There ~~is a lot of~~ isn't any money in the bag.

GRAMMAR
Adjective order

A Read the messages in Reading Exercise B again. Underline the adjectives of size or age. Circle the adjectives of color.

B WORK IT OUT Read these sentences from the messages. Choose the correct option to complete the rules.

Adjective order

I'm wearing an old blue sweatshirt and a yellow cap.

I'm wearing a long gray coat.

1 We *can* / *can't* put more than one adjective before a noun.
2 The color adjective usually goes *before* / *after* the adjective for size or age.

C Go to the **Grammar Hub** on **page 112**.

D PRACTICE Rewrite the sentences and add the extra adjectives in parentheses.

1 It's a blue shirt. (new)
It's a new blue shirt.
2 She's wearing an old dress. (green)
She's wearing an old green dress.
3 I have a new hat. (red)
I have a new red hat.
4 That's a blue skirt. (long)
That's a long blue skirt.

E SPEAK Work in pairs. Describe the clothes in the pictures.

big long short small

She's wearing a long yellow coat.

Suggested answers:
a She's wearing a long yellow coat.
b He's wearing a small black suit.
c She's wearing a big colorful sweater.
d She's wearing a short green jacket.

SPEAKING HUB

A PREPARE Imagine you are in these situations. What are you wearing? What are you doing? Write notes.

a You're in the park in the summer.

b You're traveling for business.

c You're at a concert.

B PRACTICE Work in pairs. Choose one of the situations in Exercise A. Your partner is trying to find you, but they can't. Have a phone conversation and describe what you are wearing and what you are doing.

A: What are you wearing?
B: I'm wearing a long red skirt, a white hat and sunglasses.

C REPEAT Find a new partner. Choose a new situation and describe what you're wearing and what you're doing.

Talk about clothes

Café Hub

8.3 Too loud

F– shop for clothes

COMPREHENSION

A ▶ Watch the video and answer the questions.

1 Where are Gaby and Lucy? At a (metal) music concert.

2 Who buys something? Why? Lucy buys a cap. She wants to help Gaby cover her hair.

B Are the sentences true (T) or false (F)? Correct the false sentences.

1 Gaby is waiting for Lucy. (T) / F

2 Lucy says Gaby's hair is bad. She thinks it is just different. T / (F)

3 The cap seller likes the music. (T) / F

4 Gaby wants to buy a cap. Lucy wants to buy a cap for Gaby. T / (F)

5 There's a blue cap. (T) / F

6 The caps are one size. Three sizes – small, medium and large T / (F)

7 Caps cost £10. (T) / F

8 Gaby needs a small cap. a large cap T / (F)

C ▶ Watch the video again and check your answers to Exercise B.

D What do you think of the music? Choose an adjective from the box or use your own ideas.

amazing   bad   good   horrible   OK

USEFUL PHRASES

A Match the phrases (1–4) with the pictures (a–d).

1 It's not bad. It's just different. c

2 Oh, look over there. d

3 She's joking! b

4 I have a surprise for you. a

B Which useful phrase means *She's not serious*? She's joking!

C ▶ Watch the video again and check your answers to Exercises A and B.

a

b

c

d

8.3 Too loud

LEAD-IN

Students review the pictures and guess the context for this unit's video. Ask students if they have ever been somewhere similar and give them the opportunity to share their experiences.

COMPREHENSION

A ▶ Students watch the video and confirm their ideas from the Lead-in discussion and/or answer the questions in Exercise A.

B Students review the sentences in pairs, recalling what they saw in the video, correcting any sentences they can.

C ▶ Students watch the video again and check their ideas from Exercise B.

D Encourage students' personal response to the music, asking them to choose an adjective from the box or to add their own ideas. This could be expanded to include an opportunity to identify the music they do like (particularly if they don't like the music in the video).

USEFUL PHRASES

A Model the sentences with appropriate stress and intonation. Work as a whole class for students to match the phrases with the pictures.

B Answer the question as a class. You could encourage discussion and elicit how students would say this in their language if the class is monolingual.

C ▶ Students watch the video again and check their answers for Exercises A and B.

▶ VIDEO SCRIPT

L = Lucy G = Gaby M = Man

L: Hi! I like your hair!
G: I hate it!
L: Oh.
G: Yes, it's really bad. I said, 'I'd like something different' and look!
L: It's not bad, it's just different. Oh, look over there!
M: Can I help?
G: Can you change my hair?
M: What?
L: She's joking. We're just looking, thanks.
M: OK, no problem.
L: Actually, I'm looking for …
M: Yes?
L: Actually, I'm looking for a cap.
M: Sure, we have caps. Lots of them.
L: Great. Do you have a …
M: Yes?
L: Do you have a blue one?
M: Yes, we have blue. What size would you like? Small, medium or large?
L: Can I have a medium, please?
M: Of course.
L: Perfect. How much is it?
M: £10.
L: Gaby, I have a surprise for you!
G: Thanks!
L: Maybe a large?

METHODOLOGY HUB by Jim Scrivener

Viewing activities

Other ideas

Now, if you're feeling interested, here's a mixed bag of ideas to liven up the lessons. (Don't try all of these in one lesson, but do try one or two of them sometime!)

- Don't let students mentally unplug; make them think; challenge them. Cover up the screen and ask questions: *Listen to the words/music – what's the picture? What are they describing? Where are they?* Then, look at the images and compare.
- In pairs, the above idea becomes an instant communicative activity: *Tell your partner what you think was happening.* It could lead to drawing and comparison of pictures.
- Turn off the sound: *What are they saying?* Advertisements work beautifully: in pairs, imagine and write the script. And then the two students 'lip-sync' it: *Come up to the TV; sit on either side of it and while I play the* (silent) *recording again, you speak the words.* (Hilarious – try it!)
- Watch a one- or two-minute clip a number of times with the sound down and English subtitles. Ask students to first copy these subtitles. Replay it frequently enough for them to do this. When all students have the text (and have checked it), ask them to work in pairs to decide what the subtitles would be in their own language. When they have finished writing and have compared (and acted out their versions?), they can, of course, watch the DVD with subtitles in their language and see how close they got.

8.3 Too loud

FUNCTIONAL LANGUAGE

A Highlight that the table represents a conversation and that students need to identify the correct words in the phrases. Students work in pairs to complete the exercise.

B ▶ 00:45–01:59 Play the section of the video for students to check their answers.

PRONUNCIATION

8.9 **A** Highlight the underlined sections. Focus on the word *looking* and elicit why only the first part is underlined (*it is a two-syllable word and the first syllable is stressed*). Ask students to find other examples of multi-syllable words in the conversation (*medium, Seventeen*). Play the audio for students to listen and follow the conversation in their books.

8.9 **B** Students listen to the audio again and repeat, line by line. Encourage appropriate stressing and destressing of syllables. Highlight other pronunciation points already covered in the course (e.g. the schwa sound).

C Students practice the conversation in pairs. Encourage the students to look up and say the lines rather than reading them off the page.

SPEAKING

A Students review the items of clothing and decide on a price for each one. (You could extend this by allowing students to write a brand on each item and adjust the price to fit the brand!)

B Individually, students decide what they want to buy, the color and the size. They can write a note about the key words if they need the support.

C Students work in pairs, with one student as the sales person and one as the customer. Model the conversation with a strong student first, showing how you are using the information you decided on in Exercises A and B. Also include phrases from the lesson and clear stressed syllables. When students work in pairs, monitor and write a note about language use for feedback. Provide feedback, both positive and for things which need further work.

D Students change roles and have a new conversation. Monitor and encourage and praise improved language performance from the feedback.

TEACHING IDEA by David Seymour and Maria Popova

Function: Buying and selling

Use this activity to build on the ideas of the Speaking section.

Imagine you are buying some things in a street market. Look at this conversation.

A: Good morning.

B: Good morning. A kilogram of onions, please.

A: There you go. Anything else?

B: Yes. I'll have a large beet.

A: One large beet. Anything else?

B: That's all, thanks.

A: OK. That'll be $1 please.

B: Here you are. Thanks.

A: Bye.

In pairs, choose one of these stores and write a list of the things you sell. Write a few items to buy from each of the other stores. One of you will go shopping and the other will stay to mind the store. Have conversations like the one on the board in each store.

drug store, market stall, newsstand, butcher, bakery, computer store, post office, DIY store, sports store

METHODOLOGY HUB by Jim Scrivener

When to correct

There are several factors to take into account when deciding if a correction should be made: Will it help or hinder learning? Am I correcting something they don't know? (If so, there doesn't seem much point.) How will the student take the correction? What is my intention in correcting?

The options include: immediately, after a few minutes, at the end of the activity, later in the lesson, at the end of the lesson, in the next lesson, later in the course, never. The distinction between accuracy and fluency goals is again important here. If the objective is accuracy, then immediate correction is likely to be useful; if the goal is fluency, then lengthy, immediate correction that diverts from the flow of speaking is less appropriate. We either need to correct briefly and unobtrusively as we go or save any correction for after the activity has finished or later.

One strategy used by many teachers during fluency activities is to listen in discreetly and collect a list of overheard errors. Later on, you can use this list to provide sentences to discuss, to set an exercise, to plan the next lesson, etc.

GABY

SAM

LUCY

FUNCTIONAL LANGUAGE

Shopping for clothes

A Read the conversation and underline the correct options.

Sales person	Lucy
Can I [1]*see* / *help*?	We're [2]*just* / *only* looking, thanks.
No problem.	Actually, I'm [3]*looking* / *waiting* for a cap.
Sure. We have caps. Lots of them!	Great! Do you have a blue [4]*type* / *one*?
Yes, we have blue. What [5]*size* / *color* would you like: small, medium or [6]*big* / *large*?	Can I [7]*want* / *have* a medium, please?
Of course.	Perfect. How [8]*much* / *money* is it?
Ten pounds.	

B 00:45–01:59 Watch part of the video and check your answers.

PRONUNCIATION

8.9 **A** Listen to the conversation and notice how the underlined words are stressed.

Sales person: Can I help you?
Customer: I'm just looking, thanks.
Sales person: OK, no problem.
Customer: Actually, I'm looking for a T-shirt. Do you have a red one?
Sales person: Yes. What size would you like? Small, medium or large?
Customer: Can I have a large, please?
Sales person: Of course.
Customer: How much is it?
Sales person: Seventeen dollars.

8.9 **B** Listen again and repeat the conversation. Copy the stress.

C SPEAK Work in pairs. Practice the conversation.

SPEAKING

A PLAN You are a sales person. Look at the clothes and decide how much each item costs.

$ ______

$ ______

$ ______

$ ______

$ ______

$ ______

B PREPARE You are shopping for clothes. Decide what you want to buy, the color and the size you need.

C PRACTICE Work in pairs. Decide who is the sales person and who is the customer. Have a conversation and buy the clothes you want. Use the conversation in Pronunciation Exercise A to help you.

D REPEAT Change roles and have a new conversation.

Shop for clothes

Unit 8 Writing

8 Writing

Write a short message

W – using *also* and *too*

A Read the text message conversation between two friends. Choose the correct image for where Mia is.

Hi Mia. What are you doing?

Ex B Q1 Hi Petra. I'm at a barbecue at Amy's house. It's so nice and sunny today!

Oh great! Who are you with?

Ex B Q2 I'm with Greg. Lilly's here, too. They're making the food. Ex B Q3

What are you doing?!

Ex B Q4 I'm sitting in the sun and talking to Amy. Do you want to come over?

Ex B Q5 I can't. I'm shopping with my sister right now. Also, I have to work later. Maybe next time 😃.

a 

b 

B Read the messages again. Answer the questions.

1. Where's Mia?
2. Who's with Mia?
3. What are Greg and Lilly doing?
4. What's Mia doing?
5. Why can't Petra go?

Using *also* and *too*

We use *also* and *too* to say that something is true about more than one person or thing. We usually put *also* at the beginning of a sentence or before the verb. We always put *too* at the end of a sentence.

Also, I have to work later.

Lilly's here, too.

WRITING

WRITE Write a text message conversation between two friends. Choose a situation from the pictures in Exercise A or use your own ideas.

Write a short message

Refer students to the conversation as a model for the writing task.

Answers

1 At a barbecue (at Amy's house)
2 Amy, Greg and Lilly
3 They're making the food.
4 She's sitting in the sun and talking to Amy.
5 She's shopping with her sister. She has to work later.

Remind students to write notes and plan before they start writing.

Unit 8 Review

GRAMMAR

A Complete the conversation using short answers and the verbs in parentheses in the present progressive.

A: What [1] *are* you *doing* (do)?
B: I [2] 'm/am eating (eat) lunch.
A: [3] Is Michael having (have) lunch with you?
B: No, he [4] isn't. He [5] 's/is working (work) in the library.
A: Who [6] is he working (work) with?
B: He [7] isn't working (not work) with anyone.

B Order the words to make sentences.

1. is / this / blue / new / my / sweatshirt
   This is my new blue sweatshirt.
2. has / an / gray / hat / he / old
   He has an old gray hat.
3. wearing / a / long / dress / white / she's
   She's wearing a long white dress.
4. a / short / coat / brown / the man / wearing / is
   The man is wearing a short brown coat.

VOCABULARY

A Join the halves to make sentences.

1. I'm going
2. We're watching
3. Aki and Darren are meeting
4. Luke's reading
5. My sister is having
6. Geri is talking
7. Yannick is looking
8. Luke's taking

a. to her friend on the phone.
b. a photo with his new camera.
c. to a café.
d. at the bus station.
e. TV at home.
f. at clothes in a store.
g. lunch.
h. a magazine.

B Complete the words for clothes.

1. d r e s s
2. sw e a t s h i r t
3. h a t
4. j e a n s
5. s h o e s
6. sn e a k e r s

64 THE HERE AND NOW

LEAD-IN

Ask students to stand up in a circle and join them. Say something about an item of clothing you are wearing, e.g. *I'm wearing a black jacket*. Then ask the next student to say, e.g. *John is wearing a black jacket* and *I'm wearing an old shirt*. Continue around the room.

WRITING

A Students read and answer the question, then check in pairs before you give the answer. Ask students to identify why picture *b* is correct, e.g. *they are making food*.

B Students work individually to answer the questions, then go through them with the whole class. Make sure they identify the sentences that give the reasons. Write *also* and *too* on the board and ask students to underline them in the text, then go through the *Using also and too* box in the book with the students. Give some more examples on the board that are true for your class, e.g. *Pierre is here and Noel is here, too*.

WRITING TASK

Students write individually, while you walk around and help as necessary; try to direct them back to the model conversation rather than giving them answers directly. At the end, share their conversations, either by displaying them or asking students to read them aloud.

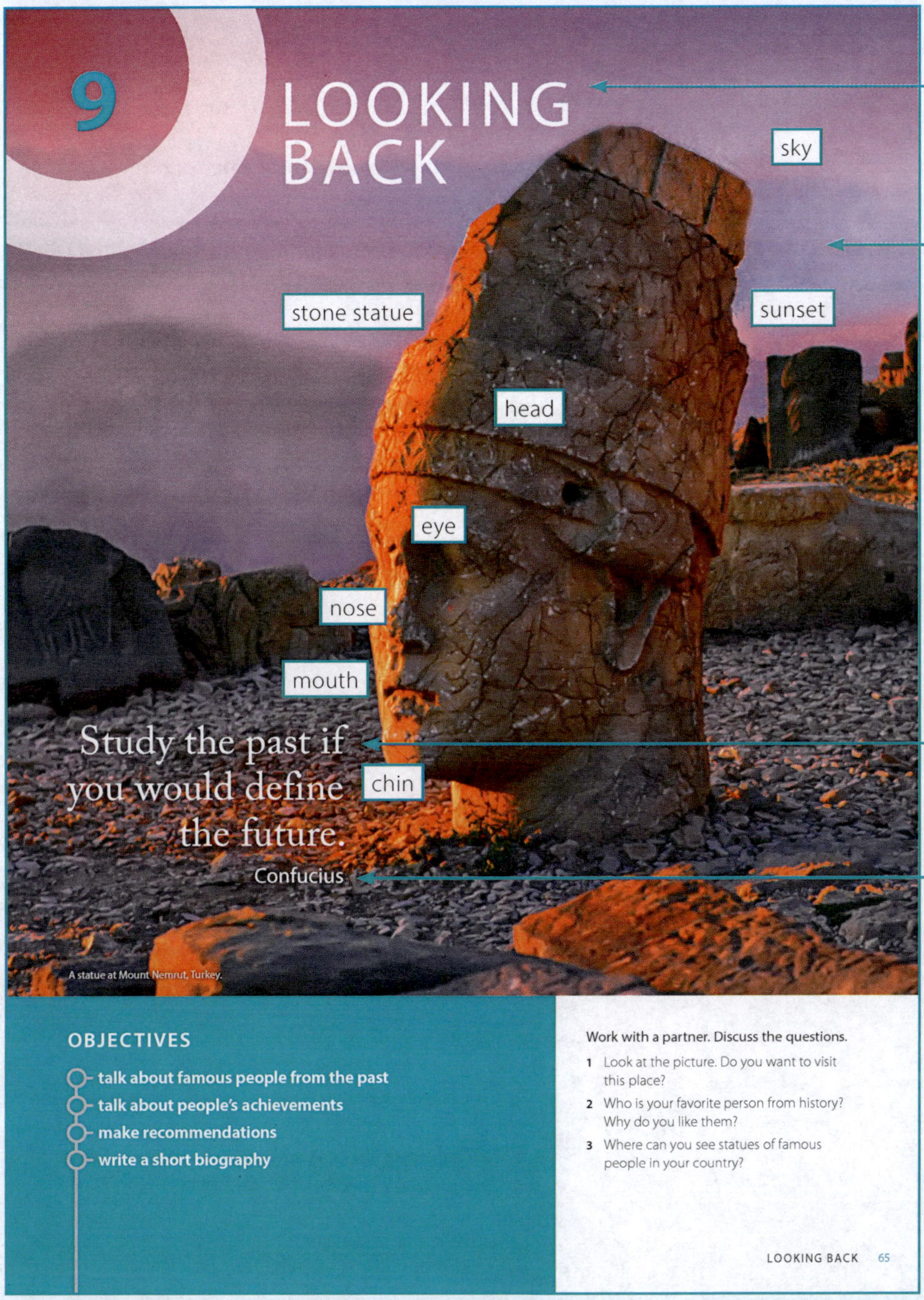
9 LOOKING BACK

Study the past if you would define the future.

Confucius

A statue at Mount Nemrut, Turkey.

OBJECTIVES

- talk about famous people from the past
- talk about people's achievements
- make recommendations
- write a short biography

Work with a partner. Discuss the questions.

1 Look at the picture. Do you want to visit this place?

2 Who is your favorite person from history? Why do you like them?

3 Where can you see statues of famous people in your country?

LOOKING BACK 65

The phrase describes thinking about a time or event in the past.

Ask students to label the photo if you need time to set up the class.

The quote suggests that to take control of the future, we need to learn from the past. There are many lessons we can take from studying past actions and events, and if we are wise, we will look backward before looking forward to the unknown.

Confucius (551 BCE–479 BCE) was a Chinese philosopher, politician and teacher. Confucius considered family and public interaction important, and he created models for his theories. These models provide rules for living, respect for elder people and the importance of disciplined behavior.

OBJECTIVES

Read the unit objectives to the class.

UNIT OPENER QUESTIONS

Working in pairs, focus the students on the picture of the statue at Mount Nemrut. Encourage students to describe the picture, also thinking about how old the statue might be, who might have carved it, who or what it was meant to represent. Ask students if they would like to visit Mount Nemrut, giving reasons for their answers.

Then ask students to look at Question 2, and name their favorite person from history. Ask students to discuss with their partners why they have chosen this person and why they like them. Elicit names from students of famous people and add the names to the board along with the vocabulary students use to describe the famous person and their achievements for use throughout the class. Add sentence stems to the board to support students, or give examples yourself. *My favorite person from history is … I like this person because he/she …*

Students then discuss where famous statues can (or cannot) be seen in their own country. If the class is an international class, a map of famous statues can be made and displayed in the classroom.

WORKSHEETS

Lesson 9.1 Famous faces

Vocabulary: Dates and years (W31)

Grammar: Simple past: *was/were* (W32)

Lesson 9.2 Voices from the past

Vocabulary: Everyday verbs (W33)

Grammar: Simple past: regular verbs (W34)

9.1 Famous faces

Talk about famous people from the past

G simple past: *was/were* **V** dates and years **P** *was he / was she*

LISTENING

A PREPARE TO LISTEN Look at the pictures in *A visit to Madame Tussauds*. Do you know these famous people? Why are they famous? **a** an actor **b** a writer **c** an artist **d** a politician

9.1 **B LISTEN FOR SPECIFIC INFORMATION** Listen and write the missing years (a–d) in *A visit to Madame Tussauds*.

9.1 **C LISTEN FOR SPECIFIC INFORMATION** Listen again and complete the information below.

1 AUDREY HEPBURN
Country: [1] Belgium
Jobs: [2] actor
[3] model
[4] dancer
She was famous for her [5] beautiful clothes.

2 WILLIAM SHAKESPEARE
Country: [6] England
Jobs: [7] writer
[8] actor
[9] Hundreds of words in everyday English come from his work.

3 MARIE TUSSAUD
Country: [10] France
Job: Famous for [11] Madame Tussauds in London. [12] waxwork maker

4 NELSON MANDELA
Country: [13] South Africa
Job: President for [14] five years.

A VISIT TO

MADAME TUSSAUDS

In cities all over the world – in London, Paris, New York and New Delhi – people come to Madame Tussauds to see waxwork statues of famous people from the past and present. Why were they famous? Were they actors? Writers? Or inspirational leaders? Enjoy a visit to Madame Tussauds to find out more about these famous faces.

9.1 Famous faces

LEAD-IN

Write three categories on the board, e.g. *painter / soccer player / scientist*. Choose a letter and ask students to write a name for each category starting with that letter. They could do this individually or in groups. Give a short time limit. Students get a point if they find someone for all three categories. (Adjust the category topics and number of categories to suit your students.)

LISTENING

A–B (9.1) Read the introduction to Madame Tussauds together and ask if students have ever visited a Madame Tussauds. Focus students on the pictures, and ask if they know any of the people. Students could predict the years the people were born. Then play the audio while students listen for the dates.

C (9.1) Focus students on the four biographies. Elicit what kind of information they should expect to hear. Ask students to predict/ guess some of the answers. Then play the audio while they listen and write. Repeat the audio until they have finished. Discuss answers as a class.

AUDIO SCRIPT

9.1

Listening, Exercise B
A = Anna Ni = Nick AG = Audio Guide

A: Oh, who's this? Was she a model?
Ni: Oh, I don't know. Push the button. Let's find out who she was.
Ex C Q2 **AG:** Meet Hollywood actor Audrey Hepburn. She was
Ex C Q1 born in Belgium on May 4, 1929. Her movies Ex B a
were very popular in the 1950s and 60s. She wasn't
Ex C Q3 & Q4 just an actor, she was also a dancer and a model. She
Ex C Q5 was famous for her beautiful clothes!
A: Hey Nick, come here. Look! Why was he famous?
Ni: I don't know. Let's listen.
AG: William Shakespeare was born in Stratford-upon-
Ex C Q6 Avon in England on April 26, 1564. He was Ex B b
Ex C Q7 a famous writer. He's famous for plays such as *Romeo and Juliet* and *Hamlet*. He wasn't just a writer, he
Ex C Q8 was an actor, too. His plays were very important for
Ex C Q9 the English language. Hundreds of the words we use in English today come from Shakespeare.
Ni: Look over here. I don't know who this is. Do you know?
A: No idea!
Ex C Q10 **AG:** Marie Tussaud was born in Strasbourg in France on
Ex B c December 1, 1761. She's now famous for the
Ex C Q11 Madame Tussauds museum in London. Marie
Ex C Q12 Tussaud was very good at making wax models of people and her waxworks were very popular. Photographs weren't common at the time, but Marie Tussaud made a waxwork of herself – was this a type of selfie?
A: That was really interesting! Now we know who this is! He was President of …
Ni: South Africa!
Ex C Q13 **AG:** This famous politician was born in South Africa on
Ex B d July 18, 1918. His name is Nelson Mandela.
Ex C Q14 He was in prison for 27 years. Later, he was president for five years from 1994 to 1999. He was the first black president of South Africa.

GRAMMAR HUB

9.1

Simple past: *was/were*

	Positive	Negative
I/he/she/it	**It was** interesting.	**She was not** young. **She wasn't** young.
you/we/they	**You were** amazing.	**We were not** there. **We weren't** there.

	Question	Positive short answer	Negative short answer
I/he/she/it	**Was he** popular?	**Yes, he was.**	**No, he wasn't.**
you/we/they	**Were they** at home?	**Yes, they were.**	**No, they weren't.**

- The simple past forms of the verb *be* are *was, were, wasn't* and *weren't*.
  Marie Tussaud was an artist from France.
  My grandparents weren't famous.
- We use *was(n't)/were(n't)* to talk about people and things in the past.
  Nelson Mandela was the first black president of South Africa.
- For *yes/no* questions, we put *was* or *were* at the beginning of the question, followed by the subject.
  Was he a popular writer?
- For *wh-* questions, we put *what, where, why*, etc at the beginning of the question, followed by *was/were* + the subject.
  Who was that man?
  Where was it?
  Why were you late?

9.1 Famous faces

GRAMMAR

A Do the first sentence as an example and then ask students to find *was* and *were* in the sentences in the exercise.

B Elicit who the *was* is talking about. Is it one person (singular) or more (plural)? Elicit the difference between *yes/no* and *Wh-* questions using real examples in the class, then put them into pairs to complete the table.

C Students complete the rules. Elicit examples from the class to illustrate it, e.g. *Tom was early today*.

D Direct students to the **Grammar Hub** (see below and TB66).

E Give an example of a celebrity you really liked when you were young, and talk about them briefly. Then ask students to do the same. Monitor the discussion, encouraging them to ask questions and add more details. Get feedback from one or two students about their partner's choices. Use the **Grammar Worksheet** on page W32 for extra practice.

VOCABULARY

9.2 **A** Students match the numbers to the words. Play the audio while they check, then listen again and repeat.

9.3 **B** Students complete the exercise. Show how the *first/second/third* difference continues with *twentieth* but not *twelfth*. Practice the pronunciation of all of them, starting with *first*.

9.4 **C** Play the audio while students listen and circle the years. Play it again and discuss any differences with students' L1.

D Ask students to stand up and mingle, asking classmates about their birthdays. Walk around joining in. Ask students to stand in a line according to birthday. Use the **Vocabulary Worksheet** on page W31 for extra practice.

PRONUNCIATION

9.5 **A** Play the audio while students read and listen, then write the first sentence on the board and play the audio again. Elicit the fact that *was* and *he* are connected, draw a line to show the link and ask students to read it. Then repeat the audio while students listen and draw lines for the remaining sentences. Demonstrate and practice the pronunciation.

9.6 **B** Play the audio while students listen and choose, then play it again and write the correct sentences on the board. Demonstrate and practice the whole sentence pronunciation, including the link between *she* and *an*.

SPEAKING

A Give an example of someone from the past (not the person you used as an example before). Ask students to choose a different person, and make sure they all choose someone different. If necessary, write some categories on the board, e.g. *sports/politics/art*. Go through the questions briefly talking about your choice, as an example. Then ask students to write the information about their person.

B Put students into pairs. Make sure they understand they must not look at each other's information or give the name of the person; use the model conversation as an example. Then let them discuss. Monitor and encourage complete questions and answers and correct pronunciation of *was/wasn't*.

C Ask students to report back to the whole class. You could make copies of the table to complete while they listen, to give them a purpose. At the end, you could lead a whole-class discussion about the people, e.g. *Who was the most famous? Who helped the world the most?* etc.

GRAMMAR HUB

9.1

Simple past: *was/were*

A Complete the conversation with *was, wasn't, were* or *weren't*.

A: Where [1] ___were___ you yesterday?
B: I [2] ___was___ in London.
A: Why [3] ___were___ you in London?
B: We [4] ___were___ at Madame Tussauds on a day trip.
A: [5] ___Was___ it fun?
B: Yes, it [6] ___was___ amazing. There were statues of writers, actors and politicians. They [7] ___were___ all so real!
A: [8] ___Were___ you there all day?
B: No, we [9] ___weren't___. We [10] ___were___ there for about three hours.

B Put the words in the correct order to make questions.

1. Charles Dickens / was / who ___Who was Charles Dickens___?
2. when / he / was / born ___When was he born___?
3. he / from London / was ___Was he from London___?
4. from / where / he / was ___Where was he from___?
5. rich / were / his parents ___Were his parents rich___?
6. his best book / what / was ___What was his best book___?

C Match the questions (1–6) in Exercise B and the answers (a–f).

_3_ **a** No, he wasn't.
_6_ **b** It was *Oliver Twist*, in my opinion.
_1_ **c** He was a famous writer.
_5_ **d** No, they weren't.
_2_ **e** He was born in 1812.
_4_ **f** He was from Portsmouth.

➤ Go back to page 67.

GRAMMAR
Simple past: *was/were*

A Read the examples from *A visit to Madame Tussauds*. Underline examples of *was* and *were*.

1 Why were they famous?
2 Were they actors?
3 Was she a model?
4 Her movies were very popular.
5 Why was he famous?
6 He was a famous writer.
7 He wasn't just a writer.
8 Photographs weren't common.

B WORK IT OUT Complete the table with the sentences from Exercise A.

was/were	Singular	Plural
positive	He was a famous writer.	Her movies were very popular.
negative	He wasn't just a writer.	Photographs weren't common.
yes/no questions	Was she a model?	Were they actors?
wh- questions	Why was he famous?	Why were they famous?

C WORK IT OUT Look at Exercises A and B. Complete the rules with *was, wasn't, were* or *weren't*.

Simple past: *was/were*

1 Was is the past form of *is*. Were is the past form of *are*.
2 Wasn't is the past form of *isn't*. Weren't is the past form of *aren't*.
3 We make *yes/no* questions with was or were + subject.
4 We make *wh-* questions with a question word + was or were.

D Go to the Grammar Hub on page 114.

E SPEAK Work in pairs. Who was your favorite celebrity when you were young? Why were they famous?

VOCABULARY
Dates and years

9.2 **A** Match the numbers (1–6) with the words in the box. Listen and check.

fifth first fourth second sixth third

1 1st first
2 2nd second
3 3rd third
4 4th fourth
5 5th fifth
6 6th sixth

9.3 **B** Listen and write the numbers that you hear.

a 7th b 8th c 9th d 10th e 12th
f 18th g 20th h 31st i 42nd j 53rd

9.4 **C** Listen and circle the years you hear.

a 1948 / 1958 c 2014 / 2040 e 2002 / 2012
b 1909 / 1999 d 1564 / 1546 f 1800 / 1900

D SPEAK Stand up and walk around. Say the day and month of your birthday to each other. Then stand in order according to your birthday.

PRONUNCIATION
was he / was she

9.5 **A** Read and listen. Draw a line (‿) to show the linked words.

1 Was‿he‿a writer?
2 Was‿she‿a writer?
3 Where was‿he born?
4 Where was‿she born?

9.6 **B** Listen to each question and choose the words you hear.

1 *Was he* / *Was she* an artist?
2 *Was he* / *Was she* an actor?
3 Why *was he* / *was she* famous?
4 When *was he* / *was she* born?

SPEAKING

A PREPARE Think of a famous person from the past. Complete the information about him or her.

Man or woman?

Country?

Job?

When were they famous?

Why were they famous?

B DISCUSS Work in pairs. Describe your famous person. Don't say the name of the person. Ask your partner questions. Who is it?

A: He was a singer in The Beatles.
B: John Lennon?

C REPORT Tell the class about your famous person.

Talk about famous people from the past

V everyday verbs S scanning G simple past: regular verbs P past tense endings: /d/, /t/ and /ɪd/

VOCABULARY
Everyday verbs

A Look at the pictures. Match the phrases in the box with the correct pictures.

collect stamps	design a building	help a friend
paint a picture	receive a present	start to run
study in college	travel to the city	

1 study in college

2 collect stamps

3 design a building

4 travel to the city

5 receive a present

6 help a friend

7 start to run

8 paint a picture

B SPEAK Work in pairs. Use the verbs to make sentences that are true for you.

A: I collect CDs.

B: I travel to Rome every fall for work.

READING

A PREPARE TO READ Which heroes from children's stories can you name?

B READ FOR GIST Read *Goodnight stories for rebel girls*. Choose the correct options to complete the summary.

Goodnight stories for rebel girls is about *real women* / *women in children's stories*.

Scanning

When you scan a text, you read it to look for specific information. Scanning helps you find information more quickly. Look for key words, names, dates and percentages.

GOODNIGHT STORIES for REBEL GIRLS

What were your favorite stories when you were young? Who were your heroes? How many were girls?

In 2011, the University of Florida studied the number of male and female characters in children's storybooks. Ex C Q1 There were male characters in every book. But 25 percent had no female characters. And in 37 percent of the books, the female characters didn't talk. Ex C Q2

Ex C Q3 Two Italian women, Elena Favilli and Francesca Cavallo, decided to change this. They wanted to make a book of stories about real women. They asked people for money online to make the book. They received over a million dollars! Here are some of the women in their book:

Maria Sibylla Merian (1647–1717)
Merian was a scientist. Ex C Q4 She was born in Frankfurt in Germany. When she was a child, she collected butterflies and insects. She discovered many new things about them. She traveled to South America and painted beautiful pictures of nature.

Ada Lovelace (1815–1852)
Lovelace was an English mathematician. She didn't study at public school or college. She studied at home with a teacher. When she was 12, she designed a flying machine. Also, she was the first computer programmer in the world. Ex C Q5

Wangari Maathai (1940–2011)
Maathai was a Kenyan politician. She studied at universities in the US and in Germany. She wanted to help people in Kenya, so she and a group of women started to plant trees. They planted hundreds of trees and the trees helped people and nature. She received the Nobel Peace Prize in 2004. Ex C Q6

9.2 Voices from the past

LEAD-IN

Write the names of three famous people from your country's past on the board and, if possible, display images of them. Ask students what they know about the three people and add correct facts and information to the board. Students work individually, or in small groups if sharing a nationality, to do the same. They then present the names and, if possible, images to the class to find out what other students know about the past of these people from their country. If students are from the same nationality group, organize a pyramid discussion in which they choose the top three most important people in their country's past.

VOCABULARY

A Students work individually to match the phrases and pictures, then check in pairs. Then go through the answers, practicing pronunciation of the whole phrases, using connected speech to make the phrases into language 'chunks'.

B Give a few sentences about yourself as an example, then students work in pairs to discuss while you monitor and help with vocabulary if needed. Ask for a few interesting things people do at the end and see what the most popular activities are. Use the **Vocabulary Worksheet** on page W33 for extra practice.

READING

A Students look at the picture. Name one or two famous children's book characters, write them on the board and ask for more ideas; write them all on the board. Ask which books students read when they were children and which ones they liked or didn't like.

B Read the summary together and elicit the answer from students asking them to explain how they made their decision.

METHODOLOGY HUB by Jim Scrivener

Approaches to reading

Reading to oneself (as opposed to reading aloud) is, like listening, a 'receptive' skill, and similar teaching procedures can be used to help learners. The task–feedback circle (Figure 9.1) works well with reading texts, as well as with listening tasks.

The most obvious differences are to do with the fact that people read at different speeds and in different ways. While a recording takes a definite length of time to play through, in a reading activity, individuals can control the speed they work at and what they are looking at.

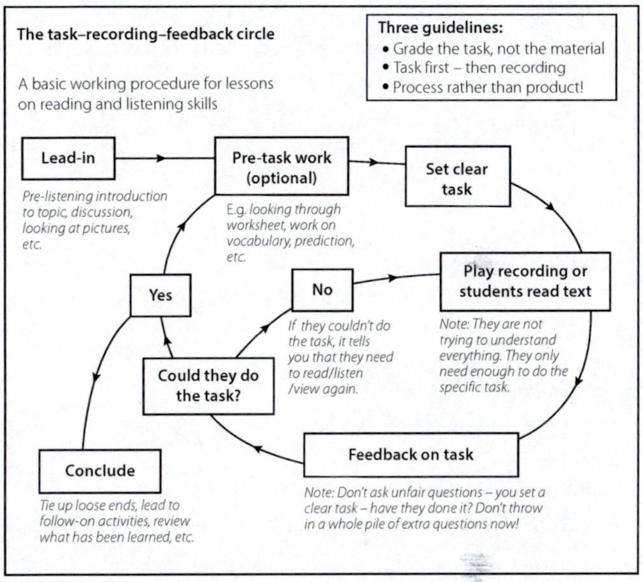

FIGURE 9.1 The task–feedback circle

GRAMMAR HUB

9.2

Simple past: regular verbs

	Positive	Negative
I/you/he/she/it/we/they	**She lived** in Mexico. **We learned** a song.	**I did not play** tennis. **I didn't play** tennis.

- We use the simple past tense to talk about actions in the past.
  Alexander Fleming discovered penicillin in 1928.
- We form the simple past tense of regular verbs by adding *-ed* to the main verb. If the verb ends in *-e*, just add *-d*. If the verb ends in *-y*, change the *-y* to an *-i* and add *-ed*.
  start → started
  live → lived
  study → studied
- To form the negative, we put *did not* (*didn't*) before the main verb.
  She didn't study math.
- To talk about a period of time in the past, we can use *for* + minutes, months, years, etc.
  He lived in Spain for three years.

Be careful!

- Use *didn't* for the negative, but don't add *-d* or *-ed* to the main verb. The main verb stays the same.
  She didn't live there. NOT ~~She didn't lived there.~~

9.2 Voices from the past

C Read through the *Scanning* box together. Then ask students to read individually and then check in pairs. Encourage students to mark the relevant passages in the text. Go over the answers, asking students to justify their answers by referring to the text.

D Students work in small groups to discuss the questions. Monitor and encourage fluency. Get feedback from all the groups at the end; did they all feel the same or were there different views?

GRAMMAR

A Do the first one together as an example, then ask students to work individually to find the rest. Write the answers on the board in a list.

B Focus students on the Ada Lovelace section of the text and ask students to find a negative verb (*didn't study*).

C Put students into pairs to work out the rules. When they finish, go through the rules, using the examples on the board and colored markers to clarify them, especially the fact that we don't use the *-ed* ending on the verb with *did*. Demonstrate some examples with other verbs, e.g. *like*, *watch*, to check understanding.

D Direct students to the **Grammar Hub** (see below and TB68). Use the **Grammar Worksheet** on page W34 for extra practice.

PRONUNCIATION

9.7 **A** Draw the table and phonemic symbols on the board. Play the audio while students read and listen. Then play it again while they repeat; write the words under the symbols in the correct column. Isolate the three sounds and ask students to say them. Practice differentiating between the sounds by associating an action with each sound. Ask students to stand up when they hear /d/, to sit down when they hear /t/ and clap when they hear /ɪd/. Say the sounds at random and see if students can recognize each sound.

9.8 **B** Play the audio while students listen and add the words to the correct columns. Elicit answers from students to complete the table on the board and ask them if they can see any patterns, e.g. *wanted/collected/started* all end in *-ted*.

SPEAKING HUB

A Put students into two groups, A and B. Direct Group B to the **Communication Hub** (see TB97). In their groups, students work together to complete the sentences with the past tense of the verbs in the box and choose the correct information.

B A student from one group reads their sentences to the other group. The other group checks the grammar and the answer to the question. A maximum of two points is available for each question, one for correct grammar and one for the correct answer. Groups take turns reading and checking the answers.

C Do the same thing with the other group. Check all the answers. Were the students surprised by any of the information?

Extra activity

The groups of students from the Speaking Hub section write their own quiz using the same format and then do the same activity as a competition. They can either research the answers in class on their digital devices or you could provide some reference materials for the groups to use.

GRAMMAR HUB

9.2

Simple past: regular verbs

A Complete the sentences with the simple past form of the verbs in parentheses.

1. Picasso __changed__ (*change*) the way we look at art.
2. We __tried__ (*try*) to find information about Frida Kahlo.
3. William Shakespeare __lived__ (*live*) in a town called Stratford-upon-Avon.
4. Kim __decided__ (*decide*) to write about Ada Lovelace for her project.
5. The women __planted__ (*plant*) trees in the park.
6. I __started__ (*start*) to read a book about famous women scientists.
7. Our history class __studied__ (*study*) the Anasazi people of North America last year.
8. Shelly __remembered__ (*remember*) to bring back my book about Wangari Maathai.

B Make the sentences negative.

1. Ada Lovelace studied art.
   Ada Lovelace __didn't study art__.
2. The female characters talked a lot in the book.
   The female characters __didn't talk a lot__ in the book.
3. Elena Favilli and Francesca Cavallo created a book about famous men.
   Elena Favilli and Francesca Cavallo __didn't create a book about famous men__.
4. Maria Sibylla Merian collected clothes.
   Maria Sibylla Merian __didn't collect clothes__
5. Wangari Maathai planted flowers.
   Wangari Maathai __didn't plant flowers__

C Complete the sentences with the past form of the verbs in parentheses.

1. I __didn't want__ (*not want*) to be a dancer when I was a child.
2. We __studied__ (*study*) French when we were at school.
3. My wife __designed__ (*design*) the house we live in.
4. He __started__ (*start*) a new yoga class last week.
5. She __didn't use__ (*not use*) her phone yesterday.
6. They __didn't receive__ (*not receive*) the letter last Monday.

➤ Go back to page 69.

C READ FOR DETAIL Are these statements true (T) or false (F)?

1 There are female characters in all children's books. T / (F) — 25% had no female characters.

2 Some female characters in children's books don't say anything. (T) / F

3 The writers of *Goodnight stories for rebel girls* are men. They are women. T / (F)

4 Maria Sibylla Merian was a mathematician. She was a scientist. T / (F)

5 Ada Lovelace was a computer programmer. (T) / F

6 Wangari Maathai was the winner of an important prize. (T) / F

D SPEAK Work in groups. Discuss the questions.

1 Do you think that this book was a good idea? Why/Why not?

2 Do you think that this book is good for boys, too? Why/Why not?

3 Do girls and boys read the same or different books? Why/Why not?

GRAMMAR

Simple past: regular verbs

A Read the introduction to the article again. Write the simple past: form of the verbs.

1 study ___studied___
2 decide ___decided___
3 want ___wanted___
4 ask ___asked___
5 receive ___received___

B Read the section about Ada Lovelace again and underline the negative verb.

C WORK IT OUT Match the two parts of each rule (1–4) with (a–d). Use the examples in Exercises A and B to help you.

Simple past: regular verbs

1 We add *-ed*	a we use *did* + *not* (*didn't*) before the verb.
2 We add *-d*	b to verbs ending in *-e*.
3 With verbs ending in *-y*,	c we cut the *-y* and add *-ied*.
4 To form the negative,	d to most verbs.

D Go to the **Grammar Hub** on **page 114**.

PRONUNCIATION

Past tense endings: /d/, /t/ and /ɪd/

9.7 **A** Read and listen to the verbs. Notice how we say the endings.

/d/	/t/	/ɪd/
studied	helped	wanted
designed	asked	decided
lived	talked	started
traveled		collected

9.8 **B** Listen to the verbs and add them to the table in Exercise A.

1 decided
2 asked
3 designed
4 lived
5 started
6 talked
7 collected
8 traveled

SPEAKING HUB

Work in groups. Group A – Stay on this page. Group B – Go to the **Communication Hub** on **page 130**.

A PREPARE Complete the sentences with the past tense of verbs from the box. Then choose the correct information (a, b or c) to complete the sentences.

discover live receive start

1 Larry Page and Segey Brin ___started___ the company Google in …
(a) 1998. b 2001. c 2008.

2 John Couch Adams ___discovered___ the planet Neptune in …
a 1696. (b) 1846. c 1906.

3 William Shakespeare ___lived___ in England in the … century.
a 15th (b) 16th c 17th

4 Malala Yousafzai ___received___ the Nobel Peace Prize in …
a 2001. (b) 2014. c 2016.

B PRACTICE Read your sentences to Group B. They will check your answers.

C PRACTICE Listen to Group B's sentences. Check their answers.

Correct sentences:

1 Ibn Battuta **traveled** from Morocco to China in the **14th century**.

2 Gabriel García Márquez **received** the Nobel Prize in Literature in **1982**.

3 Neil Armstrong **walked** on the moon in **1969**.

4 Steve Jobs and Steve Wozniak **designed** the first personal computers in **1976**.

Talk about people's achievements

9.3 Pizza Roma

F– make recommendations

COMPREHENSION

A ▶ 00.10–01:14 Watch the first part of the video and choose the correct options to complete the sentences.

1 Sam is *opening* / *closing* the café. closing
2 Sam *knows* / *doesn't know* Metal Train. doesn't know
3 Gaby *loves* / *hates* pizza. loves
4 Pizza Roma is *terrible* / *amazing*. amazing
5 Pizza Roma has *big* / *small* pizzas. big
6 The pizzas are *expensive* / *cheap*. cheap
7 Pizza Roma is *near* / *far from* Sam's Café. near

B ▶ 01:15–01:34 Watch part of the video and choose the correct set of directions from Sam's Café to Pizza Roma.

1  ☐

2  ☐

3  ☑

C ▶ 01:35–03:00 Watch the second part of the video. Discuss the questions.

1 What was Gaby's pizza like? It was bad.
2 Did she eat it? No
3 Where did she buy it? From Pizza Nova
4 What does Gaby eat? An apple
5 What does Lucy do? She gets another pizza.
6 Where was Lucy's pizza from? From Pizza Roma

USEFUL PHRASES

A Who says it? Gaby (G) or Sam (S)?

1 I'm afraid I'm closing now. S
2 Hey! That's a nice cap! S
3 Ah, I see. S
4 It's not far. S
5 It's next to the station. S
6 I've got it, thanks! G

Glossary
shop (n) (British) = store (n) (American)

B Match the useful phrases in Exercise A with the meanings.

I understand. [1] Ah, I see. [2] I've got it, thanks!
I'm sorry ... [3] I'm afraid ...
It's near here. [4] It's not far.
I like your ... [5] That's a nice ...

C Replace the underlined phrases with useful phrases from Exercise A.

Gaby: Hi, Sam. [1]I like your T-shirt. (That's a nice)
Sam: Thanks. It's from my friend's shop.
Gaby: Where's her shop?
Sam: Oh, [2]it's near here. (it's not far.) Just go out the café, turn left, turn left again and it's on your right.
Gaby: Left, left, right. [3]I understand, (I've got it,) thanks!
Sam: [4]I'm sorry. (I'm afraid) I'm going to my yoga class now. It starts in five minutes.
Gaby: Ah, [5]I understand! (I see.) Bye!

FUNCTIONAL LANGUAGE

Making recommendations

A ▶ Complete the phrases with the words in the box. Then watch the video again and check your answers.

Don't   Do you know   There's   You should

Asking for a recommendation

[1] Do you know / Is there a good restaurant near here?

Giving a recommendation

[2] There's / I know a really good pizza restaurant. It's called Pizza Roma.
I was there last week. And the pizza was amazing. It was really big and really cheap.
[3] You should / Why don't you try it.
[4] Don't / I wouldn't go to Pizza Nova! I went there last week. The pizza was bad! It was really small and really expensive.

B Circle the correct options to complete the conversation.

Liz: [1]*Do you know* / *There's* a good café near here? (Do you know)
Mark: Do you like big breakfasts?
Liz: I love big breakfasts.
Mark: OK, [2]*why don't you* / *there's* a really good café. It's called Tom's Café. I was there this morning. The breakfast is [3]*amazing* / *horrible*. It's really big and really cheap. [4]You *should* / *shouldn't* go there. (there's; amazing; should)
Liz: Thanks! Don't go to Rachel's Café. I went there yesterday. The coffee was [5]*amazing* / *terrible*. It was really small and really bad. (terrible)
Mark: Oh, I see. Thanks.

9.3 Pizza Roma

LEAD-IN

Ask students if they like pizza and if they have a favorite pizza (or other) restaurant near the English class. Take the opportunity to review directions and ask students to give you directions to their favorite (pizza) restaurants.

COMPREHENSION

A ▶ 00:10–01:14 Allow students time to read through the sentences. They could predict the answers at this point. Play the video for students to watch and choose the correct options to complete the sentences.

B ▶ 01:15–01:34 Review the direction arrows with the students. At this stage, elicit the directions for each arrow (e.g. *turn left*). Students then watch the section of the video and choose the correct set of directions.

C ▶ 01:35–03:00 Students watch the second part of the video and then discuss the questions in small groups. Check answers as a whole class.

USEFUL PHRASES

A Review the useful phrases as a whole class and ask students to recall who said each one. Replay the video as required.

B Students work in pairs to match the useful phrases with the meanings. Check answers as a class.

C Focus the students on the conversation and highlight the underlining. Students then work alone to replace the underlined phrases with useful phrases from Exercise A. Students check answers in pairs.

FUNCTIONAL LANGUAGE

A ▶ Review the box of phrases for asking for and giving recommendations. Students complete the phrases. Play the video again for students to check their answers.

B Students read the conversation and choose the correct options. Check answers as a whole class.

VIDEO SCRIPT

S = Sam G = Gaby L = Lucy

S: I'm afraid I'm closing now.
G: Oh, OK.
S: Thanks. Hey, that's a nice cap!
G: Well …
S: Ah, I see. Who are Metal Train? Nice!
G: Sam, do you know a good restaurant near here?
S: A good restaurant near here. Ooh, do you like pizza?
G: I love pizza!
S: Great. There's a really good pizza restaurant. It's called Pizza Roma.
G: Great.
S: I was there last week and the pizza was amazing. It was really big and really cheap. You should try it.
G: Where is it?
S: It's not far. Go out of the café, turn left and then right and then right again and it's next to the station.
G: So I turn left, then right, then right again?
S: Yes.
G: I've got it, thanks!
L: Hey Gaby. How are you?
G: Hi Lucy. Not great. I got a pizza, but it was terrible! Don't go to Pizza Nova!
L: You should try Pizza Roma. They do great pizzas.
S: It's called Pizza Roma.
G: Who's that?
L: Pizza Roma delivery!
G: Thank you!

METHODOLOGY HUB by Jim Scrivener

Analyzing functions

Why do people speak or write to each other? To show off their ability to make grammatically correct sentences? Obviously not. There is no point making perfectly formed sentences if we do not succeed in getting our point across. We speak or write because we have messages to communicate or there is something we hope to achieve.

Functions and their exponents

Examples of language used to achieve a particular function are known as exponents of a function. Thus *Do you have the time?* is an exponent of the function of 'asking for information'. Some exponents are fixed formulae that allow for little or no alteration: you can't really change any word in *Do you have the time?* without losing the meaning. Other exponents have more generative possibilities: *Could you tell me the way to the station?* is usable in a variety of situations by substituting different vocabulary for *station*.

For classroom purposes, teachers usually think of communicative functions under general headings such as 'complaining', 'asking for information', 'sympathizing', etc and plan lessons to introduce students to sets of useful exponents which they can practice in activities such as role plays and communication games.

9.3 Pizza Roma

PRONUNCIATION

9.9 **A** Tell students not to focus on the color of the text at this point but to notice the underlined stressed words and syllables. Play the audio for the students to listen and follow in their books.

9.9 **B** Students listen to the conversation line by line and repeat, focusing on the marked stress.

SPEAKING

A Students read through the *Restaurants near you* text and discuss the restaurants. Open this up into a whole-class discussion.

B Focus the students on the blue and red phrases in the conversation in Pronunciation Exercise A and read through the task instructions carefully. Work through an example following the instructions together on the board if your students need the support. As students work in pairs to rewrite the conversation, monitor and assist as required.

C Students practice their conversation. They could use their digital devices to record, watch and improve their delivery of the conversation. Then invite pairs to perform their conversations in front of the class.

D Students choose different restaurants, change roles and repeat the exercise.

Extra activity

Students create their own *Restaurants near you* reviews about places near to the location of the English class. They can create and practice similar role plays. When these are finished, students can post their reviews around the room. Then the whole class moves around the room to read all the reviews, using post-it stickers to add comments for the restaurants they know.

METHODOLOGY HUB by Jim Scrivener

Drama

Six types of drama activity are commonly found in English-language teaching classrooms:

- Role play – Students act out small scenes using their own ideas or from ideas and information on role cards.
- Simulation – This is really a large-scale role play. Role cards are normally used, and there is usually other background information as well. The intention is to create a much more complete, complex 'world', say of a business company, television studio, government body, etc.
- Drama games – Short games that usually involve movement and imagination.
- Guided improvisation – You improvise a scene and the students join in one by one in character, until the whole scene (or story) takes on a life of its own.
- Acting play scripts – Short written sketches or scenes are acted by the students.
- Prepared improvised drama – Students in small groups invent and rehearse a short scene or story that they then perform for the others.

All of these are good ways to get students use the language. By bringing the outside world into the classroom like this, we can provide a lot of useful practice that would otherwise be impossible in cafés, stores, banks, businesses, streets, parties, etc. There may also be a freeing from the constraints of culture and expected behavior; this can be personally and linguistically very liberating. Curiously, it is sometimes the shiest students who are usually most able to seize the potential.

Success or failure of drama activities depends crucially on your perceived attitude and that of the other students; without a certain degree of trust, acceptance and respect, the chances for useful work are greatly diminished.

TEACHING IDEA by David Seymour and Maria Popova

Conversation: Restaurants

Work in small groups. I'll give each group a different type of restaurant. Create a menu and include appetizers, main courses, side dishes, desserts and drinks. Don't forget the prices.

a steak house, a vegetarian café, an expensive French eatery, a highway service station restaurant, a seafood restaurant

In pairs, describe your last visit to a restaurant in detail.

when and where, the food and drink, who you were with, the décor, the waiter, the music, what you talked about, the other people there

If anyone has experience of working in a restaurant, answer questions about the job from the class.

GABY

SAM

LUCY

PRONUNCIATION

9.9 **A** Listen to the conversation and notice how the underlined words are stressed.

Frank: Do you know a good restaurant near here?
Emily: Do you like sushi?
Frank: I love Japanese food.
Emily: There's a really good Japanese restaurant. It's called Sushirama.
Frank: Great.
Emily: I was there last week. And the sushi was amazing. It was really fresh. You should try it. Don't go to Suzy's Sushi! It's really bad.

9.9 **B** Listen again and repeat the conversation. Copy the stress.

SPEAKING

A PLAN Work in pairs. Read *Restaurants near you*. Discuss the questions.

1 Which restaurant(s) would you like to go to? Why?
2 Which restaurant(s) would you **not** like to go to? Why?

B PREPARE Rewrite the conversation in Pronunciation Exercise A.

- Replace the blue phrases with new ideas from the Functional language section.
- Replace the words in red using the ideas in the reviews below.
- Create some directions and include three or more useful phrases.

C PRACTICE Work in pairs. Practice and then perform your conversation in front of the class.

D REPEAT Choose different restaurants. Change roles and have a new conversation.

Restaurants near you

Moo Burger Bar
★★★★☆
Great fries!

Bob's Burgers
★☆☆☆☆
Terrible burgers, bad fries.

Puk Yuk Thai
★★★★★
Amazing! Best Thai food in town.

Bangkok House
★☆☆☆☆
Expensive Thai food.

Pierre's French cuisine
★☆☆☆☆
Bad service. Terrible food.

Paris mon amour
★★★★★
Amazing French food.

Make recommendations

Unit 9 Writing

9 Writing

Write a short biography

W– organizing your notes

A Work in pairs. What can you see in the pictures? What is the connection between them?

B Read the description and complete the notes.

Leonardo da Vinci

Leonardo da Vinci was born near Florence in Italy in 1452. He was an artist, a mathematician, a scientist, a musician and a writer. He is famous for his paintings, but he also designed machines. He painted the famous *Mona Lisa*. He painted this picture in 1503 and it is now in the Louvre Museum in Paris, France. It is a picture of a woman with a beautiful smile.

Name: Leonardo da Vinci *Occupation(s):* artist, mathematician, scientist, musician, writer

Birth date: 1452 *Why famous?* for his paintings

Birth place: near Florence, Italy *Famous painting:* Mona Lisa

Organizing your notes

When you are planning your writing, think about how to organize your notes. In a biography, you can start with personal information (date and place of birth), describe their job, say why they are famous and finally describe one thing they are famous for.

C Read the notes below. Number the information in the best order for a description.

4 artist
5 changed the world of art
1 Pablo Picasso
6 Cubism, new style of painting
3 Málaga, Spain
2 1881

WRITING

A PLAN Add any more details that you know about Picasso. Decide where to write this information.

B WRITE Write a description using the information in Exercise C. Compare with a partner.

Write a short biography

Refer students to the biography as a model for the writing task.

To extend this practice, students could write a biography of another person. Give them time to research the information and organize their notes.

Unit 9 Review

GRAMMAR

A Complete the sentences with the correct past form of *be*.

1 Shakespeare ___was___ a writer and a poet.
2 Pablo Picasso and Marie Tussaud ___were___ artists.
3 A: ___Was___ Maya Angelou a poet?
B: Yes, she ___was___.
4 A: ___Was___ Gandhi a scientist?
B: No, he ___wasn't___.
5 There ___weren't___ any phone selfies in the 1700s.
6 There ___wasn't___ a black president of South Africa before Nelson Mandela.

B Complete the sentences with past tense forms in the positive (+) or negative (-).

1 Last weekend, I ___stayed___ (+ *stay*) at home and I ___painted___ (+ *paint*) my bedroom.
2 Tamara ___didn't pick up___ (– *pick up*) her computer from the store, but she ___organized___ (+ *organize*) her files.
3 Omar ___didn't visit___ (– *visit*) his grandma, but he ___called___ (+ *call*) her at home.

VOCABULARY

A Complete the sentences with words for ordinal numbers.

1 We live in the ___twenty-first___ (*21st*) century.
2 Shakespeare lived in the ___sixteenth___ (*16th*) century.
3 March is the ___third___ (*3rd*) month of the year.
4 George Washington was the ___first___ (*1st*) US president.

B Complete the description with the past form of a verb from the box.

be help return start study travel

Marco Polo

Marco Polo was born in Venice in 1254. He and his father [1] ___traveled___ to China. They [2] ___started___ their journey in 1271 when Marco Polo [3] ___was___ 17 years old. The journey was long and difficult. Marco Polo stayed in China for many years and [4] ___studied___ Chinese language and culture. When Marco [5] ___returned___ to Italy 26 years later, his friend [6] ___helped___ him to write a book about his experiences.

72 LOOKING BACK

LEAD-IN

Bring in or display some pictures of famous paintings. Write the names of the artists on strips of paper. Give one picture to half of the students and the names of the artists to the rest. Ask students to walk around and find their partner.

WRITING

A Students discuss the questions in pairs. Write some of their ideas on the board, but do not give feedback on whether they are correct or not.

B Students read the description and complete the notes. Go through the answers and see if their ideas on the board were right.

C Focus students on the *Organizing your notes* box. Ask them to compare the ideas in it against the *Leonardo da Vinci* text. Then ask them to work in pairs or individually to decide on the best order. Discuss their ideas, emphasizing that there can be more than one 'correct' order.

WRITING TASK

A Ask students to add any more information about Picasso that they have. They could research a little if there is time and they have access to the internet, but if they do, make sure they don't just copy the information; they should use the information to write notes, then write it in their own words.

B Students write their descriptions. Walk around helping, making sure they follow their plans. When they finish, encourage them to correct their own work before they show other students. After they compare, you could display their work on a board or a shared class site.

10 It's history

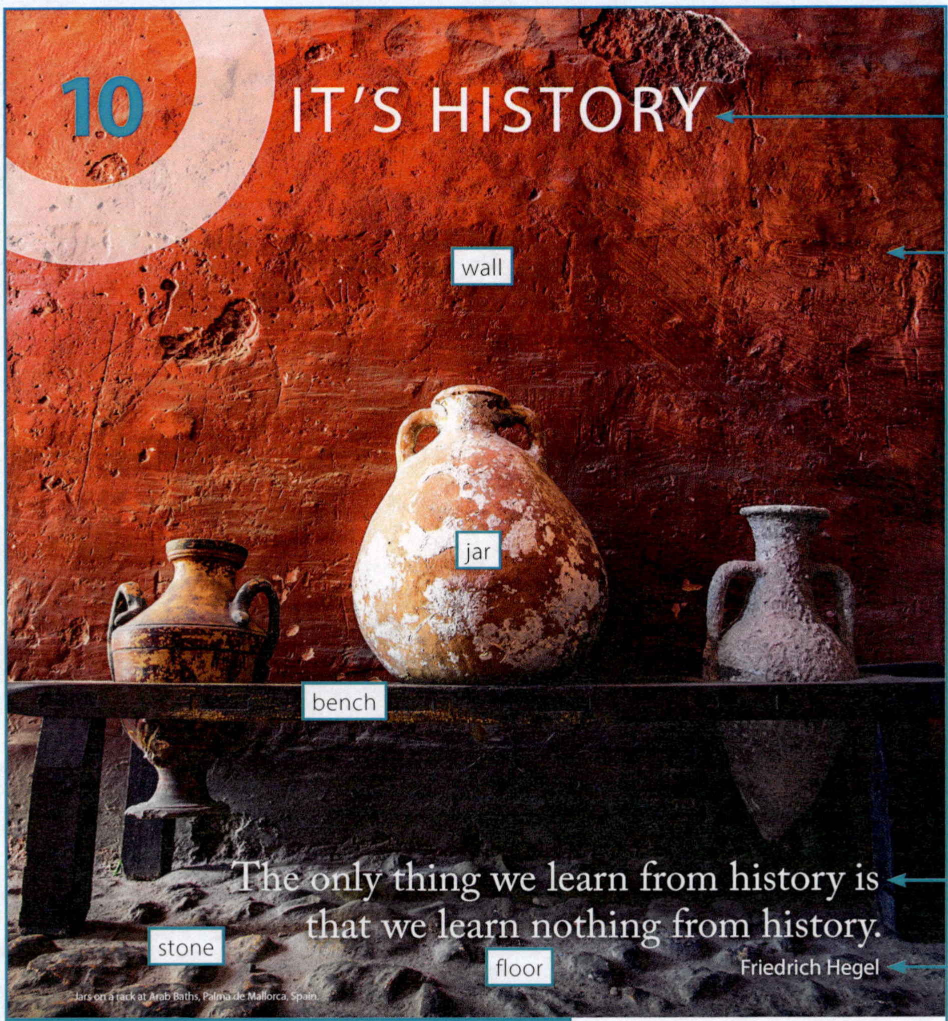

The phrase is used informally to say that something is not important anymore.

Ask students to label the photo if you need time to set up the class.

The quote argues that, though maybe we should, we do not look to the past to guide our future actions. However, paradoxically, we only see that we have not learned from the past, by looking back at history and recognizing and learning from the repeated mistakes we have made.

Friedrich Hegel (1770–1831) was a German philosopher, widely recognized as one of the most important Western philosophers of the last three centuries. Hegel was particularly interested in the concept of freedom and also the progress of history and ideas.

OBJECTIVES

- talk about past events
- talk about past experiences
- talk about what you did on the weekend
- write a paragraph about a past event

Work with a partner. Discuss the questions.

1 Look at the picture. What can you see?

2 Choose words to describe the objects in the picture.

beautiful boring important interesting old new useful

3 Are you interested in history?

IT'S HISTORY 73

OBJECTIVES

Read the unit objectives to the class.

UNIT OPENER QUESTIONS

Focus the students on the picture of the rack of jars in the Arab Baths. Encourage them to guess what the different jars could have been used for – what they would have contained, who would have used them, what was their importance. Ask students to name the things they can see and build up a list of vocabulary on the side of the board. Leave this there for the whole lesson referring to the words as and when they come up.

Then ask students to read Question 2 and use the words in the box to describe the things they can see in the picture. Add any new vocabulary students might use to the list on the board. Elicit answers from the class, encouraging a lot of students to answer and share their ideas. Finally, ask students if they are interested in history. If they are, ask them to say why they find it interesting. If they are not, again, ask students to say why they don't find it interesting. You could add some example sentences to the board for students to use: *I'm interested in history because … I think history is boring because …*

WORKSHEETS

Lesson 10.1 Precious finds

Vocabulary: Time phrases (W35)

Grammar: Simple past: irregular verbs (W36)

Lesson 10.2 Family treasures

Vocabulary: Life events (W37)

Grammar: Simple past: questions (W38)

10.1 Precious finds

Talk about past events

G simple past: irregular verbs V time phrases P vowel sounds: /ɔː/ and /oʊ/

A HISTORY OF THE WORLD IN 100 OBJECTS

The British Museum in London has a lot of important objects from the past. A few years ago, the museum director started an interesting project. He **chose** Ex B Q1 100 objects from the museum to tell a history of the world. Here are just four of the objects. What do they tell us about the past?

HAND AXE

1.2–1.4 million years old, Olduvai Gorge, Tanzania

Scientists **found** many of these hand axes in different regions of Africa. The first GRAMMAR Ex B answer humans didn't have metal. They **made** these axes from stone and used them to cut meat and wood. Ex C Q2

TWO-HEADED SNAKE

15th–16th century, Aztec Empire, Mexico

Ex C Q3 600 years ago, the Aztec people **gave** this bright blue snake to the Aztec Emperor. It **took** a lot of time and skill to make this beautiful object. We think the Emperor **wore** it to show how important he was.

GOLD MODEL CHARIOT

5th–4th century BCE, Tajikistan

The Persians **built** many new roads across their country. The man in this model **went** from town to town in his Ex C Q4 chariot. He collected money for the king and carried important messages for people.

BANKNOTE

CE 135, China

In the 2nd century, Chinese people **bought** and **sold** things using these banknotes. They made banknotes from Ex C Q1 paper. Before this, people used coins. This banknote was the same as 1,000 coins. The Emperor's name was on these notes to show that they were real.

READING

A PREDICT Look at the pictures above. Which object do you think is most interesting?

B READ FOR GIST Read the introduction to *A history of the world in 100 objects*. Choose the best option to complete the summary.

The museum director chose these objects because …

1 they show us what life was like in the past.
2 they tell us about important events.
3 they belonged to important people.

C READ FOR MAIN IDEA Read the text and match each sentence with an object from the text.

1 This was the first kind of paper money. banknote
2 People used this to cut things. hand axe
3 They made it for an important person. two-headed snake
4 This was a way to travel around the country. chariot

D SPEAK Work in pairs. Ask and answer questions about each object.

1 Where is it from? 2 How old is it? 3 What is it for?

E SPEAK Work in pairs. Discuss the questions.

1 Which objects are beautiful? Which are useful?
2 Which objects do you use today?

GRAMMAR

Simple past: irregular verbs

A Read *A history of the world in 100 objects* again. Complete the table with words in bold in the article.

Irregular verb	Past form	Irregular verb	Past form
build	1 built	go	6 went
buy	2 bought	make	7 made
choose	3 chose	sell	8 sold
find	4 found	take	9 took
give	5 gave	wear	10 wore

B Read the text again. There is one example of the simple past negative. Find and underline it.

C WORK IT OUT Choose the correct options to complete the rules. Use *A history of the world in 100 objects* to help you.

Simple past: irregular verbs

1 Irregular verbs *have* / *don't have* -*ed* in the past.
2 We *add* / *don't add* -*s* to the third person singular in the past.
3 We use *didn't* + verb / verb + -*ed* + *not* in negative sentences.

A lot of common verbs have irregular past tense endings. See the irregular verbs list on page 97.

D Go to the Grammar Hub on page 116.

10.1 Precious finds

LEAD-IN

Find some images (or draw pictures) of objects from the past that you think are important or relevant to modern life, e.g. an image of a lightbulb or a credit card or a steam train, etc. Display these images and ask students what they think the connection between them is, eliciting the theme of the reading text.

READING

A Focus students on the four pictures and elicit what they think looks most interesting.

B Ask students to read the introduction and choose the best summary. Discuss the answer as a class.

C Students read the descriptions and then match each one to an object from the text. Check in pairs, then give the answers.

D Students work in pairs to ask and answer the questions. Walk around monitoring, making sure they speak only in English and use full sentences to ask and answer.

Hand axe:	*1 Olduvai Gorge, Tanzania, Africa*
	2 1.2–1.4 million years old
	3 for cutting
Gold model chariot:	*1 Tajikistan*
	2 5th–4th century BCE (2,500 years old)
	3 for traveling
Banknote:	*1 China*
	2 CE 135 (2,000 years old)
	3 for buying and selling
Two-headed snake:	*1 Mexico*
	2 15th–16th century (500–600 years old)
	3 for decoration, to show power/importance

E Check that students understand the questions by giving a brief example of something in the classroom. Students then work in pairs to discuss the questions. Monitor, encouraging them to ask follow-up questions and provide a lot of details, using adjectives.

Suggested answers

1 *The chariot and the serpent are beautiful. The axe and the banknote are useful.*

2 *We use the axe and the banknote today.*

GRAMMAR

A Write the headings *verb* and *simple past* on the board and *make* under *verb*. Write *maked* next to it under *past form*, and cross this out. Ask students to find the correct simple past form of *make* in the first paragraph. Erase *maked* and write *made*. Then ask students to find the rest of the verbs in the text and complete the table. Explain that verbs which don't have *-ed* endings in the past are called *irregular verbs*. There are not very many irregular verbs in English, but they are very common verbs like *have*, *go* and *make*. The vast majority of verbs are regular. Add *be* to the column and elicit *was/were*; tell students that *to be* is the only English verb with two simple past forms.

B Ask students to do the exercise individually as fast as possible, scanning the text for the simple past negative (*didn't have*).

C Put students into pairs to work out the rules in the *Simple past: irregular verbs* box, using the examples from the text. Check answers and use the examples on the board to clarify the rules. Direct them to the irregular verbs list.

D Direct students to the **Grammar Hub** (see below and TB75). Use the **Grammar Worksheet** on page W36 for extra practice.

GRAMMAR HUB

10.1

Simple past: irregular verbs

Verb	Positive	Negative
build	**I built** a house.	**I didn't build** a house.
buy	**You bought** a good car.	**You didn't buy** a good car.
choose	**He chose** 100 objects.	**He didn't choose** 100 objects.
find	**She found** it yesterday.	**She didn't find** it yesterday.
give	**We gave** it to the teacher.	**We didn't give** it to the teacher.
go	**They went** from town to town.	**They didn't go** from town to town.
have	**I had** coffee this morning.	**I didn't have** coffee this morning.
make	**They made** tools.	**They didn't make** tools.
sell	**We sold** the house.	**We didn't sell** the house.
wear	**She wore** her new T-shirt yesterday.	**She didn't wear** her new T-shirt yesterday.

- Irregular verbs do not take *-ed* in the simple past. You have to learn each verb separately.

  They found an axe. NOT ~~*They finded an axe.*~~

  They went to the museum. NOT ~~*They goed to the museum.*~~

- In the negative, we use *didn't* + base form.

  I didn't have coffee yesterday. NOT ~~*I didn't had coffee yesterday.*~~

- In the negative, we usually use the contraction *didn't* but we can also use the long form *did not*.

  They didn't know the answer. OR *They did not know the answer.*

Be careful!

- Irregular verbs do not change form in the simple past.

  simple present: I make… / He makes… BUT *simple past: I made… / He made…*

10.1 Precious finds

VOCABULARY

A Write *I went to the movie theater last week* on the board. Underline *to the movie theater* and *last week* and ask which is about time, i.e. a time phrase (*last week*). Then ask students to find and underline time phrases in the text; write them on the board.

B Focus students on the time expressions in the box and get them to complete the table.

C Students work individually to complete the sentences, then check with a partner. Check answers as a class.

D Students work in pairs to discuss the questions. Monitor, encouraging fluent, long turns and follow-up questions. Use the **Vocabulary Worksheet** on page W35 for extra practice.

PRONUNCIATION

10.1 **A** Write the phonemic symbols on the board and explain that the double dots (/ː/) make a longer sound and the two symbols together (/oʊ/) are a double sound (a diphthong, where you glide from one vowel sound to the second). Play the audio while students read and listen. Then play it again and ask them to repeat after each word. Write the words under the correct phoneme. Make sure students extend the long vowel and produce a diphthong for the sound. It can help if you demonstrate the mouth movements.

10.2 **B** Students look at the words and circle and underline them. Play the audio while they listen and check. Play it again while they listen and repeat. Add these words to the ones on the board. Ask if they can see any patterns, e.g. *slow* and *show* and *nose*, *chose*, *phone*.

C Put students into pairs to do the exercise; monitor, correcting the past forms if necessary. Ask students to share the most interesting things they or their partner did.

SPEAKING

A Draw a timeline on the board, with *21st century/now* on the left, then *22nd*, *23rd*, *24th* and finally *25th* on the right. Draw stick figures talking on the right, with an arrow to show they are talking about the 21st century as if it were the past. Go through the instructions, checking that students understand that they are talking from the future to the past. Support by asking concept questions and illustrating the idea of *imagine* on the board (e.g. a person with a thought bubble). They could work in pairs or individually to think of five objects and why they are important.

B Put one person from each pair in a group, then ask them to present their ideas in turn. Make sure they understand that they have to justify their choices and answer any questions.

C When students finish presenting, ask them to agree on the top five objects from their group. It is a good idea to provide a large sheet of paper to write them on so that it can be displayed and the other groups can look and compare. When all the groups have finished, see if you all can agree on one set of five, then eliminate one object at a time until there is a single representative object.

Extra activity

Describe the oldest thing in your home to your students (this could be something special or even something like a couch or table). Don't say what the object is but give details about it, e.g. where it is from, whether it was a gift or not, whether you are going to buy a new one. Students guess the object. Students then work in small groups to continue the game.

GRAMMAR HUB

10.1

Simple past: irregular verbs

A Write the simple past form of the verbs.

1 have *had*
2 make made
3 go went
4 build built
5 sell sold
6 buy bought
7 give gave
8 wear wore

B Complete the sentences using the simple past form of the verbs in parentheses.

1 I *wore* (*wear*) a blue shirt yesterday.
2 My dad built (*build*) our house.
3 We had (*have*) coffee for breakfast.
4 Our parents gave (*give*) us money.
5 He bought (*buy*) a new phone.
6 They chose (*choose*) a present for Alan.
7 My grandmother sold (*sell*) flowers.
8 You found (*find*) us.

C Rewrite the sentences in Exercise B in the negative.

1 *I didn't wear a blue shirt yesterday*.
2 My dad didn't build our house.
3 We didn't have coffee for breakfast.
4 Our parents didn't give us money.
5 He didn't buy a new phone.
6 They didn't choose a present for Alan.
7 My grandmother didn't sell flowers.
8 You didn't find us.

D Complete the sentences with the correct simple past form of the verbs in parentheses.

A hundred years ago, life in America was very different. They [1] didn't have (*not have*) computers or cell phones. People [2] didn't send (*not send*) emails. They [3] wrote (*write*) letters and [4] sent (*send*) postcards. They [5] didn't buy (*not buy*) things online. They [6] went (*go*) to stores and markets. Stores [7] didn't sell (*not sell*) a lot of clothes. People [8] made (*make*) clothes at home. Parents [9] gave (*give*) their children homemade toys. But even without the internet, children [10] found (*find*) a lot of ways to have fun by singing and playing games at home.

➤ Go back to page 74.

VOCABULARY

Time phrases

A Read the short text below. Underline time phrases with *in*, *last* and *ago*.

> We studied this painting in our art class last year. The artist, Zhang Zeduan, painted this picture 1,000 years ago. It shows everyday life in China in the 12th century.

B Write the time expressions in the table.

the 12th century ~~fifty years~~ 1600 a long time month an hour Friday the past week

Ago	Last	In
fifty years	month	the 12th century
a long time	Friday	1600
an hour	week	the past

C Complete the sentences with *in*, *last* or *ago*.

1. A hundred years ___ago___ people didn't have cell phones.
2. Women wore long dresses ___in___ the 15th century.
3. People found some old gold coins here ___last___ year.

D **SPEAK** Work in pairs. Describe how life was different in the past. Use the topics in the box to help you.

clothes homes money shopping transportation

A: How was life different in the past?
B: People didn't buy clothes in a store very frequently. They made clothes at home.

PRONUNCIATION

Vowel sounds: /ɔː/ and /oʊ/

A Read and listen to the vowel sound in these words. Listen again and repeat.
10.1

/ɔː/	bought	saw	tall	walk
/oʊ/	chose	go	nose	phone

B Circle words with the same sound as *bought*. Underline words with the same sound as *chose*. Then listen and check.
10.2

floor four know slow show talk toe wore

C **SPEAK** Work in pairs. Describe five things you did last week. Use the past tense form of the verbs in the box.

buy call choose see talk tell walk

A: I walked to school.
B: I bought some new shoes.

SPEAKING

A **PREPARE** Work in groups. Choose five objects that explain what life is like in the 21st century and why they are important.

smartphone ___ *talk with friends*
1 ___ ___
2 ___ ___
3 ___ ___
4 ___ ___
5 ___ ___

B **PRESENT** Imagine you are in the 25th century. Explain what life was like in the 21st century. Use your ideas from Exercise A.

C **DISCUSS** Work with another group. Can you agree on the five most important objects?

Talk about past events

10.2 Family treasures

Talk about past experiences

V life events **S** identifying reasons **G** simple past questions **P** final consonant /t/ and /d/

VOCABULARY

Life events

A Read the descriptions. Underline the verbs in the simple past.

This is a picture of me and my girlfriend, Susan. I met her on the first day of college. This is the day we finished college.

I wrote a short story for the school competition when I was in school and I won first prize!

This is a picture of me and my husband on the day we got married! It was in the Bahamas – it was really beautiful.

This is the day I passed my driving test! I was really happy. This sports car belonged to my uncle and I drove it home after the test.

B Match the two parts of each phrase (1–8) with (a–h) to make collocations from Exercise A. Use each verb (1–8) only once.

1 pass	a a person
2 meet	b a story
3 finish	c a car
4 write	d a prize
5 belong	e to someone
6 get	f a test
7 win	g college
8 drive	h married

C SPEAK Describe three important events in your life. Say when they happened.

A: I passed my driving test three years ago.
B: I finished college in 2010.

LISTENING

A PREDICT Look at the pictures. What do you think is the same about all the objects? These objects are old, interesting and possibly valuable.

10.3 **B LISTEN FOR GIST** Listen to three people speaking about the objects. Write the name of the person (Janine, Alfie or Isabel) under the object they talk about.

Identifying reasons

The phrases *that's the reason* or *that's why* come **after** the reason. The reason is in the sentence **before**.

She gave me the camera *That's why* I became a photographer.

10.3 **C LISTEN FOR DETAIL** Listen again and complete the table with information from the podcast.

	Object	Who gave it to the speaker?	When did they give it?	Why is it important?
1	*silver pocket watch*	her father	when she finished college	It reminds her never to be late.
2	old camera	his mother	on his 16th birthday	That's probably why he became a photographer.
3	pearl necklace	her grandmother	when she got married	Because she loved her grandmother/it makes her think of her grandmother.

D SPEAK Tell your partner about an object that is important to you. Did someone give it to you? Did you get it for a special reason?

My parents gave me a necklace on my 18th birthday.

10.2 Family treasures

LEAD-IN

Have a review of Unit 9 vocabulary: write each half of the everyday verbs from Unit 9.2 on separate cards, e.g. *collect/ stamps*. Ask students to get up and find their 'partner'. This is also preparation for Vocabulary B in this unit.

VOCABULARY

A Write *I met my friend last week* on the board, and ask students to identify the simple past verb. Underline it, then ask students to find and underline all the simple past forms in the text. Ask for the answers and write them on the board.

B Students work individually, then check in pairs. Monitor but don't give answers until they have all finished. Write the answers on the board, then practice pronunciation, focusing on the matched whole phrase with correct stress.

C Give one or two examples about yourself, then put students into pairs to complete the activity. Monitor and help if necessary, encouraging follow-up questions. Use the **Vocabulary Worksheet** on page W37 for extra practice.

LISTENING

A Ask students the question and take all the ideas and write them on the board, without confirming or denying them.

10.3 **B** Play the audio while students listen and choose the person speaking about each object. See if they were right about Exercise A.

10.3 **C** Write *reason* on the board. Give an example to the class and write it on the board, e.g. *I love South America. That's why I teach here in Brazil.* Circle *that's why* and ask what it refers to – draw a line to the first sentence. Ask a few students questions, e.g. *Why do you study English?* Show that their answers are reasons. Then refer them to the *Identifying reasons* box and go through it with them. See if they can remember any of the answers for the information in the table, then play the audio for each object while they listen and write. Repeat until students are satisfied that they have all the information, then check answers as a class.

D Students work in pairs to talk about their objects. Make sure they give reasons; model the activity with an object of your own first, then monitor while they are speaking.

AUDIO SCRIPT

10.3

Listening, Exercise B

P = Presenter J = Janine A = Alfie I = Isabel

P: In today's podcast, we invited three people to tell us about a family object that has a special meaning for them. Janine, hi and welcome to our podcast. Please tell us about the family object you brought with you today and why it's important to you.

Ex C Q1 **J:** Hi! Yes, this silver pocket watch belonged to my great-grandfather. He gave it to his son, and his son
Ex C Q1 gave it to my father – and my father gave it to me when I finished college.

P: So it has a lot of family history. Where did this watch come from? What did your great-grandfather use it for?

J: I think he bought it in the 1880s from a famous watchmaker in New York. He worked on the railroads, and he used this watch every day. He made sure the
Ex C Q1 trains were on time. So that's why this watch reminds me never to be late!

P: That's an amazing story. Thank you! Now, let's talk to
Ex C Q2 Alfie. That looks like a nice camera, Alfie.

Ex C Q2 **A:** Thanks. My mother gave it to me. She bought it in the 1970s.

P: It was probably very modern in those days! Did your mother take a lot of photos?

A: Yes, she did. She took a lot of photos of me and my
Ex C Q2 brother when we were young. She gave me the camera on my 16th birthday, That's probably why I became a photographer.

P: That's so interesting. And finally, let's talk to Isabel. This is a beautiful necklace. Did you buy this or did someone give it to you?

Ex C Q3 **I:** Actually, these pearls belonged to my grandmother. My grandfather gave them to her on the day they
Ex C Q3 got married. Then, she gave me this necklace when I got married. I loved my grandmother very much.
Ex C Q3 I always think of her when I wear this necklace. That's why the necklace is so important to me.

P: That's wonderful! Thanks so much to all of you for sharing your stories with us today. I'm afraid that's all we have time for today, but don't forget if you have stories to share, upload your photo and a brief description on our website!

METHODOLOGY HUB by Jim Scrivener

Listening: How do we listen?

When we listen, we use a variety of strategies to help us pick up the message. Some of these are connected with understanding the 'big' picture, e.g. gaining an overview of the structure of the whole text, getting the gist (the general meaning), using various types of previous knowledge to help us make sense of the message, etc. Listening in this way is sometimes termed 'gist listening' or 'extensive listening'. Other strategies are connected with the small pieces of the text, e.g. correctly hearing precise sounds, working out exactly what some individual words are, catching precise details of information, etc. This is frequently called 'listening for detail'.

When working on listening in the classroom, there are two alternative starting points: working on the 'small pieces' (sounds, words and details) or on the 'big pieces' (background topics, overall structure and organization). The former is known as top-down, while the latter is known as bottom-up.

10.2 Family treasures

GRAMMAR

A–E Direct students to the **Grammar Hub** (see below). Use the **Grammar Worksheet** on W38 for extra practice.

PRONUNCIATION

10.4; 10.5 **A–C** Students listen and complete the activities. Check answers as a class.

SPEAKING HUB

A–D Put students into groups. Direct Group Bs to the **Communication Hub** (see TB97). Students prepare questions, and then mingle to find out about their classmates. Encourage follow-up questions. Monitor and write note about language use for feedback.

GRAMMAR HUB

10.2

Simple past: questions

Question	Positive short answer	Negative short answer
Did I tell you about the meeting?	**Yes, you did.**	**No, you didn't.**
Did you see the manager?	**Yes, I/we did.**	**No, I/we didn't.**
Did he win a prize?	**Yes, he did.**	**No, he didn't.**
Did she finish her work?	**Yes, she did.**	**No, she didn't.**
Did it rain yesterday?	**Yes, it did.**	**No, it didn't.**
Did we take a lot of photos?	**Yes, you/we did.**	**No, you/we didn't.**
Did they find the money?	**Yes, they did.**	**No, they didn't.**

- For *yes/no* questions, we put *did* at the beginning, followed by the subject + base form. We don't change the verb.

  Did you see that?

	Wh- questions
I/you/he/she/it/we/they	**What time did she get up**?
	How did you get to work today?
	Where did they study?
	When did he leave Jamaica?
	Why did you do that?
	Who did you talk to yesterday?

- For *wh-* questions, we put *what*, *where*, *why*, etc at the beginning of the question, followed by *did* + subject + base form.

  Where did she go?
  Who did they work with?
  What did she say?

Be careful!

- For negative answers to *yes/no* questions, we normally use the contraction.

  No, I didn't. NOT ~~*No, I did not.*~~

10.2

Simple past questions

A Match the questions (1–6) and the answers (a–f).

1 Did they watch TV last night? *d*
2 What time did you get up? f
3 Where did you go on vacation? a
4 Did you go to work yesterday? c
5 How did you get to work? e
6 Did it start on time? b

a To Florida.
b No, it didn't.
c Yes, I did.
d No, they didn't.
e I went by bus.
f At nine o'clock.

B Complete the sentences with the words in the box.

did ~~didn't~~ we what where why

1 **A:** Did you sell him your car?
B: No, I *didn't*.
2 **A:** Where did you buy those clothes?
B: In town.
3 **A:** How did you get here?
B: By car.
4 **A:** Did you find us OK?
B: Yes, we did.
5 **A:** Why did you buy that phone?
B: Because I liked it.
6 **A:** What time did the movie start?
B: At eight o'clock.

C Write questions in the simple past.

1 you / see / that
Did you see that?
2 when / you / go / to Miami
When did you go to Miami?
3 you / build / your house
Did you build your house?
4 where / you / buy / that hat
Where did you buy that hat?
5 she / wear / her new dress
Did she wear her new dress?
6 why / you / choose / that color
Why did you choose that color?
7 they / find / the money
Did they find the money?
8 what time / we / start
What time did we start?

➤ Go back to page 77.

GRAMMAR

Simple past questions

A Read the extracts from the podcast. Underline *did* and the base form of the verbs.

Wh- questions

1 And where did this watch come from originally?

2 What did your great-grandfather use it for?

Yes/No questions

3 **A:** Did your mother take a lot of photos?
B: Yes, she did.

4 **A:** Did you buy this?
B: No, someone gave it to me.

B WORK IT OUT Complete the rules using words from the box. There are some words you do not need.

after before past present *wh-* questions *yes/no* questions

Simple past questions

1 We use *did* to make questions in the simple past.

2 Question words (*what, where, when, why* and *how*) come before *did*.

3 We use *did/didn't* in short answers to *yes/no* questions.

C PRACTICE Reorder the words to write simple past questions.

1 you / a special gift / did / get / on your 21st birthday
Did you get a special gift on your 21st birthday?

2 win / what kind of / you / did / prizes / at school
What kind of prizes did you win at school?

3 did / your best friend / you / meet / when
When did you meet your best friend?

4 pass / you / did / tests / any / last year
Did you pass any tests last year?

D Go to the Grammar Hub on page 116.

E SPEAK Work in pairs. Ask and answer the questions in Exercise C.

PRONUNCIATION

Final consonant /t/ and /d/

10.4 **A** Read and listen to these examples. Notice the final sounds in each pair.

1 mate made
2 right ride
3 hat had

10.5 **B** Listen and choose the word you hear.

1 write / ride
2 wrote / rode
3 sent / send
4 hat / had
5 sat / sad
6 set / said

C Work in pairs. Say one word from each pair in Exercise B. Ask your partner to identify the word.

SPEAKING HUB

A PREPARE Work in groups. Group A – Stay on this page. Group B – Go to the Communication Hub on page 129. Read the survey. You need to write one person's name for each sentence and find out extra information.

Find someone who:

1 … lived in another country when they were a child.
Where?

2 … passed a test not long ago.
What?

3 … wrote an email yesterday.
Why?

4 … finished college more than five years ago.
Where?

B PLAN Write the questions you need to ask for each item.

Did you live in another country when you were a child?
Where did you live?

C PRACTICE Walk around the classroom and ask questions. Write the names and the answers.

A: Did you live in another country when you were a child?
B: Yes, I did.
A: Where did you live?

D REPORT Work with someone from Group B. Tell them what you found out.

Elsa lived in Brazil when she was young. She lived there for three years and she loved it!

Talk about past experiences

10.3 It was amazing!

F– show interest

COMPREHENSION

A Watch the video. Who had a good weekend? Who had a bad weekend? Who had a good and bad weekend? Check (✓) the boxes.

	Good weekend	Bad weekend
 Carolina	☑	☐
 Onur	☑	☐
 Mark	☑	☐
 Gaby	☑	☑

B Answer the questions. Write the names in the spaces provided.

1 Who went to Paris? Onur
2 Who watched the match? Mark, Carolina
3 Who went to the hairdresser's? Gaby, Marta
4 Who went to a concert? Gaby
5 Who had a pizza? Gaby

C Watch the video again and check your answers to Exercise B.

Glossary

match (n) (British) = game (n) (American)

FUNCTIONAL LANGUAGE

Showing interest

A Complete the responses to good and bad news with the words in the box.

great love nice Really shame sounds think too

Good news	Bad news
Oh, very [1] nice.	Oh no, that [7] sounds awful.
[2] Really? Wow!	Oh, what a [8] shame.
Cool. I [3] love Paris.	
Really? Me, [4] too.	
Well, that's [5] great.	
I [6] think it's amazing!	

B Circle the correct options (a, b or c) to complete the conversation.

Mark: Onur, what did you do?
Onur: I went to France with some friends.
Mark: Oh, [1] ______. Where did you go?
Onur: We went to Paris.
Mark: Really? [2] ______!
Onur: Yes, it was amazing.
Carolina: [3] ______, I love Paris.
Mark: And what about you, Carolina. How was your weekend?
Carolina: It was also [4] ______. I watched the match on Saturday.
Mark: [5] ______? Me too. Did you enjoy it?
Carolina: Yes, it was [6] ______.
Mark: And Gaby, what did you do this weekend?
Gaby: Well, on Saturday I went to the hairdresser's and it was bad. Then on Sunday I ate a pizza and it was bad.
Carolina: Oh no, that sounds [7] ______.
Gaby: It was.
Mark: Oh. [8] ______.

1 (a) very nice b bad c awful
2 a What a shame (b) Wow c Oh no
3 (a) Cool b Oh no c What a sham
4 a awful (b) amazing c bad
5 a Oh no (b) Really c That sounds awful
6 a great b awful (c) amazing
7 a great (b) awful c amazing
8 a Really (b) What a shame c Oh no

C Watch the video again and check your answers to Exercises A and B.

10.3 It was amazing!

LEAD-IN

Tell the students three things that happened to you yesterday, making them two good and one bad or vice versa. Then ask the students if yesterday was good or bad overall for you. Use smiley and sad faces on the board to clarify the instructions. Students then do the same thing with a partner. They say three things (a mix of good and bad) that happened to them yesterday, and their partner then decides if yesterday was good or bad overall.

COMPREHENSION

A ▶ Read through the questions with students and focus on the faces and the names. Ask the students to cover the page and then describe one of the four people for their partner to guess. They take turns for the four characters. As an extension activity, ask students what they can remember about each of the characters from previous episodes. Then play the video for the students to add check marks next to the boxes. Check answers as a whole class.

B Students work in pairs to match the people to the questions.

C ▶ Play the video again for students to watch and check their answers to Exercise B.

FUNCTIONAL LANGUAGE

A Highlight the title of each column before starting. Students then work in pairs to complete the responses. Monitor and prompt as required.

B Students work individually and complete the conversation.

C ▶ Students watch the video again and check their answers to Exercises A and B.

Extra activity

Ask students to read the conversation using very flat intonation. Draw their attention to how, in English, this can make someone sound bored or sarcastic when using this language for showing interest.

▶ VIDEO SCRIPT

M = Mark O = Onur C= Carolina G = Gaby Ma = Marta

M: Good morning, everyone!
O, C, G: Good morning, Mark.
M: So, how was the weekend? Onur, what did you do?
O: I went to France with some friends.
M: Oh, very nice! Where did you go?
O: We went to Paris!
M: Really? Wow!
O: Yes, it was amazing!
C: Cool! I love Paris.
M: And, what about you, Carolina? How was your weekend?
C: It was also amazing! I watched the match on Saturday.
M: Really? Me, too. Did you enjoy it?
C: Yes, it was amazing!
M: I agree. And Gaby, what did you do this weekend?
G: Well, on Saturday, I went to the hairdresser's and it was bad. Then on Sunday, I ate a pizza and it was bad!
C: Oh no, that sounds awful.
G: It was.
M: Oh! What a shame.
G: Yeah, but then I went to a concert and it was amazing! Then, my friend Lucy bought me a new pizza and it was amazing!
M: Well, that's great! Where's Marta?
Ma: I'm sorry I'm late. I was at the hairdresser's. What do you think?
G: Well, I think it's …
M: Amazing! OK, let's get started.

TEACHING IDEA by David Seymour and Maria Popova

Use this activity to review grammar from the unit. Say this to your students:

Grammar: Sequences

Ask me some questions about what I did using these time expressions, e.g. S – *What did you do last night?* T – *I went home and had dinner. I watched the news and …*

last night/week/year

this morning

in 1997

the day before yesterday

on Tuesday / Sunday / New Year's Eve

three months ago

(Write up one of your answers and add sequence markers, e.g. T – *First, I went home and had a dinner. Then, I watched the news and after that, I …*)

In pairs, ask and answer questions in the same way. Give a sequence of at least three things. (When everybody has finished, ask some students to report back to the class about their partners.)

10.3 It was amazing!

PRONUNCIATION

10.6 **A** Highlight the underlined stressed syllables. Before listening, students could try saying the conversation with the stress. They then listen and follow in their books to check.

10.6 **B** Play the conversation line by line for students to listen and repeat. Encourage natural stress and rhythm.

SPEAKING

A Focus the students on the images and clarify any vocabulary as required. Then tell the students you had a picnic last weekend. Ask if the picnic was good or bad, highlighting the notes next to the image (*bad*), and then why (*rain*). Do the same for the brunch example. Elicit further ideas of why a picnic might be bad and a brunch might be good. Students then work alone to complete the notes for all the activities. Highlight that students should use their imaginations. Then model a conversation with a student, asking *What did you do on the weekend?* The student uses his or her notes to reply and then you respond appropriately (e.g. *That sounds good. / Oh, what a shame.*). Students then work in pairs to talk about all the images one after another.

B Model the exercise with a student using your own examples and prompting the student to respond to your news appropriately. Students then work in pairs to complete the exercise. Monitor and write a note about phrases and pronunciation which need work. Also write a note about effective language use to highlight and praise. Have a feedback session working on the language samples you collected.

C Students mingle and find out about all their classmates, responding appropriately. As whole-class feedback, ask students to tell you about each other, e.g. *Daniela went to a party.* You then respond either appropriately, e.g. *Oh, very nice*, or inappropriately, e.g. *Oh, what a shame*, and get students to correct you if necessary.

METHODOLOGY HUB by Jim Scrivener

Errors and correction

In most things, humans largely learn by trial and error, experimenting to see what works and what doesn't. It is the same with language learning. Student errors are evidence that progress is being made. Errors usually show us that a student is experimenting with language, trying out ideas, taking risks, attempting to communicate, making progress. Analyzing what errors have been made clarifies exactly which level the student has reached and helps set the syllabus for future language work. In dealing with errors, teachers usually look for correction techniques that, rather than simply giving students the answer on a plate, help them to make their own corrections. This may raise their own awareness about the language they are using: 'What you tell me, I forget; what I discover for myself, I remember'.

Task 12.1 Different kinds of errors

Errors can be of many kinds. Match the errors in the following list with their descriptions.

Errors	Descriptions
1 Alice like this school.	**a** pronunciation (/ɪ/ vs /iː/)
2 Where you did go yesterday?	**b** pronunciation (/ʃ/ vs /tʃ/)
3 The secretary is in the office.	**c** pronunciation (word stress)
4 Give me one cakecheese!	**d** grammar (wrong tense)
5 I eat shocolate every day.	**e** lexis (incorrect collocation)
6 After three years, they made a divorce.	**f** grammar (verb–noun agreement)
7 I am here since Tuesday.	**g** grammar (word order)
8 I'm going to heat you.	**h** lexis (incorrect word) – and rude!

Commentary

Answers: **1** *f* **2** *g* **3** *c* **4** *h* **5** *b* **6** *e* **7** *d* **8** *a*

Sometimes language can be grammatically correct but completely inappropriate in the context in which it is used. Errors can also be made in intonation and rhythm; in fact, wrong intonation seems to cause more unintended offense to native speakers than almost any other kind of error. Five teacher decisions have to be made when working with oral errors in class:

1. What kind of error has been made (grammatical? pronunciation? etc).
2. Whether to deal with it (is it useful to correct it?).
3. When to deal with it (now? end of activity? later?).
4. Who will correct (teacher? student self-correction? other students?).
5. Which technique to use to indicate that an error has occurred or to enable correction.

GABY

SAM

LUCY

PRONUNCIATION

A Listen to the conversation and notice how the underlined words are stressed.

10.6

Astrid: What did you do on the weekend?
Patrick: I played tennis. It was great.
Astrid: That sounds good.
Patrick: Then I had lunch with my friend.
Astrid: Oh, very nice.
Patrick: But the food was terrible.
Astrid: Oh, what a shame.

B Listen again and repeat the conversation. Copy the stress.

10.6

SPEAKING

A PLAN Imagine you did the activities in the pictures below last weekend. Decide if they were good or bad and say why.

have a picnic

bad, rain

have brunch

amazing, delicious

go to the hairdresser's

go to a party

go to the beach

go ice-skating

B PREPARE Work in pairs. Talk about your weekends. Listen and respond to your partner.

A: On Saturday I ______________________. It was ______________________.
B: Oh, that sounds *great* / *good* / *bad* / *awful*!

C PRACTICE Go around the class and find out what other people did on the weekend. Listen and respond to what they say.

A: What did you do on the weekend?
B: I went to a birthday party. It was great.
A: Oh, very nice.
B: But then I watched a movie and it was bad.
A: Oh, what a shame.

Show interest

Unit 10 Writing

10 Writing

● Write a paragraph about a past event

W using sequencing words

A Look at the picture. What is it? Where is it from? How old is it?

B Read the story. What do you think happened next?

About | **Submit** | Contact

Every picture tells a story! Write a story in 100 words.

A lucky coin

On Saturday morning, Jack got up early and went running in the park. After half an hour, he sat down for a break and he saw something gold under the bench. It was an old gold coin. He picked it up. Then, he put it in his pocket and went home. The next day, on his way to work, he saw a poor man and gave the gold coin to him. A few days later, Jack saw the poor man again. The man walked over to Jack and said, 'I sold the coin for $100 yesterday. Here's $50 for you.'

C Read the story and answer the questions.

1. What did Jack find? an old gold coin
2. Where did he find it? in the park, under a bench
3. What did he do with it? He gave it to a poor man.
4. What happened in the end? The poor man gave him $50.

Using sequencing words

Sequencing words, for example *after*, *then*, *later*, help the reader to understand the order of events in a story.

D Underline the sequencing words in the story. Put the actions in the order they happened in the story.

- 2 Jack sat down for a break.
- 5 Jack gave the coin to the poor man.
- 4 Jack put the coin in his pocket.
- 6 The poor man offered Jack money.
- 1 Jack went running.
- 3 Jack found a coin.

E Choose the correct options to complete the story. Finish the last line of the story.

Last week, Vicky saw a lamp in the window of an old furniture store. It was very beautiful and she looked at it for a long time. [1]*Then* / *After*, she went to work. A week [2]*next* / *later*, she came back to the store, but the lamp wasn't in the window. [3]*Later* / *After* a couple of minutes, she decided to …

WRITING

A PLAN Choose one of the story starters and write notes about what happened next.

B WRITE Write the story in 100 words.

- Last summer, we were on vacation in Greece. We walked on the beach every day and one day we found …
- Yesterday morning, Julia went to a market. There were a lot of old paintings. After a few minutes, she saw …
- About three weeks ago, I found a lot of old boxes in my grandparents' garage. I opened one of them and there was …

○ Write a paragraph about a past event

Suggested answers

Jack gave the money back. / Jack said, 'Thank you very much!'

Suggested answers

go into the store and ask about the lamp. / forget about the lamp. / go inside and look for the lamp.

Students could use their own ideas here if they want to.

Refer students to the story as a model for the writing task.

Unit 10 Review

GRAMMAR

A Complete the sentences in the positive or negative form of the simple past.

1. She didn't buy (*buy*) a new watch last Saturday. (-)
2. He drove (*drive*) to work on Monday. (+)
3. My father sold (*sell*) his car two weeks ago. (+)
4. They didn't find (*find*) the hotel last week. (-)
5. I didn't wear (*wear*) a coat yesterday. (-)
6. We gave (*give*) her a present for her birthday. (+)

B Complete the conversation with the simple past forms of the verbs in the box.

go see take

Kit: Where [1] did you go last weekend?
Ben: We [2] went to the art museum.
Kit: Really? What [3] did you see there?
Ben: We [4] saw some art from Ancient Greece.
Kit: Really? [5] Did you take any photos?
Ben: Yes, I did. I [6] took a lot of photos.

VOCABULARY

Complete the sentences with the simple past form of verbs from the box and the correct time expressions.

ago finish give go in (x2) last (x2) meet win

1. We went to Switzerland for our vacation last summer.
2. Sushila finished college in 2014.
3. Tony won first prize in the art competition two years ago.
4. Eliana met her new friend on vacation in Greece last year.
5. They gave this watch to my father in 2009.

LEAD-IN

Say the first line of a story, e.g. *Last Saturday, I got up late*. Then ask the next student to continue the story. Go around the class adding to the story. When you have gone all the way around, see if the students can remember the whole story – gesture to different students to say the parts of the story.

WRITING

A Ask students for their ideas and answers to the questions and write them on the board.

B Students read and check their ideas to Exercise A. Ask students for their predictions for what happens next.

C Students see if they can remember any of the answers, then read the text again to answer. Focus students on the *Using sequencing words* box. Write a few examples on the board from what happened in the class that day, e.g. *I started the class, then Alia arrived*. Explain that these words help the reader see the order of events.

D Students work alone and then check ideas with a partner. Check answers as a class, referring to the text to support answers.

E Students choose the correct words; give answers, then ask them to finish the final sentence in pairs. You could ask them to read their answers aloud and ask the class to vote on the best one.

WRITING TASK

A Students read the story starters. Go through them to check they understand, then ask students to choose one. Make sure they don't all choose the same one. Then ask them to write brief notes on their story, putting the events in order.

B Students write their stories, using their notes to guide them. When they finish, it is good to 'publish' the stories, either by swapping them with other students or posting them on a wall or a shared social media site. Encourage them to give positive feedback on each other's work.

Senior man with hands raised, riding a rollercoaster.

Ask students to label the photo if you need time to set up the class.

The quote suggests that we cannot make ourselves happy with activities, possessions and experiences. Our happiness lies within us and not on other people or objects. Our feelings about life, and the way we experience it, are truly our own responsibility.

Aristotle (384 BCE–322 BCE) was a Greek philosopher and is still widely regarded as one of the greatest thinkers of Western history. He created systems of philosophical and scientific thought and theory which have become the foundations for different belief systems over the past 2,000 years. As a young man, he studied with Plato in Athens and then traveled to other areas of the region to continue his own teaching and writing.

OBJECTIVES

- talk about things you like doing
- talk about favorite sports, music and movies
- make and respond to suggestions
- write a personal profile

Work with a partner. Discuss the questions.

1. Look at the picture. How do you think the man feels?
2. Do you like theme parks?
3. Read the quote. Tell each other about things you enjoy.

HAVING FUN 81

OBJECTIVES

Read the unit objectives to the class.

UNIT OPENER QUESTIONS

Focus the students on the picture. Ask them how they feel when they look at the picture. Use mime and facial expression (e.g. *excited*, *happy*).

Students work in pairs to discuss the remaining questions. Ask them if they enjoy riding rollercoasters like the man in the picture. Ask them to tell their partner how they would feel if they were on the rollercoaster. Add vocabulary on the side of the board and keep it there for students to use throughout the lesson. Finally, ask students to think about the quote regarding happiness. Ask them if they agree or disagree and to give reasons for their answers. Encourage several students to share their view, before discussing in pairs, and then as a class, all the things that students enjoy doing that make them happy.

WORKSHEETS

Lesson 11.1 In or out?

Vocabulary: Recreational activities (W39)

Grammar: *like/love/hate/enjoy* + verb + *-ing* (W40)

Lesson 11.2 Super fans

Vocabulary: Entertainment (W41)

Grammar: Object pronouns (W42)

11.1 In or out? Talk about things you like doing

V– recreational activities
READING Ex B answers

G– *like/love/hate/enjoy* + verb + *-ing*
picture b

P– verb + *-ing* /ŋ/
picture a

Is STAYING IN the new GOING OUT?

There are a lot of things you can do to relax on the weekend. You can go to a restaurant or the movie theater. Or you can go to a concert or maybe a soccer game. Did you do any of these things last weekend? For a lot of people, the answer is no. **They don't like going out.** They just want to stay at home. We talked to three people to find out why.

a

b

Why do you like staying in? READING Ex D answers

Agnes

Ex E Q1
I love movies. [1] ___b___, but I don't like going to the movie theater. I don't like the food they sell there. **I love getting takeout food**, spending time with my family and watching TV and movies at home.

Lee

Ex E Q2
I'm a soccer fan, [2] ___c___. You can watch games from all over the world on TV. My friends come to my house, and we chat and eat snacks, and **we enjoy watching sports together**. It's a great way to spend time with friends.

Frieda

My favorite type of music is rock. [3] ___a___, and in my car. **My husband loves going to concerts** and he goes out all the time. But **I hate going to concerts** – they're expensive and there are too many people! **I like staying at home** and listening to my favorite music really loud! Ex E Q3

READING

A SPEAK Work in pairs. Ask your partner about last weekend.

A: What did you do last weekend?
B: I went to an Italian restaurant. What about you?

B PREPARE TO READ Read the headline of *Is staying in the new going out?* and look at the pictures. Match the underlined words with the pictures (a and b).

C READ FOR GIST Read the first paragraph of the article. Choose the correct options to complete the summary.

There [1]*are* / *aren't* a lot of things that people do to relax [2]*in the week* / *on the weekend*. The article says people these days mostly want to [3]*stay in* / *go out*.

D READ FOR DETAIL Read the rest of the article. Choose the correct phrase to fill in the blanks in the text.

a I listen to it at home
b I watch them every weekend
c but I don't go to games

E READ FOR SPECIFIC INFORMATION Read the article again and choose the correct options.

1 Agnes doesn't go to the movie theater because …
  a it's expensive.
  b she doesn't live near a movie theater.
  (c) she doesn't like the food.
2 Lee doesn't go to games because …
  (a) he can watch a lot of sports at home.
  b they're expensive.
  c he doesn't like the snacks.
3 Frieda doesn't go to concerts because …
  (a) it costs a lot of money.
  b she doesn't like music.
  c she doesn't like loud music.

F SPEAK Work in pairs. Are you similar to Agnes, Lee or Frieda? Give examples.

VOCABULARY
Recreational activities

A Complete the phrases with the words in the box.

~~family~~	friends	a museum	the park	TV	a video online

1 spend time with ___family___

2 go to ___the park___

3 watch ___TV___

4 watch ___a video online___

5 spend time with ___friends___

6 go to ___a museum___

B Go to the **Vocabulary Hub** on **page 126**.

C SPEAK Talk to your partner. Ask and answer questions about the recreational activities you like.

A: Do you watch a lot of TV?
B: Yes! I love it! Where do you usually spend time with your friends?
A: At a café, or sometimes at home.

11.1 In or out?

LEAD-IN

Ask students to write down three activities they enjoy and one they don't like. Then get them up take turns reading aloud all four, without saying which they don't like. The other students guess which one they don't like. You can make this into a game by giving points for correct guesses. Use this as an opportunity to test prior knowledge of language students will encounter in the unit.

READING

A Students discuss what they did last weekend. Write *staying in/going out* on the board. Ask for a few activities that they did, saying, e.g. *Oh, so you went out/stayed in* and write them under the headings.

B Read the headline with the students, then ask them to match the underlined words to the pictures. Check the answers.

C Students read the summary first, then read the first paragraph; give them a short time limit to complete the exercise in order to encourage fast gist reading. Ask them to check in pairs, then give the answers, asking them to identify the parts of the text that give the answers.

D Read the phrases together first, then students read the rest of the article and complete the exercise. Go through the answers with the whole class, discussing why the phrases fit where they do.

E See if students can remember any answers, then ask them to read the article again and choose the correct options individually before checking in pairs. Go through the answers with the whole class.

F Give an example using yourself and explain why, then put students into pairs to discuss the question. Get feedback from the pairs and find out which of the three is most like people in the class.

VOCABULARY

A Students complete the activity in pairs. Go through the answers, practicing pronunciation of the phrases.

B Direct students to the **Vocabulary Hub** (see TB97).

C Model the conversation with a strong student, then ask students to discuss their recreational activities. Go around helping with vocabulary if necessary. Use the **Vocabulary Worksheet** on page W39 for extra practice.

TEACHING IDEA by David Seymour and Maria Popova

Conversation: Hobbies

Arrange the students so that they are standing/sitting in a circle. Stand in the middle. Ask each of these questions to individual students at random. After they answer it, tell them to repeat the question to the next student and write a note about the student's answer. Indicate that they should continue the chain so the question progresses around the class. Meanwhile, introduce the other questions so that in the end, there are a lot of questions moving around the class.

What sports do you play, if any?
How much time do you spend watching TV?
What hobby would you like to take up?
What do you do on Sunday afternoons?
How much free time do you have?
What do you read for enjoyment?
What hobbies did you use to have as a child?
When and where did you last go to the beach?
Turn your notes into full sentences, e.g. Maria plays tennis.

GRAMMAR HUB

11.1

like/love/hate/enjoy* + verb + *-ing

	Positive	Negative	Question
I/you/we/they	**I enjoy going** to the theater. **They love going** to restaurants.	**We don't enjoy staying** at home on weekends.	**Do they like spending** time with friends?
he/she/it	**He likes watching** TV. **Joanna loves playing** soccer.	**She doesn't like listening** to loud music.	**Does Frank enjoy watching** videos on his laptop?

- In positive phrases, we use *like/love/hate/enjoy* + verb + *-ing*.
  I like going to concerts.
  We love getting takeout food.
- In negative phrases, we use *don't/doesn't* + *like/love/hate/enjoy* + verb + *-ing*.
  I don't enjoy watching movies on my laptop.
  He doesn't like going to soccer games.
- In questions, we use *do/does* + subject + *like/love/hate/enjoy* + verb + *-ing*.
  Do you enjoy listening to music?
  Does Harriet like watching videos online?

Be careful!

- Make sure you put only the activity verb in the *-ing* form and not *like/love/hate/enjoy*.
  I like spending time with my friends. NOT ~~*I'm liking spending time with my friends.*~~

11.1 In or out?

GRAMMAR

A Ask students to find the bold phrases in the article and call them out; write them on the board. Then refer them to the exercise and ask them to choose the correct option. Give the answer, then underline the activities in each phrase, e.g. *I love getting takeout food*.

B Students complete the exercise to match words to emojis: write the answers on the board. Practice the pronunciation.

C Put students into pairs to complete the rules. Then go through the answers, using the phrases on the board to reinforce and clarify the rules.

D Direct students to the **Grammar Hub** (see below and TB82). Use the **Grammar Worksheet** on page W40 for extra practice.

PRONUNCIATION

11.1 **A** Play the audio while students listen, then refer them to the statement. Play it again while they choose. Give the answer, then isolate the sound for *-ing* (/ŋ/) and get students to repeat it.

11.2 **B** Play the audio while students listen, then play it again and get them to repeat each sentence, focusing on the *-ing* sound.

11.3 **C** Play the audio while students listen and choose. Write the answers on the board.

11.4 **D** Play the audio stopping after each question for students to write. Play it again, stopping and asking students to repeat the questions. Then ask them to ask you the questions; give full answers, as a model for the Speaking exercise.

E Students work in pairs to ask and answer the questions from Exercise D. Go around monitoring and making sure they try to produce the target sound.

SPEAKING

A Set the task, copy (or display) the table onto the board, then walk around helping students with vocabulary for their personal activities. Ask two students to read aloud the conversation, and show how the answer is recorded using the table on the board.

B Get students to stand up and walk around, interviewing different students to fill in the survey.

C When students finish, get them to work in pairs to write sentences; show that they can give exact numbers, as in the first example, and summarize, as in the second. Then ask them to report back to the rest of the class.

Extra activity

Extend the Speaking activity by having students work in pairs to produce a display of survey results. This could be on a poster or using presentation slides on a computer. The pairs can prepare and practice their presentation, recording themselves on their digital devices to help them to improve their performance.

GRAMMAR HUB

11.1

like/love/hate/enjoy* + verb + *-ing

A Choose the correct options to complete the sentences.

1 We (*enjoy*) / *enjoys* going to the movie theater.
2 He (*likes*) / *like* watching TV shows on his laptop.
3 They (*love*) / *loves* spending time with family.
4 *Do* / (*Does*) Jenny hate going to concerts?
5 I (*don't*) / *doesn't* like playing tennis.
6 You (*like*) / *likes* seeing friends on weekends.
7 *Does* / (*Do*) they enjoy playing soccer?
8 He *don't* / (*doesn't*) like listening to music.

B Complete the sentences with the correct form of the verbs in parentheses.

1 I don't like ___doing___ (*do*) homework on weekends.
2 She loves ___going___ (*go*) out in her free time.
3 Do you hate ___staying___ (*stay*) in the house all day?
4 Henry doesn't like ___talking___ (*talk*) to his friends online.
5 They love ___chatting___ (*chat*) with people from all over the world.
6 We don't enjoy ___making___ (*make*) dinner at home.
7 Does Jim like ___getting___ (*get*) takeout food?
8 I enjoy ___seeing___ (*see*) my friends on the weekend.

C Use the words in parentheses to complete the text.

My friend Lukas [1] ___hates staying___ (*hate / stay*) in. He's a writer and he works at home, so in the evening he [2] ___doesn't like watching___ (*not like / watch*) TV. He wants to go out. Every evening! He [3] ___enjoys going___ (*enjoy / go*) to a café or a restaurant, and he [4] ___loves going___ (*love / go*) to the movie theater and the theater. I frequently go out with him, but I [5] ___don't like going___ (*not like / go*) out every night – it's too expensive!

➤ Go back to page 83.

GRAMMAR

like/love/hate/enjoy + verb + *-ing*

A WORK IT OUT Read the phrases in bold in *Is staying in the new going out?* Choose the correct option.

In these phrases, the people are talking about their feelings about *activities* / *objects*.

B Match the words with the emojis.

enjoy hate like love

1 love 2 like / enjoy 3 hate

C WORK IT OUT Complete the rules with the words in the box.

negative phrases positive phrases questions

1 In positive phrases, we use *like/love/hate/enjoy* + verb + *-ing*.

2 In negative phrases, we use *do/does* + *not* + *like/love/hate/enjoy* + verb + *-ing*.

3 In questions, we use *do/does* + subject + *like/love/hate/enjoy* + verb + *-ing*.

D Go to the Grammar Hub on page 118.

PRONUNCIATION

Verb + *-ing* /ŋ/

11.1 **A** Read and listen to the sentence. Choose the correct option to complete the statement.

I like listening to music in the kitchen.

The underlined letters have *the same sound* / *different sounds*.

11.2 **B** Listen and repeat the sentences.

1 He likes going out and spending time with his friends.

2 She likes staying in and watching TV.

11.3 **C** Listen and circle the word you hear.

1 ban / bang 2 thin / thing 3 win / wing

11.4 **D** Listen to the questions. Write the missing words.

1 Do you like getting takeout food?

2 Do you and your friends like listening to the same music?

3 What do you enjoy doing on the weekend?

4 Who do you enjoy spending time with on the weekend?

5 What do you hate watching on TV?

6 Where do you like going out to eat?

E SPEAK Work in pairs. Ask and answer the questions in Exercise D.

A: Do you like getting takeout food?

B: No, I don't. I like going to restaurants.

SPEAKING

A PREPARE Take a class survey about free-time activities. Write three activities from the lesson and add three new activities of your own. Include some 'staying in' activities and some 'going out' activities, too.

Activity	Love	Like/Enjoy	Hate	Extra info
go to the park	✓			near school
watch TV				

B PRACTICE Ask other students about the activities they like, enjoy, love and hate.

A: Do you like going to the park?

B: Yes, I love it!

A: Which park do you like?

B: I like the park next to the school.

C REPORT Work in pairs. Look at your results. Answer the questions. Tell the class.

1 What activities do people like, enjoy, love and hate?

2 Do the people in the class like staying in or going out?

Ten people love going to the park. No one hates going to the park.

In general, the people in this class like going out.

Talk about things you like doing

11.2 Super fans

Talk about favorite sports, music and movies

S listening for opinions G object pronouns V entertainment P vowel sounds: /ʊ/ and /uː/

LISTENING

11.5 **A** Look at the picture below. Who is the man, and where is he from? Listen to the radio show interview and check. Mo Salah, Egypt

11.5 **B** Listen again. Choose the correct options to complete the summary.

They are at a [1]*basketball* / *soccer* game in the [2]*Olympic* / *Athletic* Stadium between [3]*England* / *Germany* and Egypt.
They are waiting to [4]*play* / *watch* their favorite player, Mo Salah.

Listening for opinions

When we want to give our opinion about something we can use the phrase *I think* to start the sentence. We can also use adjectives, for example *interesting*, *boring*, to show how we feel about something. We use *because* to introduce reasons for our opinion.

I think he's great … I also like him because he's a nice person.

My boyfriend loves soccer, but I hate it – it's so boring.

11.5 **C** Answer the questions. Listen again and check your answers.

1 Who says Mo Salah is number one in the world? *Wendy* / *Kelly* / *Ryan*
2 Who says Mo Salah is a nice person? *Wendy* / *Kelly* / *Ryan*
3 Who says Mo Salah is good to his fans? *Wendy* / *Kelly* / *Ryan*
4 Who doesn't like any other soccer players? *Wendy* / *Kelly* / *Ryan*
5 Who isn't interested in soccer at all? *Wendy* / *Kelly* / *Ryan*

D SPEAK Work in pairs. Do you like soccer? Why/Why not?

GRAMMAR

Object pronouns

A Read these sentences from the radio show interview. Answer the questions.

Wendy: I'm here to see Mo Salah.
Interviewer: Why do you like him?

1 What or who is the object of Wendy's sentence? Mo Salah
2 Which word does the interviewer use to replace the object of Wendy's sentence? him

B Read more sentences from the listening. Underline the object pronouns and circle the people or things they refer to.

1 Kelly: My boyfriend loves soccer, but I hate it.
2 Interviewer: What do you think about Mo Salah?
Kelly: My boyfriend likes him.
3 Interviewer: So, Ryan, what do you think about the other soccer players?
Ryan: I'm not interested in them.

C WORK IT OUT Complete the table with the object pronouns in the box.

her him it ~~me~~ them us you (x2)

Subject pronouns	Object pronouns
I play tennis with Luke.	Luke plays tennis with [1] me.
You watch TV with Harry.	Harry watches TV with [2] you.
He knows a lot of people.	A lot of people know [3] him.
She plays soccer.	I play soccer with [4] her.
It is a great movie.	I love watching [5] it.
We like staying in with Mike.	Mike likes staying in with [6] us.
You can all come to my house.	I'm happy to see [7] you all.
They are musicians.	I like listening to [8] them.

D Go to the Grammar Hub on page 118.

E SPEAK Complete the sentences with your own ideas. Then complete the questions with the correct object pronoun. Work in pairs and ask and answer the questions.

1 ______ is a famous pop singer in my country. Do you know ______?
2 ______ is the name of a stadium in my town/city. Do you know ______?
3 ______ is a sports (soccer/basketball, etc) team in my country. Do you know ______?

11.2 Super fans

LISTENING

11.5 **A–D** Students look at the picture and listen to the audio. Complete the exercises, giving students time to discuss ideas in pairs. Check answers as a class.

GRAMMAR

A–E Direct students to the **Grammar Hub** (see below and TB85). Use the **Grammar Worksheet** on page W42 for extra practice.

AUDIO SCRIPT

11.5

Listening, Exercise A

I = Interviewer W = Wendy K = Kelly R = Ryan

Ex B **I:** This is the *Sports Talk* soccer show and I'm at the Olympic Stadium in Berlin for this international
Ex B friendly game between Germany and Egypt … and as you can hear, there are a lot of people here. They come from all over the world, and many of
Ex B them are here to see one man: Mo Salah, the
Ex A soccer superstar from Egypt. Hi! Can I ask you a few questions?

W: Sure. No problem.
I: What's your name?
W: I'm Wendy.
I: Who are you here to see, Wendy?
W: Mo Salah – I'm such a big fan!
I: Why do you like him?
Ex C Q2 **W:** I think he's great. I love watching him play. I also like
Ex C Q3 him because he's a nice person. He's always good to his fans.
I: Thanks, Wendy. Hi, can I ask you a few questions?
K: Um … OK.
I: What's your name?
K: Kelly.
I: OK Kelly, what do you think about Mo Salah?
K: Um … My boyfriend likes him. I don't know.
I: Are you a soccer fan?
Ex C Q5 **K:** No, I'm not. My boyfriend loves soccer, but I hate it – it's so boring.
I: Oh … OK, well … is this your boyfriend?
K: Yeah, that's him.
I: Hello, can I ask you …
R: He's Egyptian and he's amazing and Mohammed's his name.
I: OK, great. So, what's your name?
R: Ryan.
I: So, why are you …
R: Mo Sa–la–la–la–lah! Mo Sa–la–la–la–lah!
I: Why are you a big Mo Salah fan, Ryan?
Ex C Q1 **R:** Because he is the number one in the world!
I: Do you watch Mo Salah play a lot?
R: I watch every game he plays – club and country.
I: So, Ryan, what do you think about the other soccer players?
Ex C Q4 **R:** I'm not interested in them. I only like Salah!
I: Thanks, Ryan. I hope you enjoy watching the game. Well, the game starts in one hour.

GRAMMAR HUB

11.2

Object pronouns

Subject pronoun	Object pronoun
I like soccer.	Sam plays soccer with **me**.
You know many people.	Many people know **you**.
He enjoys movies.	Mike watches movies with **him**.
She doesn't like TV.	Audrie doesn't watch TV with **her**.
We are musicians.	People like listening to **us**.
Do **they** play tennis?	Do Raphael and Sue play with **them**?

- We can use object pronouns to refer to object nouns.
  *The children like **Raphael**. = The children like **him**.*
  *Erin doesn't like **the videos**. = Erin doesn't like **them**.*
  *Does Helen know **Paulina**? = Does Helen know **her**?*
- Subject pronouns are *I, you, he, she, it, we* and *they*. Object pronouns are *me, you, him, her, it, us* and *them*.
  I like my teachers. My teachers like me. I like them.
  Tennis is a sport. It is fun, but Gus and Vicky don't like it.
  Leslie sings in a band. She's a good singer, and I love her.
- Object pronouns can follow *with* and *to*.
  Josh plays soccer with him.
  Do you like listening to them?

Be careful!

- Use *it* for singular object nouns, and *them* for plural object nouns.
  Mary likes that show. She watches it online. NOT ~~She watches them online.~~
  Tom hates soccer games. He doesn't watch them. NOT ~~He doesn't watch it.~~

11.2 Super fans

VOCABULARY

A–D Students read the text and complete the table. Check answers as a class. Direct students to the **Vocabulary Hub** (see TB97). Students complete Exercise C in pairs or individually. Go through the answers with the class. Model some example sentences for Exercise D, then put students into pairs to complete the exercise. Use the **Vocabulary Worksheet** on page W41 for extra practice.

PRONUNCIATION

11.6 **A** Play the audio for students to identify the different sounds. Then isolate the sounds and get students to repeat them; practice the words. Show them the different mouth movements if appropriate.

11.7 **B** Play the audio while students listen and choose. Play it again and write the answers on the board. Play it again and ask students to repeat, focusing on the target sounds.

11.8 **C** Ask students to predict the answers, then play the audio while they listen and underline.

D Monitor and help with the sentences and sounds if necessary. At the end, ask a few students to say their sentences to the class to see if anyone came up with the same ones.

SPEAKING HUB

A Ask students what they enjoy doing. Write a few examples on the board, then let them write notes for themselves.

B Write *What?/Where?/Who?/Why?* on the board, then point at them one at a time and ask students questions using them to remind them of the meanings. Then go through the words in the box before they work on the questions. Monitor and help if needed.

C Put students into pairs to ask and answer the questions. Demonstrate the activity, showing how they need to ask follow-up questions to get more information. At the end, get some students to share what they found out about their partners.

Extra activity

In small groups, students decide on a 'Super Team' to appear on a TV show. The 'Super Team' needs to have one sports person, one actor, one musician and one singer. (You could ask students to suggest another category, too, as appropriate.) Individually, students choose their favorite person for each category. They then discuss their choices and choose one for each category. They then present their 'Super Team' to the class. See how many similarities and differences there are between teams.

GRAMMAR HUB

11.2

Object pronouns

A Choose the correct options to complete the sentences.

1 I usually play soccer with my brother. He likes playing with ___.
(a) me b I

2 Danielle watches movies with her sister. She usually goes to the movie theater with ___.
a she (b) her

3 We like pop music, but we don't listen to ___ all the time.
a them (b) it

4 There are a lot of games at our stadium, but I don't frequently see ___.
(a) them b it

5 My favorite actor is Ryan Gosling. I like ___ and his movies a lot!
(a) him b he

6 Simon and I play tennis with my neighbor, Dina. She really enjoys playing with ___.
a her (b) us

B Rewrite the words in bold using object pronouns.

1 Cat videos are funny. Jill enjoys watching **cat videos**. *them*
2 Lionel Messi is a great player. Mike and I love **Lionel Messi**! him
3 Rihanna is a famous singer. Michelle likes listening to **Rihanna**. her
4 Jake loves playing soccer. I don't like **soccer**. it
5 Jan and I watch TV with my little brother. He likes spending time with **me and Jan**. us

C Choose the correct options to complete the conversation.

Thomas: Who's a famous person in your home country, Anika?
Anika: Aishwarya Rai is a famous actress in India. Do you know [1]*it* / (*her*)?
Thomas: Yes, I think so. She's famous in the US, too. Do you enjoy watching her movies?
Anika: Yes, I do. I frequently watch [2]*her* / (*them*). Who's your favorite actress or actor?
Thomas: I really like Benedict Cumberbatch. He's great in the TV show *Sherlock*. I enjoy seeing [3](*him*) / *he* as Sherlock Holmes.
Anika: Yes, he's very good. *Sherlock* is a good show, but I don't watch [4](*it*) / *him* regularly.
Thomas: And what about sports? Do you like [5](*them*) / *us*, too?
Anika: I love tennis. My favorite player is Serena Williams. [6]*Her* / (*She*) is amazing!
Thomas: Yes, she is. My friend Paul and I watch tennis all the time, too. Would you like to watch tennis with [7]*her* / (*us*) some time?
Anika: That sounds great, thanks! I know your friend Paul. I sometimes see [8]*it* / (*him*) at college.

➤ Go back to page 85.

VOCABULARY
Entertainment

A Look at the pictures and read the sentences. Put the words in bold in the correct category.

Rihanna's one of my favorite **pop stars**. I go to all her **concerts**.

The **stadium** is always full when Brazil plays. They're really good **players** and the **games** are usually exciting.

My favorite **movie stars** were at the **movie theater** on Hollywood Boulevard to watch the **premiere**.

People:	pop stars	players	movie stars
Events:	concerts	games	premiere
Places:	stadium	movie theater	

B Go to the **Vocabulary Hub** on **page 126**.

C Choose the correct option to complete the sentences.

1 My favorite *actor* / *player* is Scarlet Johansson; I have all her movies on DVD.
2 I think Antoine Griezmann is a really good soccer *player* / *singer*.
3 Justin Timberlake was a famous *pop star* / *player* when I was a teenager.
4 There are many famous pop *players* / *stars* in my country.
5 My brother's in a *classical* / *rock* band. He plays the electric guitar.
6 I love watching *action movies* / *comedies*. All of my favorite movies are funny!

D **SPEAK** Work in pairs. Discuss the sentences in Exercise C. Make sentences that are true for you.

My favorite actor is …

PRONUNCIATION
Vowel sounds: /ʊ/ and /uː/

11.6 **A** Listen and repeat.

/ʊ/ took, sugar, book /uː/ two, June, blue

11.7 **B** Listen to the sentences. Which sound do the underlined words have?

1 My father is a good cook. /ʊ/ /uː/
2 Moon is my favorite sci-fi movie. I like horror movies, too. /ʊ/ /uː/

11.8 **C** Listen and read the sentences. Underline the word that includes the sound in parentheses.

1 The soccer game starts soon. (/uː/)
2 I like cooking Italian food. (/ʊ/)
3 My daughter loves going to school. (/uː/)
4 I know that woman. (/ʊ/)
5 I always go out on Tuesday evening. (/uː/)
6 There are a lot of interesting things to look at in the museum. (/ʊ/)

D **SPEAK** Work in pairs. Make a short sentence that includes one of the words in the box. Say it to your partner. Listen and check your partner's pronunciation.

book foot good look museum the news too Tuesday

I watch the news on TV every evening.

SPEAKING HUB

A **PREPARE** Think about the things that you enjoy doing. Why do you like them? Write some notes.

B **PLAN** You are going to find out if your partner is a superfan. Write some questions. Use the words in the box to help you.

actor movies music player singer sports star

What …? Where …? Who …? Why …?

Do you like watching movies?
What movies do you like watching?
Who is your favorite actor?

C **DISCUSS** Work in pairs. Ask and answer the questions from Exercise B. Is your partner a superfan? Why/Why not?

Talk about favorite sports, music and movies

Café Hub

11.3 Short run

F– make and respond to suggestions

COMPREHENSION

A ▶ Watch the video. Underline the correct words or phrases. Then write *Gaby*, *Lucy* or *Both*.

1 *She* / *They* dyed *her* / *their* hair. Gaby
2 *She's* / *They're* free tomorrow. Both
3 *She wants* / *They want* to go to the gym. Lucy
4 *She likes* / *They like* breakfast a lot. Both
5 *She's* / *They're* sporty. Lucy
6 *She says* / *They say* they love running. Gaby
7 *She doesn't* / *They don't* run far. Both
8 *She has* / *They have* breakfast at Sam's Café. Both

B Correct the information in Gaby's diary. There are five mistakes.

Today	Tomorrow
~~Wash~~ Dye hair.	Meet Lucy at Newton Green at ~~9~~ 8 am.
Call ~~Sam~~ Lucy.	Go ~~swimming~~ for a run in the park.
	Go for breakfast at ~~Pizza Roma~~ Sam's Café.

FUNCTIONAL LANGUAGE

Making and responding to suggestions

A ▶ 00:18–01:23 Put the telephone conversation in the correct order. Then watch part of the video and check your answers.

a What about going to the gym and then we can have a big breakfast afterwards? 6
b Cool. Do you want to do something? 3
c Sure. Why don't we do something sporty? 4
d No, I'm free all day. 2
e Great, see you there. 11
f OK, how about going for a run and then breakfast? 8
g Yeah, OK. 5
h Perfect. I love running. That sounds really nice. Where do you want to meet? 9
i Er, I'm not sure about the gym, but I like breakfast a lot. 7
j Hi Lucy. Are you busy tomorrow? 1
k Let's meet at Newton Green at eight o'clock tomorrow. 10

B Complete the table with examples from the conversation in Exercise A.

Make a suggestion	Saying yes
What about + verb + *-ing* …	Sure / Great / Perfect
[1] What about going to the gym?	That sounds [5] really nice.
How about + verb + *-ing* …	**Saying no**
[2] How about going for a run?	I'm not sure about [6] the gym.
Why don't we …	**Arrange a place and time**
[3] do something sporty?	Where do you want to meet?
Let's …	Are you busy … + time/day? [7] Are you busy tomorrow?
[4] meet at Newton Green at eight o'clock tomorrow.	See you there.

11.3 Short run

LEAD-IN

Elicit from students what they enjoy doing in their free time. What would they do if they suddenly had some free time? Ask students to look at the pictures and predict what will happen in this episode.

COMPREHENSION

A ▶ Read through the questions with students and check vocabulary meaning as necessary (e.g. *dyed her hair = colored her hair*). Then play the video. Allow time afterward for students to compare answers before checking as a whole class.

B Students work in pairs to review and correct the diary. Highlight that the five mistakes are in content, not spelling or grammar. Check answers as a class, playing the video again as necessary.

FUNCTIONAL LANGUAGE

A ▶ 00:18–01:23 Students work alone for a few minutes, putting the conversation in order. They then compare and confirm their ideas in pairs. Monitor and give assistance as required. Then play the section of the video again for students to check answers.

B Highlight the title of each section of the table. Students then complete the table with examples from the conversation in Exercise A. Build up the answers together on the board.

METHODOLOGY HUB by Jim Scrivener

Viewing activities

As with audio recordings, it usually helps to set clear viewing tasks. The task–text–feedback circle still works well as a basic procedure for video. Tasks might be in the form of oral instructions or in the form of a worksheet, or they might be a natural follow-on from the preview activities. You may want to play the recording through many times with harder tasks.

Follow-up activities

There are many activities that you can do after viewing; here are just a few ideas.

- Discussion, interpretation, personalization (e.g. 'What would you have done?' or 'Has this ever happened to you?')
- Study of new language
- Role-play the scene (or its continuation)
- Inspiration for other work: 'What did the newspaper / Hello magazine say the next day? Design the front page'
- Write a letter from one character to another
- Plan what they should do next

▶ VIDEO SCRIPT

G = Gaby L = Lucy S = Sam C= Customer

L: Hi, Gaby.
G: Hi, Lucy. Are you busy tomorrow?
L: No, I'm free all day.
G: Cool. Do you want to do something?
L: Sure. Why don't we do something sporty?
G: Yeah, OK.
L: What about going to the gym and then we can have a big breakfast afterwards?
G: Er, I'm not sure about the gym. But I like breakfast! A lot!
L: OK. How about going for a run and then breakfast?
G: Perfect! I love running. That sounds really nice. Where do you want to meet?
L: Let's meet at Newton Green at eight o'clock tomorrow.
G: Great. See you there.
L: Go! Gaby?
G: Lucy?
L: Gaby, why don't we go for …
G: … breakfast!
L: Now?
G: That sounds …
L, G: perfect!
S: There you go.
C: Thanks.
S: Are you going for a run?
G: Er, no. We went for a run this morning.
L: Yes. A really good run.
G: It was very difficult.
L: Yes, and very long.
G: Very, very long.
L: And we're really tired.
G: And really hungry.
S: Amazing! Well done. Enjoy your breakfast.

11.3 Short run

PRONUNCIATION

11.9 **A** Highlight the underlined stressed syllables in the conversation. Then play the audio while students listen and follow along in their books.

11.9 **B** Play the audio line by line for students to listen and repeat. Encourage, notice and praise natural stress and rhythm.

Extra activity

Encourage students to change the mood of the conversation. Draw up a list of different moods on the board, e.g. happy, moody, excited, etc. Students read the conversation in different moods, changing their tone to show their mood. If you want to play it as a game, then pairs could choose one of the moods, then perform their conversation for the class and the class can guess which mood they are demonstrating.

SPEAKING

A Model the task for students by writing the things you would and wouldn't like to do on the weekend on the board under the appropriate emojis. Students then complete the task in pairs.

B Model the conversation with the students. Indicate for a student to suggest something from your 'wouldn't like to do' list. Say no to the suggestion using the functional language from the lesson. Repeat with something from your 'would like to do' list. Students then work in pairs to have the conversation.

C Model the mingling activity, completing a line of the arrangements table on the board for students to see. Students then mingle and complete the table in their books with their arrangements. Monitor and make a note of successful and less successful language use for a feedback session at the end of the class.

METHODOLOGY HUB by Jim Scrivener

Voice settings

One interesting approach to pronunciation may sound a little odd at first. It's based on the idea that, rather than work on all the small details of pronunciation (such as phonemes, stress patterns, etc), it might be better to start with the larger holistic picture – the general 'settings' of the voice. If you think about a foreign language you have heard a number of times, you are probably able to quickly recall some distinctive impressions about how the language is spoken – the sorts of things that a comedian would pick on if they wanted to mimic a speaker of that language, for example, a distinctive mouth position with the lips pushed forward, a flat intonation with machine-gun delivery, a typical hunching of shoulders, frequently heard sounds, a generally high pitch, etc.

Do your students have such an image about American speakers of English? Or Australians? Or Canadians? One useful activity would be to (a) watch one or more native speakers on video, (b) discuss any noticeable speech features, (c) try speaking nonsense words using this 'voice setting' ('comedian' style), (d) practice reading a simple short conversation in as 'native' a way as they can. (This will probably seem very funny to your students, who will initially tend to do fairly bland copies, never completely believing that a voice setting may be so different or exaggerated compared with their own language; encourage them to risk looking and sounding really like a native speaker.)

TEACHING IDEA by David Seymour and Maria Popova

Grammar: Likes and dislikes

In pairs, find out about your partner's likes and dislikes, e.g.:

A – *What do you like doing in the evening?* B – *I like cooking.*
A – *Do you like doing the dishes?* B – *No. I hate doing the dishes.*

Use these words to help you.

do/evening, eat/breakfast, watch/TV, play/sports, read/book, do/weekend, talk/friends

Tell me a few of the things you found out about your partner.

On your own, write five sentences about yourself using a gerund. Choose from these adjectives, e.g. *Dancing makes me feel happy.*

sad, tired, excited, sick, dizzy, proud, happy, insecure, relaxed, guilty, embarrassed, angry

GABY

SAM

LUCY

PRONUNCIATION

11.9 **A** Listen to the conversation and notice how the underlined words are stressed.

Charlie: Are you free on Saturday?
Beccie: Yes, I'm free all day.
Charlie: Cool. Do you want to do something?
Beccie: Sure. Why don't we go for a run?
Charlie Uh, I'm not sure about running.
Beccie: OK. How about going for a walk?
Charlie: Great, I love walking. Where do you want to meet?
Beccie: Let's meet at Sam's Café at nine o'clock.
Charlie: Great! See you there.

11.9 **B** Listen again and repeat the conversation. Copy the stress.

SPEAKING

A PLAN Work in pairs.

- Make a list of things you like doing on the weekend. 🙂
- Make a list of things you don't like doing on the weekend. 🙁

B PREPARE Practice the conversation. Then change roles.

Student A: Suggest something from the 🙁 list.
Student B: Say no.
Student A: Suggest something from the 🙂 list.
Student B: Say yes.

C REPEAT Go around the class and make an arrangement with five other students. Use the activities in Exercise A or your own ideas. Complete the table below.

Name	Activity	Place	Time
Sam	*Play soccer*	*The park*	*5 pm*

Make and respond to suggestions

11 Writing

Write a personal profile

W– using *so*

ABOUT ME

Sign up | Login

Helena H.

Ex A Q1 I'm an artist and a designer, so I love going to museums and art galleries. Ex A Q2 I have a dog; her name's Kia, and we go on a lot of walks together. I live near the ocean, so we spend a lot of time on the beach. Ex A Q3 Kia really enjoys running after the birds! I live with my husband and three sons, and they all love football. It's always on TV in our house, and I hate it. Ex A Q4 I'm not a sports fan at all, so I'm happy to go out for a walk with Kia, or to work on my art.

A Read the text. Join the beginnings (1–4) to the ends (a–d) to make sentences.

1 Helena is — d
2 She likes — a
3 She spends time — b
4 She doesn't like — c

a going to museums and galleries.
b on the beach with her dog.
c watching sports.
d an artist and a designer.

Using *so*

When we want to talk about a result, we can use *so*.

I'm an artist and a designer, so I love going to museums and art galleries.

I live near the ocean, so we spend a lot of time on the beach.

I'm not a sports fan at all, so I'm happy to go out for a walk.

When we write, we usually put a comma (,) before *so*.

B Use *so* to write short endings to the sentences. Use the ideas in the box to help you.

go to the gym | go shopping | go to the stadium | go to the theater | listen to music at home | spend time in the park

1 I like baseball …
2 I don't enjoy going to concerts …
3 I have three dogs …
4 I love fashion …
5 I enjoy exercise …
6 I'm a fan of Shakespeare …

WRITING

A PLAN You are going to write a personal profile. Write notes about what you like doing and why.

B WRITE Write a short personal profile for the website.

Write a personal profile

Suggested answers

1 *I like baseball, so I frequently go to the stadium to watch a game.*
2 *I don't enjoy going to concerts, so I usually listen to music at home.*
3 *I have three dogs, so I spend a lot of time at the park.*
4 *I love fashion, so I go shopping every week.*
5 *I enjoy exercise, so I frequently go to the gym.*
6 *I'm a fan of Shakespeare, so I go to the theater a lot.*

Refer students to the personal profile as a model for the writing task.

Unit 11 Review

GRAMMAR

Find and correct eight mistakes.

WHAT DO YOU LIKE DOING?

Home | Soccer | Basketball | Football | Tennis | Golf | More…

This week: Basketball star Orson Orlando

I'm a professional basketball player, but I don't like ~~watch~~ watching basketball on TV. I have three children, and I like ~~spend~~ spending time with ~~they~~ them. We ~~enjoying~~ enjoy going to the park on the weekend and having fun. My wife is an actor. I love watching ~~she~~ her but ~~her~~ she doesn't want to watch movies on the weekend. She doesn't ~~liking~~ like going to the movie theater, but I love ~~its~~ it.

5h | 3

VOCABULARY

Complete the sentences with the words in the box.

actor | basketball | concert | game | premiere | restaurant | singer | takeout

1 Josh Brolin is my favorite __actor__. I have all his movies on DVD.
2 I don't like cooking. I like staying in and getting __takeout__ food.
3 There's an international soccer __game__ on TV tonight.
4 I went to a pop concert last night but I didn't like the __singer__. He wasn't very good.
5 I went to a movie __premiere__ and I met all the actors. It was really exciting!
6 I like sitting very close to the players when I go to a __basketball__ game.
7 The __concert__ was very loud but I loved it!
8 I love Chinese food but I don't eat it at home. I like going to the __restaurant__ in the town center.

88 HAVING FUN

LEAD-IN

Write the answers to five questions about yourself on the board, e.g. *playing the guitar*. Students ask questions, e.g. *What do you like?* If they are correct, cross out the answer. Continue until all the answers are crossed out. The person who asks the last question comes up and does the same thing. Continue for as long as you have time, or switch to pairs if time is short.

WRITING

A Students read the text and complete the exercise individually, then check in pairs. Go through the answers with the class, making sure students can justify their answers from the text.

B Write two sentences that are true about you, e.g. *I like music. I go to concerts*. Show how we can connect them with *so*. Focus students on the *Using so* box and go through it with them, checking they understand by asking them to identify the result in each example. Do the first sentence of the exercise with the whole class, then students work individually to complete the exercise. Write the answers on the board.

WRITING TASK

A Model the activity by writing a plan for yourself on the board, using short notes rather than sentences. Show how you can then put your ideas into a logical order. Give students time to write their own notes, helping with vocabulary if needed.

B Students write their profile. Ask them to work with a partner to correct it before you look at it. If you can, get them to share their profiles on a class site, or display them on the board.

Female hiker walking through Red Cave, Utah, United States.

The phrase is used to describe leaving your home for a period of time, especially for a vacation.

Ask students to label the photo if you need time to set up the class.

The quote highlights that all tasks we face, no matter how big or small, begin with a simple action – 'one step'. We do not need to face all the parts of the big task ahead at once. We need to focus on what needs to be done now which will, in turn, lead us to the next step. In this way, we can accomplish great things, without feeling overwhelmed at the start. All we need to do is begin, with that one first step.

Lao Tzu (born 601 BCE) was a Chinese philosopher credited with creating the philosophy of Taoism. Not all the facts are known or agreed on about Lao Tzu. However, the work attributed to him has been very influential from his time of writing to the present day. Taoism is a system of thought which promotes living a simple life.

OBJECTIVES

- describe a trip
- talk about vacation plans
- ask for and give opinions
- write a postcard

Work with a partner. Discuss the questions.

1. Look at the picture. Do you enjoy long trips?
2. When do you usually go on vacation?
3. What makes long trips difficult?

GOING AWAY 89

OBJECTIVES

Read the unit objectives to the class.

UNIT OPENER QUESTIONS

Working in pairs, focus the students on the picture of the tourist walking through the cave. Ask them what they can see in the picture and how it makes them feel. Ask students if they enjoy long trips and to give reasons for their answers. Elicit answers from several students so that a wide range of views is expressed by the students. Add vocabulary on the side of the board for students to use throughout the lesson and keep adding to it as new words are used by the students.

Ask students to then look at Question 2 and ask them to say when they usually go on vacation. Ask if there are any special reasons for choosing a particular time of year, e.g. good weather, national holidays or a good time for a break from work. Finally, ask students what they think makes long trips difficult. You could add some sentence stems to the board for students to use, such as *I think that … make(s) long trips difficult. Sometimes, … can make long trips difficult.*

Students work in pairs to answer the question. Monitor and assist as required, then answer and discuss as a whole class. Ask students if they know quotes in their own languages about trips.

WORKSHEETS

Lesson 12.1 Trips

Vocabulary: Travel (W43)

Grammar: Countable and uncountable nouns (W44)

Lesson 12.2 A prize vacation

Vocabulary: Types of vacation (W45)

Grammar: Present progressive (W46)

12.1 Trips

Describe a trip

V travel   P consonant clusters   G countable and uncountable nouns

READING

A Work in pairs. Make a list of the problems people sometimes have when they travel.

B READ FOR GIST Read *A bad trip*. Choose the correct summary.

(a) Kate McCallister didn't take her son when she went on vacation. She tried to get home, but she had a very bad trip.

b Kate McCallister didn't take her passport when she went on vacation. She went home with her son.

C READ FOR DETAIL Put the events (a–e) in the order they happened (1–5). Read the article again to check your answers.

a Kate got on a plane to Paris. 2

b Kate remembered Kevin was at home. 3

c Kate went to Chicago in a van. 5

d Kate went to the airport in Chicago. 1

e Kate got on a plane to Pennsylvania. 4

D SPEAK Work in pairs. Answer the questions.

1 Do you ever go on a plane or a train?

2 Do you sometimes forget things when you travel?

A BAD TRIP

A lot can go wrong when you travel. For example:

- Your train to the **airport** is late, so you miss your plane.
- You take a taxi to the airport, but there is a lot of **traffic**, so you miss your plane.
- You forget your **passport**.
- Your **luggage** is too big to take on the plane.
- You forget the **bag** with all of your **money**, your **credit card** and your **ticket** in it.

These are all things that can happen, but I think the worst thing is what happened to Kate McCallister in the 1990 movie *Home Alone*. She went to Paris on vacation with her family. At first, she didn't have any problems. She got to the airport on time, she didn't forget her passport, her luggage wasn't too big, and she had all her bags and all her money with her. She also had all of her credit cards and tickets. But she forgot one very important thing.

When she was on the plane from Chicago to Paris, Kate remembered: her 8-year-old son, Kevin! Kevin was not with them. He was at home … alone! Ex B

When they got to Paris, there weren't any planes back to Chicago, so she took a plane to Pennsylvania in the United States. Then, Kate tried to get a plane from Pennsylvania to Chicago but there weren't any. So, she traveled home in a van with a traveling group of musicians. Did she get back to Kevin? Was he okay? Watch the movie to find out!

VOCABULARY

Travel

A Match the images with the words in bold in the article.

1 passport

5 luggage

2 bag

6 airport

3 money

7 ticket

4 traffic

8 credit card

B Go the the Vocabulary Hub on page 127.

12.1 Trips

LEAD-IN

Elicit the difference between a journey and a trip. Give examples of, e.g. your trip to work and a journey you went on. Ask students to think about their trip to class. You could ask questions like *How long does it take? Is it busy? Do you listen to music or read a book on your way?* You could elicit other trips students frequently go on, such as regular vacation destinations or going home to visit family, etc.

READING

A Give an example of a small problem you had when traveling, e.g. missing a connection because a plane was delayed. Put students into pairs and give them a time limit, e.g. three minutes, to think of as many problems as they can. You could show them how to make a mind map, e.g. write and circle *travel* in the middle of the board, then add branches off with different types of travel, e.g. *plane/bus*, then add branches off each of those with, e.g. *airport/security*, and then problems, e.g. *strike/stopped for baggage check* and so on. Then students can make their own mind map to generate ideas.

B Students read the summaries first; check that they understand them. Then ask them to read the article quickly to decide which one is correct. Show students that they should skim down the article rather than reading every word; a short time limit helps, e.g. one minute. Check the answer and ask which words helped them decide. Ask which of their ideas in Exercise A were in the text.

C Students look at the events and see if they can guess/remember which order any of them happened, then read the text again checking their ideas and completing the task. Ask students to read aloud the order and put it on the board.

D Give an example from your life in answer to the two questions, then put students into pairs to discuss their answers to the questions. Monitor, encouraging fluency and discussion.

VOCABULARY

A Students do the exercise individually, then check in pairs. Give the answers and write them on the board, practicing the pronunciation of the items. If you can, bring some of the items into class to use as realia; use the objects to practice the meanings by pointing at them and asking individual students and/or the whole class to name them.

B Direct students to the **Vocabulary Hub** (see TB97).

GRAMMAR HUB

12.1

Countable and uncountable nouns

Countable nouns	Uncountable nouns
bag/bags	cash
card/cards	information
dollar/dollars	luggage
hour/hours	money
ticket/tickets	traffic
train/trains	water

- A countable noun is a noun we can count – we can have one, two or more.

  one passport   two passports
  I don't have a passport.
  My friend has two passports – he's American and Italian.

- We can't count uncountable nouns.

  water NOT ~~one water, two waters~~
  What's happened? There's water all over the floor!

- We use a singular verb with uncountable nouns.

  Money is … NOT ~~Money are …~~
  I think money is very important.
  Money isn't important. It's more important to be happy!

- We never use *a* or *an* with uncountable nouns.

  Money … OR The money … OR Some money … NOT ~~A money …~~
  The money for the taxi is on the table.

Be careful!

- Never make an uncountable noun plural. Uncountable nouns do not have plural forms.

  information NOT ~~informations~~

C Students work in pairs to read the conversation and choose the correct answers. Check with the whole class. Use the **Vocabulary Worksheet** on page W43 for extra practice.

PRONUNCIATION

12.1 **A** Demonstrate how it is easy to say a consonant followed by a vowel or the reverse but harder to say two consonants together. Focus students on the exercise and play the audio while they listen. Play it again and get them to repeat the underlined consonant clusters.

12.2; 12.3 **B–C** Play the audio while students listen and underline the consonant clusters in Exercise B. Students then listen and circle the words they hear in Exercise C.

GRAMMAR

A Students read the sentences. Elicit the fact that *bag* in the second sentence has an *s*, which makes it plural. Write *singular* and *plural* on the board.

B Ask students to look at the underlined word in each sentence (*money*). Ask students under which heading on the board, *singular* or *plural*, should they write *money* (*singular*).

C Put students into pairs to read the *Countable and uncountable nouns* box and work out the rules. Demonstrate why it is uncountable; take out a bill or coin and ask, e.g. *How much money? One? Two?* Elicit the fact that students have to use a currency to answer, e.g. *two dollars*. Elicit some more uncountable things, e.g. *water*; again, show that we can count it but we need a unit, e.g. *a liter / a bottle / a glass*.

D Students do the exercise individually, then check in pairs. Go through the answers, giving more examples and using the examples on the board to help with the concepts and use of *some*, *all* and *a lot of*.

E Direct students to the **Grammar Hub** (see below and TB90). Use the **Grammar Worksheet** on page W44 for extra practice.

SPEAKING

A Students read the description and answer the questions. Go through the answers with the class. Ask if anyone ever had a similar experience.

B Students use the questions to plan what they are going to say. Encourage them to write notes rather than write full sentences at this stage.

C Students then tell their stories in groups. Encourage those listening to ask follow-up questions and practice active listening. They can use the example questions on the page to help them.

Extra activity

Play a game of 'consequences'. Students write the first sentence of a story at the top of a piece of paper. Then they pass the paper to the left. They read the first sentence of the new story they have just received and add the next sentence on a new line. Having written their sentence, they fold the paper so only the latest sentence is visible. The activity continues in this way. When it is time, instruct the students to write a final sentence for the story. Students then unfold the paper and read the complete story!

GRAMMAR HUB

12.1

Countable and uncountable nouns

A Complete the table with words from the box to make pairs of countable and uncountable nouns.

credit cards homework hours luggage music sandwiches ~~traffic~~ water

Countable nouns	Uncountable nouns
cars	1 *traffic*
bags	2 luggage
3 credit cards	money
songs	4 music
exercises	5 homework
6 sandwiches	food
7 hours	time
bottles	8 water

B Choose the correct options to complete the sentences.

1 Australian passports ***is*** / ***are*** blue.
2 These exercises ***is*** / ***are*** really difficult!
3 The traffic ***was*** / ***were*** bad today.
4 The sun ***is*** / ***are*** too hot today!
5 The taxi ***was*** / ***were*** late and we missed our flight!
6 The cash ***isn't*** / ***aren't*** here!
7 The music ***was*** / ***were*** great at the party!
8 The food ***is*** / ***are*** on the table.

C If the phrase in bold is correct, put a check mark (✓). If it's wrong, put an (✗).

1 I want **an information** about train times, please. ✗
2 We made **a plan** to meet tomorrow. ✓
3 Do you like **a music**? ✗
4 I don't have **a credit card**. ✓
5 Do you want **a sandwich**? ✓
6 Do you want **a food**? ✗
7 Here's **a bag** for the plane. ✓
8 Do you have **a luggage** for the plane? ✗

D Complete the sentences with the words in the box and choose C (countable noun) or U (uncountable noun).

cash dollars information plane ticket

1 We took a ___plane___ from Madrid in Spain to Bogotá in Colombia. *C* / *U*
2 I changed my euros into ___dollars___ at the airport. *C* / *U*
3 I asked for some ___information___ about the trip at the train station. *C* / *U*
4 I need some ___cash___. Some stores don't take credit cards. *C* / *U*
5 I got a(n) ___ticket___ for the train to Ankara. *C* / *U*

➤ Go back to page 91.

C Choose the correct options to complete the conversation.

Leo: Do you have your [1]*passport* / *taxi*? You need it to get on the [2]*plane* / *airport*.

Mia: Yes, I do. It's in my bag.

Leo: Do you have some [3]*money* / *luggage*? We need to exchange it at the airport for [4]*dollars* / *tickets*.

Mia: Yes, I do. It's in my bag.

Leo: Do you have the [5]*tickets* / *credit cards* for the train to the [6]*airport* / *station*?

Mia: Yes, I do. They're in my bag.

Leo: Do you have your bag?

Mia: Yes, I … Oh wait. No, I don't. I think it's at home.

PRONUNCIATION

Consonant clusters

12.1 **A** Listen to the sentences. Notice how we say the underlined letters.

You need your ticket to get on the plane.

I took a train at the station.

12.2 **B** Listen to the words. Underline the consonant clusters.

blue class fly plane travel

12.3 **C** Listen and circle the words you hear.

1 rain / train
2 tea / tree
3 top / stop
4 red / bread
5 back / black

GRAMMAR

Countable and uncountable nouns

A Read the sentences from the article. What do you notice about the words in bold? Are they talking about one bag, or more than one?

1 You forget the **bag** that has your money, your credit card and your ticket in it. one bag

2 … her luggage wasn't too big, and she had all her **bags** and all her money with her. more than one

B What do you notice about the underlined words?
no change, it has no plural form

C **WORK IT OUT** Choose the correct option to complete the sentences.

Countable and uncountable nouns

1 *Bag* / *Money* is a countable noun: it has a singular and a plural form.

2 *Bag* / *Money* is an uncountable noun: it doesn't have a plural form.

D **PRACTICE** Choose the correct options. Use examples from the article *A bad trip* to help you.

1 *all of your monies* / *all of your money*
Money is a(n) *countable* / *uncountable* noun.

2 *all of her credit cards* / *all of her credit card*
Credit card is a(n) *countable* / *uncountable* noun.

3 *her luggages* / *her luggage*
Luggage is a(n) *countable* / *uncountable* noun.

4 *a lot of traffic* / *a lot of traffics*
Traffic is a(n) *countable* / *uncountable* noun.

E Go to the **Grammar Hub** on **page 120**.

SPEAKING

A **PREPARE** Work in pairs. Read the description of a trip. Answer the questions.

I took a train from New York to Philadelphia. The train left on time but soon after we got to Pennsylvania the train stopped. There was a tree on the track and the train couldn't move! In the end, we got on a bus. We arrived in Philadelphia two hours late.

1 Where did she start? New York
2 Where did she finish? Philadelphia
3 How did she travel? by train and then by bus
4 What was the problem? The train stopped, there was a tree on the track, she took a bus and got to Philadelphia two hours late.

B **PLAN** Think about a bad trip you went on. Prepare the answers to these questions.

1 Where did you start?
2 Where did you finish?
3 How did you travel?
4 What was the problem?

C **DISCUSS** Work in groups. Tell each other about your bad trips. Listen and ask questions.

And then what happened?
What did you do?
What happened next?
Oh wow, how did you …?

Describe a trip

12.2 A prize vacation

Talk about vacation plans

S – listening for feelings V – types of vacations G – present progressive P – vowel sounds: /ɪ/, /iː/ and /aɪ/

LISTENING

A SPEAK Work in pairs. Talk about your last vacation. Where did you go? What did you do?

A: I went to Lake Como in Italy. I went hiking, and I ate a lot of great Italian food.

B: For my last vacation, I didn't go away, but I didn't go to work – I just relaxed at home. It was great!

B PREPARE TO LISTEN Read the web page. Answer the questions.

Home | Listen live | Schedule Search

HUB LIVE – ONLINE RADIO

Mikey Greene's afternoon show

In this week's competition, you can win a vacation for you and a friend.

Enter online. We will call the winner live on the radio. Listen to Tuesday's show and have your phone with you.

1 What is HUB Live?
  - (a) a radio station
  - b a TV station
  - c a news website

2 Who is Mikey Greene?
  - a a vacation expert
  - b a singer
  - (c) a radio presenter

3 What is the prize?
  - a a radio
  - (b) a vacation
  - c a phone

4 How does a listener know they are the winner?
  - (a) They get a phone call on Tuesday.
  - b They look online.
  - c They get an email on Tuesday.

12.4 **C LISTEN FOR GIST** Listen to the conversation. Choose the picture (a, b, c or d) that shows the vacation. Is the winner happy? No, she isn't.

12.4 **D LISTEN FOR DETAIL** Listen again. Answer the questions.

1 What's the name of the competition winner? Jo

2 What's the name of the competition winner's friend? Charlotte

3 On what day of the week does the vacation start? Wednesday

4 In which month does the vacation start? November

5 How long is the vacation? two weeks

Listening for feelings

How we say things can tell the listener how we're feeling. When we're unhappy about something, we usually pause.

Jo: … No beach?

When we're angry or surprised, we usually speak loudly.

Jo: TWO WEEKS?

12.5 **E LISTEN FOR FEELINGS** Listen to Mikey and Jo. Match Jo's words (1–2) with the actions (a–b). What do they tell us about her feelings?

1 Camping. In a tent? — b pause

2 Mountains? — a loud

a loud
b pause

She is not happy, she doesn't want to stay in a tent near mountains.

F SPEAK Work in pairs. Role-play the conversation when the winner tells her friend about the vacation.

A: Hi. I won a vacation for you and me.

B: That's great! Where is it?

A: Uh …

G SPEAK Work in pairs. Imagine you won this vacation. How do you feel?

12.2 A prize vacation

LEAD-IN

Put some magazine pictures of vacation destinations on the walls. Ask students to walk around and choose their favorite destination, and stand next to it. See which is the most popular and ask the students who chose it and why they like it. Then do the same with the least favorite destination.

LISTENING

A–B Put students into pairs to talk about their last vacations. Students then read the webpage and then answer the questions.

12.4 **C–D** Give students time to read the questions, then play the audio again while they listen and answer them.

12.5 **E** Go through the *Listening for feelings* box with the students. Then play the audio while students listen and match. Check answers as a class.

F Students work in pairs to role-play the conversation.

G Change pairs and ask students to discuss how they would feel if they won. When they finish, ask some of them to share their feelings with the class.

AUDIO SCRIPT

12.4

Listening, Exercise C
M = Mikey Greene J = Jo

M: Now listeners, it's three o'clock on Tuesday afternoon and it's time to call this week's competition winner. Have your phone with you – we are calling … now!
J: Hello?
Ex D Q1 **M:** Is this Jo?
J: Yes, yes, yes! Is this Mikey?
M: It's Mikey Greene and you're on the radio! Congratulations, Jo – you are this week's competition winner!
J: Wow! That's amazing. I never win anything.
M: Well, you're a winner today.
J: I can't believe it. Me?
M: That's right, Jo. Your prize is a vacation for you and a friend.
J: Wow! I don't usually enter competitions, but I saw the picture on the website of the beach and the ocean, and I thought, 'This is the vacation for me!' I'm so excited.
M: The picture on the website? Oh, right, yeah. Um … that's not a picture of the vacation you're going on.
J: Oh, really?
GRAMMAR Ex B **M:** Yes, you're going on a different kind of vacation. But don't worry. It's an amazing vacation.
J: Oh. OK then.
GRAMMAR Ex B **M:** Who are you taking with you?
Ex D Q2 **J:** I'm taking my friend, Charlotte. She loves going to the beach.
GRAMMAR Ex B **M:** That's great, Jo, but just to be clear: you're not going on a beach vacation this time.
J: No beach?
M: Um, … no.
J: What kind of vacation is it, Mikey?
Ex C **M:** Well, Jo … it's a camping vacation!
J: Camping. In a tent?
Ex C **M:** That's right. You're going to the countryside, and you're staying in a tent, next to some mountains.
GRAMMAR Ex B **J:** Mountains? Charlotte hates walking and she doesn't like cold weather. When are we going?
Ex D Q3 **M:** You're going … next Wednesday!
Ex D Q4 **J:** Next Wednesday? It's November, Mikey. It's really
GRAMMAR Ex B cold. How long are we going for?
Ex D Q5 **M:** It's a two-week vacation, Jo. Isn't that great?
J: Two weeks? In a tent? In the cold?
M: Next to a mountain. That's right, Jo. Have a great time. Bye, Jo. Well listeners, I think Jo's really excited about her vacation. Next week's competition is … a beach vacation in Brazil.

GRAMMAR HUB

12.2

Present progressive

	Positive	Negative	Question
Present progressive	**I'm taking** my camera with me.	**They aren't staying** in a hotel.	**Is Tina going** skiing?

- You know that we use the present progressive to talk about things happening now (see Unit 8). We can also use the present progressive to talk about the future. In this sentence, the people aren't traveling right now – the trip is in the future.
  We're traveling to France next week.
- We use the present progressive like this to talk about our plans for the future.
  Helga is staying in a hotel. (She booked it last week.)
  The girls are flying to the US. (They have their tickets and passports.)
- We frequently use future time expressions with the present progressive when we are talking about future plans:
  e.g. *tomorrow, next week, soon, in the summer, this evening.*

Be careful!

- You can only use the present progressive for the future if there's a plan.
  I'm watching a soccer game tomorrow. NOT ~~*I'm winning a soccer game tomorrow.*~~

12.2 A prize vacation

VOCABULARY

A Students work in pairs to match the words and pictures. Check the answers as a class. Practice the pronunciation of the phrases and personalize by asking who has experienced them.

B Direct students to the **Vocabulary Hub** (see TB97).

C Students work individually to complete the exercise, then check in pairs. Give the answers.

D Students work in pairs to decide. Give the answers, demonstrating and giving more examples to clarify the usages.

E Ask students to ask you the three questions, then put students into pairs to ask and answer. Walk around encouraging them to ask further questions and to give extra details and to express their feelings about the vacations. Use the **Vocabulary Worksheet** on page W45 for extra practice.

PRONUNCIATION

12.6 **A** Write the phonemic symbols on the board and demonstrate the individual sounds. Then play the audio while students listen and read. Write the words under the symbols for the sounds and practice pronunciation – demonstrate the mouth movements if appropriate, and remind students that the two dots in one symbol represent lengthening the sound, while the two symbols are a combination sound, a diphthong, so the mouth moves when producing it.

12.7 **B** Play the audio while students listen and add the words to the table. Check answers as a class.

12.8 **C** Students work in pairs, saying the words and matching. Then play the audio for them to listen and check. Give the answers.

D Students choose individually, then check with a partner. Give the answers and model the words for students to repeat.

E Put students into different pairs to ask and answer the questions. Monitor, correcting pronunciation if necessary.

GRAMMAR

A Ask students to read the sentences, then refer them to the *Present progressive* box to choose the rules. Write the present progressive expressions on the board using different colors for each part of the form: the subject, *to be* and the *-ing* form. Give an example from your own life of fixed future arrangements, then elicit a few more examples for people in the class and write them up using the same colors as before, to highlight the pattern.

B Students go to the relevant pages and read the audio script and complete the task individually.

C Direct students to the **Grammar Hub** (see below and TB92). Use the **Grammar Worksheet** on page W46 for extra practice.

SPEAKING HUB

A Put students into pairs and ask them to choose who they want to be, then direct students to the **Communication Hub** (see TB97).

B Students work on their role play in pairs.

C Students use the cues in the box to discuss their plans for the vacation they want to go on.

D Ask each pair to summarize their conversations, encouraging the use of the present progressive to show that they have made a plan with their partner.

Extra activity

Students work in small groups to plan a class vacation. They should choose the type of vacation, where and when to go, and the activities to do there. The groups then present the vacation to the class. At the end of all the presentations, the class votes on the vacation to go on.

GRAMMAR HUB

12.2

Present progressive

A Are these sentences about what's happening now or a plan in the future? Choose (N) for Now or (P) for Plan.

1 Ssh! The children are doing their homework. **(N)** / P
2 We're flying to Paris next week. N / **(P)**
3 I'm staying in a tent and it's cold! **(N)** / P
4 We're meeting at the train station. Don't be late! N / **(P)**
5 Gemma is waiting to get on her flight. She's bored. **(N)** / P
6 What time are we meeting Lauren? N / **(P)**

B Complete the conversation using the present progressive. Use the words in parentheses to help you.

Axel: What [1] are you doing (*you / do*) this summer?
Ben: [2] I'm/I am going (*I / go*) on a sightseeing vacation in Istanbul.
Axel: Great! Who [3] are you going (*you / go*) with?
Ben: [4] I'm/I am going (*I / go*) with my sister. She's a photographer.
Axel: [5] Is she taking (*she / take*) her camera?
Ben: No, [6] she isn't (*she / be*). She doesn't like working when she's on vacation.

C Complete the sentences and questions with the correct present progressive form of the verbs in parentheses.

1 *Are you traveling* (*you/travel*) by train or by bus?
2 My parents aren't/are not taking (*not/take*) a lot of luggage with them.
3 Alexander 's/is going (*go*) skiing next week.
4 Where are you staying (*you/stay*)?
5 The students are going (*go*) sightseeing around Kyoto tomorrow.
6 We 're/are camping (*camp*) in the mountains for the summer.
7 What 's/is Ali taking (*Ali/take*) with him on vacation?
8 Sara isn't/is not working (*not/work*) next week.

➤ Go back to page 93.

VOCABULARY
Types of vacations

A Match two words or phrases with each of the pictures (a–d) on page 92.

a beach vacation | a camping vacation | a chalet | the ocean | a sightseeing vacation | a skiing vacation | a tent | tourists

B Go to the **Vocabulary Hub** on **page 127**.

C ~~Cross out~~ the option that is not correct.

When you go on vacation, you can …

1 stay in a *tent* / *hotel* / ~~*beach*~~ / *chalet*.
2 take your *sunglasses* / *camera* / ~~*skiing*~~ / *snorkel*.
3 use a *guidebook* / *stove* / ~~*sightseeing*~~ / *camera*.

D Choose the correct option to complete the sentences.

1 We usually go *in* / *on* a beach vacation in August.
2 You can see the ocean *from* / *to* our hotel window.
3 We went sightseeing *around* / *of* Kyoto in Japan.
4 We usually go skiing *in* / *at* the mountains in January.
5 I enjoy camping *with* / *for* my friends.
6 I take a lot of photos *by* / *with* this camera.

E SPEAK Work in pairs. Discuss the questions.

1 What is your favorite type of vacation? Why?
2 How often do you go on this type of vacation?
3 What things do you take?

PRONUNCIATION
Vowel sounds: /ɪ/, /iː/ and /aɪ/

12.6 **A** Read and listen to the examples.

/ɪ/	/iː/	/aɪ/
sit	green	why
a winner	b beach	c time

12.7 **B** Read and listen to the examples from the radio show. Then put the words (1–3) in the correct place in the table.

No [1]beach? Well, you're a [2]winner today. Have a great [3]time.

12.8 **C** Join the first half of the sentences (1–3) to the second half of the sentences (a–c) with underlined letters that have the same sound. Then, listen and check.

1 /ɪ/ This is
2 /aɪ/ My prize was
3 /iː/ He enjoyed

a a week at the ski resort.
b an interesting vacation.
c a guidebook.

D Choose the correct sound for each underlined word.

1 Do you like beach vacations? /ɪ/ /iː/ /aɪ/
2 Do you frequently win competitions? /ɪ/ /iː/ /aɪ/
3 Do you like Jo's prize? /ɪ/ /iː/ /aɪ/

E SPEAK Work in pairs. Ask and answer the questions in Exercise D.

GRAMMAR
Present progressive

A WORK IT OUT Read the sentences from the radio show. Choose the correct option to complete the rules.

Mikey: **You're going** … next Wednesday!

Mikey: **You're going** to the countryside, and **you're staying** in a tent, next to some mountains.

Present progressive

1 He is talking about an arrangement in the *present* / *future*.
2 He is talking about something that *is* / *isn't* fixed.

B Read the **audio script** on **page 137**. Find six more sentences or questions when Mikey and Jo use present progressive.

C Go to the **Grammar Hub** on **page 120**.

SPEAKING HUB

A PREPARE You are going to role-play a conversation between a radio presenter and a prize winner. Work in pairs. Choose roles.

Student A – You are the prize winner. Go to the **Communication Hub** on **page 133**.

Student B – You are the radio presenter. Go to the **Communication Hub** on **page 129**.

B PRACTICE Role-play the conversation with your partner.

C DISCUSS Have a conversation with your partner. Imagine and plan a vacation you both want to go on. Think about:

- the type of vacation
- the place
- when to go
- where to stay
- how long to go for
- things to take

D REPORT Tell the class about your vacation.

We're going on a beach vacation!

Talk about vacation plans

Café Hub

12.3 Istanbul

F – ask for and give opinions

COMPREHENSION

A 00:10–00:40 Watch the first part of the video. What do you think Lucy's idea is? Choose a, b or c.

a Why don't you come with me to Madrid?

(b) Let's go on a city break!

c How about going to see Metal Train tonight?

B 00:41–03:04 Watch the second part of the video and check your answer to Exercise A.

C Match Sam's comments (1–4) with the different places (a–d).

1 It's too rainy. ____d____

2 It's really expensive. ____a____

3 It's too busy. ____c____

4 It's really cold there right now. ____b____

a Copenhagen

b Helsinki

c Venice

d Dublin

D Watch the video again and check your answers to Exercise C.

E SPEAK Work in pairs. Answer the questions.

1 Which cities in the video would you like to visit?

2 Which cities in your country are like descriptions 1–4 in Exercise C?

3 Which city in the world would you most like to visit?

FUNCTIONAL LANGUAGE

Asking for and giving opinions

A Complete the phrases in the table with the words in the box.

about busy ~~going~~ Good How No really think

Ask for an opinion	Agree
What about [1] ___going___ on a city break? What [2] ___about___ Dublin? [3] ___How___ about Istanbul?	That's a great/nice idea. Perfect!
	Disagree
	[4] ___No___ way!
Give an opinion	**Agree**
I think it's [5] ___really___ expensive. It's really cold there right now. It's too [6] ___busy___ with long queues everywhere. It's too rainy.	Oh yeah. [7] ___Good___ point. That's true.
	Disagree
	I don't [8] ___think___ it's *that* cold/busy/rainy etc.

B Watch the video again and check your answers to Exercise A.

Glossary

city break **(n) (British)** = a getaway in the city **(n) (American)**
queues **(n) (British)** = lines **(n) (American)**

12.3 Istanbul

LEAD-IN

Ask the students to describe the different cities they can see in the photos. Ask students if they have visited the cities and invite them to share their experiences.

COMPREHENSION

A ▶ 00:10–00:40 Allow time for students to read the three options. Then play the video for students to predict.

B ▶ 00:41–03:04 Play the next part of the video for students to check their predictions.

C Students work in pairs to match the comments to the different places. Highlight that *too* gives a negative meaning to the sentence. It is not simply the same as *very*, i.e. *very busy* could still be acceptable to someone; however, *too busy* is not.

D ▶ Students watch the video again and check their answers to Exercise C.

E Answer the questions with your views for the class to hear examples. Encourage students to ask you questions (e.g. *Why?*). Students then answer the questions in pairs. Invite students to report their partner's answers back to the class.

Extra activity

Students work individually to create a list of places they would like to visit and why. These could be in their own country or anywhere in the world. Put students into pairs to discuss their ideas and agree on a final list of three. Then, put pairs together to create groups of four. Together as a group they must discuss and agree on the top place to go of the six ideas brought to the group. Then put groups together to agree on the place they want to visit. Continue until the class agrees on one place.

FUNCTIONAL LANGUAGE

A Highlight the titles of the different sections of the table. Students then complete the table with the words in the box. Build up the phrases on the board or ask students to transfer the information to large sheets of paper which can be posted on the walls to support the students during the rest of the lesson.

B ▶ Students watch the video again to check their answers to Exercise A.

VIDEO SCRIPT

G = Gaby L = Lucy S = Sam

G: Muy bien, Lucy. Well done. Your Spanish is very good now.
L: Thanks, Gaby. I'm moving to Madrid in only two weeks!
G: Lucy! I'm going to miss you!
L: Oh, I'm going to miss you, too. But I have a very cool idea!
G: Really?
L: What about going on a city break?
G: A weekend away together? Before you go?
L: Yes! Somewhere in Europe.
G: That's a great idea. But where?
L: OK. How about Copenhagen?
S: Copenhagen? I think it's really expensive.
L: Oh, yeah. Good point. OK, how about Helsinki?
S: Helsinki? No, it's really cold there right now.
L: Oh. I don't think it's that cold.
G: Is it colder than London?
L: Well, yes.
G: That's too cold.
L: OK then, somewhere warmer …
G: How about Venice?
S: No, it's too busy with long queues everywhere.
L: Oh, yeah. Good point. What about Dublin?
G: Oh, Dublin! That's a nice idea. And it's not too far.
S: Dublin? No way! It's too rainy!
G: That's true. I don't like rain. How about Istanbul?
S: Perfect!
L: Perfect!
G: Perfect!

METHODOLOGY HUB by Jim Scrivener

Approaches to speaking: Pyramid discussion

A 'pyramid discussion' is an organizational technique that works particularly well with simple problem-based discussions and especially with item-selection tasks, e.g. 'What are the four most useful things to have with you if you are shipwrecked on a desert island?', or list sequencing tasks, e.g. 'Put these items in order of importance'. Here's how to do it:

1. Introduce the problem, probably using a list on the board or on handouts.
2. Start with individual reflection – learners each decide what they think might be a solution.
3. Combine individuals to make pairs, who now discuss and come to an agreement or compromise. If you demand that there must be an agreed compromise solution before you move on to the next stage, it will significantly help to focus the task.
4. Combine the pairs to make fours; again, they need to reach an agreement.
5. Join each four with another four or – in a smaller class – with all the others.
6. When the whole class comes together, see if you can reach one class solution.

What's the point of doing a discussion in this way? (After all, it will take some time to do.) Well, most importantly, the technique gives students time to practice speaking in smaller groups before facing the whole class. Even the weaker speakers tend to find their confidence grows as the activity proceeds and they are able to rehearse and repeat arguments that they have already tested on others. Learners who would usually never dare state their views in front of the entire class will still get a number of chances to speak and, because they have practiced a little, may even get the courage to say them again to everyone. It also tends to lead to a much more exciting and well-argued whole-class discussion. The smaller groups are seedbeds for a variety of ideas and opinions; if we jumped in the deep end with the whole-class stage, we would probably get silence or possibly just one or two students dominating.

12.3 Istanbul

PRONUNCIATION

12.9 **A** Highlight the stressed syllables. Then play the audio for students to listen and follow along in their books.

12.9 **B** Play the audio line by line and have the students say each line. Try 'back chaining' to help students. Say the last word in the sentence, then second to last and the last, then the third to last, second to last and the last and so on (e.g. *rainy – that rainy – it's that rainy – think it's that rainy* – etc). Focus on natural stress and rhythm in these short segments.

SPEAKING

A Elicit which cities the pictures show. Students work in pairs to list good and bad points about the cities shown. This section could be extended if students have access to digital devices, by allowing time to research information about the cities (e.g. temperature, cost, etc).

B Model the conversation with a strong student. Take the role of Student B and model explaining why you don't agree with the suggestion. Make sure to use functional phrases in your reply. Students then work in pairs to have the conversation. Monitor and give feedback on samples of language use. This will help students to improve for the next exercise.

C Invite students to perform their conversation in front of the class.

D Students can discuss the question in groups, conduct a survey or mix and mingle, asking and answering. Share ideas as a whole class and take a vote on the most popular city if it hasn't been decided on already.

Extra activity
For further practice, the same language could be practiced in an alternative situation. Tell students they are going to organize a social event for the class. You could set a context for this, such as a meal in a restaurant, or you could leave it open for students to make their own suggestions. Students individually think of a few suggestions. They then work with a partner to discuss and decide on what to do. You could extend this to be discussed in groups and then as a class to eventually decide together on the final event.

METHODOLOGY HUB by Jim Scrivener

Stages in a speaking lesson

The following are some likely elements:

Once you have explained the specific speaking task, the learners may need to:

- plan how they will do the task
- rehearse parts (or all) of it
- hear examples of competent speakers doing the same task
- get input from you on possible structures, phrases, vocabulary, etc
- reflect on how well they did the task after they finish
- replan or review their original ideas
- have another try at doing the task a second (third?) time.

At various points, the learners may want correction and advice on how to do it better.

Here are those elements arranged into a basic lesson sequence, together with a worked example for 'making a business appointment over the phone'. The stage marked with a star could come at any point of your choosing.

Basic lesson sequence:

1. Set task
2. Plan the speaking
3. Rehearse the speaking
4. Do the task
5. Feedback / review the success
6. Add / correct / review
7. Redo the task

* Exposure to example

Worked example

1. **Set task**: Tell learners that they must call a business contact to make an appointment for a meeting to discuss future plans.
2. **Plan the speaking**: Ask learners to work in pairs to decide what the caller will say and how the receptionist will respond. Learners should not write out a whole script but can write notes of particular phrases.
3. **Rehearse the speaking**: Learners practice in pairs. You listen in and suggest corrections and improvements.
4. **Do the task**: Make new pairs. Without further discussion, learners 'call' each other and do the task.
5. **Feedback / review the success**: The pairs meet and reflect on whether the task was done well. Maybe the whole class also discusses the question and you offer notes. You may draw attention to specific language that learners could use and specific ways of interacting appropriate to the genre.
6. **Add / correct / review**: The pairs work out how they could improve their task next time.
7. **Redo the task**: Make new pairs. The task is done again.

* **Exposure to example**: Play a recording of competent speakers doing the same task. The class is asked to write down notes about the language they use.

GABY

SAM

LUCY

PRONUNCIATION

A Listen to the conversation and notice how the underlined words are stressed.
12.9

Michael: I have a cool idea. Let's go on a getaway.
David: A weekend away? Together? But where?
Michael: How about Paris?
David: I think Paris is very expensive.
Michael: Good point.
David: What about San Sebastián?
Michael: No way, it's too rainy.
David: I don't think it's that rainy!
Michael: But, at this time of year, it rains a lot.
David: That's true.
Michael: OK, how about Amsterdam?
David: Perfect!

B Listen again and repeat the conversation. Copy the stress.
12.9

SPEAKING

A **PREPARE** Work in pairs. List good and bad points about the cities below.

B **PRACTICE** Work in pairs. Write and practice a conversation using your ideas from Exercise A.

- Student A: Suggest a city for a getaway.
- Student B: Disagree with Student A three times and explain why.
- Finish the dialogue when Student B agrees with Student A.

C **PRESENT** Perform your conversation for the other students in the class.

D **DISCUSS** Find out which is the most popular city in your class.

Rome, Italy

ykjavík, Iceland

San Francisco, US

Prague, Czech Republic

Dubai, United Arab Emirates

Ask for and give opinions

Unit 12 Writing

12 Writing

Write a postcard

W– editing your writing

A Read the postcard. Find:

1. the type of vacation — sightseeing
2. the place — Casablanca
3. a useful item — camera
4. a place to visit — markets / Hassan II Mosque
5. the first day of the vacation — last Thursday
6. the last day of the vacation — tomorrow

Hi Juan,

I'm on vacation in Casablanca. There are a lot of people, and it's very hot, but I love it! Every day, I go sightseeing. There are some great markets, and I really liked the Hassan II Mosque. It's beautiful. I have a new camera, and I'm taking a lot of photos. I got here last Thursday, and I'm going home tomorrow but I don't want to leave! See you soon.

Kyra

Editing your writing

When you write something, it's a good idea to check for any spelling, grammar or punctuation mistakes.

Im on Vaccation at paris ✗

I'm on vacation in Paris. ✓

B Find and correct the mistakes in this postcard text.

~~hi~~ Hi Ellie.

Im on vacation in ~~peru~~ Peru. I ~~lov~~ love it here! We went to Machu Picchu yesterday. It was beautiful. Tomorrow ~~we~~ we're going to Lake Titicaca. I can't ~~wate~~ wait.

See you when I get back,

~~wendy~~ Wendy

WRITING

A PLAN Plan a postcard. Follow the instructions.

- Choose a place to write about.
- Write notes for each of the categories in Exercise A.

B WRITE Imagine you are on vacation now. Write a postcard. Use all of the information you prepared in Exercise A.

C EDIT Check your postcard for mistakes. Think about spelling, grammar and punctuation.

O– Write a postcard

Refer students to the postcard as a model for the writing task.

Remind students that it is good practice to edit their work.

Unit 12 Review

GRAMMAR

A Choose the correct options to complete the sentences.

1. I have some *moneys* / ***money*** in my bag.
2. Can I have two *ticket* / ***tickets*** to Buenos Aires, please?
3. I asked the staff for more ***information*** / *informations* about the trip.
4. My friend Anna goes on a lot of *vacation* / ***vacations***.
5. I don't have any *credit card* / ***credit cards***, but I have some cash.
6. Our taxi was late because there was a lot of *traffics* / ***traffic***.

B Complete the conversation with the verbs in the box in the present progressive.

drive go take visit be

Sam: Where [1] ___are___ you ___going___ on vacation this year?
Tom: I [2] ___'m visiting___ my brother in Virginia.
Sam: [3] ___Are___ you ___taking___ the train?
Tom: No, I [4] ___'m not___. I [5] ___'m driving___ there.

VOCABULARY

Match the words with the descriptions. Use each word only once.

airport chalet guidebook passport skiing snorkel taxi tent

1. a type of vacation, usually in the mountains — skiing
2. a type of transportation — taxi
3. something you need when you go to another country — passport
4. a place you can stay in when you are on a skiing vacation — chalet
5. something tourists use when they are sightseeing — guidebook
6. a place where you can get on a plane — airport
7. something you stay in when you are camping — tent
8. something you can use when you are on a beach vacation — snorkel

LEAD-IN

Ask students to write down three places they want to visit in their lives. Then ask them to walk around the class and find someone that wants to go to one of the same places. When they find them, they quickly plan their trip. If nobody has the same places, students can try and convince someone to come with them to one of their places. Ask students to report back to the class.

WRITING

A Students look at the postcard. Ask them what and where it shows. Students read the postcard and answer the questions. Check answers as a class.

B Write one or two sentences on the board with spelling, grammar and punctuation mistakes, e.g. *I,m you teacher sam. I live on girona*. Elicit and make the corrections, asking if they are grammar, punctuation or spelling corrections. Focus students on the *Editing your writing* box and go through it together. Then ask them to find the mistakes in the postcard text, labeling the mistakes *G* (grammar), *P* (punctuation) or *S* (spelling), and then check in pairs before you go through it with the whole class.

WRITING TASK

A Students work individually to plan their postcard. Walk around helping with vocabulary.

B Students write their postcards. It would be good to give them postcard-sized pieces of card to do this on, or they could write it on paper and then copy it after editing.

C Write *G/P/S* on the board and remind students what the letters refer to, and then ask them to check and edit for each in turn. When students have finished, ask them to 'send' their postcards to other students in the class to read; you can act as the delivery person. At the end, display the postcards; students could add pictures of their destination from the internet if appropriate and possible.

Vocabulary and Communication Hub

Contents

Vocabulary Hub

1.2 Jobs

Match the words in the box with the pictures.

an actor   a builder   a chef   a musician   a photographer   a police officer   a receptionist   a sales person   a soccer player   a writer

1 a builder

2 a chef

3 a photographer

4 a soccer player

5 a receptionist

6 a sales person

7 a writer

8 a police officer

9 a musician

10 an actor

➤ Go back to page 4.

2.1 Nationalities

Look at the flags. Use *-an*, *-ian*, *-ese* or *-ish* to write the nationality for each country.

Algeria

Algerian

Chile

Chilean

Denmark

Danish

Italy

Italian

Lebanon

Lebanese

Morocco

Moroccan

Russia

Russian

Scotland

Scottish

Venezuela

Venezuelan

Vietnam

Vietnamese

➤ Go back to page 10.

2.2 Numbers 11–100

Write these words in numbers.

a thirty-seven 37
b ninety-two 92
c twenty-four 24
d fifty-one 51
e eighty-three 83
f sixty-five 65
g forty-six 46
h seventy-nine 79

➤ Go back to page 12.

3.1 Objects and colors

Match the words with the colors.

black blue brown green gray red white yellow

a ___green___ b ___black___ c ___red___ d ___brown___ e ___blue___ f ___white___ g ___gray___ h ___yellow___

➤ Go back to page 18.

4.1 Daily activities

Look at the pictures and complete the phrases with the verbs in the box.

go (x2) have read talk watch

1 ___have___ breakfast

2 ___go___ home

3 ___go___ to bed

4 ___watch___ TV / a movie

5 ___talk___ to my friends/family

6 ___read___ a book

➤ Go back to page 26.

5.2 Food and meals

A Look at the pictures. Practice the words with a partner.

1 fruits

banana

pear

orange

grapes

2 vegetables

tomato

broccoli

cucumber

onion

3 drinks

tea

milk

juice

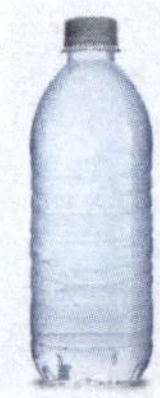
water

4 snacks

chocolate

chips

peanuts

cookies

B Label the food groups.

drinks fruits snacks vegetables

C Add two more words to each group. Tell the class.

➤ Go back to page 36.

6.2 Furniture and rooms

A Look at the picture. Write the correct word next to each number.

coffee table couch fridge mirror oven rug shower toilet

1	shower	5	rug
2	toilet	6	couch
3	mirror	7	oven
4	coffee table	8	fridge

B Label the rooms (a–c) with the words in the box.

bathroom kitchen living room

➤ Go back to page 44.

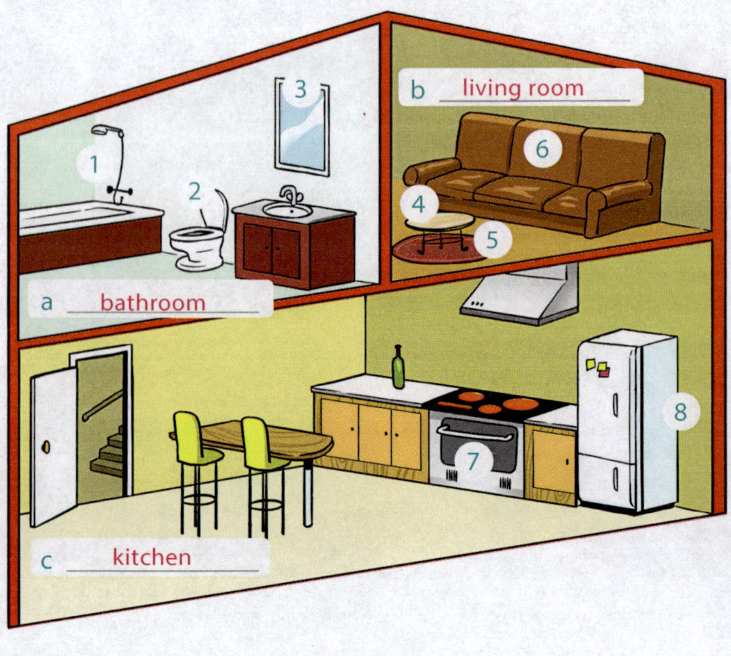

7.1 Abilities

Look at the pictures. Use the verbs *make*, *play*, *ride* and *speak* to make phrases about abilities.

make play ride speak

1 ride a bicycle

2 make a cake

3 speak Chinese

4 make an omelette

5 speak Spanish

6 play tennis

7 play the piano

8 ride a horse

➤ Go back to page 51.

8.2 Clothes

Match the words in the box with the pictures.

cap coat dress hat jacket jeans pants shirt shoes skirt suit sweater

1 skirt

2 cap

3 coat

4 shoes

5 pants

6 dress

7 jeans

8 shirt

9 hat

10 suit

11 jacket

12 sweater

➤ Go back to page 60.

Vocabulary Hub

11.1 Recreational activities

Complete the table with the recreational activities in the box.

get takeout food | go to a concert | go to a soccer game | go to a restaurant | ~~listen to music~~ | watch soccer on TV

Going out	Staying in	Both
go to a concert	get takeout food	listen to music
go to a soccer game	watch soccer on TV	
go to a restaurant		

➤ Go back to page 82.

11.2 Entertainment

Match the words in the box with the pictures.

~~action~~ | baseball | basketball | classical | comedy | horror | jazz | pop | rock | sci-fi | soccer | tennis

Types of music

1 classical

2 jazz

3 pop

4 rock

Types of sports

1 basketball

2 soccer

3 baseball

4 tennis

Types of movies

1 action

2 comedy

3 horror

4 sci-fi

➤ Go back to page 85.

12.1 Travel

Match the phrases to the pictures.

by bike   by bus   by car   by plane   by taxi   by train   by trolley   on foot

a on foot

b by taxi

c by bus

d by train

e by plane

f by trolley

g by car

h by bike

➤ Go back to page 90.

12.2 Types of vacations

A Match the words with the pictures.

a camera   a guidebook   skiing goggles   skis   a snorkel   a stove   sunglasses   a tent

a a tent

b sunglasses

c a camera

d a guidebook

e a stove

f skis

g a snorkel

h skiing goggles

B Choose two things from Exercise A that you use when you go on …

- a beach vacation: sunglasses, a snorkel
- a camping vacation: a stove, a tent
- a sightseeing vacation: a camera, a guidebook
- a skiing vacation: skis, skiing goggles

➤ Go back to page 93.

6.2

Student A

Look at your picture. Your partner has a similar picture but there are eight differences. Ask questions to find the differences.

A: Is there a bed in your picture?
B: Yes, there is.

➤ Go back to page 44.

1 There are three cushions on the bed in picture 1. There aren't any cushions on the bed in picture 2.

2 There is one chair in picture 1. There are two chairs in picture 2.

3 There's a laptop on the desk in picture 1. There isn't a laptop in picture 2.

4 There are five books on the shelf in picture 1. There are four books on the shelf in picture 2.

5 There's a view of a wall in picture 1. There's a view of trees in picture 2.

6 There's one jacket in the closet in picture 1. There are two jackets in picture 2.

7 There's a bag under the chair in picture 1, but not in picture 2.

8 There's a picture on the wall in picture 1. There's a mirror on the wall in picture 2.

1.2

Student B

A PLAN Imagine this woman is your friend. Complete the information about her with your own ideas.

First name ________________
Last name ________________
Country ________________
City ________________
Job ________________

B PREPARE Prepare to introduce your friend to your partner. Practice by yourself.

This is a picture of my friend. Her name is Cristina. She's from ...

C PRACTICE Work in pairs. Listen to your partner's introduction.

D REPEAT Introduce your friend to your partner.

➤ Go back to page 5.

10.2

Group B

A PREPARE Read the survey. You need to write one person's name for each sentence and find out extra information.

B PLAN Write the questions you need to ask for each item.

Did you win a prize or a competition at school?
What kind of competition did you win?

Find someone who:

1 … wanted to be a doctor when they were a child
Why?

2 … won a prize or a competition at school.
What?

3 … collected something when they were young.
What?

4 … had a favorite toy when they were a child.
What?

C PRACTICE Walk around the classroom and ask questions. Write the names and the answers.

A: Did you want to be a doctor when you were a child?
B: Yes, I did.
A: Why did you want to be a doctor?

D REPORT Work with someone from Group A. Tell them what you found out.

Paolo won an art competition when he was at school. He won first prize.

➤ Go back to page 77.

3.1

Coatroom attendant

Turn your back, or leave the room, for two minutes.

You are a coatroom attendant. The others are customers.

Look for their objects and check that you have the correct things. Ask about:

1 the name of the object/objects (hat, bag, headphones, etc)

2 the color/colors (red, blue, black and white, gray and brown)

Remember: *this/these.*

Change roles and repeat.

Are these your glasses?

➤ Go back to page 19.

12.2

Student B

You are the presenter of a radio show. You are going to call your partner and tell them they are the winner of a vacation. Write notes about what to say:

Vacation type: skiing

Place: mountains, Switzerland

Start: next Thursday

How long: ten days

Hello, is that …?
Congratulations! You are the winner.

➤ Go back to page 93.

Communication Hub

9.2

Group B

A PREPARE Complete the sentences with the past tense of the verbs in the box. Then choose the correct information (a, b or c) to complete the sentences.

design receive travel walk

1 Ibn Battuta ___traveled___ from Morocco to China in the …
  a 10th century. b 12th century. (c 14th century.)
2 Gabriel García Márquez ___received___ the Nobel Prize in Literature in …
  a 1972. (b 1982.) c 1992.
3 Neil Armstrong ___walked___ on the moon in …
  a 1959. (b 1969.) c 1979.
4 Steve Jobs and Steve Wozniak ___designed___ the first personal computers in …
  a 1966. (b 1976.) c 1986.

B PRACTICE Read your sentences to Group A. They will check your answers.

C PRACTICE Listen to Group A's sentences. Check their answers.

Correct sentences:

1 Larry Page and Sergey Brin **started** the company Google in **1998**.
2 John Couch Adams **discovered** the planet Neptune in **1846**.
3 William Shakespeare **lived** in England in the **16th century**.
4 Malala Yousafzai **received** the Nobel Peace Prize in **2014**.

➤ Go back to page 69.

6.2

Student B

A PREPARE You want to rent a room from your partner. Read the description of what you need. Write five questions to ask your partner.

- a table. *Is there a table?*
- lamps.
- a large window.
- the internet.
- near museums and theaters.
- near restaurants.

B SPEAK Answer your partner's questions. Use the information in the advertisement.

C REPEAT Ask your partner questions about their room. Find out if it is the right place for you.

A: Can I ask about the room for rent?
B: Yes, of course. How can I help you?
A: Is it near museums and theaters?
B: Yes, it is.

D REPORT Tell the class about the room.

I like / don't like my partner's room because …

➤ Go back to page 45.

Your room:

- Comfortable room in quiet area.
- 10 minutes from train station.
- Near stores and restaurants.
- Has a bed, desk, chair and lamp.

$250 per week.

4.2

Student B

A PREPARE Look at the picture. Write questions to find the missing information.

1 what / called What are they called?
2 where / live Where do they live?
3 where / go / in the fall Where do they go in the fall?
4 where / go / in the spring Where do they go in the spring?
5 how far / go *How far do they go every year*?

B DISCUSS Ask your partner the questions in Exercise A. Complete the missing information.

C DISCUSS Read the information about Arctic terns. Answer your partner's questions.

Name: Arctic terns
Where: The Arctic and the Antarctic
When: In August or September they go to the Antarctic. In May or June they go to the Arctic.
How far: About 44,000 miles per year (70,800 kilometers)

➤ Go back to page 29.

8.1

Student B

Look at the instructions below.

- Look at the picture.
- Describe the people and what they are doing to your partner.
- Listen to your partner's description of their picture.
- Find six differences.

➤ Go back to page 59.

6.2

Student B

Look at your picture. Your partner has a similar picture but there are eight differences. Ask questions to find the differences.

A: Is there a bed in your picture?

B: Yes, there is.

➤ Go back to page 44.

1 There are three cushions on the bed in picture 1. There aren't any cushions on the bed in picture 2.

2 There is one chair in picture 1. There are two chairs in picture 2.

3 There's a laptop on the desk in picture 1. There isn't a laptop in picture 2.

4 There are five books on the shelf in picture 1. There are four books on the shelf in picture 2.

5 There's a view of a wall in picture 1. There's a view of trees in picture 2.

6 There's one jacket in the closet in picture 1. There are two jackets in picture 2.

7 There's a bag under the chair in picture 1, but not in picture 2.

8 There's a picture on the wall in picture 1. There's a mirror on the wall in picture 2.

2.2

Student B

A PREPARE Read the information. What questions can you ask to find the missing information?

Write your questions here.

1 *Where's Victor Moretti from?*

2 What's his job ?

3 What's her name ?

4 How old is she ?

5 Where is Dev Gupta from ?

6 What's his job ?

7 Where is Zehra Yilmaz from ?

8 How old is Zehra Yilmaz ?

B PRACTICE Ask your partner questions to complete the information about each person.

a

Name	Victor Moretti
Country	1 Argentina
Age	28
Job	2 Designer

b

Name	3 Tomoko Kogawa
Country	Japan
Age	4 35
Job	Doctor

c

Name	Dev Gupta
Country	5 India
Age	42
Job	6 Engineer

d

Name	Zehra Yilmaz
Country	7 Turkey
Age	8 25
Job	Computer programmer

➤ Go back to page 13.

12.2

Student A

You are the listener of a radio show. You entered a competition on the radio show's website to win a vacation. Read the information below, then answer your phone and talk to the radio presenter.

- You don't like cold weather.
- You don't have a passport.
- You're a doctor. You're working at the hospital next week.

➤ Go back to page 93.

7.2

Student B

B PREPARE Read the information about this person. Write questions to find the missing information.

UTA ABE and her brother Hifumi are from Japan. Hifumi is very good at [1] ___judo___ and is a world champion. Uta is good at [2] ___judo, too___. She's the 2017 Junior World Champion. Hifumi and Uta are the winners of [3] ___the 2017 Tokyo Grand slam___.

1 What is Hifumi good at?
2 What ...?
3 What ...?

C DISCUSS Now ask your partner questions to complete the missing information. Answer your partner's questions.

D REPEAT Repeat with the information below.

ALISTAIR BROWNLEE is from [1] ___England___. He is good at triathlons – three events in one race. He can [2] ___swim, ride a bicycle and run___ and he's fast! His brother is good at triathlons, too. His brother's name is [3] ___Jonathan___. They both have Olympic medals.

➤ Go back to page 53.

1.1 Vocabulary

Countries

Work in pairs. Label the pictures of the countries with the words in the box.

Britain Canada Egypt Italy Japan Mexico Morocco Spain

1 ____________

2 ____________

3 ____________

4 ____________

5 ____________

6 ____________

7 ____________

8 ____________

Numbers 0–9

A Write each word from the box next to the correct number.

eight five four nine one seven six three two zero

0 ________	**1** ________	**2** ________	**3** ________	**4** ________
5 ________	**6** ________	**7** ________	**8** ________	**9** ________

B Work in pairs. Student A, say a phone number from below. Student B, listen and point at the number. Swap roles.

12:16 PM

Recent missed calls

3329 2256
414 987 1320
00 3889977
0770 155 2989
441 987 3120
022 259 2255
0202 598 3232
0038 889977
077 015 5298
419 225 672

Simple present *be*: *I, you*

A Complete the sentences with *am*, *am not*, *are* and *are not*. Use the short form *'m* where possible.

1 **John:** Hi! I __________ John. I __________ from Canada.

2 **Eleanor:** __________ you from Morocco?
Hector: No, I __________ from Mexico!

3 **Heath:** I __________ from Australia. __________ you from Turkey?

4 **Sara:** __________ you from Spain?
Maria: No, I __________ from Italy!

5 **Keiko:** Hi, I __________ Keiko. I __________ from Brazil. I'm from Japan.

6 **Louisa:** __________ you from Mexico?
Juan: No, I __________ from Argentina.

7 **Hussam:** I __________ Hussam, and I __________ from Egypt.

8 **Viktor:** Hi, __________ you from Britain?
James: Yes, I __________.

9 **Amy:** I __________ Amanda! I'm Amy!

10 **Dexter:** __________ you from Egypt?
Haifa: Yes, I __________.

B Work in pairs. Write a list of five countries. On your own, choose one of the countries from your list. Your partner can ask three questions.

A: Are you from Italy?

B: No, I'm not.

A: Are you from Britain?

B: No, I'm not.

A: Are you from Mexico?

B: Yes, I am!

1.2 Vocabulary

Jobs

A Reorder the letters to make the names of jobs.

1 tordco ______
2 rngdeise ______
3 nereegin ______
4 hcteaer ______
5 nemarga ______
6 hcartitce ______
7 tsutend ______
8 rptucmoe rgrpmmreoa ______

B Complete the sentences with *a* or *an*.

1 Are you ______ engineer?
2 Are you ______ designer?
3 Are you ______ doctor?
4 Are you ______ computer programmer?
5 Are you ______ architect?
6 Are you ______ teacher?
7 Are you ______ manager?
8 Are you ______ student?

C Work in pairs. Choose a job from Exercise B. Mime it to your partner. Can they guess what it is? Swap roles.

D How many questions did you ask? How many questions did your partner ask?

1.2 Grammar

Simple present *be*: *he, she, it*

A Complete the sentences with the simple present of *be*. Use contractions where possible.

1 Roberto ______ from Mexico. He's from Argentina.
2 Anna isn't from Canada. She ______ from Spain.
3 ______ Jules an architect or ______ he a doctor?
4 Maria is a computer programmer and she ______ from Italy.
5 ______ she an engineer or ______ she a student?
6 He ______ an engineer. He's a teacher.

B Work in pairs. Make sentences about all the people in your class.

Maria is from Barcelona.

Roberto is a computer programmer.

C Ask other students to see if your guesses from Exercise B are correct.

A: Maria, are you from Barcelona?

B: Yes, I am.

A: Roberto, are you a computer programmer?

B: No, I'm not.

Languages and nationalities

A Complete the crossword with the nationalities of the countries.

Across

1 England
3 America
4 Jamaica
6 Brazil
8 Norway
10 Japan
11 Sweden
12 Mali

Down

2 Iceland
5 Portugal
7 Spain
9 Italy

B Work in pairs. Take turns naming someone from one of the countries in Exercise A. Your partner guesses the nationality. Get one point for each correct answer.

A: Usain Bolt.

B: He's Jamaican.

A: Correct – one point.

Simple present *be*: *we, you, they*

Replace the words in bold with *we*, *you* or *they*.

1 **James and Andy** are French musicians. ______ are French musicians.

2 **Maria and I** are Spanish. ______ are Spanish.

3 **You and Marco** are in the same class. ______ are in the same class.

4 **The songs** are in different languages. ______ are in different languages.

5 **My classmates and I** are all from different countries. ______ are all from different countries.

Possessive adjectives

A Complete the sentences with the correct possessive adjectives.

a I'm a musician and [1]______ name is Ed. This is [2]______ album. [3]______ name is *In the World*.

b My sister is a singer. [4]______ music is cool. [5]______ songs are in Italian.

c We're Spanish singers. We play world music. [6]______ music is sad.

d He's from Brazil. [7]______ songs are in Portuguese. [8]______ music is good.

B Work in pairs. Complete the sentences with names and types of music.

1 My name is ______.

2 My partner's name is ______.

3 My favorite music is ______.

4 My partner's favorite music is ______.

C Work in different pairs. Tell them about you and your partner from Exercise B.

A: Hi, our names are Ella and Sami. His favorite music is Spanish, and my favorite music is …

2.2 Vocabulary

Days of the week

A Write the days of the week in order, starting with Monday.

1 Monday
2 ______
3 ______
4 ______
5 ______
6 ______
7 ______

B Work in pairs. Take turns saying a day of the week. Your partner says the next day of the week.

Numbers 11–100

A Write the words for the numbers. Underline the stressed syllable.

18 ______ 16 ______ 19 ______
80 ______ 60 ______ 90 ______

B Work in pairs. Say the numbers you can see in each picture.

a

b

c

d

e

2.2 Grammar

Wh- questions with *be*

A Complete the questions with the *wh-* question words in the boxes.

What (x2) Where How

What When Where Who

1 Sam: ______ is your name?
Liz: My name's Liz.

2 Sam: ______ old are you?
Liz: I'm 25.

3 Sam: ______ is your job?
Liz: I'm an engineer.

4 Sam: ______ are you from?
Liz: I'm from France.

5 Sam: ______ is your teacher?
Liz: My teacher is Mr. Jones.

6 Sam: ______ is your teacher from?
Liz: He's from America.

7 Sam: ______ is your English class?
Liz: It's at eight o'clock every Wednesday.

8 Sam: ______ is your favorite music?
Liz: I love classical music.

B Work in pairs. Ask and answer the questions so they are true for you.

Objects and colors

A Write the correct word from the box next to each picture.

a bag a coat glasses a hat headphones
a smartphone a sweatshirt an umbrella

1 ______________

2 ______________

3 ______________

4 ______________

5 ______________

6 ______________

7 ______________

8 ______________

B Work in pairs. What color are these objects usually? Choose the correct words from the box.

black blue brown green gray red white yellow

1

2

3

4

5

6

7

1 A traditional stop sign in the US. ______________

2 A traditional taxi in New York. ______________

3 A 'go' signal to cross the road. ______________

4 A zebra. ______________ and ______________

5 A grizzly bear. ______________

6 A swimming pool. ______________

7 An elephant. ______________

C Work in pairs. Point at or name things you can see in the classroom or out of the window. Your partner says what color they are. Swap roles.

a/an and plural nouns

A Complete the conversations with *a*, *an* or no article (–).

John: What's in your bag, Susie?

Susie: I have [1] ____________ umbrella, [2] ____________ headphones and [3] ____________ pen.

Johanna: What's your job, Frank?

Frank: I'm [4] ____________ teacher. What's your job, Johanna?

Johanna: I'm [5] ____________ architect.

Pedro: I like your new coat.

Sofia: It isn't [6] ____________ coat! It's [7] ____________ sweatshirt.

Pedro: Ha ha! Oh yes! I need [8] ____________ glasses.

B Decide if the underlined nouns are correct. If they are wrong, change them to the correct form – singular or plural.

1 There are two <u>book</u> on the table.

2 My <u>computers</u> is very good.

3 My <u>teacher</u> is Mr. Jones?

4 They are <u>a tomato</u>.

5 Her <u>songs</u> is great.

6 Where are your <u>baby</u> today?

7 They're very good <u>songs</u>.

8 What's your <u>names</u>?

C Work in pairs. Tell your partner …

- what's in your bag
- what's on your table
- what's in the classroom.

3.1 Grammar

this, that, these, those

A Choose the correct option to complete each sentence.

1 ***This*** / ***That*** television is big.

2 ***Those*** / ***That*** monkeys are gray and brown.

3 ***These*** / ***This*** shoes are nice.

4 Do you understand ***this*** / ***that*** diagram?

B Look at the pictures. Complete the sentences with *this*, *that*, *these* or *those*.

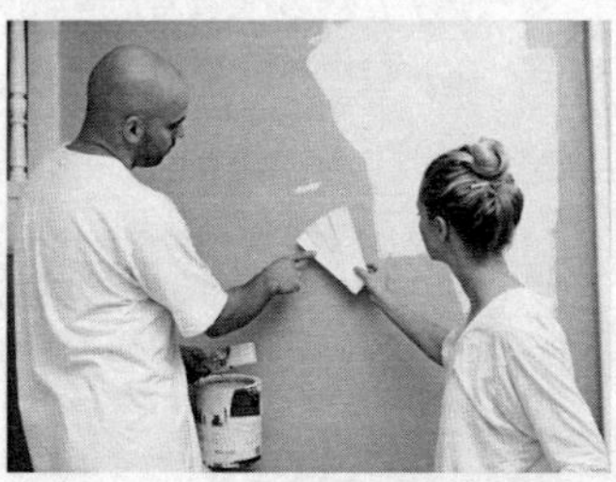

1 I like ______________ color.

2 Do you like ______________ picture?

3 ______________ picture is called the *Mona Lisa*.

4 Look at ______________ eggs.

5 Look at ______________ houses.

6 ______________ question is difficult.

C Tell your partner about the things that you can see in the classroom.

A: I like that picture.

B: Those headphones are black.

3.2 Vocabulary

Family

A Label the people in the pictures with the words in the box.

brother daughter father granddaughter grandfather grandmother grandson husband mother sister son wife

B Complete the sentences with the words in the box.

children grandparents parents

1 A mother and father are ______________.

2 A son and daughter are ______________.

3 A grandmother and grandfather are ______________.

C Work in pairs. Use the words to talk about you and your family relationships.

A: I'm a son. My mother is Claire. My father is Frank.

B: I'm a grandson. My grandfather is Eric. My grandmother is Vera.

3.2 Grammar

have/has

A Write the words in the correct order to create sentences.

1 have / I / sisters / two

______________________________.

2 any / you / brothers / Do / or / sisters / you

______________________________?

3 don't / a / daughter / have / We

______________________________.

4 grandchildren / any / Does / mother / your / have

______________________________?

5 don't / have / You / any / children

______________________________.

6 daughters / have / do / you / How many

______________________________?

7 My / have / grandparents / grandchildren / three

______________________________.

8 sisters / brothers / have / doesn't / any / She / or

______________________________.

9 any / he / sisters / have / Does

______________________________.

10 three / have / sons / They

______________________________.

B Work in pairs. Describe your family. Talk about who's in your family and their jobs.

> I have a brother and a sister.
> My brother is an engineer and my sister is a teacher.
> My sister is married, and her husband is named Alex.
> They have two children – a son and a daughter.
> My brother has two sons, Sam and Michael.
> My mother is a businesswoman and my father is a mechanic.

C Work in groups. Tell the group something about your partner from Exercise B.

Daily activities

A Match pictures (a–g) with the sentences (1–7).

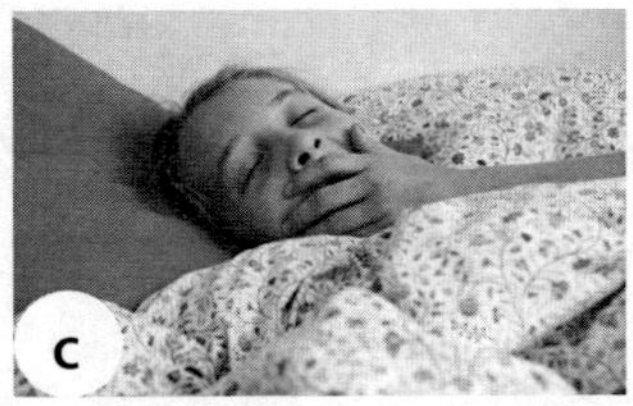

1 I watch TV in the evening. ___

2 I have breakfast at eight fifteen in the office. ___

3 I get up at seven o'clock in the morning. ___

4 I go to bed at 11 o'clock. ___

5 I go to work at seven forty-five in the morning. ___

6 I get home at about seven o'clock in the evening. ___

7 I finish work at five thirty and go home. ___

B Work in pairs. Put the pictures in the correct order to make the daily routine.

Time

A Match the times. Write the numbers next to the words.

12:45 1:15 1:45 2:00 5:30 5:20 4:05 1:25 1:50 7:30 6:35 6:25

a one fifty ______________

b one twenty-five ______________

c one fifteen ______________

d seven thirty ______________

e six thirty-five ______________

f five twenty ______________

g two o'clock ______________

h five thirty ______________

i six twenty-five ______________

j twelve forty-five ______________

k four oh five ______________

l one forty-five ______________

B Work in pairs. Answer the questions.

1 What time is it now?

2 What time is your English class?

3 What time do you get up?

4 What time do you go to bed?

Simple present: *I, you, we, they*

A Write down the times that you do each of the things in the 'me' column.

	Me	My partner
get up		
have breakfast		
go to work/school		
finish work/school		
get home		
have dinner		
go to bed		

B Cover the table in Exercise A. Take turns saying a time and an activity. Your partner says if that is the correct time that you do the activity or not.

A: Six o'clock. Get up.

B: You get up at six o'clock.

A: Correct!

B: Nine o'clock. Have dinner.

A: You don't have dinner at nine o'clock.

B: Correct! I don't have dinner at nine o'clock. I have dinner at eight o'clock.

C Work in new pairs. Tell your new partner about anything that is the same about the daily routines of you and your first partner.

We go to work at eight o'clock. We get home at seven o'clock. We have dinner at …

D Tell the class about anything that is the same about the daily routines of your partner and their first partner.

They go to work at eight o'clock. They get home at seven o'clock. They have dinner at …

Months and seasons

A Reorganize the letters to write the months. Then put the months in the correct order.

a tuAusg ______ __
b ayM ______ __
c eeerbmSpt ______ __
d bFuraeyr ______ __
e luyJ ______ __
f moverbNe ______ __
g ryauJna *January* *1*
h Jnue ______ __
i cebrDeme ______ __
j oOctrbe ______ __
k hcraM ______ __
l ilArp ______ __

B Label the pictures with the names of the seasons.

1 ______

2 ______

3 ______

4 ______

C Work in pairs. Complete the sentences about yourself. Then ask your partner questions to complete the information about them.

My favorite month is ______.
My favorite season is ______.
My birthday is in (month) ______.

Your favorite month is ______.
Your favorite season is ______.
Your birthday is in (month) ______.

Simple present questions: *I, you, we, they*

A Correct the mistakes in the questions.

Questions

1 What time you do get up?

2 What your favorite season?

3 You go to another country in the summer?

4 Who do talk to you in the morning?

5 Live do you in Japan?

6 What month your birthday?

B Match the answers to the questions in Exercise A.

Answers

a Winter.

b No, in Sweden.

c Yes, I go to Brazil.

d It's in January.

e My parents.

f At seven o'clock.

C Work in pairs. Ask and answer questions using words from the list.

birthday
get up
Italy
favorite month
watch TV
favorite music
start work
favorite season
work at night
go to bed

A: When's your birthday?

B: My birthday is in September. What time do you get up?

A: I get up at six o'clock. What's your favorite type of music?

Free-time activities

A Choose the correct verb to complete each sentence.

1 I ***go* / *play* / *have*** for a walk.
2 We ***go* / *cook* / *play*** a meal.
3 You ***go* / *sit* / *take*** a bath.
4 I ***go* / *play* / *sit*** to the gym.
5 We ***go* / *cook* / *play*** chess.
6 I ***have* / *go* / *play*** running.
7 You ***go* / *have* / *cook*** shopping.
8 We ***have* / *go* / *sit*** in the backyard.

B **You are going to interview your classmates. Write the questions to find the information below. Then ask your classmates and write down a name for each activity.**

Find someone who …

	Name
1 goes running three times a week.	______
2 takes a bath to relax.	______
3 goes for a walk on the weekend.	______
4 goes shopping every Saturday.	______
5 goes to the gym before work.	______
6 cooks dinner every day.	______
7 sits in the backyard in the summer.	______
8 plays chess with friends or family.	______

A: Do you go running three times a week?

B: No, I go running on the weekend.

A: Do you take a bath to relax?

B: Yes, I do!

C **Work in pairs. Tell your partner about your classmates.**

A: Roberto goes running three times a week.

B: Alexandra takes a bath to relax.

5.1 Grammar

Simple present: *he, she, it*

A Complete the sentences with the words from the box.

do does get up gets up go goes

1 What time does Paulo ____________ to the gym?

2 What time does Julie ____________ in the morning?

3 Martha ____________ at seven o'clock in the morning.

4 My grandmother ____________ to the library in the afternoon.

5 What does Ben ____________ to relax on the weekend?

6 What kinds of games ____________ your brother play?

B Work in pairs. Write the names of five people you know in your notebook and show them to your partner. Ask and answer questions about the people.

A: Who is Martin?

B: He's my brother.

5.2 Vocabulary

Food and meals

A Write the words from the box into the correct places in the table.

apple banana beans bread broccoli cereal cheese chicken chips chocolate cookies cucumber eggs fish grapes juice milk noodles onion orange pasta peanuts pear potatoes rice tea tomato water

Fruits	Vegetables	Dairy products	Drinks	Snacks	Other

B Work in pairs. Talk about how to make a nice meal with the foods in Exercise A.

Adverbs of frequency

A Write the adverbs of frequency in the box in the correct place.

always frequently never seldom sometimes usually

2 ____________ **4** ____________ **6** ____________

0% **100%**

1 ____________ **3** ____________ **5** ____________

B Where does the adverb of frequency go, position *a* or *b*? Write the adverb in the correct place.

1 I (a) ____________ am (b) ____________ late for work. (*never*)

2 My father (a) ____________ cooks (b) ____________ on the weekend. (*always*)

3 My grandmother (a) ____________ eats (b) ____________ fish. (*frequently*)

4 We (a) ____________ are (b) ____________ busy in the evening. (*usually*)

5 My daughter (a) ____________ takes (b) ____________ a bath in the morning. (*sometimes*)

6 Mirka (a) ____________ is (b) ____________ early. (*always*)

C You are going to interview your classmates. Read the questions below, then add three of your own ideas.

How often do you …	Name	Name	Name	Name
cook fish?				
have an apple?				
eat meat?				
eat in a restaurant?				
go to the gym?				
play chess?				
go running?				
drink juice?				

Places in a town

A Use a word in the box to answer each question.

art gallery	café	hotel	market	museum	park	restaurant	station	store	theater

Where do people go to …

1 see a play? ____________

2 learn about history? ____________

3 catch a train? ____________

4 sleep on their vacation? ____________

5 have coffee? ____________

6 go out for dinner? ____________

7 see paintings and art? ____________

8 buy fresh fruit? ____________

9 go running? ____________

10 buy clothes? ____________

B Write the names of five places in your town or city. Tell the class:

- how often you go there
- what you do there
- the location of the places.

I sometimes go to the Metro Theater. I see plays there. It's near the train station.

6.1 Grammar

there is / there are; some and *any*

A Write sentences using the correct form of *there is / there are* and *some* and *any*.

1. a bank ✓ — *There's a bank.*
2. theaters ✗ — *There aren't any theaters.*
3. a museum ✗ — ______
4. parks ✓ — ______
5. a market ✗ — ______
6. station ✓ — ______
7. cafés ✓ — ______
8. restaurants ✓ — ______
9. an art gallery ✗ — ______
10. a hotel ✓ — ______

B Work in pairs. Look at the plans of two different towns. Describe the two towns and find ten differences.

Town A

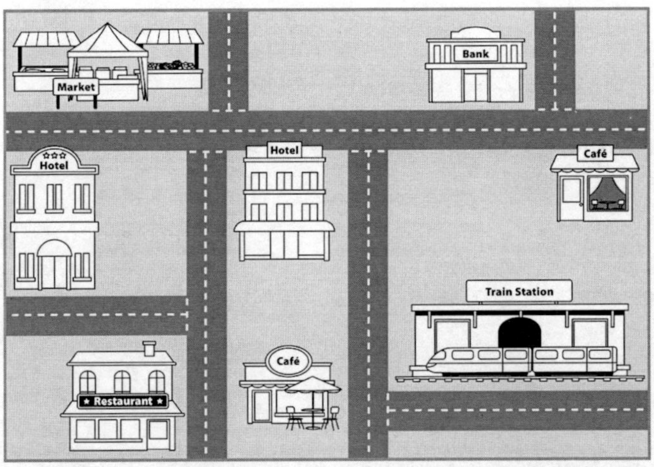

Town B

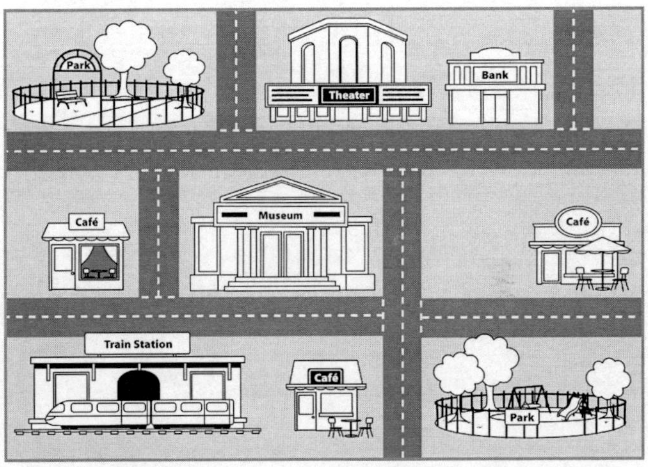

1. ______
2. ______
3. ______
4. ______
5. ______
6. ______
7. ______
8. ______
9. ______
10. ______

Furniture and rooms

Draw a picture for each word.

1 clock

2 window

3 couch

4 shower

5 bed

6 oven

7 desk

8 chair

9 lamp

10 bookshelf

11 cushion

12 closet

Prepositions of place

Work in pairs. Student A, describe Picture 1. Student B, describe Picture 2. Include sentences using *in*, *on* and *under*.

Picture 1

Picture 2

is there / are there question forms

A Put the words into the correct order to form questions.

1 couch / a / there / Is

______________________________?

2 any / there / Are / windows

______________________________?

3 a / there / mirror / Is

______________________________?

4 Is / coffee table / a / there

______________________________?

5 television / there / Is / a

______________________________?

6 any / shoes / there / Are

______________________________?

7 pictures / any / Are / there

______________________________?

8 any / there / people / Are

______________________________?

9 rug / there / Is / a

______________________________?

10 cushions / any / there / Are

______________________________?

B Answer the questions (1–10) from Exercise A about the picture of a living room.

1 ______ *Yes, there is.* ______

2 ______________________________

3 ______________________________

4 ______________________________

5 ______________________________

6 ______________________________

7 ______________________________

8 ______________________________

9 ______________________________

10 ______________________________

C Work in pairs. Take turns asking and answering questions about what is in the picture below.

A: Is there a fridge?

B: Yes, there is. Is there a coffee table?

Abilities

A Complete the boxes with the activities in the pictures.

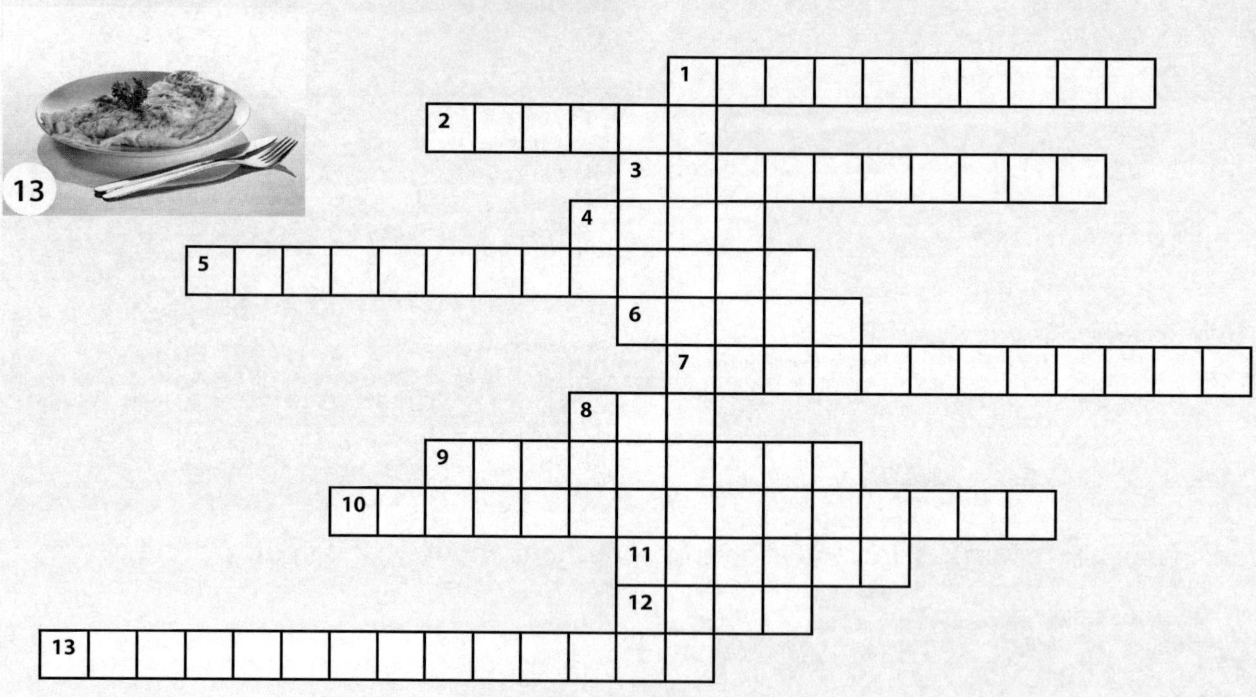

B Work in pairs. Interview your partner about the activities in Exercise A. What can they do? What can't they do?

A: Can you play the piano?

B: Yes, I can.

C Work in new pairs. Tell your new partner about the person you interviewed in Exercise B.

can/*can't*

A Four of the sentences have mistakes. Find and correct them.

1 He can't to swim.

2 They can run very far.

3 We not can speak Icelandic.

4 I can't dive for very long.

5 He can cook Chinese food.

6 She can climbs high.

7 I can't eating spicy food.

8 They can play chess.

B Write questions with *Can you …?* and the verbs in the box. Or use your own ideas.

climb cook dive run far sing speak Chinese speak Spanish swim

1 ______________________ **5** ______________________

2 ______________________ **6** ______________________

3 ______________________ **7** ______________________

4 ______________________ **8** ______________________

C Work in pairs. Ask the questions you wrote in Exercise B. Then tell the class what your partner can do.

Adjectives

A Decide which adjective is positive and which is negative.

	Positive	Negative
1 Soccer is a ***great*** / ***boring*** sport.	______	______
2 Spanish is a/an ***difficult*** / ***amazing*** language to learn.	______	______
3 I am a very ***bad*** / ***talented*** singer.	______	______
4 Math is an ***interesting*** / ***awful*** subject.	______	______
5 Running is a/an ***easy*** / ***terrible*** hobby.	______	______
6 My cooking is ***OK*** / ***terrible***.	______	______

B Choose an adjective to complete the sentences so they are true for you.

C Work in pairs. Compare your sentences. Are they the same or different?

D Read the questions below. Then add three more questions of your own.

1 Do you think English is easy?

2 Do you think soccer is interesting?

3 Do you think chocolate is healthy?

4 ______________________________?

5 ______________________________?

6 ______________________________?

E Work in pairs. Ask and answer the questions in Exercise D.

Possessive 's

A Look at the picture of the family. Complete the description with the correct names and possessive 's.

James has a great family. His [1] ________________ name is Emma. They have three children – two boys and a girl. Their [2] ________________ names are Matt and Tom. Their [3] ________________ name is Katie. James's [4] ________________ names are Violet and Bill.

B Work in pairs. Ask questions about the people in the picture.

A: Who is Violet's husband?

B: Bill is Violet's husband.

B: Who are Katie's brothers?

A: Katie's brothers are Matt and Tom.

C Work in groups. Talk about your friends and family.

My parents' names are Anna and Mark.
My brother's name is Phil and his wife's name is Sam.
They have two children.
My best friend's name is Karen. She's married. Her husband's name is Chris …

Verb phrases

A Choose the correct option to complete the sentences.

1 He has ***mirror*** / ***coffee*** before work.

2 She watches ***messages*** / ***videos*** to learn English.

3 I read ***messages*** / ***shopping*** on my phone.

4 They go ***shopping*** / ***station*** every Saturday.

5 We talk on the ***work*** / ***phone*** every week.

6 He takes a ***coffee*** / ***break*** every two hours.

7 I look in the ***mirror*** / ***message*** three times a day.

8 We meet at the ***coffee*** / ***station*** at 8:30 every morning.

B Work in pairs. Talk about how often you do the activities in Exercise A.

I always have coffee before work. I go to the café near my apartment and get it to go. Then I drink it on the train on the way to work.

I don't usually watch videos to learn English. But I always listen to English music. I love it.

Present progressive

A Use the prompts to write sentences and questions in the present progressive. Use contractions where possible.

1 They / walk in the park. (+)

____

2 They / sit on the bench. (–)

____

3 She / take a break in the park. (+)

____

4 I / wait to call my friend. (–)

____

5 You / listen to me? (+)

____

6 He / talk on the phone. (–)

____

7 We / watch a video online. (–)

____

8 He / drink coffee. (–)

____

B Work in pairs. Describe the two pictures. What is the same? What is different?

Clothes

A Label the picture with the words in the box.

dress handbag jacket jeans pants shirt shoes shorts skirt sneakers sweatshirt suit

1 ______ 5 ______ 9 ______
2 ______ 6 ______ 10 ______
3 ______ 7 ______ 11 ______
4 ______ 8 ______ 12 ______

B Work in pairs. Student A, choose someone in your class and think about what they are wearing. Student B, ask Student A questions to find out who the person is. Then change roles and repeat.

B: Is the person wearing black sneakers?

A: No, he isn't.

B: Is the person wearing a blue T-shirt?

A: Yes, he is.

B: Is the person Omar?

A: Yes, it is.

Adjective order

A Check (✓) the correct sentences. Correct the mistakes in the other sentences.

1 He's wearing a black old coat. ☐ *He's wearing an old black coat.*
2 She has a large blue shirt. ☐ ______
3 That's a yellow big hat! ☐ ______
4 He has a new white sweatshirt. ☐ ______
5 I have long red socks. ☐ ______
6 They have green new caps. ☐ ______
7 I have a blue beautiful dress. ☐ ______
8 They're wearing old blue jeans. ☐ ______
9 He has a black new suit. ☐ ______
10 She has a long red skirt. ☐ ______

B Work in pairs. Tell your partner about some of the clothes you have.

A: I have an old brown jacket. I wear it every day.

B: I have a long red dress. I wear it to parties.

Dates and years

A Complete the list of numbers and words.

1st	1 ______
2nd	2 ______
3rd	3 ______
4th	4 ______
5 ______	fifth
6 ______	tenth
11th	7 ______
8 ______	twelfth
20th	9 ______
10 ______	twenty-first
22nd	11 ______
12 ______	thirtieth

B Write the years in words.

1967	1 ______
1981	2 ______
2008	3 ______
2011	4 ______
1643	5 ______
1715	6 ______
1816	7 ______
1997	8 ______
1464	9 ______
2023	10 ______
1977	11 ______
2019	12 ______

C Interview your classmates.

Find someone who ...	Name
was the first to arrive today.	
passed their driving test on the fifth time.	
lives on the third floor.	
is the second child in their family.	
went to a 50th birthday party last year.	

Simple past: *was/were*

A Find the five mistakes in the use of *was* and *were* in the sentences below. Rewrite the incorrect sentences.

1 My grandmother was a teacher.
2 My dad's first phone weren't a smartphone.
3 My friends was late for class today.
4 The sandwiches wasn't very good yesterday.
5 My neighbors were very loud last night.
6 My brother and I was tired.
7 Tom wasn't at the party.
8 The trip was very dangerous.
9 My mom wasn't at home.
10 The food weren't expensive.

B Add *was* or *were* to the correct place in the questions below.

Question	Student 1	Student 2	Student 3
1 What the last movie you saw?			
2 Where the last selfie you took?			
3 Who the last celebrity you watched on TV?			
4 What on TV last night?			
5 Where you born?			

C Ask three people in your class the questions in Exercise B. Write a note about the answers in the table.

D Present the information from Exercise C to your class.

Everyday verbs

A Choose the correct verb to complete the questions.

1. How many hours a week do you ***design*** / ***study*** English?
2. Do you know someone who ***collects*** / ***starts*** stamps?
3. Would you like to ***design*** / ***travel*** a building?
4. How often do you ***travel*** / ***receive*** to different countries?
5. Do you like to give or ***receive*** / ***study*** presents?
6. When was the last time you ***traveled*** / ***helped*** a friend?
7. When did you ***start*** / ***study*** learning English?
8. Do you enjoy ***painting*** / ***helping*** pictures?

B Complete the table with your answers to the questions in Exercise A. Then interview another student.

	My answers	Another student's answers
1		
2		
3		
4		
5		
6		
7		
8		

C Are you and your partner similar? Tell the class.

Simple past: regular verbs

A Find and correct one error with the verb in each sentence.

1 I didn't ~~used~~ use my phone yesterday.

2 We study English for three hours last week.

3 My best friend not received a present from her brother.

4 I design the slides for our last presentation.

5 They didn't wanting to help anyone.

6 She traveling to the US for work last month.

7 He ask the police officer for help last night.

8 She didn't planted the tree yesterday.

9 We live there from 2006 to 2012.

10 They didn't tried to help me last week.

B Complete the sentences so they are true for you.

1 When I was younger, I wanted to be a ________________.

2 When I was a child, I didn't like ________________.

3 When I started learning English, I used a ________________.

4 When I was at school, I didn't ________________.

5 When I was a teenager, I decided to ________________.

6 When I got home yesterday, I ________________.

C Work in groups. Compare your sentences. Are any of the ideas the same?

10.1 Vocabulary

Time phrases

A Complete the sentences so three are true for you and three are not true for you.

1 I saw my best friend ________________ ago.

2 I finished elementary school in ________________.

3 I bought ________________ last ________________.

4 I went on vacation ________________ ago.

5 I started learning English in ________________.

6 I spoke to ________________ last ________________.

B Work in pairs. Guess which sentences in Exercise A are true for your partner.

C Work in pairs. Read the actions below and write a time expression for when you think your partner last did these things.

My partner …

bought a phone … *18 months ago*

spoke to a friend … ________________

wore sunglasses … ________________

left school … ________________

went on vacation … ________________

visited a museum … ________________

had a history class … ________________

visited a place built a long time ago … ________________

went shopping … ________________

D Show your partner your answers to Exercise C. Are they correct?

Simple past: irregular verbs

A Complete the sentences with the simple past form of the verbs in parentheses.

1 I ____________ dinner at home yesterday evening. (*have*)

2 I ____________ at five o'clock this morning. (*get up*)

3 I ____________ a jacket yesterday afternoon. (*buy*)

4 I ____________ to the movie theater yesterday. (*go*)

5 I ____________ anywhere last weekend. (*not go out*)

6 I ____________ someone a present last week. (*give*)

B Change the sentences in Exercise A so they are true for you.

C Imagine you are a famous celebrity. You are going to talk about what you did last weekend. Write about what you did. Use the verbs in the box to help you or use your own ideas.

buy call choose eat find give go have make

____

____

____

____

____

____

D Work in pairs. Tell each other about the day you described in Exercise C. Which sounds fun?

Life events

A Choose the correct options to complete the sentences.

1 I ***drove*** / ***finished*** / ***met*** my best friend at college.

2 My sister ***belonged*** / ***wrote*** / ***passed*** her first blog post last year.

3 My teacher ***got*** / ***won*** / ***met*** married last month.

4 My best friend ***passed*** / ***wrote*** / ***won*** a prize for her essay.

5 I was so happy. I ***wrote*** / ***passed*** / ***won*** my driving test on the first time.

6 This house ***belonged*** / ***got*** / ***finished*** to my grandparents.

B Write important events from your life on the timeline.

I was born **Now**

C Tell your partner about the events from your life. Your partner will complete the timeline below for your life.

D Listen to your partner talk about their life. Add the important events from their life to the timeline below.

My partner was born **Now**

10.2 Grammar

Simple past questions

A **Find and correct the mistakes in the simple past questions.**

1 Where you study last year?

____

2 When you did get your phone?

____

3 You did give someone a present last month?

____

4 How get you here today?

____

5 What did you bought yesterday?

____

B **Match the answers (a–e) to the questions (1–5) in Exercise A.**

a Yes, I gave my mom a book. __

b I didn't buy anything. __

c At college. __

d I got it two months ago. __

e By bus. __

C **You are going to interview someone about their life. Write six questions.**

1 ______________________________?

2 ______________________________?

3 ______________________________?

4 ______________________________?

5 ______________________________?

6 ______________________________?

D **Work in pairs. Interview your partner. Ask other questions to find out more information, for example, *Why?***

E **Tell the class about the person you interviewed.**

11.1 Vocabulary

Recreational activities

A Complete the verb phrases with *go*, *get*, *watch*, *listen* or *spend*.

1 ______________ to a concert
2 ______________ takeout food
3 ______________ to a soccer game
4 ______________ time with family
5 ______________ to a restaurant
6 ______________ to the park
7 ______________ to a museum
8 ______________ soccer on TV
9 ______________ a video online
10 ______________ to music
11 ______________ time with friends

B Complete the questions with your own ideas. Then interview a partner.

Where do you usually …?
How often do you …?
When was the last time you …?
Who do you usually … with?
Why do you …?
Why do you like …?

C Tell the class what you found out about your partner in Exercise B.

11.1 Grammar

like/love/hate/enjoy* + verb + *-ing

A Choose the correct word to complete the text about Kai and his brother.

I'm Kai. I love [1]***spend* / *spending*** time with my friends. I like [2]***go* / *going*** to a café for lunch with them. I [3]***enjoy* / *enjoys*** going to the movie theater, too. It's a great way to relax. I don't like staying at home in the evening. My brother is very different. He [4]***enjoy* / *enjoys*** studying at home. He loves [5]***cooking* / *cook*** for the family. But he [6]***hates* / *hate*** doing the cleaning!

B Tell your group about what you and someone in your family or a friend enjoy doing in your free time. Listen to the others in the group and ask questions.

A: I like staying at home in the evening. My sister is different. She enjoys meeting friends.

B: Do you like going to the movie theater with your sister?

A: Yes, I love it!

B: Why?

A: It's a great way to relax.

11.2 Vocabulary

Entertainment

A Complete the sentences with the words in the box.

action actor band concerts game movie theater musicians player pop star premiere rock songs stadium

a She's my favorite [1] ________________. I love all her [2] ________________ and she did some great [3] ________________ on her tour last year.

b He is an excellent soccer [4] ________________. I went to the [5] ________________ in the city last week and I watched a very exciting [6] ________________.

c I love this [7] ________________. I saw her at the [8] ________________ of her new [9] ________________ movie in New York. She was at the [10] ________________ near my house! It was amazing.

d This is my favorite [11] ________________. They play a lot of [12] ________________ music, but some of them are classical [13] ________________!

B Write an example for each item below.

action movie ________________

singer ________________

movie star ________________

soccer player ________________

rock band ________________

popstar ________________

comedy ________________

soccer stadium ________________

C Work in pairs. Discuss your answers to Exercise B. Do you know all the examples on your partner's list?

11.2 Grammar

Object pronouns

A Find and correct the mistakes with object pronouns in the sentences below. Three sentences are correct.

1 My friends want to go and see that new horror movie but I don't want to see it.

2 Mario called I last night and told me the news.

3 I gave my brother some new shoes for his birthday but he didn't like they.

4 That's Helen's sister – I play tennis with she.

5 Who's that man over there? I don't know he.

6 I need to talk to your.

7 Your friends are here. Let's talk to them.

8 The teacher gave we a test yesterday.

9 This is for John – can you give it to him, please?

10 Where are my glasses? I can't find us!

11 I like your new coat. Where did you buy him?

12 I met Alfonso's brother yesterday. I talked to her for a long time.

B Who or what are your favorites? Complete the sentences with your own ideas.

My favorite movie is ______________. I like ______________ because ______________ …

My favorite sports team is ______________. I like ______________ because ______________ …

My favorite musician is ______________. I like ______________ because ______________ …

My favorite town is ______________. I like ______________ because ______________ …

My favorite food is ______________. I like ______________ because ______________ …

C Work in pairs. Compare your answers to Exercise B. Are any of your sentences the same?

A: My favorite movie is ***The Lion King***. I like **it** because it has a really interesting story.

B: My favorite musician is **Beyoncé**. I like **her** because she's a great singer.

12.1 Vocabulary

Travel

A Match the words in the box with definitions below.

airport bag credit card money passport plane ticket traffic

1 An official document saying which country you are a citizen of. It has your photograph on it and you show it when you travel. ________
2 What you earn, save and use to pay for things. ________
3 The vehicles that are traveling in an area at a particular time. ________
4 Something made of material that is used for carrying things. ________
5 A place where planes arrive and leave, with a terminal for passengers. ________
6 A piece of paper that shows you have paid for a trip on a train or plane. ________
7 A small plastic card you use to buy things now and pay for them later. ________
8 An aircraft with wings. ________

B Work in pairs. Talk about the places you travel to using the transportation below.

- by bike
- by bus
- by car
- by plane
- by taxi
- by train
- by trolley
- on foot

A: I usually go to work by bike. It's only about half an hour.

B: I never go anywhere by bike. I usually go to work by train.

Countable and uncountable nouns

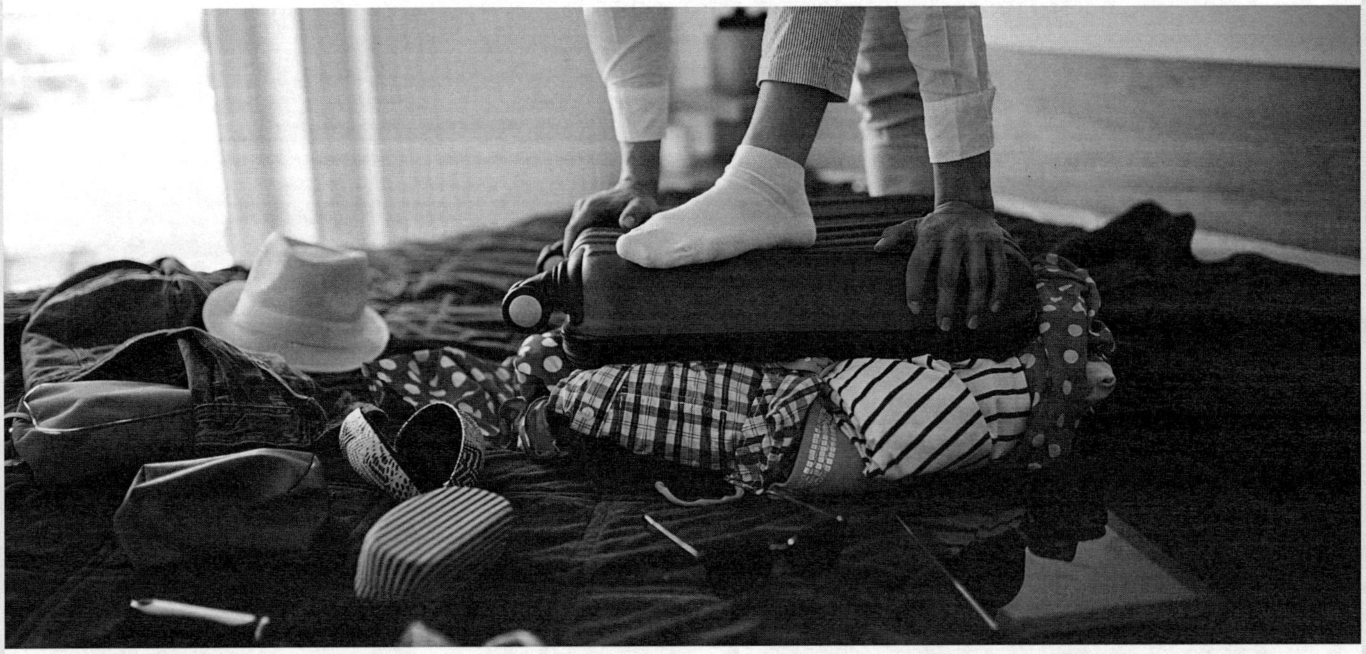

A Find and correct the errors in the sentences. There is a mistake with one of the words in bold in each sentence.

1 I have 500 **dollar**. Do you think I need more **money**?

2 Are you going to use one of your **credit card** or **cash**?

3 There is a lot of **traffics** today. We're going to be late for the **plane**.

4 I only have two **bag**. You have a lot of **luggage**!

5 Is there any **informations** about the arrival time on the **ticket**?

B Work in pairs. Complete the conversation with the words in the box.

bags cash dollars luggage

A: I think I have everything. Let me count … one, two, three, four [1]________________.
B: That's a lot of [2]________________. You can't carry all that!
A: Don't worry. I have [3]________________ for a taxi when we get there.
B: A taxi will cost about 45 [4]________________! You're rich.

C Work in pairs. Continue the conversation from Exercise B. Use the words in the box to help you or use your own ideas.

credit card information money plane ticket traffic

D Practice and then perform your conversations from Exercise C to the class. Listen to the other conversations. Do other students have the same situation as you?

Types of vacations

A Complete the paragraphs with the words in the box.

beach vacation camping vacation chalet guidebook hotel (x2)
sightseeing vacation skiing vacation snorkel stove sunglasses tent

Maria: When I go on a [1]________________, I like to stay in a really nice hotel, as close to the ocean as possible. I spend a lot of time in the water, and I like to swim and look underwater at the fish and coral, so I always take a [2]________________. The weather is usually warm and really sunny, so I always wear my [3]________________.

James: Every winter, a big group of my friends and I go on a [4]________________. We never go to the same place and we always check to see where the best snow is before we book. We're a big group, so we like to rent a traditional [5]________________ to stay in. It's better than a room in a [6]________________ because we can also cook a meal together and relax there in the evenings.

Pierre: Every year, I try to visit a new city somewhere in Europe. I don't really like going on vacation and sitting on the beach, so a [7]________________ is perfect for me. I usually go with a friend and we get a cheap room in a [8]________________ for a couple of nights. I like to just arrive and explore, but my friend is a bit more organized, so she usually reads a [9]________________ on the plane and makes a list of things she wants to see.

Samantha: I'm never going on a [10]________________ again! It was awful. The weather was terrible and really windy – it took hours to put up the [11]________________. It rained every day and I didn't enjoy hiking at all. The showers at the campsite didn't work and I couldn't wash my hair for days. Then, on the final night, we didn't have enough gas for the [12]________________, so we couldn't have any hot food. This vacation was a disaster. In the future, I'm only going to stay in five-star hotels!

B Work in pairs. Which vacation in Exercise A would you like to go on? Why?

C Work in pairs. Describe your last vacation to your partner.

American Language Hub Starter Teacher's Book.

Present progressive

A Complete the conversation with the present progressive form of the words in parentheses.

Laura: Hi Amelia! How are you?

Amelia: I'm fine, thanks! I [1] ________________ (*go*) on vacation tomorrow, so I need to go home and pack.

Laura: Oh, very nice! Who [2] ________________ (*go*) with? And where [3] ________________ (*go*)?

Amelia: I'm going to Budapest with an old friend from college. We [4] ________________ (*stay*) in a five-star luxury hotel right in the city center – my friend works for a travel company, so she got a special deal!

Laura: That sounds amazing. How long [5] ________________ (*stay*) for?

Amelia: Just a couple of days, we [6] ________________ (*come back*) on Thursday.

Laura: Great. Let's meet up when you're back and you can tell me about it.

Amelia: Yes, that sounds great. I [7] ________________ (*work*) on Friday, but I'm free on the weekend. I'll call you on Saturday.

Laura: Perfect. Have a great vacation! See you on Saturday.

Amelia: Bye!

B Complete the diary below with your plans for next week.

Monday ________________

Tuesday ________________

Wednesday ________________

Thursday ________________

Friday ________________

Saturday ________________

Sunday ________________

C Work in pairs. Organize to do something with your partner next week. If you are already busy, say why.

A: Hi. Do you want to go to the movie theater on Wednesday night next week?

B: Oh, sorry. I'm playing soccer next Wednesday. What about Thursday night?

A: Yes, great. I'm free on Thursday.

Answer key

1.1 Vocabulary

Countries

1 Canada 2 Britain 3 Japan
4 Morocco 5 Italy 6 Mexico
7 Spain 8 Egypt

Numbers 0–9

A

0 zero 1 one 2 two 3 three
4 four 5 five 6 six 7 seven
8 eight 9 nine

1.1 Grammar

A

1 'm; 'm 2 Are; 'm
3 'm; Are 4 Are; 'm
5 'm; 'm not 6 Are; 'm
7 'm; 'm 8 are; am
9 'm not 10 Are; am

1.2 Vocabulary

A

1 doctor 2 designer
3 engineer 4 teacher
5 manager 6 architect
7 student 8 computer programmer

B

1 an 2 a 3 a 4 a 5 an 6 a
7 a 8 a

1.2 Grammar

A

1 isn't 2 's 3 Is; is 4 's
5 Is; is 6 isn't

2.1 Vocabulary

A

Across
1 English
3 American
4 Jamaican
6 Brazilian
8 Norwegian
10 Japanese
11 Swedish
12 Malian

Down
2 Icelandic
5 Portuguese
7 Spanish
9 Italian

2.1 Grammar

Simple present *be*: *we, you, they*

1 They 2 We 3 You
4 They 5 We

Possessive adjectives

A

1 my 2 my 3 Its 4 Her 5 Her
6 Our 7 His 8 His

2.2 Vocabulary

Days of the week

A

2 Tuesday 3 Wednesday 4 Thursday
5 Friday 6 Saturday 7 Sunday

Numbers 11–100

A

18 eighteen 16 sixteen 19 nineteen
80 eighty 60 sixty 90 ninety

B

a sixty-six b twenty-three
c eighteen and nineteen d ten
e twenty-four and seven

2.2 Grammar

A

1 What 2 How 3 What 4 Where
5 Who 6 Where 7 When 8 What

3.1 Vocabulary

A

1 a hat 2 a smartphone
3 a sweatshirt 4 an umbrella
5 a bag 6 a coat
7 glasses 8 headphones

B

1 red 2 yellow 3 green
4 black and white 5 brown 6 blue
7 gray

3.1 Grammar

***a/an* and plural nouns**

A

1 an 2 – 3 a 4 a 5 an 6 a
7 a 8 –

B

1 book**s** 2 computer~~s~~ 3 correct
4 ~~a~~ tomato**es** 5 song~~s~~ 6 bab~~y~~**ies**
7 correct 8 name~~s~~

this, that, these, those

A

1 This 2 Those 3 These 4 that

B

1 this 2 this 3 That 4 these
5 those 6 This

3.2 Vocabulary

A

1 grandmother 2 granddaughter
3 husband 4 wife
5 grandson 6 grandfather
7 brother 8 sister
9 father 10 son
11 mother 12 daughter

B

1 parents 2 children 3 grandparents

3.2 Grammar

A

1 I have two sisters.
2 Do you have any brothers or sisters?
3 We don't have a daughter.
4 Does your mother have any grandchildren?
5 You don't have any children.
6 How many daughters do you have?
7 My grandparents have three grandchildren.
8 She doesn't have any brothers or sisters.
9 Does he have any sisters?
10 They have three sons.

4.1 Vocabulary

Daily activities

A

1 d 2 g 3 b 4 c 5 f 6 a 7 e

B

1 b 2 f 3 g 4 e 5 a 6 d 7 c

Time

A

a 1:50 b 1:25 c 1:15 d 7:30
e 6:35 f 5:20 g 2:00 h 5:30
i 6:25 j 12:45 k 4:05 l 1:45

4.2 Vocabulary

A

a August; 8 b May; 5
c September; 9 d February; 2
e July; 7 f November; 11
h June; 6 i December; 12
j October; 10 k March; 3
l April; 4

B

1 spring 2 winter 3 fall
4 summer

4.2 Grammar

A

1 What time **do you** get up?
2 What**'s** your favorite season?
3 **Do you go** to another country in the summer?
4 Who **do you talk to** in the morning?
5 **Do you live** in Japan?
6 What month **is** your birthday?

B

1 f 2 a 3 c 4 e 5 b 6 d

5.1 Vocabulary

A

1 go 2 cook 3 take 4 go 5 play
6 go 7 go 8 sit

B
1 Do you go running three times a week?
2 Do you take a bath to relax?
3 Do you go for a walk on the weekend?
4 Do you go shopping every Saturday?
5 Do you go to the gym before work?
6 Do you cook dinner every day?
7 Do you sit in the backyard in the summer?
8 Do you play chess with friends or family?

5.1 Grammar

A
1 go 2 get up 3 gets up
4 goes 5 do 6 does

5.2 Vocabulary

A
Fruits: apple, banana, grapes, orange, pear
Vegetables: beans, broccoli, cucumber, onion, potatoes, tomato
Dairy products: cheese, milk
Drinks: juice, milk, tea, water
Snacks: chips, chocolate, cookies, peanuts
Other: bread, cereal, chicken, eggs, fish, noodles, pasta, rice

5.2 Grammar

A
1 never 2 seldom 3 sometimes
4 frequently 5 usually 6 always

B
1 b 2 a 3 a 4 b 5 a 6 b

6.1 Vocabulary

A
1 theater 2 museum
3 station 4 hotel
5 café 6 restaurant
7 art gallery 8 market
9 park 10 store

6.1 Grammar

A
3 There isn't a museum.
4 There are some parks.
5 There isn't a market.
6 There's a station.
7 There are some cafés.
8 There are some restaurants.
9 There isn't an art gallery.
10 There's a hotel.

B
In Town A, there's a market, but in Town B there isn't a market.
In Town A, there are two hotels, but in Town B there aren't any hotels.
In Town A, there are two cafés, but in Town B there are three cafés.
In Town A, there's a restaurant, but in Town B there isn't a restaurant.
In Town A, there aren't any parks, but in Town B there are two parks.
In Town A, there isn't a museum, but in Town B there's a museum.
In Town A, there's a theater, but in Town B there isn't a theater.

6.2 Grammar

A
1 Is there a couch?
2 Are there any windows?
3 Is there a mirror?
4 Is there a coffee table?
5 Is there a television?
6 Are there any shoes?
7 Are there any pictures?
8 Are there any people?
9 Is there a rug?
10 Are there any cushions?

B
2 Yes, there are. 3 No, there isn't.
4 Yes, there is. 5 No, there isn't.
6 No, there aren't. 7 Yes, there are.
8 No, there aren't. 9 Yes, there is.
10 Yes, there are.

7.1 Vocabulary

A

Down
1 paint a picture

Across
1 play tennis 2 do yoga
3 ride a horse 4 sing
5 play the guitar 6 dance
7 play the piano 8 ski
9 make a cake 10 ride a motorcycle
11 juggle 12 draw
13 make an omelette

7.1 Grammar

A
1 He can't ~~to~~ swim.
2 Correct
3 We ~~not~~ can'**t** speak Icelandic.
4 Correct
5 Correct
6 She can climb~~s~~ high.
7 I can't eat~~ing~~ spicy food.
8 Correct

7.2 Vocabulary

A

	Positive	Negative
1	great	boring
2	amazing	difficult
3	talented	bad
4	interesting	awful
5	easy	terrible
6	OK	terrible

7.2 Grammar

A
1 wife's 2 sons' 3 daughter's
4 parents'

8.1 Vocabulary

A
1 coffee 2 videos 3 messages
4 shopping 5 phone 6 break
7 mirror 8 station

8.1 Grammar

A
1 They're walking in the park.
2 They aren't / They're not sitting on the bench.
3 She's taking a break in the park.
4 I'm not waiting to call my friend.
5 Are you listening to me?
6 He isn't / He's not talking on the phone.
7 We're not/We aren't watching a video online.
8 He isn't / He's not drinking coffee.

8.2 Vocabulary

A
1 dress 2 shorts 3 jeans
4 handbag 5 suit 6 pants
7 shoes 8 sneakers 9 jacket
10 skirt 11 sweatshirt 12 shirt

8.2 Grammar

A
2 ✓
3 That's a big yellow hat.
4 ✓
5 ✓
6 They have new green caps.
7 I have a beautiful blue dress.
8 ✓
9 He has a new black suit.
10 ✓

9.1 Vocabulary

A

1 first 2 second
3 third 4 fourth
5 5th 6 10th
7 eleventh 8 12th
9 twentieth 10 21st
11 twenty-second 12 30th

B

1 nineteen sixty-seven
2 nineteen eighty-one
3 two thousand and eight
4 two thousand and eleven
5 sixteen forty-three
6 seventeen fifteen
7 eighteen sixteen
8 nineteen ninety-seven
9 fourteen sixty-four
10 twenty twenty-three
11 nineteen seventy-seven
12 twenty nineteen

9.1 Grammar

A

1 Correct
2 My dad's first phone **wasn't** a smartphone.
3 My friends **were** late for class today.
4 The sandwiches **weren't** very good yesterday.
5 Correct
6 My brother and I **were** tired.
7 Correct
8 Correct
9 Correct
10 The food **wasn't** expensive.

B

1 What **was** the last movie you saw?
2 Where **was** the last selfie you took?
3 Who **was** the last celebrity you watched on TV?
4 What **was** on TV last night?
5 Where **were** you born?

9.2 Vocabulary

A

1 study 2 collects 3 design
4 travel 5 receive 6 helped
7 start 8 painting

9.2 Grammar

A

2 We **studied** English for three hours last week.
3 My best friend **didn't receive** a present from her brother.
4 I **designed** the slides for our last presentation.
5 They didn't **want** to help anyone.
6 She **traveled** to the US for work last month.
7 He **asked** the police officer for help last night.
8 She didn't **plant** the tree yesterday.
9 We **lived** there from 2006 to 2012.
10 They didn't **try** to help me last week.

10.1 Grammar

A

1 had 2 got up 3 bought
4 went 5 didn't go out 6 gave

10.2 Vocabulary

A

1 met 2 wrote 3 got
4 won 5 passed 6 belonged

10.2 Grammar

A

1 Where **did** you study last year?
2 When **did you** get your phone?
3 **Did you** give someone a present last month?
4 How **did you get** here today?
5 What did you **buy** yesterday?

B

a 3 b 5 c 1 d 2 e 4

11.1 Vocabulary

A

1 go 2 get 3 go 4 spend
5 go 6 go 7 go 8 watch
9 watch 10 listen 11 spend

11.1 Grammar

A

1 spending 2 going 3 enjoy
4 enjoys 5 cooking 6 hates

11.2 Vocabulary

A

1 pop star 2 songs 3 concerts
4 player 5 stadium 6 game
7 actor 8 premiere 9 action
10 movie theater 11 band
12 rock 13 musicians

11.2 Grammar

A

1 Correct
2 Mario called **me** last night and told me the news.
3 I gave my brother some new shoes for his birthday but he didn't like **them**.
4 That's Helen's sister – I play tennis with **her**.
5 Who's that man over there? I don't know **him**.
6 I need to talk to **you**.
7 Correct
8 The teacher gave **us** a test yesterday.
9 Correct
10 Where are my glasses? I can't find **them**!
11 I like your new coat. Where did you buy **it**?
12 I met Alfonso's brother yesterday. I talked to **him** for a long time.

12.1 Vocabulary

A

1 passport 2 money 3 traffic
4 bag 5 airport 6 ticket
7 credit card 8 plane

12.1 Grammar

A

1 I have 500 **dollars**. Do you think I need more money?
2 Are you going to use one of your **credit cards** or cash?
3 There is a lot of **traffic** today. We're going to be late for the plane.
4 I only have two **bags**. You have a lot of luggage!
5 Is there any **information** about the arrival time on the ticket?

B

1 bags 2 luggage 3 cash 4 dollars

12.2 Vocabulary

A

1 beach vacation 2 snorkel
3 sunglasses 4 skiing vacation
5 chalet 6 hotel
7 sightseeing vacation 8 hotel
9 guidebook 10 camping vacation
11 tent 12 stove

12.2 Grammar

A

1 am/'m going 2 are you going
3 are you going 4 're/are staying
5 are you staying 6 are/'re coming back
7 am/'m working